The Complete Guide
to
New Zealand
Trout Lures

Indeed, my good scholar, we may say of angling, as Dr Boteler said of strawberries, *'Doubtless God could have made a better berry, but doubtless God never did;'* as so (If I might be judge) *'God never did make a more calm, quiet, innocent recreation than angling.'*

IZAAC WALTON – The Compleat Angler

The Complete Guide to New Zealand Trout Lures

Derek Quilliam

The Halcyon Press

Published by
The Halcyon Press
(A division of Halcyon Publishing Ltd)
P O Box 360, Auckland, New Zealand

Printed through
Colorcraft Ltd.

Typeset by
HPL

Cover design:
Process Art Studios

ISBN 0 908685 34 3

First Published 1999

CONTENTS

DEDICATION

This is the part my wife has been waiting for.

She has even offered to write it!

All of which underscores the patient and long-suffering sacrifices Wendy has made while I disappeared to my fly-tying room night after night. She would have been asleep some hours by the time I emerged, around midnight. Not to mention all the clutter and fluff and feathers. Wendy has endured my hobby (which she regards unkindly as an obsession) with a stoicism and cheerful fortitude, which is given only to other anglers' wives to comprehend.

To you Wendy,

I dedicate this book.

ACKNOWLEDGMENTS

I started this work in the naive expectation that I could do everything myself. I was quickly disabused of that aspiration. A book of this nature could not have been possible without the valuable and considerable assistance of others. I acknowledge and record my grateful appreciation for the unstinting encouragement and help from people too numerous to mention but they know who they are. I would be remiss, however, if I did not specifically include the following:

Hugh McDowell of Rotoura. There is no question in my mind that this project would have faltered and died at an early stage but for Hugh's encouragement and support. He was a valuable source of information as well as inspiration, as well as being one of the most engaging personalities it has been my pleasure to meet.

Garth Coghill of Rotoura. Garth is a supreme fly-tier who offered to assist in the tying of lures and made good his offer. In addition, he offered very helpful advice, information, and encouragement, and was generous with the materials he supplied me.

Pat Swift of Rotorua. It was Pat who first sowed the seeds of the Appendices to this book with his suggestion of regional smelt patterns. The book was then at the stage where I regarded the suggestion with some dismay. "Where does it end?" I asked. "Where does it start?" he countered. I needed that refreshing inoculation of positive thought. Pat, also a superb fly-tier, offered to assist with tying up patterns. If he ever regretted opening his mouth he never let on, and his application to the numerous patterns I sent him (which I bet he didn't expect, not the quantity), considerably shortened this project.

Bronwyn Wilson of Taupo. Bronwyn embraced my venture with almost missionary zeal. She showered me with undiminished kindnesses: from tying patterns, supplying me with an unbelievable amount of materials, taking me fishing, introducing me to others of interest, researching of her own volition, and plying me with food and coffee. She gave me valuable instructions in the art of tying flies, when I thought I needed none. I certainly did. Her contribution to this book, both tangible and intangible, is beyond measure.

Barry Kent of Te Puke. At the material time Barry worked out of Guns & Tackle in Ahuriri, Napier. I purchased the majority of my materials through him and he always ensured I had the best, either in quality or value. He assessed some of my fly-tying efforts, and gave me valuable tips, hints, and instructions.

Photoz of Napier. The personnel at this photo developing shop were unfailingly pleasant, courteous, and helpful, and the quality of their photo developing never once slipped below excellent.

And finally, to a doctor from Stratford or Eltham or thereabouts whose name I regret I have long forgotten. In early January 1976, Wendy and I, and our 15 month old son Peter, had the use of a relation's bach at Kuratau, Taupo. Fly rods, all set up with lures, adorned the walls. Temptation finally overcame me, and I resolved to have a go at this fly fishing thing. I don't know how long the doctor watched me flailing away on the bank of the Kuratau River, but eventually he approached and unassumingly inquired if he could offer his assistance and advice. Could he! I then spent some time in his company learning the finer art of casting, during which time, I almost, *almost* hooked a trout. He lent me Greg Kelly's *Fishing For Trout* to read overnight, which I did. The good doctor gave me a bug, which afflicts me still.

INTRODUCTION

This book evolved out of a perceived shortage of images of New Zealand trout lures. There are many overseas publications which fulfil that brief, but nothing comparable in New Zealand. This book is an attempt to fill that gap.

It must be stressed at the outset that this is not a fly-tier's manual. Anyone wishing to acquire the reasonably easy basic skills of fly-tying is directed to read Hugh McDowell's superb book: *New Zealand Fly-Tying – The ten-thumbed beginner's guide.* Not only is it a very readable and instructive book, but it classifies for the first time the categories into which various trout lures fall, from a fly-tier's perspective. This nomenclature of fly 'types' is an important contribution to fly-tying knowledge and it is hoped that fly patterns of the future will include this information. I discuss this aspect more fully later.

This book attempts to be a compendium of New Zealand trout lures, past and present. It is limited to lures only. As a compilation of trout lures, I have attempted to include as many patterns as I can find – not just of modern, commercially available dressings, but also patterns which once enjoyed popularity as the distinctively dressed New Zealand patterns evolved.

It is recognised that new lures – and new fly-tying materials – will continue to evolve. Inevitably, a work such as this will be out of date even before it is published. Nevertheless, it is hoped that this book will provide a comprehensive reference to those wishing to tie up their own stock of proven lures. On that point, it is worth noting that more than 70% of the lures listed have been published in one form or another, or are commercially available somewhere.

When I began this book, the classic reference source was the pre-eminent publication by Keith Draper *Trout Flies in New Zealand.* My starting point was to work my way systematically through his lure section from beginning to end, photographing each fly as it was tied, and adding such other patterns as I could locate through research, or which are currently available in most sports shops. Subsequently, Keith published his updated book *New Zealand Trout Flies – Traditional & Modern.* By and large, I found it unnecessary to amend my manuscript but I have made it clear, when quoting from his works, to which of Keith's books I am referring.

Both of Keith's books are more comprehensive than mine in that they cover the whole range of trout flies available. They are valuable resources which no angler should be without. It has been necessary to quote extensively from his books because, as New Zealand's foremost authority on angling history, his writings are, in many instances, the only available literature.

If I have any criticism at all with Keith's books, it is that I find the plates of photos of lures to be indicative, because of their size, rather than definitive. The same might be said of those appearing in Hugh McDowell's book. The photos are better, but of a very limited representation. *Deceiving Trout – The Flytier's Art* by the very well known John Parsons is a superb book with a very high standard of photographs of trout flies. However, it barely touches on lures, and that is the focus of this book. [I make no attempt to define "lure". There is an excellent commentary in Keith Draper's 1997 book on this point to which pedants are referred.]

The popularity of trout lures is a fickle thing. Undoubtedly, some enjoy commercial success because they look appealing, and it has been said many times before that some flies are more successful at catching fishermen than fish! We all know of the phenomenon of discarding a tried and trusted fly for a new variety that catches our eye. For years, at Lake Waikaremoana, I used nothing but a Rabbit, with considerable success. I have no doubt that the Rabbit is still catching trout there, and always will. But then I got a "whisper" that a Mrs. Simpson tied on a No. 2 hook was the answer. And so it was. And so my tastes changed.

Tastes have also changed historically and commercially. The reasons are many and varied. In some instances, the materials used for particular flies became non-existent, scarce and expensive, difficult to obtain, or just plain illegal. New synthetic materials spawned a whole new set of creations, and will continue to do so in the future. Few fly-tiers can resist the temptation to try and create the ultimate weapon – a fly which is absolutely irresistible to all trout over 10lbs. I imagine, and hope, that the ultimate is unattainable. Part of the fascination and allure of angling is the challenge – the pitting of one's wits, skills, and ingenuity against the finely honed survival instincts of the quarry. Just as in cricket one would deprecate a bowler who developed an unplayable delivery that took a wicket every bowl without fail, so, too, in angling where the infallible lure would reduce a sport to a mechanical function devoid of art, mystery, hope, emotion, and soul. Naturally, I do not tie flies, which are designed *not* to catch trout. I will continue to search for a lure which outperforms others, but my quest ends there.

Just because a particular lure has fallen out of favour does not mean that it is ineffective. Patterns of yore were cast just as expectantly and with the same degree of success, as those which are popular today. And it should not be forgotten that a number of erstwhile very popular lures only disappeared from the scene because the materials became too scarce or expensive for commercial production. However, those materials are still available to the home fly-tier who is prepared to make the necessary enquiry. Also, if you are a hunter and duck shooter (or know someone who is), then you can get an inexhaustible supply of feathers and fur for very little outlay.

Although I have attempted to depict as extensive a range of lures as possible, inevitably decisions as to inclusion or exclusion arose. Rightly or wrongly, I have omitted tube flies. Equally, I have tended not to include luminous night flies where the effectiveness derives from the glowing nature of the material rather than any particular style or dressing. Anyone with a supply of aurora skirt or similar can create an infinite variety of luminous lures.

Again, I have not included silicon imitations of smelt. These are not particularly difficult to make, and I have made up quite a quantity using a tube of silicon (any hardware store) and plastic foodwrap for ease of shaping and moulding the sticky gel. Leave for a week in a cool place to set, then trim to shape with a razor blade or craft knife.

I have not included every smelt fancy ever created, many of which last but one season and then disappear. Nor have I included every variation of the Rabbit. There are enough variations of that pattern alone to fill a book.

My policy of inclusion, however, is not infallible and I have no doubt that someone, somewhere, will draw my attention to a particular lure deserving of inclusion but which has escaped my notice. I welcome such advice.

I enjoy my trout fishing but I am by no means an expert. I enjoy tying up trout lures but I am by no means an expert for all of Hugh McDowell's helpful instructions. I do admit to some expertise as a photographer (although that is not my profession). The raison d'etre of this book was the provision of good quality images of trout lures, and those photos should not be used as examples of the fly-tier's skills (or lack of!). They may not attain the level of an art form but I am encouraged to think that the average home tier will identify with my quality while we all strive to emulate the extraordinary expertise of such tiers as Pat Swift, Garth Coghill, John Morton, and others.

It is my intention that this book should be regarded as a work of reference. Brief observations from my own limited experience, and borrowing heavily from Keith Draper, Tony Orman, Hugh McDowell, and others, are included wherever it is considered appropriate. This book should be considered as a companion to Keith Draper's books, not a substitute.

I have deliberately photographed all flies facing from left to right because, for the majority of fly-tiers I suggest, this is how they present in the vice.

Unless otherwise stated, all flies tied by the author have been tied on a Mustad No. 6 hook.

THOSE MYSTERIOUS LETTERS IN BRACKETS

A trout fly pattern is a description of the material used to create a particular fly or lure. However, it does not always illuminate the style with which the fly is to be dressed. Sometimes, the only clues lie in accompanying photos, or in the type of material to be used - e.g. hackle feathers are used in a different way to pheasant rump feathers. The novice fly-tier might therefore be perplexed with the pattern for All Black, the first lure described in Keith Draper's 1971 book which is described thus:

'Body, wing and hackle: All tied of black materials with a silver rib.'

There is no accompanying photo. (A photo does appear in the 1997 book).

Hugh McDowell, in *New Zealand Fly-Tying – The ten-thumbed beginner's guide* has identified five categories of fly-tying styles or techniques. These are as follows:

Hackle (H)

where the "wing" is formed from hackle feathers wound around the body, usually at the mid-point and at the head, but sometimes just at the head.

Examples are Fuzzy-Wuzzy, Red Setter, Dappled Dog.

Pukeko (P)

where the wing is tied in flat on top of the body, like a canopy.

Examples are Craig's Night-time, Scotch Poacher.

Matuku (M)

where the wing is laid vertically along the top of the body and bound to the body with ribbing which passes through the hackle fibres. Tied in this manner, the feathers can form both the wing and the tail.

Examples are Parsons' Glory, Orbit, Rabbit, and Taupo Tiger.

Killer (K)

where the feathers are tied in alongside the body, sometimes in two or more pairs per side.

Examples are Mrs Simpson, Hamill's Killer, Lord's Killer.

Other (O)

where the style does not fit readily into any of the four basic techniques.

Examples are Hairy Dog, Muddler Minnow.

The simple notation in parenthesis – (H), (P), (M) etc. used when giving any pattern, quickly and easily identifies the style of the fly and the method to be employed when dressing it.

Neither I, nor Hugh McDowell, claim this classification to be sacrosanct. There are differing opinions. Garth Coghill of Rotorua, and others, feel strongly that the Matuku style should be classified as Fixed Wing Streamer (F). It is argued that the term 'Matuku' applies only to a lure tied using the feathers of the now-protected bittern, or in substitution thereof. The logic of this view is difficult to gainsay.

On the other hand, a contrary argument is to the effect that the manner of fixing the wing to the body along the length of the shank is a *style* of tying, and which was uniquely New Zealand. The classification as Matuku style simply derives from the name of the lure which first used that style.

In a similar vein, there are those who prefer to describe the Pukeko style as Craig style (after Craig's Night-time), or even Cowl style. There is merit in both alternatives although the same criticism over the Matuku designation could apply to a Craig designation. I once felt that lures employing a wing tied in at the head on top of the body, not being feathers, such as Bucktails, Blondie, Squirrel Nutkin, Furry Butcher, etc. should be classified as Pukeko style (P) rather than Other (O). I had argued that I could not see the difference between tying in a Pukeko feather at the head, and a bunch of hair or other material at the same place and in the same manner. On reflection, however, it is recognised that (with reference to Pukeko style), the synonymous Cowl style conjures up a very different image to that envisaged by Hairy Dog for example.

If I have preference at all, it would be for Cowl style (C). This defines more accurately what the dressing intends. For instance, Black Max employs a Pukeko feather wing tied in by the butts at the head, but it is not tied in the Pukeko (or Cowl) style.

The list of tying classifications is capable of further refinement. Lures such as Badger Smelt, Golden Demon, Hughie's Mallard, and old ties of Tamati and Turkey flies, to name but a few, could be classified as Streamer style (S), adding persuasion to the Fixed Wing Streamer lobby. Then again, one could have a Muddler style (M) but only if there was a Fixed Wing Streamer style, otherwise the designation (M) might be confused for Matuku.

In raising these matters, my intent is not to advocate any particular nomenclature, but rather to advocate the use of some universally recognised designation which immediately and clearly identifies the technique involved (or indicates by Other that it is outside those classifications).

Most experienced tiers will have no difficulty recognising the style to be employed just by looking at the pattern. However, there have been occasions, during the course of my research for this book where the answer was not obvious, and I lamented on those occasions the lack of the simple, but helpful, style designation. The Black Phantom dichotomy is unique, and is not a justification in itself for having accepted categories, but it is a case in point.

For the purposes of this book, I am content to adopt Hugh McDowell's categories and nomenclature throughout.

There are abbreviations and repetitions which require explanation. I have referred throughout to seven principal sources of information. These are as follows:

Keith Draper - *Trout Flies in New Zealand* (1971).

Keith Draper - *New Zealand Trout Flies - Traditional & Modern* (1997).

Hugh McDowell - *New Zealand Fly Tying - The ten-thumbed beginner's guide* (1984).

John Veniard - *Reservoir and Lake Flies* (1970 - UK), specifically a section of that book titled New Zealand Lake Patterns.

Tony Orman - *Trout & Salmon Sport in New Zealand* (1980), compiled by Tony Orman.

Nancy and Bryan Tichborne - The 'Tichborne calendars' (1985-1991) and subsequent book *Anglers' Paradise* (1990).

Robert K. Bragg - *New Zealand Fishing Flies* (1997). I have referred to this throughout as 'Bragg's book'.

All references to any of those authors, any quotes attributed to them, and any abbreviated book references are from, or refer to, the above works. A full bibliography appears at the rear of this book.

It was my original intention, evidenced by my manuscript, to ascribe one page for each lure pattern with the photo enlarged to approximately 110 x

170mm. Regretfully, I have had to bow to the realities of publication economics. Nevertheless, I have achieved my aim whereby each entry is intended to stand alone. The method of tying up a particular style of fly, e.g. Hackle flies, is pretty much the same for all hackle-style flies. It would have been simple to give a brief tying guide to just one fly in a particular category and refer all other lures of that style to that entry. That would have involved constant cross-referencing. By avoiding that, it has been necessary to repeat tying instructions ad nauseam, but that was considered the best option. Anyone interested in tying up virtually any fly listed can do so without having to refer constantly to other pages.

As a pupil of the Hugh McDowell school of fly-tiers (but by no means a graduate) I have followed his methods closely. Individual styles and preferences should prevail. The guide is not intended to be anything other than a brief outline and presupposes some familiarity with at least the basics of fly-tying, e.g. winding the thread onto the hook, forming and completing the head, and other obvious techniques which are not given in detail.

I have researched carefully and extensively. I believe that this book may be accepted as authoritative. If, by chance, errors of fact exist, the responsibility for such errors is mine alone.

DEREK QUILLIAM
NAPIER

PHOTOGRAPHIC INDEX OF TROUT LURES

For ease of reference the photographs follow the same order as the text.

AFTER-BURNER (O)

ALBINO (3) (M)

AFTER DARK (M)

ALEXANDRA (O)

ALBINO (1) (M)

ALL BLACK (M)

ALBINO (2) (M)

ANNA'S BLUE GHOST (M)

AURORA (O)

BADGER SMELT (O)

AWAHOU SPECIAL (K)

BALCARASTER (M)

AWESOME AUCK (M)

BALLARD'S BEAUTY (M)

BADGER (M)

B AND B (M)

BANTAM (M)

BARRY'S SMELT (O)

BARRED KILLER (K)

BASIL'S INANGA (M)

BARRED ROCK (M)

BASIL'S SMELT (P)

BARRED ROCK SILVER (M)

BASIL'S WHITEBAIT (O)

BAXTER'S SPECIAL (O)

BLACK ARROW (O)

BETHLEHEM CAT (O)

BLACK BOOBIE (H)

BILL'S KILLER (M)

BLACK DEMON (M)

BISHOP'S BLESSING (M)

BLACK MARABOU (O)

BLACK MATUKU (M)

BLACK PHANTOM (K)

BLACK MAX (O)

BLACK PHANTOM (P)

BLACK AND ORANGE (M)

BLACK PRINCE (M)

BLACK PETE (K)

BLACK SMELT (H)

BLACK AND YELLOW (DEVIL) (H)

BLOODY MARY (O)

BLONDIE (1) (O)

BLUE DUN MATUKU (M)

BLONDIE (2) (O)

BLUE DUN SMELT (M)

BLOODY BUTCHER (M)

BLUE MALLARD (O)

BLYTHE'S SPECIAL (O)

BOTTLETOP (M)

BMS (O)

BRIGGS' BROADHEAD (O)

BOCKETT'S GHOST (M)

BRIGGS' SILVERY (M)

BOOBY (O)

BROADHEAD (K)

BROWN BOMBER (H)

BRUNTON NO.2 (O)

BROWN KILLER (K)

BRUNTON RED (O)

BROWN MATUKU (M)

BUCKTAILS (P)

BRUNTON NO. 1 (O)

BUDGIE (O)

BUGS BUNNY (O)

BULLY (RED & YELLOW) (K)

BULLHEAD (O)

BUM FLY (P)

BULLY (P)

BUM FLY VARIATION 1 (P)

BULLY FLY (O)

BUM FLY VARIATON 2 (P)

BUM FLY VARIATION 3 (P)

CARDINAL (O)

BUNNY (O)

CASEY (O)

BURGLAR (O)

CASUAL DRESS (O)

CAPTAIN MILNE (O)

CHAMBERLAIN'S LURE (O)

CHARLIE'S FAVOURITE (O)

CLARET (M)

CHINAMAN (M)

CLEARWATER MATUKU (M)

CHRISTIE (M)

CLIFF'S KILLER (H)

CLAIRE'S CHARM (O)

COACHMAN LURE (O)

COCK-A-BULLY (K)

CRAIG'S KILLER (K)

COMETS (O)

CRAIG'S NIGHT-TIME (P)

CORONATION (O)

CRAYFISH (P)

COTTEE'S SILVERY (M)

DAINTY VEIL (H)

DAMSEL NYMPH NO. 1 (O)

DELUXE HARLER (M)

DAMSEL NYMPH NO. 2 (O)

DEMON SQUIRREL (O)

DANDY (O)

DEVIL DODGER (M)

DAPPLED DOG (H)

DIANNE'S KILLER (K)

DIRTY HARRY (P)

DOROTHY, SILVER (M)

DISCO DOLL (H)

DOUBLE PUFF (O)

DOLL FLY (O)

DRIFTER (H)

DOROTHY (M)

DUCHESS (K)

DUKE (K)

ETHIOPIAN (M)

EARLY SEASON MATUKU (M)

EWE WASP (O) (OLD TIE)

ENGLAND'S DEMON (M)

EWE WASP (M) (MODERN TIE)

EPOXY SPRAT (O)

EWE WASP (BARRED) (M)

EXOCET (H)

FIREBALL (O)

FERRIS (M)

FRANCIS BUTCHER (O)

FERRIS (RED & YELLOW) (M)

FRUIT SALAD (P)

FERRIS VARIATION (M)

FURNACE SMELT (M)

FURRY BARRED WASP (O)

FUZZY WUZZY (H)

FURRY BUTCHER (O)

GAMELAN (M)

FURRY EWE WASP (O)

GARY'S GREEN MARABOU (O)

FURRY TAMATI (O)

'GEE WHIZ' KEELER (M)

GILLIES LODGER (M)

GLO-BUG (O)

GINGER MICK (M)

GOLDEN DEMON (O)

GINGER SMELT (O)

GOLDEN LION (M)

GLACIER FLY (O)

GOLDEN QUEEN (M)

GOLDEN REAPER (M)

GREEN DRAGON (M)

GOLDIE HAWN (O)

GREEN FROG (M)

GOTCHA (O)

GREEN MATUKA (M)

GREEN DOG (O)

GREEN MATUKU (M)

GREEN PARSONS (M)

GREY GHOST (M)

GREEN PRINCE (K)

GRIZZLE SMELT (O)

GREEN SLEEVES (K)

GRIZZLY BEAR (O)

GREYFRIARS (O)

GRIZZLY GREEN (H)

GT SMELT, SILVER (M)

HAIRY DOG (O)

GUARDSMAN (P)

HALL'S NIGHT-TIME (O)

HAEMORRHOID (O)

HAMILL'S KILLER (K)

HAIR FLIES (O)

HAMILL'S SILVER SMELT (O)

HAMILL'S SMELT (O)

HATEPE SMELT (O)

HARLEY'S BULLY (K)

HAWK (M)

HARRY (M)

HAWK AND POSSUM (O)

HART'S CREEK (M)

HAWK AND RABBIT (O)

HEN PHEASANT (K)

HERB'S GLOW SMELT (O)

HILDA (O)

HOB NAILED BOOT (O)

HOPE'S DARK (O)

HOPE'S LURE (M)

HOPE'S SILVERY (M)

HOPKIN'S FANCY (O)

HUGHIE'S MALLARD (O)

IRISH SETTER (H)

HYDRO HUSTLER (H)

ITALIAN STALLION (O)

IHI (O)

JACK'S SPRAT (M)

IRISH REBEL (H)

JOCK (M)

JOCK MILLER (O)

KEELER (P)

JOCK MILLER VARIATION (O)

KEITH'S KRAWLIE (O)

JOCK SCOTT (O)

KILWELL BLONDE (O)

JO JO JUGGINS (M)

KILWELL BULLY (O)

KILWELL NO. 1 (K)

KLONDIKE KATE (M)

KILWELL NO. 2 (K)

KOKAPU (M)

KIWI PARMACHENEE (M)

LA GIACONDA (H)

KIWI TEASER (H)

LAMPREY (M)

LESLIE'S LURE (K)

LISA (H)

LES'S FANCY (M)

LISA SIMPSON (M)

LIGHT BROWN AND PARADISE (O)

LITTLE GREEN FATAL (O)

LIMEY (O)

LITTLE RAINBOW (O)

LOGAN'S LURE (H)

MALLARD (1) (K)

LORD'S KILLER (K)

MALLARD (2) (K)

LOUIE'S LURE (H)

MALLARD AND BLACK (P)

LOU'S GREEN PARROT (M)

MALLARD AND CLARET (O)

MALLARD HEN (K)

MARABOU KING (O)

MALLARD SMELT (O)

MARABOU KING VARIATION (O)

MAORI ALL BLACK (H)

MARABOU KOURA (P)

MAORI CHIEF (O)

MATUKU (M)

MATUKU MUDDLER (O)

MISSIONARY (O)

MELLOW YELLOW (M)

MIZOOLIAN SPOOK (O)

MICHELLE'S MAGIC (H)

MOHAKA NO.1 (O)

MIDNIGHT (M)

MOHAKA SPECIAL (H)

MOLINEAUX'S SILVERY (M)

MOTHER SUPERIOR (M)

MONSUM'S BULLY (O)

MR SIMPSON (K)

MOONSHINE (M)

MRS SIMPSON (K)

MORTON'S SMELT (M)

MUDDLER MINNOW (O)

MURPHY (O)

NIGHT-TIME (K)

MUSKRAT (1) (M)

NORTHERN RABBIT (M)

MUSKRAT (2) (M)

O'KEEFE'S KILLER (K)

NAILER (O)

O'KEEFE'S SMELT (O)

OLD JACK (M)

O'NEIL'S SPECIAL (M)

OLD NICK NO.1 (O)

OPOSSUM LURE (M)

OLD NICK NO.2 (O)

ORANGE HAWK (M)

OLIVE SMELT (M)

ORANGE LONGTAIL (M)

ORANGE RABBIT (M)

ORSIM (M)

ORANGE ROUGHIE (M)

PADDLE TAIL (O)

ORANGE WITCH (K)

PALAMINO (O)

ORBIT (M)

PARADISE KILLER (K)

PARADISE WRIGGLER (M)

PARSONS' SUNSET (M)

PARSONS' GLORY (M) (OLD TIE)

PEPPERMINT TWIST (O)

PARSONS' GLORY (M) (MODERN TIE)

PETERKEN'S POACHER (O)

PARSONS' GLORY VARIATION (M)

PETERKEN'S POSSUM (O)

PHANTOM BURGLAR (O)

PLUTO (M) & (K)

PINK AND GREY (H)

POLECAT SMELT (M)

PINK DAWN (M)

POODLE (O)

PINK LADY (H)

POTT'S PET (O)

PRETTY PRETTY (O)

PURPLE MARABOU PRINCE (O)

PROSPECTOR (O)

PURPLE PARSONS' GLORY (M)

PULLEY LURE (O)

QUAIL (K)

PUNTER'S BLACK RABBIT (O)

RABBIT (M)

RABBIT BULLY (M)

RASTAFARIAN (M)

RABBIT MUDDLER 1 (M)

RECKLESS WILLIAM (K)

RABBIT MUDDLER 2 (O)

RECKLESS WILLIAM'S MATE (K)

RAINBOW TROUT (M)

RED AND BLACK MATUKA (M)

REDFIN MATUKU (M)

RED TERROR (M)

RED SETTER (H) (OLD TIE)

ROTODYERAN SPECIAL (H)

RED SETTER (H) (MODERN TIE)

ROYAL COACHMAN LURE (O)

RED SHADOW (M)

ROYAL TAN (M)

RUSTLER (M) & (K)

SIERPINSKI RED (O)

SCOTCH POACHER (P)

SILVER DOCTOR (O)

SIERPINSKI (O)

SILVER GREY (M)

SIERPINSKI DOG (O)

SILVER FITCH (M)

SILVER POSSUM (M)

SIMPLE SALMON (O)

SILVERY (M)

SIMPSON FLY (O)

SILVERY RED BODY (M)

SINGLE PUFF (O)

SIMPKIN (M)

SKINNY MAC (M)

SNAIL FLY (P)

SPA SPECIAL (K)

SNOW QUEEN (O)

SPLIT PARTRIDGE (M)

SORCERER (P)

SPLIT TURKEY (O)

SOUTHERNER'S COMFORT (P)

SPOTTY GOLD (M)

SQUIRREL NUTKIN (O)

SUCCESS (M)

STARLING (H)

SUNSET FLY (H)

STOAT (M)

SUNSET RABBIT (M)

STRING FLY (O)

SWAGGER (M)

SWEEP (M)

TAIHAPE TICKLER (P) (OLD TIE)

SYD'S GINGER (M)

TAIHAPE TICKLER (P) (MODERN TIE)

TADPOLE (M)

TAIL-LIGHT (H)

TAGARTI (O)

TAMATI (O) (OLD TIE)

TAMATI (M) (MODERN TIE)

THAT PURPLY-BLUE THING (H)

TAUPO TIGER (M)

THE BOSS (H)

TEAL (O)

THE SMELT FLY (M)

TE TAUIWHA (O)

THUNDER & LIGHTNING (O)

TINOPAI (O)

TURKEY (M) (MODERN TIE)

TIPPET RED (O)

TURKEY (O) (YELLOW & RED) (OLD TIE)

TOMMO (H)

URCHIN (M)

TONGARIRO QUEEN (O)

VERON ARGENTE (M)

WAIHORA (O)

WHANGANUI SMELT (M)

WARDEN'S WORRY (K)

WHITEBAIT NO. 1 (O)

WATER RAT (O)

WHITEBAIT NO. 2 (M)

WATSON'S FANCY (O)

WHITEBAIT NO. 3 (O)

WHITEBAIT NO. 4 (O)

WHITEBAIT NO.5 (M)

WHITEBAIT NO. 6 (M)

WHITEBAIT NO. 7 (M)

WHITEBAIT NO. 8 (M)

WHITEBAIT NO. 9 (O)

WHITEBAIT NO. 10 (O)

WHITEBAIT NO. 11 (O)

WHITEBAIT NO. 12 (O)

WILLIS SMELT (M)

WHITEBAIT NO. 13 (O)

WILLY'S WONDER (M)

WHITEBAIT NO.14 (O)

WILSON'S WUNDER (H)

WHITE VEIL (H)

WISP (O)

WOOLLY BUGGER (H)

YELLOW FUZZ (O)

WOOLLY WORM (H)

YELLOW LADY (M)

WOOSTER'S SILVERY (M) (MODERN TIE)

YELLOW RUDDEL (M)

WOOSTER'S SILVERY (O) (OLD TIE)

YELLOW TERROR (M)

ZONKER (O)

ZULU (M)

BRONWYN WILSON'S SERIES

CHANGE OF LIGHT (M)

COMMANDER (M)

BRONWYN'S RABBIT (M)

EARLY DAWN (M)

BRONWYN'S ZONKER (M)

ELF (M)

EXTINGUISHER (M)

GALAH (M)

FERNIE FLASH (M)

MARABOU SCOTCH POACHER (P)

FIRST LIGHT (O)

MARSHMALLOW (M)

FUZZY WUZZY RABBIT (H)

MONARCH (M)

MOODY BLUE (P)

PINK DUSK (O)

MOODY RABBIT (M)

PURPLE SPLENDOUR (M)

MOTHER'S CHOICE (M)

RUFUS (M)

NIGHT RIDER (M)

TANGELO (M)

TARAWERA CHIEF (M)

THREE-IN-ONE (M)
(RABBIT VERSION)

TARAWERA PRINCESS (M)

UNCLE HARRY (M)

THREE-IN-ONE (H)
(FUZZY WUZZY VERSION)

WHITE RABBIT (M)

ROTORUA REGIONAL PATTERNS

EPOXY SMELT (O)

GREY GHOST PEARL (M)

HELEN'S SMELT (M)

L.B. FUZZY WUZZY (H)

JACK'S SPRAT PEARL (M)

LUMO ALEX (O)

JAFFABOU (O)

LUMO BLACK MARABOU (O)

KELLY GREEN DOLL FLY (O)

LUMO CRAIG'S NIGHT-TIME (P)

MALLARD SMELT PEARL (O)

SCOTCH POACHER VARIATION (P)

MARA DOLL CHARTREUSE (O)

TARAWERA RABBIT (M)

MARA DOLL GREEN (O)

WEEDLESS LUMO WALLABY (O)

ROTOITI RABBIT (M)

GT SMELT, GREEN (M)

GT SMELT, YELLOW (M)

TAUPO REGIONAL SMELT PATERNS

EDDIE'S MALLARD SMELT (O)

MADEIRA SMELT (BLUE) (O)

GOLDEN PHEASANT SMELT (O)

MADEIRA SMELT (GREEN) (O)

HAWK AND POSSUM (PEARL) (O)

MADEIRA SMELT (PINK) (O)

MALLARD SMELT (O)

SALMON SMELT (O)

BRUNO KEMBALL PATTERNS

GOLDEN PHEASANT SMELT (O)

GREY GHOST SMELT (O)

GOLD-OLIVE SMELT (O)

MALLARD SMELT (O)

GREEN ORBIT SMELT (O)

OLIVE SMELT (O)

SQUIRREL SMELT (O)

PARTRIDGE BULLY (K)

TURKEY SMELT (O)

SILVER SMELT (O)

BLACK DEMON SMELT (O)

TIGER ROSS SMELT (O)

GOLD SMELT (O)

A BEVY OF BURGLARS

BOTTLE-TOPS AND BIROS

THE BOTTLE-TOP LURE

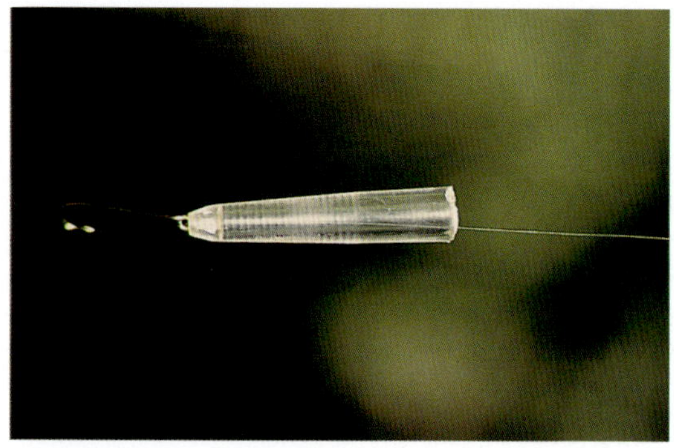

THE BIRO LURE

DEERHAIR LURES

RUNNA MUK MUDDLER

BULLY MUDDLER (M)

BRER MUDDLER (O)

PUDDLER (O)

FUZZY BAMBI (O)

TYING KILLER LURES AND THE SOUTH ISLAND WAY

BLACK PETE

KILWELL NO 2 (MRS SIMPSON)

HAMILL'S KILLER

WALKER'S KILLER (KILWELL NO 1)

FOR THE RECORD

NO NAME 1 (O)

NO NAME 2 (O)

OLD TAUPO LURES

WHITE MATUKA (M)

WHITE KIWI (O)

AWAHOU (K)

RED MATUKA (O)

NAMELESS (O)

WHITE RAT (M)

YELLOW KIWI (M)

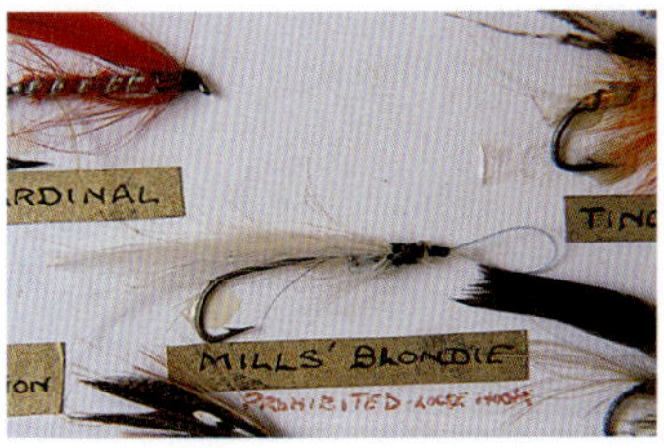

MILL'S BLONDIE (O)

SPUDDLER (O)

RED SETTER (M)

MCMILLAN (O)

HOPE (O)

TINOPAI (O)

BLACK DOCTOR (O)

RUKI BUG (O)

TAUPO LURES 1974

KIRKLEY'S ABORTION ("K.A.") (O)

PETER ROSS (O)

HATEPE BUG (O)

BRADSHAW'S FANCY (O)

BULLY (K)

MRS SIMPSON KEA

ORANGE & CLARET BLACK RABBIT (M)

BUM FLY (O)

TAUPO LURES 1974

TROUT LURES ALPHABETICAL SECTION

AFTER-BURNER (O)

ORIGIN: NOT KNOWN
HOOK: NOT STATED BUT PROBABLY 2-8
TAIL: RED HACKLE FEATHER
BODY: STRIP OF BLACK RABBIT FUR
HEAD: BLACK

The effect, when wet, can be imagined, and don't you just love the name. The fur (black feral cat would also be an excellent option) pulses beautifully, and I am told that it is a deadly night fly. It is obviously a variation of Bugs Bunny and tied the same way. When I finish my present love affair with the Woolly Bugger, I may well look to this fly, tied with red marabou for the tail, and with Jungle Cock 'eyes'. Ideally the strip of fur should be cut across the pelt so that the fur naturally lies back towards the tail, but I have tied up very effective flies like this using commercially available zonker strips.

The example has been tied on a Kamasan B830 No. 6 long shank.

Tie in the tail. The feather should not extend more than half the length of the hook beyond the bend. Tie in the strip of fur.

Wind the strip of fur along the shank with the fur lying back, each succeeding turn slightly overlaying the previous one. Secure and trim.

If you wished, you could experiment with a red or black hackle, and/or Jungle Cock cheeks.

AFTER DARK (M)

ORIGIN: NOT KNOWN
HOOK 4-8
BODY: RED CHENILLE OR WOOL
RIB: OVAL SILVER
WING: PALE YELLOW HEN HACKLE
HEAD: BLACK

This is an Australian lure which has been included in Keith Draper's 1997 book *New Zealand Trout Flies - Traditional & Modern*. It has to fall under the 'Modern' designation, and while I have never come across it, it has to be assumed that it is now established on the New Zealand scene. The name implies that it is a night lure, but the colouring leads Keith to offer the suggestion that it might be favoured on moonlit nights.

Tie in the body material and ribbing.

Wind on the body material and trim. Tie in the wing feathers by the butts.

Wind on the ribbing, tying down the wing in the Matuku style.

ALBINO (1) (M)

ORIGIN: NOT KNOWN
HOOK: 2-8
BODY: WHITE CHENILLE, FLOSS, OR WOOL
RIB: OVAL SILVER
WING: TWO WHITE COCK HACKLES, BACK TO BACK, AND TIED DOWN ON TOP OF HOOK WITH RIBBING TINSEL
HACKLE: WHITE COCK, WOUND AS A COLLAR
HEAD: BLACK

This appears in John Veniard's book. It is a predictable smelt imitation, popular in the Taupo region. Somewhere along the way, red bits were added and these are shown in the next entry. I have no doubt that this pattern came first.

Tie in the chenille and ribbing.

Wind on the chenille and secure. Tie in the wings at the butt and trim.

Wind on the ribbing, tying down the wing in the Matuku style. Tie in a hackle feather and wind on the hackle

ALBINO (2) (M)

ORIGIN: NOT KNOWN
HOOK: 2-8
TAIL: RED WHISKS
BODY: WHITE CHENILLE, FLOSS, OR WOOL
RIB: OVAL SILVER
WING: WHITE COCK HACKLES
HACKLE: WHITE
HEAD: RED

I have seen a reference to a tail of red ibis and this was obviously the forerunner to the stock dressing which is given above, and which is widely used today - at least in the Taupo region. It is also sold under the name Rotoiti, and Keith Draper recounts in his 1997 book how Bruno Kemball of the Red Spinner at Hatepe would mischievously enquire if one wanted a Red

Nosed Virgin!

This is a very successful lure where smelt abound, especially harling or trolling, and I know of one angler at Taupo who uses this lure to the virtual exclusion of all others - day and night, 365 days of the year.

In some outlets, particularly in the Taupo area, you may see this selling under the name of White Knight.

Tie in the tail. Tie in the chenille and the ribbing.

Wind on the chenille and secure. Tie in the wings by the butts and trim.

Wind on the ribbing, tying down the wing in the Matuku style. Tie in a hackle feather and wind on to form a hackle collar.

ALBINO (3) (M)

ORIGIN: BRONWYN WILSON OF TAUPO
HOOK: 2-8
TAG: RED WOOL OR HACKLE WHISKS
BODY: GREEN, PINK, OR BLUE BARBIE DOLL MATERIAL
RIB: OVAL SILVER FOR THREE-QUARTERS OF BODY, THEN ONE TURN AT HEAD TO HOLD WING DOWN
WING: FOUR WHITE COCK HACKLES
TOPPING: FLASHABOU OR HOLOGRAPHIC TINSEL - MATCH COLOURS TO BODY COLOUR USED
HACKLE: WHITE
HEAD: BLACK

This is a successful smelt pattern, which incorporates the flash and dazzle which is absent from the other Albino patterns. Barbie Doll material is available from fabric shops (see my comments under Success).

The method of ribbing described adds strength while retaining movement to the wing. It is a matter of opinion whether this justifies the Matuku designation or whether it is a streamer tie.

Tie in the tag. Tie in a thin strip of body material and the ribbing.

Return the thread back three-quarters of the way along the shank. Wind on the Barbie Doll material and the ribbing to this point and secure.

Continue the thread and body material nearly to the head and secure. Tie in the wing feathers by the butts. Take one final turn with the ribbing catching down the wing.

Tie in the topping. Tie in a hackle feather and wind on to form a hackle collar.

ALEXANDRA (O)

ORIGIN: NOT KNOWN
HOOK: 2-14
TAG: RED IBIS OR DYED WHISKS
BODY: FLAT SILVER
WING: GREEN PEACOCK HERL
HACKLE: BLACK
CHEEK: JUNGLE COCK
HEAD: BLACK

This is more commonly tied as a 'wee wet' (as Hugh McDowell describes them), but for a period they were tied up in the larger sizes as a lure. Two examples tied in this manner appear in Bragg's book, noted in one instance as being a Canterbury pattern. It does, of course have a far older origin beginning in England about 1860 during the time of Princess (later Queen) Alexandra after whom the fly was named. Tied up in the larger sizes it was once popular in the Taupo and Rotorua regions where rainbow trout, in particular, succumbed to Her Majesty.

Tie in the tail whisks. Tie in the body tinsel.

Wind on the tinsel to form the body. (My method is to tie the tinsel in at the head and wind it down to the bend and back.)

Tie in the peacock herl for the wing. Tie in the hackle feather and wind on to form the hackle collar.

Add Jungle Cock cheeks and complete the head in the usual way.

ALL BLACK (M)

ORIGIN: NOT KNOWN
HOOK: 2-8
BODY: BLACK CHENILLE
RIB: OVAL SILVER
WING: BLACK COCK HACKLES
HACKLE: BLACK
HEAD: BLACK

Given that night lures are generally of dark material, this is an inevitable creation, although its exact origin remains a mystery. Just as predictable is the name, inspired no less by our national rugby team I presume, as by the materials used. A night fly which has all the credentials to be successful.

Tie in the chenille and ribbing.

Wind on the chenille body and secure. Tie in the wings at the butt and trim.

Wind on the ribbing, tying down the wing in the Matuku style. Tie in a hackle feather and wind on to form a hackle collar.

ANNA'S BLUE GHOST (M)

ORIGIN: ROB LIMMER OF TAURANGA
HOOK: 2-10
TAIL: RED WHISKS
BODY: SOLDIER BLUE CHENILLE
RIB: OVAL SILVER
WING: GREY COCK HACKLE
HACKLE: GREY COCK HACKLE
TOPPING: PEARL POLAR FLASH
HEAD: BLACK

This was tied up for Anna who, with her husband Dave, manage the Ohau Channel Lodge. Anna wanted something with blue in it, and this was the result. It has been fishing very well in the Ohau Channel, and Dave claims that it is deadly in Lake Tarawera.

Basically, it is a dark-bodied smelt fly, which is fished with a fast, jerky retrieve, or slower on a starry night. Rob notes that at certain times of the year smelt are not all silver or transparent white but can have a dark hue in the body.

Tie in the whisks. Tie in the chenille and ribbing.

Wind on the chenille body. Tie in the wing feathers by the butts.

Wind on the ribbing, tying down the wing in the Matuku style. Tie in a hackle feather.

Wind on the hackle feather to form a collar.

AURORA (O)

ORIGIN: MAUREEN BUTLER OF ROTORUA
HOOK: 4-8
TAG: FLUORESCENT GLO-BUG YARN (SULPHUR YELLOW),TEASED OUT
BODY: FLUORESCENT GLO-BUG YARN (SULPHUR YELLOW)
RIB: FLAT SILVER BRAID ("VERNA" BRAND)
THROAT: FLASHABOU ACCENT WHITE
WING: WHITE ARCTIC FOX FUR
TOPPING: OLIVE MARABOU
HEAD: BLACK

This is an attractor pattern, which has proved very successful at any time, but it is particularly good in discoloured water and even at night. Alphabetically this is the first of several of Maureen's innovative hair style type lures, all of which have shown themselves to be tried and true over many years. In 1990 Maureen was privileged to be elected the first ever lady life member of TALTAC, the Turangi based angler's organisation. Maureen uses 'Verna' brand tinsel, or braid, gold and silver. I have referred to it by name in this pattern of hers only. I have a small amount left of the quantity she kindly gave me. I do not know where to get any more. If you ever come across it, buy it. it is easily the best I have come across.

Tie in a length of glo-bug yarn leaving a short extension for the tag. Tie in the ribbing.

Wind on the glo-bug yarn followed by the ribbing. Secure.

Tie in the Flashabou under the throat. Tie in the hair wing followed by the marabou topping.

AWAHOU (See Leslie's Lure)

AWAHOU SPECIAL (K)

ORIGIN: NOT KNOWN

HOOK: 2-8
TAIL: COCK PHEASANT RUMP FIBRES
BODY: RED, YELLOW, OR GREEN CHENILLE
RIB: OVAL SILVER TINSEL
WING: TWO PAIRS OF COCK PHEASANT RUMP FEATHERS TIED IN TO LIE ALONGSIDE BODY
HEAD: BLACK

This appears in an English book by John Veniard called *Reservoir and Lake Flies*, under a section titled New Zealand Lake Patterns. This is tied in the Killer style, and is very similar in many respects to Mrs Simpson. Indeed, it has been unwittingly resurrected commercially in some parts of the North Island under the name of Bart Simpson.

It was presumably named after the Awahou Stream, which flows into Lake Rotorua north of Ngongotaha. As with all Killer lures, the ribbing is probably unnecessary

Tie in the tail, chenille, and ribbing.

Wind on the chenille and ribbing and secure. Depending on the size of hook used, you may wish to tie in a pair of wing feathers at the mid-point, in which case proceed as for a Mrs Simpson. My interpretation is that only one set of wing feathers is used.

Tie in a pair of feathers, on each side of the shank in the Killer style.

AWESOME AUCK (M)

ORIGIN: RITCHIE BUCHANAN OF TAUPO
HOOK: 2-8
TAIL: RED WHISKS
BODY: WHITE WOOL OVER-WRAPPED WITH BLUE WOOL
RIB: OVAL SILVER
WING: WHITE COCK HACKLES
TOPPING: RED DMC EMBROIDERY YARN
HEAD: BLACK

This is Ritchie's tribute to the successful Auckland Blues and provincial rugby team. The success of the Auckland side is reflected in the success of this lure. It is a good seller for either, or both, reasons.

It is mainly a summer smelting pattern for the months December to March, particularly from February onwards. For some reason, it seems to be at its best at stream mouths flowing into the Western Bay at Lake Taupo.

Tie in the tail whisks. Tie in the two body colours and the ribbing.

Wind on the white wool body followed by the blue wool, spiralling it over the white. Tie in the wing feathers.

Wind on the ribbing, tying down the wing in the Matuku style. Tie in the topping, which should reach back to the end of the wing.

BADGER (M)

ORIGIN: NOT KNOWN
HOOK: 2-8
BODY: WHITE CHENILLE
RIB: OVAL SILVER
WING: BADGER HACKLE
HACKLE: BADGER HACKLE
HEAD: BLACK

Keith Draper says of this fly: "This lure is fairly well known in the South Island. In the north it would have its head painted red and be called a white Taupo Tiger. Either way, it is basically the same pattern. There can be no doubt the Badger evolved separately from the Tiger". (1971)

Tie in the chenille and ribbing.

Wind on the chenille and secure. Tie in the wing at the butt and trim.

Wind on the ribbing, tying down the wing in the Matuku style. Tie in the hackle feather and wind on to form a hackle collar.

BADGER SMELT (O)

ORIGIN: KILWELL'S OF ROTORUA
HOOK: 2-8
TAIL: GOLDEN PHEASANT TIPPETS
BODY: WHITE CHENILLE
RIB: OVAL SILVER
WING: BADGER HACKLE TIED IN AT THE HEAD ONLY
HACKLE: BADGER HACKLE
HEAD: BLACK

By changing the wing feather from badger to ginger or grizzle, Kilwell created three otherwise identical smelt patterns. The trailing wing, which is not tied down in the Matuku style, is better suited to harling as there would be less chance of the wing catching around the hook, as it would be prone to do when casting.

Tie in the tail tippets. Tie in the chenille and the ribbing. Secure and trim.

Wind on the chenille, followed by the ribbing. Secure and trim.

Tie in the wing feathers at the butt so that they are trailing free and not secured to the body. Tie in the hackle feather and wind to form a hackle collar.

BALCARASTER (M)

ORIGIN: BRONWYN WILSON OF TAUPO

HOOK: 2-6

TAG: RED HACKLE WHISKS

BODY: REAR THREE-QUARTERS: PEARL LUREX YARN. FRONT QUARTER: YELLOW ICE CHENILLE.

RIB: OVAL SILVER

WING: WHITE

TOPPING: THIN SILVER HOLOGRAPHIC TINSEL.

HACKLE: YELLOW

HEAD: RED.

This is another smelt pattern from Bronwyn's vice and which has proved successful at Taupo, principally harling. The name comes from an old family name of one of her relatives. Bronwyn gives an alternative body dressing of yellow sparkle yarn and dubbed Antron for the rear and front sections respectively. (See my comments under Albino 3 with regard to the ribbing.)

Tie in the tag whisks. Tie in the first section of body material and the ribbing.

Take the thread back three quarters of the way along the shank. Wind on the lurex and ribbing to this point and secure. Tie in the second body section and wind on to the head.

Tie in the wing feathers by the butt. Finish the ribbing with one turn at the head to hold the wing down. Tie in the topping.

Tie in the hackle feather and wind on to form a hackle collar.

BALLARD'S BEAUTY (M)

ORIGIN: RAY PUNTER OF ROTORUA

HOOK: 4

BODY: DANVILLES MONO CORD, LIGHT GREY

WING: CHENILLE 'FISH SHAPES' (AVAILABLE FROM CRAFT SHOPS)

TOPPING: APPROXIMATELY 6 STRANDS EACH OF FLASHABOU ACCENT AND SILVER KRYSTAL FLASH TINSEL

HEAD: BLACK

This was named after a former colleague, Malcolm Ballard, "whose very first trout fishing trip was made memorable by the outstanding success of this fly." (Bryan Tichborne - *Anglers' Paradise*). It does not cast well, and the body tends to lose its shape after trout have chewed on it. However, it has proved itself as an excellent and successful harling pattern, particularly when trout are smelting. The lure should be thoroughly dried after use to prevent the wire core in the body material rusting. The chenille 'shapes' are supplied in lengths consisting of six 'shapes', approximately 10 lengths to a packet.

Take the grey tying thread down to the bend, then wind back to the eye, and back down to the bend again, all the time in close, even turns. This forms a light grey, slender body on which to attach the wing.

Select a chenille 'shape' and decide which way round you want it on the hook (the chenille sometimes lies better one way than the other). Snip through the wire close to the beginning of the fish shape at the chosen head end, and slightly further back at the tail end.

Cut away the underside of the 'shape' which is to sit on top of the body.

Using the grey tying thread, carefully tie the shape onto the shank top in the Matuku style, winding in evenly spaced turns about 1mm apart towards the head. Stroke the chenille back after each turn. Tie down the head securely.

Tie in the topping and complete the head in the usual way.

B and B (M)

ORIGIN: BRONWYN WILSON OF TAUPO

HOOK: 2-6

TAG: RED HACKLE WHISKS

UNDER-BODY: LIGHT YELLOW GLO-BUG YARN

OVER-BODY: YELLOW KRYSTAL FLASH, WELL GLUED

RIB: OVAL SILVER

WING: TWO YELLOW FEATHERS INSIDE TWO WHITE FEATHERS

HACKLE: WHITE

HEAD: RED

No, the name does not stand for Bed and Breakfast, although trout might certainly be on the morning menu! The name originated when Bronwyn caught a Brown the first time she used this lure. The 11lb specimen, in beautiful condition, has been mounted and graces her living room. The lure is not a one-fish-wonder, and has gone on to catch many more.

Tie in the tag. Tie in the under-body material, a strand of Krystal Flash, and the ribbing.

Wind on the glo-bug yarn under-body followed by the Krystal Flash wound closely over the glo-bug yarn to the head. Secure.

Tie in the wing feathers. Wind on the ribbing, tying down the

wing in the Matuku style.

Tie in a hackle feather, and wind on to form a hackle collar.

BANTAM (M)

ORIGIN: NOT KNOWN
HOOK: NOT STATED BUT PROBABLY 2-8
BODY: WHITE
RIB: OVAL SILVER
WING: PALE NATURAL BROWN
HACKLE: PALE NATURAL BROWN
HEAD: BLACK

This appears in Bragg's book as a Taupo and Rotorua lure during the 1960s. It is very similar to Hope's Silvery without the tail and topping. The name suggests that the wing feathers come from a Bantam. For the above example I have used ordinary natural pale brown (ginger) hackles. The end result seems to be the same. Following the single example portrayed in Bragg's book, I have kept the head hackle on the long side.

Tie in the body material and ribbing.

Wind on the body material. Tie in the wing feathers by the butts.

Wind on the ribbing, tying down the wing in the Matuku style.

Tie in a hackle feather, and wind on to form a hackle collar.

BARRED KILLER (K)

ORIGIN: NOT KNOWN
HOOK: 2-8
TAIL: RED-SQUIRREL TAIL
BODY: WOOL OR CHENILLE, USUALLY RED OR YELLOW, BUT ANY OF THE POPULAR COLOURS
WING: GREY PARTRIDGE
HEAD: BLACK

This is a stablemate of Kilwell No.1 and Kilwell No.2 and tied commercially by Kilwell's at least as late as 1974. Difficulties in obtaining the plumage in sufficient quantities for commercial production led to its demise and relegation to a place on the wall in Kilwell's museum.

However the plumage is still obtainable for the home tier. Another reason for its demise, so I am told, is that its performance as a fish taker has never come up to expectations, although it is difficult to see why that might be so. The same barred feathers, dyed green, appear on many modern versions of Hamill's Killer.

Tie in the tail fibres, and tie in the body material.

Take the thread part way back along the shank. Wind on the body material to this point. Tie in a pair of wing feathers on either side of the shank in the Killer style.

Take the thread back to the head.

Wind on the body material to this point and tie off. Tie in another pair of wing feathers on either side of the shank.

BARRED ROCK (M)

ORIGIN: THE BARRED ROCK LURES (WHITE, SILVER, AND RED) ARE ASSOCIATED WITH MR. W. (BILL) WINCHESTER OF LEESTON.
HOOK: 2-8
BODY: WHITE OR RED CHENILLE
RIB: OVAL SILVER
WING: BARRED ROCK
HACKLE: BARRED ROCK
HEAD: BLACK

Canterbury lures which are very similar to Dorothy if dressed conventionally and would probably be regarded as such in the North Island. However, if tied in the original manner (as I have done here), using soft hen and spade hackles, the effect is of a shorter and chunkier lure than the Dorothy and is altogether a different fly. "Barred Rock" is another name for Grizzle Hackle (from the Plymouth Rock) which is readily available. Depending on the body colour, the lures are known as Barred Rock White, Barred Rock Red, etc

Tie in the chenille and silver ribbing.

Take the thread and the chenille back nearly to the head and secure. Tie in the wing feather.

Wind on the ribbing, tying down the wing in the Matuku style. Tie in the hackle feather and wind on to form a hackle collar.

BARRED ROCK SILVER (M)

ORIGIN: ASSOCIATED WITH MR. W. (BILL) WINCHESTER OF LEESTON.
HOOK: 2-8

BODY: SILVER
RIB: OVAL SILVER
WING: BARRED ROCK (GRIZZLE)
HACKLE: BARRED ROCK, THROAT ONLY
WING OVERLAY: GREY MALLARD
HEAD: BLACK

One of the range of Barred Rock Lures shown on the previous entry. This has been separately listed because of the wing overlay, which has considerations for the fly-tier, and removes it somewhat from the previous pattern. Again, I have tied it in the original manner. "Barred Rock" is another name for Grizzle Hackle.

Tie in the flat silver for the body, and the oval silver for the ribbing.

Form a body with the flat tinsel and secure. Tie in a grizzle hackle for the wing.

Wind on the ribbing, tying down the wing in the Matuku style. Tie in the wing overlay. Tie in a hackle feather and wind on to form a hackle collar.

BARRY'S SMELT (O)

ORIGIN: BARRY BIRCHALL OF KAIKOHE
HOOK: 2-6
TAIL: BUNCH OF YELLOW HACKLE TOPPED WITH A BUNCH OF YELLOW MARABOU, PREFERABLY OF A LIGHTER SHADE THAN THE HACKLE FIBRES
BODY: SILVER LUREX YARN
WING: PALE GREY RABBIT STRIP CUT ACROSS THE GRAIN AND WOUND ALONG THE SHANK BUGS BUNNY STYLE BUT SPACED OUT SO THAT THE BODY SHOWS
OVERWING: A FEW STRANDS OF PEARL FLASHABOU
THROAT: A TUFT OF RED MARABOU
HEAD: BLACK

This pattern appeared in one of Nancy Tichborne's renowned calendars and subsequently the book *Angler's Paradise* co-authored with her husband Bryan. Barry says that this is a very effective summertime lure, succeeding when others fail.

Tie in the tail fibres and the yellow marabou. Tie in the lurex and the strip of rabbit so that the end fur extends over the top of the marabou tail.

Take the thread back nearly to the head. Wind on the lurex body and tie off. Follow with the strip of rabbit fur Bugs Bunny style (perhaps more accurately, Palmerwise). Secure and trim.

Tie in a few strands of pearl Flashabou , which should reach back to about the bend in the hook, but not so as to foul the hook. Tie in a tuft of red marabou at the throat.

BASIL'S INANGA (M)

ORIGIN: BASIL JACKSON OF ROTORUA
HOOK: 2-8, LONG SHANK
TAIL: DARK MALLARD FIBRES
BODY: SILVER TINSEL
RIB: OVAL SILVER
WING: BADGER
CHEEK: JUNGLE COCK
HEAD: BLACK

This features in Nancy and Bryan Tichborne's book, *Anglers' Paradise*, under the name of Whitebait. It is intended to represent the adult form of the whitebait known as inanga. Like Jack's Sprat (which this closely resembles), it is likely to be most effective at the later stage of the whitebait run, in the mid and lower river sections during November and December, although it will serve as a smelt pattern at any time. I believe the adult whitebait is correctly known as 'inanga' although it is often spelt 'enunga' or 'inunga' being a phonetic corruption of the original. There are quite a few Maori words which are specific to various stages of the whitebait, but 'inanga' seems to be the generic term.

Tie in the tail. Tie in the body tinsel and ribbing.

Wind on the tinsel body and secure. Tie in the wing feathers.

Wind on the ribbing, tying down the wing in the Matuku style.

Add cheeks of Jungle Cock 'eyes'.

BASIL'S SMELT (P)

ORIGIN: BASIL JACKSON OF ROTORUA
HOOK: 2-8, LONG SHANK
TAIL: YELLOW HACKLE FIBRES
BODY: WHITE CHENILLE
RIB: OVAL SILVER AND AURORA SKIRT
UNDERWING: ARTIFICIAL POLAR BEAR FUR OR ANY SUBSTITUTE
OVERWING: DARK MALLARD BREAST FEATHER
HACKLE: DARK MALLARD (THROAT ONLY)
HEAD: BLACK

This is a good smelt pattern, which has been very successful for Basil. I have spoken with Rotorua anglers who claim it to be one of the best smelt patterns available. It features in the Tichborne book, *Anglers' Paradise*. The effect of the two ribbings is that the body takes on a yellowish hue, with little of the chenille showing. Any white fur can be used for the underwing, and also calf-tail and bucktail. The underwing should not be too thick. The trick with the overwing is to lightly varnish the mallard feather and then run the thumb and forefinger down the feather forming a cowl shape. Allow to dry before tying it in.

Tie in the tail. Tie in the chenille, tinsel ribbing, and the Aurora skirt.

Wind on the chenille body. Follow with the tinsel ribbing, and then the Aurora skirt.

Tie in the throat hackle. Tie in the underwing at the shoulder. It should lie along the top of the body to bolster the overwing, and not be too thick.

Tie in the varnished and dried overwing.

BASIL'S WHITEBAIT (O)

ORIGIN: BASIL JACKSON OF ROTORUA

HOOK: 4-8, LONG SHANK

BODY AND TAIL: ARTIFICIAL WHITE WOOL (BABY WOOL)

RIB: OVAL SILVER

EYES: STICK-ON OR PAINTED, YELLOW WITH A BLACK PUPIL

HEAD: BLACK

This appears in the Tichborne book, *Anglers' Paradise*, under the name of Fritter, juxtaposed immediately above Basil's Whitebait in a clever by-play of symbolic imagery. However, Basil wishes it to be known as Whitebait, as that is what it is intended to represent.

The "Whitebait" shown in the same publication is the adult form (inanga), and has been renamed Basil's Inaga for this book with Basil's consent. Basil prefers a body of Baby Wool, available from craft shops, as it does not go soggy like natural wool, and has a luminescence which is absent from natural wool.

Although this is a whitebait pattern it is, of course, equally effective as a smelt pattern. Basil based this lure on the String Fly as depicted in John Parson's book, *Deceiving Trout - The Flytyer's Art*, altering it principally by the addition of eyes.

Tie in the wool and the ribbing. Leave a short overhang of wool to form the tail, which is teased out.

Return the thread nearly to the head. Wind on the wool to this point and secure. Wind on the ribbing between the turns of wool and secure.

Form the head in the usual way, but incorporating eyes using any of the usual methods.

BAXTER'S SPECIAL (O)

ORIGIN: DR. RQ QUENTIN-BAXTER OF WELLINGTON

HOOK: NOT STATED BUT PROBABLY 2-8

BODY: WHITE

RIB: FLAT SILVER

WING: PALE GINGER

CHEEK: GUINEA FOWL DYED OLD GOLD

HACKLE: GRIZZLE

HEAD: BLACK

Created in 1940, this was a successful lure in Lake Ellesmere. This featured in Bragg's book. I cannot be certain about the hackle collar material, but the photographed example looks very close to the original, and if there is a difference between the dressing I am sure it will be lost on the trout. My attempts to create 'old gold' can certainly be bettered, but I am happy enough with the end result.

I have no doubt that this is tied in the loose-winged Streamer style.

Tie in the body material and ribbing.

Wind on the body material and follow with the ribbing.

Tie in the wing feathers by the butts at the shoulder. For this pattern I use only two hackle feathers.

Tie in cheek feathers. Tie in a hackle feather and wind on to form a collar.

BETHLEHEM CAT (O)

ORIGIN: DR. JOHN KENT OF CHRISTCHURCH

HOOK: 2-10

TAIL: SHORT BUNCH OF BLACK CAT FUR

BODY: BLACK OR RED CHENILLE OR WOOL

WINGS: TWO BUNCHES OF BLACK CAT FUR TIED ON TOP OF THE HOOK (POSSUM FUR OR- PREFERABLY,

PROVIDED IT IS REALLY BLACK- DYED BLACK RABBIT CAN BE USED AS A SUBSTITUTE)

TOPPING: 2 PUKEKO FEATHERS (OPTIONAL)

HEAD: BLACK

This pattern appears in *North Island Trout Fishing Guide*, by John Kent, and also featured in the Tichborne calendar and book. It is a night lure and John believes it is as good as any night lure he has used. Mostly, he uses it at stream mouths on a floating line, but in the right circumstances a sinking line can also be used to good effect. The lure evolved, and acquired its name, after John found a dead black cat on the side of the road at Bethlehem, near Tauranga, which he took home and skinned, much to the amusement of a friend who caught him in the act. On its first outing, the Cat was spectacularly successful, and John called unannounced on his friend to show him his haul. He found his friend in the process of skinning a cat for himself! John reckons he ran it down deliberately! All of which goes to show that it is a demand lure.

Tie in the tail. At the same point tie in a length of body material - colour of choice.

Wind the thread and the body material part way along the shank and tie in a bunch of fur for the wing.

Take the thread and body material nearly to the head and repeat the process. Trim off the chenille or wool. Add Pukeko feathers if using (tied Pukeko style).

BILL'S KILLER (M)

ORIGIN: NOT KNOWN

HOOK: 2-8

TAG: GREEN WOOL

BODY: REAR HALF: GREEN WOOL. FRONT HALF: RED WOOL. A FURNACE HACKLE IS WOUND BETWEEN THE TWO SECTIONS

RIB: OVAL SILVER

WING: FURNACE

HACKLE: FURNACE

HEAD: BLACK

This is an old pattern that was put out by Kilwell's of Rotorua. Although called a "Killer", it is in fact tied in the Matuku style. I would guess that it is best fished in the evening.

Tie in the tag. Tie in the first segment of wool and the ribbing. Trim.

Take the thread part way back along the shank. Wind on the green wool to this point. Tie in a hackle feather and wind on. Tie in the wool for the second segment.

Take the thread back nearly to the head. Wind on the red wool and tie off. Tie in the wing feathers.

Wind on the ribbing, tying down the wing in the Matuku style. Tie in a hackle feather, and wind on to form a hackle collar.

BISHOP'S BLESSING (M)

ORIGIN: KILWELL'S OF ROTORUA

HOOK: 2-8

TAG: RED

BODY: FLAT SILVER TINSEL

RIB: OVAL SILVER TINSEL

WING: HONEY GRIZZLE

HACKLE: HONEY GRIZZLE

HEAD: BLACK

Sometimes known as a Silver Parsons, it is popular as a harling fly, and kills well as a stream fly. Keith Draper says of this lure (1971): "Most anglers prefer it to be tied with pale feathers ... As John Wells told me: 'We had a Parsons' Glory, a Pope's Nondescript, a Silver Priest, so why not a Bishop's Blessing?' "

Tie in the tag, the body tinsel, and the ribbing.

Wind on the tinsel body and secure. Tie in the wing at the butt and trim.

Wind on the ribbing tying down the wing in the Matuku style. Tie in a hackle feather and wind on to form a hackle collar.

BLACK ARROW (O)

ORIGIN: JOHN MORTON OF CHRISTCHURCH

HOOK: 2-4, LONG SHANK

TAIL: FAIRLY LONG STRAIGHTISH POSSUM TAIL

BODY: 3-4MM WIDE STRIP OF BLACK RABBIT FUR FROM A NATURAL BLACK RABBIT

SIDE WINGS: 4MM WIDE STRIP OF NATURAL BLACK RABBIT FUR

COLLAR: DYED RED ROOSTER HACKLE, FAIRLY LONG AND SOFT

TOPPING: TWO IRIDESCENT BLUE FEATHERS FROM A PEACOCK NECK WITH THE CENTRE REMOVED.

HEAD: BLACK.

John describes this as his 'numero uno' night fly, the one he turns to when it matters. When one considers the astonishing effectiveness of Black Pete and Hob Nailed Boot, then it is clear that this lure is very special. It is remarkably effective with very large trout, particularly browns, night cruising in deep still pools such as large river backwaters, as well as on the drop-off shelves on the lakes at river mouths. John fishes this on a floating line with a long (about 18 feet) leader. He tells me 'there are a few fish out there now wearing this fly as lip furniture because this fly attracts the really big brownies that are tackle smashers.'

It is not a particularly difficult fly to tie, but the tying instructions are very difficult to articulate and have therefore been given in far greater detail than is normally the case.

Some experimentation may be necessary to get the right proportions for the side wings, which form the 'arrow' head.

From the hook eye, leave the first third of the hook shank bare. Attach the thread and bind the remaining two-thirds of the shank down to the bend. Tie in a bunch of possum tail.

Take a strip of rabbit fur. Cut the end of the skin to a point and tie it in at the bend. If the free end is extended beyond the bend, the grain of the fur will lie towards the bend. That determines which end of the strip to cut and tie in.

Take the thread back two-thirds the way along the shank to the starting point. Palmer wind the fur strip along the shank to this point. Comb the fur rearwards to form a thick body.

Take another strip of rabbit fur. Hold it so that the grain of the fur runs from left to right. Trim off a section of fur working from right to left i.e. against the grain. The amount to be trimmed will be a matter of experimentation.

Place the prepared strip against the Palmered body on the far side of the hook. The end of the bare strip of skin will be cut to a tapered point and tied in at the body tie off point. The other end, the tip, will extend towards the bend with the fur against the body, skin side out, and the grain of the fur will run towards the head.

Fold the strip at the intersection of the fur and the trimmed skin and tie in the tip just forward of the last tie in point. This forms half the 'arrow' head.

Repeat the process on the near side of the hook, forming the other half of the 'arrow' head.

Tie in the hackle feather and wind on. Tie in the topping. Complete the head in the usual way.

BLACK BOOBIE (H)

ORIGIN:	ADAPTED BY HUGH MCDOWELL FROM AN ENGLISH PATTERN OF THE SAME NAME.
HOOK:	6-8
BODY:	POLYSTYRENE PACKING BALLS
TAIL:	BLACK MARABOU
WINGS:	BLACK HACKLE
HEAD:	POLYSTYRENE BALLS WRAPPED IN PANTYHOSE OR NYLON.

This is a very buoyant fly which is fished with a fast sinking line. The fly remains suspended above the line, and retrieving it causes the fly to wriggle downwards. A pause in the retrieve lets it rise, suggesting an injured creature struggling to regain its equilibrium or trying to seek cover on the bottom. The amount of movement and the extent of the rise can be varied and controlled by the length of the leader, the duration and speed of the retrieve, and the length of the pause while retrieving. Hugh's favourite colour is black, but a friend of his swears by orange. Hugh says: 'Burgundy, purple, pink, yellow, lime and white all take fish, but for whatever reason I have yet to take a trout on green, red or any two tone or multi-coloured combinations.'

Apparently, the 'Dolly Parton' profile inspired the name.

Tie in a bunch of marabou for the tail. Secure, cement, and cut thread.

Cut a postage-stamp sized piece of black pantyhose or other nylon, force the eye of the hook through the centre, and slide it down the shank as far as possible. Pierce a polystyrene ball with a toothpick on both sides (to prevent splitting) and thread it down against the nylon. Reattach the thread. Stretch the nylon over the top of the ball to envelop it tightly and secure with the thread. Colour the ball with a black felt-tip pen. Tie in the hackle feather and wind on. Secure, cement, and cut thread.

Repeat the ball and hackle process. For the head, wrap two coloured balls in pantyhose, secure firmly behind the eye, stretch surplus nylon away from the fly and cut free. Criss-cross the thread between the balls, then tie off. (The balls are easily damaged by trout teeth, but it is an easy fly to tie.)

BLACK DEMON (M)

ORIGIN:	NOT KNOWN
HOOK:	4-6, LONG SHANK

TAIL: GOLDEN PHEASANT TIPPETS
BODY: GOLD TINSEL
RIB: OVAL GOLD
WING: FOUR BLACK COCK HACKLES
HACKLE: ORANGE, THROAT ONLY
CHEEK: JUNGLE COCK
HEAD: BLACK

This appears in Bragg's book (see my comments under Klondike Kate). It was Bragg's view that Matuku style flies should avoid buoyant materials and should not be overdressed as those factors reduce mobility and depth of 'swim'.

Golden pheasant tippets are listed in the pattern given but are not apparent on Bragg's photo example. I have included them in my example.

The photographed example has been tied on a Kamasan B830 No. 6 long shank.

Tie in the golden pheasant tippets for the tail. Tie in the body tinsel and ribbing.

Wind on the body tinsel. Tie in the wing feathers by the butts.

Wind on the ribbing, tying down the wing in the Matuku style.

Tie in the throat hackle and the Jungle Cock cheeks.

BLACK MARABOU (O)

ORIGIN: NOT KNOWN
HOOK: 2-8
TAIL: A SHORT TUFT OF RED WOOL UNDER A BUNCH OF BLACK MARABOU
BODY: BLACK CHENILLE
RIB: OVAL SILVER
WING: A BUNCH OF BLACK MARABOU
HACKLE: (OPTIONAL) BLACK COCK HACKLE
HEAD: BLACK

This is now a popular style of lure, which can be found in every conceivable colour. It differs from Murphy and Poodle in several respects but most noticeably in that the dressing calls for a single bunch of marabou for the wing. In this colouring, it is highly regarded as a night lure.

I have taken this pattern from Keith Draper's 1997 publication.

Tie in the tuft of wool and the marabou tail.

Tie in the chenille and the ribbing. Wind on the chenille to the head followed by the ribbing.

Tie in a bunch of marabou at the shoulder for the wing. If using, tie in a hackle feather and wind on to form a hackle collar.

BLACK MATUKU (M)

ORIGIN: NOT KNOWN
HOOK: 4-8
BODY: BLACK CHENILLE OR WOOL
RIB: OVAL SILVER
WING: BLACK HEN HACKLES
HEAD: BLACK

This is an Australian lure which has found its way into Keith Draper's 1997 book. It differs from All Black in that hen, not cock, hackles are used in the wing. It differs form Hart's Creek through the absence of a red tag, and it differs from Red and Black Matuka (another Ozzie import) through the body colour. A night lure.

Tie in the body material and ribbing.

Wind on the body material nearly to the head. Tie in the wing feathers by the butts at the shoulder.

Wind on the ribbing, tying down the wing in the Matuku style.

BLACK MAX (O)

ORIGIN: MAX SHEFFIELD OF REREWHAKAAITU
HOOK: 6-8
TAG: RED WOOL
TAIL: BLACK SQUIRREL, ALTHOUGH THE ORIGINAL USED HAIR SNIPPED FROM MAX'S BLACK LABRADOR DOG.
BODY: BLACK WOOL
RIB: THIN COPPER WIRE
WING: 2 PAIRS OF BLACK PUKEKO FEATHERS BACK TO BACK, TIED IN AT THE HEAD.
HACKLE: BLACK, BEARD STYLE
HEAD: BLACK

This evolved from Black Prince, and was tied up to imitate the koura found on the sandy ledges around the margins of Lake Rerewhakaaiitu, although it has enjoyed success further afield. It is best fished slowly on the bottom at times of changing light, especially the evening, but Max has taken a limit bag in the middle of the day.

The preferred method of fishing is to let the lure lie on the bottom, and then retrieve with short sharp twitches causing the fly to send up small puffs of sand.

There is some confusion as to whether this is tied as shown or Pukeko style. The painting by Nancy Tichborne in the 1991 calendar is unclear on this point. Maureen Butler sent me a version tied Pukeko style - that was her interpretation of the painting. Mine differed. Max, himself, could not recall, but seemed to recall that it was tied as I have shown it and gave the go-ahead for it to be tied in this fashion. If, as he says, it evolved from the Black Prince, then logically this must be the correct style. The addition of Jungle Cock eyes is my own vision.

Tie in the tag. Tie in the tail on top of the tag. Then tie in the wool and ribbing.

Wind on the wool body and secure. Follow with the ribbing and tie off.

Tie in the hackle under the throat, beard style.

Tie in the wing feathers by the butts at the head but so they stand vertically rather than the cowl-shape of Craig's Night-time.

BLACK AND ORANGE (M)

ORIGIN:	POSSIBLY 'BUDGE' HINTZ OF AUCKLAND
HOOK:	4
TAIL:	GOLDEN PHEASANT TIPPETS
RIB:	OVAL GOLD
BODY:	EQUAL SECTIONS OF ORANGE AND BLACK CHENILLE, WITH THE BLACK SECTION AT THE HEAD.
WING:	A STRIP OF DARK DYED RABBIT
HACKLE:	COCH-A-BONDDU
HEAD:	BLACK

This pattern is given by O.S. ('Budge') Hintz in his book *Fisherman's Paradise*. This is really just a version of Claret given in the same publication, which is really just a variation of Rabbit. Hintz recommends this fly for dawn fishing. 'Coch-a-bonddu' has acquired an amazing variety of spellings. Hugh McDowell's etymological research leads him to insist that this - and only this - is the correct spelling. Coch-a-bonddu originally referred to black tipped furnace hackles which are no longer available. Substitute with a dark furnace hackle, although you can, if you wish, create a coch-a-bonddu feather with the judicious use of a black felt-tipped pen.

Tie in the tail whisks, ribbing, and the first section of chenille.

Take the thread part way back along the shank. Wind on the orange chenille to this point and secure. Tie in the second section of chenille.

Wind on the black chenille to the head. Tie in the strip of rabbit.

Wind on the ribbing, tying down the rabbit strip in the Matuku style. Tie in the hackle feather and wind on as a collar.

BLACK PETE (K)

ORIGIN:	JOHN MORTON OF CHRISTCHURCH
HOOK:	4 OR 6
TAIL:	FULL BUNCH OF BLACK SQUIRREL
BODY:	RED CHENILLE
WING:	IRIDESCENT BLUE PEACOCK NECK
HEAD:	BLACK

John Morton designed this fly specifically for night fishing for brown trout in the South Island. It is said that it will take brown trout when most other patterns fail. It is best fished on the bottom and very, very slowly. Although it excels for this purpose, it is of little use during the day.

The feathers are tied in the Killer style. I have it direct from John that the feathers are tied in as follows: one pair is tied in at the tail, a single feather on either side of the shank. A second pair is tied in at mid-section again with a single feather on each side of the shank. Two pairs are tied in at the head with two feathers on each side of the shank - a total of eight individual feathers. Such is John's regard for this fly, he backs himself to beat all comers at night fishing provided he is the only one using Black Pete.

Tie in the tail. Tie in the first pair of peacock feathers, one feather on each side of the shank. Tie in the chenille.

Wind on the chenille to about the mid-point. Tie in another pair of peacock neck feathers, with one feather on either side of the body. Continue the thread and chenille back along the shank until nearly at the head.

Tie in a pair of feathers on either side of the body. Trim, finish the head and varnish.

BLACK PHANTOM (K)

ORIGIN: KILLWELL'S OF ROTORUA

HOOK: 2-8

TAIL: BLACK SQUIRREL

BODY: BLACK OR RED CHENILLE, THOUGH BLACK IS THE GENERALLY ACCEPTED PREFERENCE.

RIB: OVAL SILVER

WING: BLACK PUKEKO FEATHERS FROM BACK AND RUMP OF PUKEKO

CHEEK: JUNGLE COCK

HEAD: BLACK

This is a well-known and excellent night-time lure. According to Hugh McDowell, the only claim to the name is that it uses the same materials as the much older original of the same name which was tied in the Pukeko style (see next entry).

Pukeko substitute (suitably dyed mallard) is readily available. It is illegal to buy or sell Pukeko feathers, but it is not illegal to use them as they are a restricted game bird which can be shot during the season and their feathers thus obtained.

Jungle Cock is very expensive and is often omitted. However, there is no doubt that Jungle Cock eyes improve the effectiveness of lures, particularly night lures, and in the absence of Jungle Cock, the white-centered flank feathers of a Californian quail make a passable substitute. Also, the spotted plumage of a quinea fowl, and even the spotted breast feathers of a young thrush can be used. The silver ribbing is surely a hangover from the Pukeko style dressing because it is invisible and serves no discernible purpose. I believe it can be omitted.

Tie in the tail. Trim, and tie in the chenille and ribbing.

Take the thread, chenille, and ribbing part way back along the shank and secure. Tie in a pair of wings alongside the body in the Killer style. Continue the thread, chenille and ribbing almost to the head.

Repeat the process with the wings and add Jungle Cock cheeks.

BLACK PHANTOM (P)

ORIGIN: NOT KNOWN

HOOK: 2-8

TAG: (OPTIONAL) A SMALL BUNCH OF RED WOOL OR HACKLE FIBRES UNDER THE TAIL.

TAIL: BLACK SQUIRREL

BODY: BLACK OR RED CHENILLE

RIB: OVAL SILVER

WINGS: BLACK PUKEKO FEATHERS

TOPPING: JUNGLE COCK

HEAD: BLACK

This is the much older original dressing of the more common Killer style (see previous entry). It is one of the few Pukeko style lures which does not incorporate a hackle. No matter which way it is tied, it is an effective night-time lure whether fished deep or shallow as water depths dictate.

Tie in the tail, the chenille and the ribbing.

Wind on the chenille to form the body, then the ribbing, secure and trim.

Tie in two or more Pukeko feathers to lie along the top of the shank. Trim. Tie in a Jungle Cock 'eye' to lie on top of the wing.

BLACK PRINCE (M)

ORIGIN: NOT KNOWN, BUT IT PROBABLY ORIGINATED IN THE ROTORUA DISTRICT

HOOK: 2-8

TAG: RED WOOL OR BUNCH OF DYED RED HACKLE FIBRES

BODY: BLACK OR RED CHENILLE, THOUGH BLACK IS THE COMMONLY ACCEPTED PREFERENCE

RIB: OVAL SILVER

WING: BLACK COCK HACKLES

HACKLE: BLACK COCK HACKLES

HEAD: BLACK

With the exception only of the red tag, this is identical to All Black and is sometimes known by (confused with?) that name. It is also identical to a fly used in the South Island called Hart's Creek. Hugh McDowell suggests that Hart's Creek is the red bodied version, but Keith Draper makes no mention of a red body. He claims the correct name depends on where you come from. In addition to the two names mentioned you may see this lure referred to as a Black Matuka, or Red Matuka depending on the body colour, particularly in Australian publications, which explains the Matuka spelling. It is a night fly, but overseas it is valued as a daytime fly also.

Tie in the tag. Trim, then tie in the chenille and ribbing.

Take the thread and chenille back nearly to the head, secure, and tie in the wing at the butt and trim.

Wind on the ribbing, tying down the wing in the Matuku style. Tie in a hackle feather and wind on.

BLACK SMELT (H)

ORIGIN: NOT KNOWN
HOOK: NOT STATED BUT PROBABLY 6-8
TAIL: BLACK SQUIRREL
BODY: SILVER TINSEL
RIB: OVAL SILVER
HACKLE: BLACK
HEAD: RED

This features in Bragg's book as a Taupo and Rotorua districts lure during the 1960s. It is one of four different coloured, but otherwise identical lures. The others being orange, blue, and yellow with squirrel tail dyed to match, and respectively called Orange Smelt, Blue Smelt, and Yellow Smelt.

I am not entirely certain about the body and the rib, but I would be a little surprised if it is not as I have stated.

Tie in a bunch of squirrel tail. Tie in the body tinsel and ribbing.

Wind on the tinsel body followed by the ribbing.

Tie in a hackle feather. Wind on to form a hackle collar.

BLACK and YELLOW (DEVIL) (H)

ORIGIN: NOT KNOWN
HOOK: NOT STATED, BUT PROBABLY 2-8
TAIL: BLACK BUCKTAIL FIBRES
BODY: TWO EQUAL PARTS OF BLACK AND YELLOW MOHAIR
JOINT: BLACK COCK HACKLE TRIMMED TO ABOUT 1/4 INCH (6MM)
HACKLE: BLACK COCK HACKLE
HEAD: BLACK

This pattern is from John Veniard's book under a section titled New Zealand Lake Patterns. The mid-section hackle in the photographed example is the described length without resorting to trimming. It may be that the particular effect which is achieved by cutting hackles is deliberate, but I personally eschew that practice. The same pattern is also given in *Modern Fly Dressings*, by C.H. Kendrick along with a Red and Yellow (Devil), with the first body section colour altering accordingly. In that dressing, the mid-body hackle is not trimmed.

Tie in the tail, and tie in the black mohair.

Wind the thread part way along the shank, take the black body material to this point and secure and trim. Tie in a hackle feather, wind on and secure.

Tie in the yellow body material. Take the thread nearly to the head, and follow with the mohair. Tie in another hackle feather and wind on.

BLONDIE (1) (O)

ORIGIN: NOT KNOWN
HOOK: 4-8, PREFERABLY LONG SHANK
BODY: SILVER WITH A FEW WHISKS OF DYED RED HACKLE
WING: BLONDE HAIR, PREFERABLY THAT OF A CHILD, WHICH IS SOFTER AND FLOWS BETTER IN THE WATER
HEAD: BLACK

Keith Draper says: "This is a great killer when the trout are chasing whitebait in the shallows of a river or lake. It does have a problem, however: If tied too long the hair is inclined to wrap around the shank during casting. The best way to overcome this is to shorten the hair - and if you make your own flies you should procure some long-shanked hooks. There have been many variations of the Blondie. I have seen pale floss used, although it soon matted and lost its effectiveness. Today a popular commercial substitute is the synthetic fibre used for making dolls' hair." (1971) Commercial stock I have come across have a green floss body with silver ribbing.

The hair in the photographed example came from a four month old child, according to my hairdresser, who obtained the sample for me.

Tie in the tail whisks and the silver tinsel. Secure and trim off the surplus.

Wind on the tinsel to form the body, secure at the head and trim. Tie in the hair wing.

Finish the head, and varnish. The home tier could add

painted eyes for extra realism.

BLONDIE (2) (O)

ORIGIN: NOT KNOWN
HOOK: 4-8
TAIL: BUNCH OF WHITE OR CREAM MOHAIR CUT OFF FLAT, ABOUT 3/4 INCH (20MM) LONG
BODY: FLAT SILVER TINSEL
WING: ANOTHER BUNCH OF WHITE MOHAIR TIED IN AT THE HEAD AND CUT OFF LEVEL WITH THE END OF THE TAIL
HEAD: BLACK

This pattern is from John Veniard's book and is presumably one of the many variations referred to by Keith Draper (see previous entry). It is described by John Veniard as a good example of a whitebait or smelt lure.

Tie in the tail and cut to length. Tie in the silver tinsel.

Wind on the tinsel to form the body.

Tie in the mohair wing. (Once secured, I would saturate the tied area with clear head cement to prevent the hair from being pulled out.)

Finish the head, and varnish. The home tier could add painted eyes for extra realism.

BLOODY BUTCHER (M)

ORIGIN: NOT KNOWN
HOOK: NOT STATED BUT PROBABLY 2-8
TAIL: RED WHISKS
BODY: SILVER TINSEL
RIB: OVAL SILVER
WING: BLACK COCK HACKLES
HACKLE: NATURAL BROWN OR PALE GINGER UNDER DYED RED
HEAD: BLACK

A Canterbury pattern of unknown origin (possibly Bob Bragg), which appears in Bragg's book. Presumably it is a night lure.

There are two dressings in the two examples shown in Bragg's book. In one, the head hackle appears to be red without any other colour added. The other, with red over a light coloured hackle (it looks like pale ginger to me), caught my eye. If I have it wrong, the example nevertheless looks exactly like the one portrayed in Bragg's book.

Tie in the tail whisks. Tie in the body tinsel and the ribbing. Take the thread back nearly to the head.

Wind on the body tinsel (I prefer to tie the tinsel in at the head and wind it down to the bend and back). Tie in the wing feathers by the butts.

Wind on the ribbing, tying down the wing in the Matuku style. Tie in the ginger hackle.

Wind on the hackle to form a hackle collar. Repeat with a shorter-fibred red hackle.

BLOODY MARY (O)

ORIGIN: MAX CHRISTENSEN OF TASMANIA
HOOK: 6-10
TAIL: TOMATO-RED SILK OR NYLON
BODY: ORANGE-RED LUREX (NO. 273)
RIB: FINE GOLD WIRE
HACKLE: SOFT BLACK COCK WOUND ENTIRE LENGTH OF HOOK AS WING (PALMERED)
HEAD: RED OR BLACK

This was created in 1956 and called simply "Mary". The colouring - not its performance - led anglers to add the colourful epithet. Although an Australian lure, this pattern is included in a little-known publication called *58 NZ Lure Patterns* (about 1977 - see my comments under Furnace Smelt). It had obviously earned a place in the minds of some as a New Zealand lure - if not by origin, then by adoption in much the same way as Zonker, Muddler, and Woolly Bugger have (to name but a few). In *Freshwater Fishing in Australia and New Zealand* (1971), edited by Rodger Hungerford, an entire chapter is devoted to this lure which, if tied and fished correctly "is amongst the deadliest fish-getters in the game". One of its greatest features is that "without changing rod, line, cast, or anything you can fish Bloody Mary either wet or dry. Flick it in the air a few times before setting it down gently and it floats like a cork. With no flicking and a more positive landing it sinks. In addition, if you want it to sink while floating all that is needed is a gentle but definite little tug." Choosing the correct hackle is all-important for "Bloody Mary can neither be made nor fished correctly without the right hackles". If fished wet, retrieve slowly to let the hackles pulsate properly.

The author of the above article suggest that the colour of the head is less important that the 'shine' which is given to the head.

Tie in the tail tag, lurex, and ribbing.

Tie in the hackle feather. Wind on the lurex to the head

Wind the hackle Palmerwise along the length of the shank to the head. Secure and trim. Wind on the ribbing. Form the head. Add tinsel eyes if desired, although it is claimed that they do not add to its effectiveness.

BLUE DUN MATUKU (M)

ORIGIN: TOM KEMPER OF MANGAWEKA
HOOK: 8-10
BODY: SILVER GREY YARN
RIB: STRONG COPPER WIRE
WING: 4 OLIVE DYED GRIZZLE HACKLES
THROAT: WHITE MARABOU
HACKLE: OLIVE DYED GRIZZLE HACKLE
HEAD: BLACK

Tom is an American who divides his time between Jackson, Wyoming, and New Zealand. This lure, which features in the 1989 Tichborne calendar and book, was tied up to resemble the colouration of juvenile rainbow trout: green from above, white from below, and silvery-grey from the side. It is fished conventionally across and down, and deep, retrieving with short erratic twitches. It also takes well as a smelt imitation at river mouths after dark, or harling during the day.

Tom says that the wing from the bend of the hook to the tip should be slightly shorter than the length of the hook. He also strips the bottom feather fibres equal to the length of the shank.

Tie in the copper wire and body yarn. Return the thread back nearly to the head.

Wind on the yarn, making one wrap behind the tied-in ribbing, and then forward to the head. Secure. Tie in the wing feathers by the butts.

Wind on the ribbing, tying down the wing in the Matuku style. Tie in the throat marabou to just reach the point of the hook.

Tie in the hackle feather and wind on to form a hackle collar.

BLUE DUN SMELT (M)

ORIGIN: NOT KNOWN
HOOK: NOT STATED BUT PROBABLY 4-8
BODY: SKY BLUE FLOSS SILK
RIB: OVAL SILVER
WING: TWO LIGHT BLUE DUN COCK HACKLES
HACKLE: LIGHT BLUE DUN COCK, FAIRLY LONG IN THE FIBRE
HEAD: BLACK

This is an old pattern, which appears in John Veniard's 1970 book, and also a later similar publication in 1980. Gary Kemsley can recall fishing with this lure in the Waitahanui River back in the 1960s.

I have been unable to obtain blue floss silk, and the above example has been tied using pure silk, the colour probably being more important than the material.

A pale lightly marked grizzle hackle, or even a pale grey hackle could be used in substitution for the light blue dun hackle.

Tie in the body material and the ribbing.

Wind on the body material and secure. Tie in the wing feathers by the butts.

Wind on the ribbing, tying down the wing in the Matuku style.

Tie in a hackle feather. Wind on to form a hackle collar.

BLUE MALLARD (O)

ORIGIN: NOT KNOWN
HOOK: 6-10
TAIL: MALLARD FLANK DYED BLUE
BODY: SILVER
RIB: OVAL SILVER
WING: STRIP OF MALLARD FLANK DYED BLUE
HEAD: BLACK

This is listed in Keith Draper's *Trout Flies In New Zealand* and is the only reference to it that I can find.

Keith Draper says: "This pattern is a smelt fly, effectively fished fast on a floating line and cast among smelting trout." (1971)

The wing is constructed from narrow matching strips of feather tied in the Streamer style rather than the Pukeko style sweeping back over the body to just beyond the bend of the hook.

Tie in a bunch of mallard flank fibres for the tail.

Tie in the silver tinsel for the body and ribbing. Trim.

Wind on the tinsel to make the body. Follow with the ribbing. Secure and trim.

Tie in the strip of mallard flank to form the low sweeping wing.

BLYTHE'S SPECIAL (O)

ORIGIN:	JACK BLYTHE OF HAWERA
HOOK:	NOT STATED BUT PROBABLY 2-8
TAIL:	GINGER WHISKS UNDER BLACK SQUIRREL TAIL
BODY:	YELLOW
RIB:	OVAL SILVER (OPTIONAL)
WING:	COCK PHEASANT RUMP TIED IN ON TOP OF THE SHANK AT THE BEND AND AT THE HEAD
CHEEK:	JUNGLE COCK (OPTIONAL)
HACKLE:	GINGER OR NATURAL RED, THROAT ONLY
HEAD:	BLACK

This appears in Bragg's book. It has been dressed in two ways with Jungle Cock cheeks and ribbing appearing in one only. It differs from Mrs Simpson in that the wing has been tied in on top of the shank, which differs also from the South Island style of tying Killer-style lures.

This is a good example of the desirability of a tying style designation. Without more the pattern could be interpreted as being tied in the Pukeko style.

Tie in the whisks and the squirrel tail.

Tie in the first set of wing feathers on top of the shank. Tie in the body material and ribbing if using.

Take the thread back nearly to the head.

Wind on the body material to this point followed by the ribbing if using.

Tie in the throat hackle. Tie in the second set of wing feathers by the butts. Add Jungle Cock cheeks if desired.

BMS (O)

ORIGIN:	MURRAY WILSON OF VICTORIA, AUSTRALIA
HOOK:	6-12 LONG SHANK
TAIL:	BLUE/GREY (MIXED) SYNTHETIC LIVING FIBRE (SLF) IN HANK FORM
RIB:	FLAT PEARL MYLAR
BODY:	ROUGHLY DUBBED BLUE/GREY SLF IN DUBBING FORM
TOPPING:	(OPTIONAL) 4 STRANDS PEARL KRYSTAL FLASH
HEAD:	RED HEAD BEHIND A SILVER GLASS BEAD

It can also be tied in white or olive.

Lyndsay Lyons, a Rotorua fishing guide, got one from Murray and showed it to Pat Swift who waxes lyrical about its qualities, and with good reason. Murray told me that it has caught salmon, mackerel, bass, kahawai and other sea fish as well as trout. It has been said "it will catch anything with a mouth!" It is particularly effective in New Zealand as a smelt lure.

The name stands for Bullen Merri Special after a lake near Camperdown in Western Victoria. SLF is a superb product produced by Davy Wotton in the USA. Currently, it is not easy to obtain in New Zealand although that may be about to change. An Umpqua product called Crystal Seal would be a good substitute. The glass beads are available at craft or wool shops.

Place bead on the hook. Take thread down to the bend. Tie in a teased out tuft of SLF. Tie in the rib.

Roughly dub on a body of SLF, wind on the ribbing and tie off. Tease out the body with velcro or a dubbing needle.

Tie in the topping if using. Form a head with red thread behind the glass bead.

BOCKETT'S GHOST (M)

ORIGIN:	BRAD BOCKETT OF TAUPO
HOOK:	6-10
BODY:	GREY WOOL TIED SLIM
RIB:	OVAL SILVER
WING:	PALE GREY COCK NECK HACKLES
HEAD:	BLACK

This has been around for some time and makes its appearance in Keith Draper's 1997 book but not, so far as I am aware, in any tackle shops. It is a variation of Grey Ghost, most effective in the smaller sizes. Tied even thus, it has been more popular as a harling fly, but whether harled or cast it is a very effective smelt pattern.

In common with Grey Ghost and others, it omits a head hackle.

Tie in the wool and the ribbing.

Wind on the wool body and secure. Tie in the wing feathers by the butts at the shoulder.

Wind on the ribbing, tying down the wing in the Matuku style.

BOOBY (O)

ORIGIN: GORDON FRASER OF MELTON MOWBRAY, LEICESTERSHIRE, ENGLAND

HOOK: NOT STATED BUT PROBABLY 4-10

TAIL: BUNCH OF MARABOU WITH (OPTIONAL) A FEW STRANDS OF FLASHABOU OR SIMILAR

BODY: SPARKLE CHENILLE - E.G. ICE, FRITZ, ESTAZ, ETC., (ALL BASICALLY THE SAME BUT WITH DIFFERING FIBRE LENGTHS FOR USE WITH DIFFERING SIZED HOOKS)

EYES: POLYSTYRENE BEADS WRAPPED IN WHITE NYLON/PANTYHOSE.

This fly is now firmly established in New Zealand and is a very popular lure. The polystyrene beads give buoyancy and also a side-to-side swimming motion as an added bonus.

The method of fishing this lure is set out under Black Booby.

Commercially, this is tied up in a wide range of colours but not combinations of colours, as combinations, for some reason, have not been successful. Single colour boobies, however are deadly and few lakeside anglers in particular, would be without one of these in their arsenal.

I have taken the liberty of adding eyes to Alf's immaculately tied example.

Tie in a bunch of marabou for the tail. Tie in the chenille.

Wind on the chenille nearly to the head and tie off.

Wrap two polystyrene balls in white pantyhose or nylon. Secure firmly to the shank behind the eye with thread. Cut away surplus material. Criss-cross the thread between balls in a figure of eight and tie off. Add paint work for the eyes if desired.

BOTTLETOP (M)

ORIGIN: "BOTTLETOP" THOMPSON OF ROTORUA

HOOK: 6-8

BODY: SILVER BRAID

RIB: SAME AS BODY

WING: FOUR LIGHT-COLOURED HAWK FEATHERS

HEAD: BLACK

"Bottletop" Thompson was a World War I veteran well known to Maureen Butler, who tied the example illustrated. He was renowned for his tales of trout battles, 'up the front', at the Ohau Channel in the early 1960s. He used to create silver bodies from the first silver milk bottle tops which replaced the old cardboard ones. As a result, he became known to everyone as "Bottletop", and no-one seems able to recall his real name.

"Bottletop" used to remove a short section of fibres from the underside of the wing before tying it in as he believed this made a neater head and throat.

It is fished conventionally on a slow sinking line, making sure it is kept up from the bottom. See my comments under Hawk regarding the use of hawk feathers.

Tie in the body material and ribbing.

Wind on the body material and tie off.

Remove a short section of fibres from the wing feathers (if desired).

Tie in the wing feathers. Wind on the ribbing, tying down the wing in the Matuku style.

BRIGGS' BROADHEAD (O)

ORIGIN: CLIFF BRIGGS OF CHRISTCHURCH

HOOK: 8

TAIL: GRIZZLED SQUIRREL (THIN)

BODY: REAR HALF, SILVER TINSEL; FRONT HALF, BROWN CHENILLE

HACKLE: (OPTIONAL) ONE TURN OF GRIZZLE OR RED BROWN

There are numerous Muddler or Broadhead variations, all designed to represent the cock-a-bully. Tony Orman, in his book *The Sport In Fishing* obtained the favourite patterns of thirteen experts. This pattern was recommended by Al Creedon (who certainly fits that description) and is a variation on the Taupo Broadhead, a pattern I have been unable to locate.

Tie in a few fibres of squirrel tail. Tie in the silver tinsel, secure and trim.

Take the thread half-way back along the shank. Wind on the tinsel to that point. Tie in the brown chenille.

Take the thread nearly to the head. Wind on the chenille. Tie in a hackle feather if using.

Take one turn of the hackle, tie off, complete the head, and varnish.

BRIGGS' SILVERY (M)

ORIGIN: CLIFF BRIGGS OF CHRISTCHURCH
HOOK: NOT STATED BUT PROBABLY 2-8
TAIL: BLACK SQUIRREL
BODY: WHITE
RIB: OVAL SILVER
WING: WHITE COCK HACKLES
TOPPING: PEACOCK SWORD
HEAD: BLACK

This appears in Bragg's book under the listing of high country patterns. It appears to have been popular at Lake Ellesmere and the Selwyn River mouth, but with its distinct Albino appearance, it could be expected to perform well anywhere.

Tie in the squirrel tail. Tie in the body material and the ribbing.

Wind on the body material to the head. Tie in the wing feathers by the butts.

Wind on the ribbing, tying down the wing in the Matuku style.

Tie in the topping.

BROADHEAD (K)

ORIGIN: NOT KNOWN
HOOK: NOT STATED BUT PROBABLY 6-8
TAIL: BUNCH OF NATURAL RABBIT
WING: HEN PHEASANT FEATHERS TIED IN AT THE MID-POINT
HEAD: BROWN CHENILLE

This is a Canterbury pattern, which appears in Bragg's book. It is fairly similar to Cock-a-Bully (or, more likely, the other way around). It is difficult to be precise about the dressing, and the above pattern has to be acknowledged as my best guess. For example, it is impossible to tell from the photo in Bragg's book what the body is, or whether it even has one. As with most Killer patterns, however, I do not believe body details are important. I have used a very short strip of rabbit on the skin for the tail.

Tie in the rabbit fur for the tail, extending about a hook length beyond the bend.

Take the thread back to the mid-point of the shank. Tie in the wing feathers on either side of the shank in the Killer style.

Tie in the brown chenille. Wind on the chenille to form a large head. Secure and tie off.

BROWN BOMBER (H)

ORIGIN: IVAN BODLEY OF WAIROA
HOOK: 2-8
TAIL: BLACK OR BROWN SQUIRREL TAIL
BODY: RUSTY-COLOURED BROWN WOOL
WINGS: RHODE ISLAND RED COCK HACKLE
HEAD: BLACK

This fly was first tied up about 1977. An angler returning from Lake Waikaremoana had picked up a lost or discarded lure, which Ivan identified as "probably a Red Setter that had rusted and discoloured the original body colour." If you look at the original tie of Red Setter, some credence is given to this account. The angler who had found the lure had used it with some success and asked Ivan to tie up something similar, and Brown Bomber evolved from there.

It is a fly, which has had considerable success in the Rotorua and Taupo Lakes, as well as Lake Waikaremoana. It probably imitates the Koura (fresh water crayfish). It is best fished from the shore, particularly early and late in the day and also at night.

The pattern is tied commercially but in what might be described as a modern dressing with chenille and brown (even chocolate brown) hackles. A very similar pattern (brown chenille body) is given in Keith Draper's 1997 book. Keith was shown what appeared to be a 'brown Fuzzy Wuzzy' by a Taupo butcher, Don Grant, 30 years ago - ten years before Ivan's creation - and Keith tied up a good number of them, which were called Brown Bomber. I am inclined to the view that this is probably yet another instance of two people independently coming up with the same creation (although coming up with the same name by coincidence tends to arch the eyebrows). Although Joe Louis' reign as world heavyweight boxing champion ended in 1949, his epithet "The Brown Bomber", and his reputation, lived on for a long time after. It was a name very much in vogue just as Mrs Simpson was, so perhaps it was not too much of a coincidence after all.

Ivan's Brown Bomber was featured in the 1986 Tichborne calendar.

Tie in the tail. Trim. Tie in the wool.

Take the thread part way back along the shank. Wind on the wool to this point and secure. Tie in a hackle feather.

Take the thread back nearly to the head, continue with the wool, and repeat the process with the hackle feather. Tie off and trim..

BROWN KILLER (K)

ORIGIN: KEITH DRAPER OF TAUPO
HOOK: 4-8
TAIL: BLACK OR BROWN SQUIRREL
BODY: YELLOW FLOSS, WOOL, OR CHENILLE
WINGS: THE DARK CHESTNUT-BROWN BREAST FEATHERS OF A SHOVELLER DRAKE
HEAD: BROWN

Keith Draper says: "This fly is one of my own inventions and is a great little lure. It will never become a commercial proposition as the plumage is not easily obtained. While the shoveller, or spoonbill duck, is still found in some areas in reasonable numbers, in most districts its population is rather sparse. The breast of the female is also of a reddish-brown hue, but not with the same intensity as the drake." (1971). My impression, as a duck hunter, is that numbers are reasonably plentiful as shooters tend to ignore shovellers as being too small, preferring the larger mallard.

One of the virtues of shoveller plumage is that it ties in quite easily, unlike that of some other Killer patterns. In the absence of shoveller plumage, a good alternative is mallard breast feathers dyed a deep brown.

Tie in the tail. Trim. Tie in the body chenille.

Take the thread and chenille part way back along the shank and secure. Tie in a pair of feathers on either side of the shank.

Take the thread and chenille almost to the head and secure. Repeat the process with the feathers, securing and cementing as you go, if you wish.

Trim off surplus. Complete head and varnish.

BROWN MATUKU (M)

ORIGIN: NOT KNOWN
HOOK: 6-8
BODY: OLIVE BROWN CHENILLE OR WOOL
RIB: OVAL GOLD TINSEL
WING: GRIZZLE HACKLE DYED BROWN
HEAD: NOT STATED. BLACK OR POSSIBLY BROWN

This is another Australian import, which has found its way into Keith Draper's 1997 book.

No doubt, in Australia this would be known as a Brown Matuka and I assume that Keith has given it the Kiwi spelling.

This should be fished deep where its resemblance to bullies and minnows prompts Keith to write: "(This lure) just begs to be used."

Tie in the body material and the ribbing.

Wind on the body material and secure. Tie in the wing feathers by the butts at the shoulder.

Wind on the ribbing, tying down the wing in the Matuku style.

BRUNTON No. 1 (O)

ORIGIN: LOU BRUNTON OF CHRISTCHURCH
HOOK: 2-6
TAIL: A BUNCH OF BROWN HACKLE FIBRES
BODY: WHITE FLOSS
RIB: SILVER TINSEL
WING: WIDE BROWN HACKLES
CHEEKS: SPECKLED PARADISE SHELDUCK BREAST FEATHERS
HACKLES: BROWN
HEAD: BLACK

This is the first of a series of South Island patterns created by Lou Brunton. "These patterns were Canterbury favourites twenty years ago and were designed by Lou Brunton, a Christchurch angler, for use at the Selwyn mouth at Lake Ellesmere." - Keith Draper (1971). Therefore, they were created around 1950. Although ribbed, it appears from the photo in Keith's 1971 book (omitted from the 1997 release), that they are tied up in the Streamer style, that is, not tied down to the body but trailing free, with the addition of cheeks or topping as the case may be.

In Bragg's book, this is occasionally called Brown and Paradise.

Tie in the tail hackles. Tie in the body material and the ribbing.

Wind on the floss to the head and secure. Wind on the ribbing and secure.

Tie in the wing feathers by the butts at the shoulder. Tie in the cheeks on either side of the body.

Tie in a hackle feather, and wind on to form a hackle collar.

BRUNTON No.2 (O)

ORIGIN: LOU BRUNTON
HOOK: 2-6
TAIL: A BUNCH OF GINGER HACKLE FIBRES
BODY: WHITE FLOSS
RIB: SILVER TINSEL
WING: GINGER HACKLES
HACKLE: GINGER
TOPPING: GREEN PEACOCK SWORD
HEAD: BLACK

This is the second of Brunton's series. The colouring is ginger instead of brown, and the cheeks give way to a peacock sword topping.

Tie in the tail hackles. Tie in the body material and the ribbing.

Wind on the floss to the head and secure. Wind on the ribbing and secure.

Tie in the wing feathers by the butts at the shoulder.

Tie in a topping of peacock sword.

Tie in the hackle feather and wind on to form a hackle collar.

BRUNTON RED (O)

ORIGIN: LOU BRUNTON
HOOK: 2-6
TAIL: A BUNCH OF FURNACE HACKLE FIBRES
BODY: RED
RIB: SILVER TINSEL
WING: RED FURNACE
HACKLE: RED COCK
TOPPING: GREEN PEACOCK SWORD
HEAD: BLACK

This is the third in the Brunton trilogy. This pattern is taken from Keith Draper's 1971 book in which the word 'floss' is omitted from the body description, but added in the 1997 book. The photo in the 1971 book (omitted from the later publication) shows an example tied by R.K. Bragg which has a questionable furnace wing, and a body of red wool or seal's fur or similar. It is also tied in the chunkier Canterbury style.

Tie in the tail hackle. Tie in the body material and the ribbing.

Wind on the body material to the head and secure. Wind on the ribbing and secure.

Tie in the wing feathers by the butts at the shoulder.

Tie in the peacock sword topping.

Tie in a hackle feather and wind on to form a collar.

BUCKTAILS (P)

HOOK: 2-6
TAIL: (OPTIONAL) SQUIRREL TAIL OR HACKLE FIBRES
BODY: TINSEL, THE COLOUR OF CHOICE
WING: BUCKTAIL
HACKLE: (OPTIONAL) HACKLE FIBRES, THROAT ONLY
HEAD: BLACK

These are hair flies tied from bucktail. In his book *Trout Flies in New Zealand* (1971) Keith Draper says: ' "This is an American term for a fly made from the tail hairs of a whitetail buck. All of these flies are streamers, to use another American term, and there can be no doubt that they are extremely effective. The term has now been broadened so that a bucktail may be tied from several other types of hair or a mixture such as polar bear, calf or kip, eland, or squirrel - you name it and it's probably been tried. I have used this type of fly for several years now, adding the appropriately coloured hair to tie bucktail versions of old New Zealand favourites such as the Taupo Tiger, Parsons' Glory and Ewe Wasp, to name but a few. I would not suggest that these flies are better than the standard type of lure but I am sure they are equally as good. I mention this because the materials used are all obtainable in New Zealand as home-grown products, and as many of the imported materials used in fly-tying are of Asiatic origin, there is no guarantee that supplies will always be available."

I am not sure that polar bear fur was ever a "home grown product", but in any event it is certainly not obtainable now. In the photo plates at the end of the lure section of Keith's earlier book are photos of two Bucktails, one tied with a gold tinsel body and the other with a silver mylar body.

Given the above description as to what constitutes a Bucktail fly, the pattern given may suffice, although see Comets for a more specific pattern.

Tie in the tail, if using. Tie in the tinsel body material.

Wind on the tinsel to form the body and secure. Tie in the throat hackle if using.

Tie in the bucktail wing and cement firmly.

BUDGIE (O)

ORIGIN:	NIGEL WOOD OF ROTORUA
HOOK:	2-6
TAG:	RED WOOL TEASED OUT
TAIL:	A GOOD BUNCH OF BLACK MARABOU
BODY:	EQUAL SECTIONS OF DUBBED YELLOW, ORANGE, AND RED MARABOU
WING:	BUNCHES OF BLACK MARABOU TIED IN AT EACH BODY SECTION
HACKLE:	THIN BLACK COCK BETWEEN EACH BODY SECTION AND AT HEAD
HEAD:	BLACK

Nigel Wood is the manager of Hamill's Hunting & Fishing in Rotoura. Budgie is tied professionally for Hamill's and is a popular seller. This is a big chunky fly which has proved devastating to Rotorua trout at night. This was based on, and evolved from, Sunset Fly. Originally called Sundowner, it was changed by an angler when one whistled past his ear in a manner that evoked an image of a bird. The marabou for the body is dubbed using the loop method. The wing marabou is tied in to lie along the top of the body. Each succeeding bunch is longer than the one before so that they all reach back to the end of the first bunch tied in (tail). The length of the tail will therefore be determined by the length of the marabou which will be tied in last. Do not overdo the amount of marabou. Strive for slimness rather than bulk.

Tie in the tag and tail. Form a dubbing loop. Take the thread part way back along the shank.

Place a bunch of yellow marabou in the dubbing loop and wind on the first section. Secure. Tie in a black hackle feather and wind on Hackle style. Tie in a generous bunch of black marabou wing.

Repeat the process for each of the other two sections, making sure that each bunch of marabou wing reaches back to the end of the first bunch. Form head and complete in the usual way.

BUGS BUNNY (O)

ORIGIN:	WALTER WILLIS OF TE KUITI
HOOK:	2-8
TAIL:	BARRED SQUIRREL TAIL
BODY:	STRIP OF RABBIT FUR
HACKLE:	(OPTIONAL) GRIZZLE, GREY, OR BLUE DUN HACKLE
HEAD:	BLACK

Originally known as the Willis Rabbit, it is now tied by Kilwell under the above name. The strip of rabbit fur should be cut across the pelt so that the 'grain' of the fur lies naturally towards the tail when it is wound around the shank.

The fur pulses beautifully in the water, and it is a very effective fly, particularly on migratory fish. Colour choice is personal. I prefer cock-a-bully brown, but I have used olive green, grey, and black for night-time, in all cases varying the squirrel tail colour to suit. You can enhance the look with a painted eye, and the addition of Jungle Cock 'eyes' on the night-time version adds to its effectiveness. I omit the hackle. Wild feral cat's fur is equally as good as the rabbit.

Tie in the tail. Tie in the strip of fur. It helps, when cutting the strip, if the ends are tapered.

Wind on the fur strip with each succeeding turn overlaying the previous one.

Secure the fur body and trim off any excess. At this point a hackle collar can be added, if desired.

BULLHEAD (O)

ORIGIN:	KEVIN FITZGERALD OF CHRISTCHURCH
HOOK:	6 OR 8, LONG SHANK
TAIL:	SPARSE GREY RABBIT FUR
BODY:	GREY FLUORESCENT FLOSS ON REAR HALF, FOLLOWED BY PEACOCK HERL, RIBBED WITH

THIN SILVER TINSEL
HACKLE: LONG "SOFT" BROWN HACKLE BEHIND HEAD
HEAD: BROWN CHENILLE

This pattern appears in the book *Trout and Salmon Sport in New Zealand -An Angling Anthology,* compiled by Tony Orman.

It is recorded there that it is a "good cock-a-bully imitation and in smaller sizes a good daytime lure. Fish it slowly on a floating line."

Kevin Fitzgerald worked very closely with Al Creedon and had some input into the creation of Creedon's Creeper, which will be well known to those who fish with nymphs.

Tie in the tail. Tie in the floss.

Take the thread part way along the shank. Follow with the floss to this point and secure. Tie in the peacock herl and the ribbing.

Take the thread back nearly to the head. Follow with the peacock herl to this point and tie off. Wind on the ribbing. Tie in the hackle feather.

Wind on the hackle collar. Secure and trim. Tie in the chenille and wind on to form the head. Tie off and trim.

BULLY (P)

ORIGIN: RON BERRY OF AUCKLAND
HOOK: 6 OR 8, LONG SHANK
TAIL: BROWN MINK
BODY: LIGHT BROWN CHENILLE
RIB: GOLD TINSEL
WING: RED FOX TAIL, WITH BROWN MOTTLE TURKEY
HEAD: CLIPPED DEER HAIR

This pattern can be found in *Trout and Salmon Sport in New Zealand - An Angling Anthology*, compiled by Tony Orman. It is claimed that this is "immensely successful in Lake Rotorua, fished on either a sinking or floating line".

Ron tells me that it is an imitation of a 'Bully Fish' and the lure is a great favourite of his when fishing the shallow waters of Lake Rotorua. He says that it does not matter how the fly is retrieved - if the fish are 'on' he has always had success.

Start the thread one third of the way along the shank (from the eye) and wind down to the bend. Tie in the tail fibres. Secure and trim. Tie in the chenille and ribbing.

Take the thread two thirds of the way back along the shank. Wind on the chenille and ribbing to this point.

Tie in a bunch of fox tail fibres on top of the shank. Tie in the turkey fibres at the same place to form a topping over the foxtail. If using ordinary thread, tie off and tie in very strong thread such as kevlar.

Place a bunch of deer hair on to the bare shank. Take one or two turns of the thread, then pull down hard to make the hair spin around the shank and flare out. Push the deer hair away from the eye to form a bunch, and repeat the process until the hook is full. Tie off. Trim the deer hair to shape.

BULLY FLY (O)

ORIGIN: PAT O'KEEFE OF ROTORUA
HOOK: 2-6
BODY: DUBBED OLIVE SQUIRREL
WING: OLIVE DYED GRIZZLE
CHEEK: BACK OR SCAPULAR FEATHERS FROM A PEACOCK
EYE: JUNGLE COCK
HEAD: BLACK

This is tied in the Streamer style with the wing trailing free. For that reason it is better employed as a harling lure, and in that capacity it has proved very successful. It is obviously a bully imitation, and shares a lot in common with the Green Orbit.

Dub on the body using your own preferred method.

Tie in the wing feathers by the butt at the shoulder.

Tie in the peacock cheeks. Add Jungle Cock 'eyes'.

BULLY (Red & Yellow)(K)

ORIGIN: R.K. BRAGG
HOOK: 4-8
TAIL: BLACK SQUIRREL TAIL
BODY: RED OR YELLOW WOOL OR CHENILLE
WING: GREY OR SPECKLED PARTRIDGE, OR MALLARD FLANK, DYED GREEN.
HEAD: BLACK

Although, superficially, the pattern is nearly identical to Hamill's Killer, the colouring used by Bragg was a cross between green, yellow, and brown, and it was tied - as here - in the South Island style.

Mallard feathers dyed a 'Hamill's Killer' shade of green

(usually an olive colour), would make a suitable alternative.

Tie in the tail fibres. Tie in the body material.

Tie in a pair of wing feathers on either side of the shank to veil the base of the tail.

Take the thread back nearly to the head. Wind on the body material to this point and tie off. Tie in another pair of wing feathers on either side of the shank angled upwards to reveal the body. Trim. Complete the head and varnish.

BUM FLY (P)

ORIGIN: NOT KNOWN
HOOK: 4-8
TAIL: CHESTNUT-COLOURED RUMP FEATHERS OF A COCK PHEASANT
BODY: CHEVIOT WOOL DYED TO SUIT, USUALLY GREEN, YELLOW, ORANGE, OR RED
WING: CHESTNUT-COLOURED RUMP FEATHERS OF A COCK PHEASANT
HEAD: BLACK

Keith Draper in *Trout Flies in New Zealand* says: "The tail and two bunches of wing are tied in progressively, building the body as they go. The fly was originated in a Gisborne tackle shop and apparently after inspecting it someone remarked that it was a 'bum-looking sort of fly' .... Cheviot wool, which is very fine and crimply, is ideal for this type of body. It spins on to the thread well, still retaining that slightly scraggy look which the fly's supporters insist must be part of its character."

When it comes to performance, the only "bum" thing about it is where the feathers come from, and that, I suspect, is the truer origin of its name. Indeed, I am told that it was originally named Pheasant's Arse until decorum (up to a point) prevailed! However, it is a difficult fly to tie and it may be that the original offering justified the description. This fly becomes deadlier the more it is chewed by trout, so if you make a mess of tying one it may still be a potent weapon.

Barry Kent, once a professional fly-tier in Napier now at Te Puke, tells me that this was originally designed for use at Lake Waikaremoana. For 'those in the know' this is a highly sought after fly and people have been known to pay professional fly-tiers a premium to have one tied. All of which goes to prove that this is a cracker fly, although strictly for the home tier.

Tie in the tail. Tie in a short section of body material. Tie in a small rump feather on top of the body, Pukeko style.

Tie in another short section of body and then another feather, only bigger than the last. Repeat until the shank is full, with the last feather covering all the previous ones.

BUM FLY VARIATION 1 (P)

ORIGIN: BARRY KENT OF TE PUKE
HOOK: 4-8
TAIL: BLACK SQUIRREL TAIL
BODY: YELLOW SEAL'S FUR OR SUBSTITUTE
THROAT: RED SEAL'S FUR OR SUBSTITUTE
WING: GREEN PHEASANT RUMP ('MRS. SIMPSON') FEATHERS
HEAD: BLACK

This is a variation of the previous entry, which is preferred by Barry Kent, a professional fly-tier formerly of Napier. The rationale behind this dressing is that brown is generally regarded as a South Island colour, while green is perceived as being more effective in the north, notwithstanding that the original Bum Fly originated in Gisborne.

All versions shown in this book are deadly, and a prized possession in any fly-box.

Tie in the squirrel tail. Dub on a short section of body. Tie in a small wing feather on top of the shank, Pukeko style.

Tie in another section of body and another wing feather. The wing should extend back to cover (but not exceed) the previous wing feather.

Repeat the body and wing process until the shank is full, with the last feather covering all the previous ones. Form the head and complete in the usual way.

BUM FLY VARIATON 2 (P)

ORIGIN: PAT SWIFT OF ROTORUA
HOOK: 2-6
TAIL: BROWN SQUIRREL TAIL
BODY: LOOP DUBBED YELLOW SEAL'S FUR OR SYNTHETIC LIVING FIBRE (SLF)
THROAT: LOOP DUBBED RED SEAL'S FUR OR SLF
WING: LONG FIBRED PHEASANT RUMP
CHEEK: STRIPED BROWN PARTRIDGE
HEAD: BLACK

Pat Swift is an immaculate fly-tyer from Rotorua. He

knew how good (albeit under-rated) the Bum Fly was, and devised this variation to give it a colouring which he felt would be more effective in the North Island waters. Hence he prefers the greeny-coloured feathers to the chestnut-coloured ones. It is one of his favourite patterns which has proved deadly time and time again, one single lure having taken more than 30 trout. Pat believes it will only stop catching trout when the hook breaks.

Two or three feathers are used at each stage.

Tie in the squirrel tail. Tie in short rump feathers to lie over part of the tail.

Form a dubbing loop. Dub on a section of body material to the mid-point of the shank. Tie in a second lot of wing feathers reaching back to the end of the first.

Dub on more yellow body material as far as the throat. Dub in the red throat. Tie in a third lot of wing feather reaching back to cover the previous two.

Tie in the cheeks. Form the head and complete in the usual way.

BUM FLY VARIATION 3 (P)

ORIGIN: PAT O'KEEFE OF ROTORUA

HOOK: 6

TAIL: RUSTY PHEASANT RUMP FIBRES DYED OLIVE

BODY: DUBBED OLIVE BASAL FLUE FROM BASE OF PHEASANT BACK FEATHERS

WING: THREE SETS OF RUSTY PHEASANT RUMP FEATHERS DYED OLIVE

HEAD: BLACK

It was appropriate to keep all three Bum Fly variations together instead of listing this alphabetically as Pat's Pheasant Bum by which it is correctly known (commonly abridged to Pat's Bum!)

It is interesting that three very expert anglers and fly-tiers should come up with their variations of a very highly regarded, but otherwise little-known, lure. It is also interesting that all three, from the North Island have chosen a green version over the natural rusty brown original. Pat's version, here, is a very effective daytime pattern, best fished in flowing streams and rips. Pat tied this up for his team, which was competing against Australia in 1997, and, as he puts it, 'it cleaned them up'.

Tie in the rump feather fibres for the tail. Tie in rusty (dyed olive) rump feathers Pukeko style to lie over the tail.

Dub on a section of basal flue to the mid-point of the shank. Tie in a second lot of rump feathers, Pukeko style, to lie over the previous one.

Continue the dubbed body back nearly to the head. Tie in the last rump feathers to lie over the previous ones.

BUNNY (O)

ORIGIN: MEL KRIEGER OF SAN FRANCISCO, USA

HOOK: 2-8

WING: STRIP OF RABBIT FUR

HEAD: RED

Mel is a professional angler who makes frequent trips to New Zealand. It was on his first visit in the late 1960's that he discovered, and was taken by, our Rabbit lure. It was the inspiration for his Bunny, which initially he used on black bass in America with great success. Within a year or so he found that it was extremely effective on trout in both still and moving water.

The first Bunny was black, but Mel has since used a wide variety of colours, including natural. Variations have seen muddler heads, eyes and tinsel variously added, but Mel still prefers the basic original pattern which catches all varieties of trout and salmon, and also many species of saltwater fish. The secret, he believes, is in the lifelike undulating action of the fur. He favours rabbit but says that possum, feral cat - indeed, any fur (plus skin) - make perfect Bunnys, which is wound on in the Bugs Bunny style, but in this case the rabbit strip is not cut across the grain. Interesting enough he discovered that pre-European American Red Indians used strips of fur wound around sharpened sticks to catch fish, which goes to prove that there is nothing new in fly-tying!

Take a long strip of trimmed and tapered rabbit fur (about 110mm or 5 inches long for a No.6 long shank). Tie it in at the bend so that the 'tail' extends beyond the bend two to three times the length of the shank.

Wind on the rabbit strip Palmer style to the head. Pick out any trapped fur with a bodkin.

Trim the bottom hair at an angle narrowing towards the bend so that the fur will not twist around the bend of the hook.

BURGLAR (O)

ORIGIN: GEORGE GATCHELL OF HAVELOCK, MARLBOROUGH SOUNDS

HOOK: 4-8

TAG: RED WOOL DOUBLED OVER FOR THICKNESS, AND WELL TEASED

TAIL: SQUIRREL TAIL OR 2-4 HACKLE FEATHERS IN PAIRS

BODY: FUR, USUALLY POSSUM BUT ALSO RABBIT, TIED IN BUNCHES PROGRESSIVELY ALONG THE SHANK

CHEEK: (OPTIONAL) JUNGLE COCK EYES

HEAD: BLACK

For many years, George owned the Crystal Brook Tackle Shop at Waitahanui, Taupo. People would come from miles to see examples of his incomparable Burglar patterns adorning the walls of his shop. When George tied up his original Burglar, he wandered across the road to the famous Picket Fence and really got amongst the trout while others went fishless. "What have you got on, George?" they wanted to know. He showed them. Someone remarked that it was "stealing all our fish". Stealing? Theft? "Yeah, it's a burglar alright" came George's instinctive response, and in a flash the lure got its name.

The beauty of this lure, says George, is that you can use any combination of colours for the fur body and the tail. Provided it is tied exactly as it should be, it will still be a Burglar. George originally wound a hackle feather between the tufts of fur, and at the head, but dropped this as it served no discernible benefit. The important elements in tying this fly are: 1. The tail must be the same length as the hook shank in use. 2. The fur tufts must wrap around the shank. 3. The fur tufts should get progressively smaller so that the finished outline is vaguely delta wing.

By simply changing the colours, George produced a series of Burglars, hence Black Burglar, Grey Burglar, Green Possum Burglar. Royal Burglar, for example, employs white rabbit fur, grizzle tail, peacock herl topping, and a gold (for royalty) head. The only slight variation is Phantom Burglar which is separately listed alphabetically.

Tie in the tag of wool which is doubled and teased out. Tie in the tail, either squirrel tail or hackle feathers (either a single pair back to back or two backed pairs).

Take a tuft of fur. Hold it firmly between thumb and forefinger. Tie in, winding back towards the bend, and at the same time pushing down on the fur with thumb and forefinger. This causes the fur to wrap around the shank.

Continue to build the body using tufts of fur getting progressively smaller. Add Jungle Cock eyes if using.

CAPTAIN MILNE (O)

ORIGIN: DAVE HOPE OF CHRISTCHURCH

HOOK: 2-6

BODY: BLACK CHENILLE OR WOOL

RIB: SILVER TINSEL

WING: 2 LARGE PARADISE DUCK SPECKLED FEATHERS TIED IN AT THE HEAD AND SECURED AT THE BUTT WITH SEVERAL TURNS OF BLACK THREAD. IN THIS MANNER THE FEATHERS FORM BOTH WINGS AND TAIL.

HACKLE: BLACK

HEAD: BLACK

This is a Canterbury lure designed for fishing the mouth of the Selwyn River at night, and has proved to be effective. Keith Draper has fished a pattern "of this type" with success at Taupo.

The dark speckled feathers come from the drake. The ones used to tie the fly in the photograph came from the back of the duck.

Tie in the chenille and ribbing.

Tie in a piece of black thread with which to secure the wing/tail feather. Take the first thread back nearly to the head. Wind on the chenille body, followed by the ribbing, which in this case is not used to secure the wing to the shank in the usual Matuku style. Secure and trim off surplus.

Tie in two feathers. Using the second piece of thread at the bend, tie down the feathers to form the tail. Tie in a hackle at the head, finish the head and varnish.

Alternatively, after tying in the chenille and ribbing, tie in the wing feathers at this stage, and carefully bend them out of the way while you take the thread, chenille, and ribbing up to the head. Arrange the feather along the shank and tie in at the head, add the hackle and complete in the usual way.

CARDINAL (O)

ORIGIN: NOT KNOWN

HOOK: 2-8

BODY: RED WOOL OR CHENILLE

RIB: FLAT SILVER TINSEL

WING: COCK HACKLE DYED CARDINAL RED

HACKLE: COCK HACKLE DYED CARDINAL RED

HEAD: BLACK

Keith Draper says: "This is an old Taupo fly which was used a long time ago but has never really taken on. But like all trout flies it will of course take trout provided it is used at the right time in the right place. It is regarded as a night fly." (1971).

Until I came across an example of this lure in Charles Nott's collection (see For The Record), I had assumed that it was tied Matuku style. The pattern described the ribbing as simply silver tinsel. It is, in fact, tied in the Streamer style and is a good example of the desirability of having a fly-tying style designation.

Tie in the body material and the ribbing. Secure and trim.

Wind on the wool or chenille and secure. Follow with the ribbing.

Tie in the wing feathers by the butts at the head.

Tie in a hackle feather at the head. Complete the hackle collar with a few turns.

CASEY (O)

ORIGIN: BRONWYN WILSON OF TAUPO

HOOK: 2-4

UNDER-BODY: FLUORESCENT GREEN

OVER-BODY: GLOW-TUBING

WING: TWO YELLOW FEATHERS INSIDE TWO SLIGHTLY NARROWER BLACK FEATHERS.

CHEEK: YELLOW DYED BADGER HACKLES

HACKLE: YELLOW

HEAD: BLACK

This was named after a friend of Bronwyn who caught her first ever trout, a 7lb brown, using this lure on light harling gear. It is a night fly utilising the glow tubing, but it will also catch trout during the day. This can have a topping of lime Flashabou if desired.

Tie in the body material and wind back nearly to the head. Tie off.

Slip a length of glow tubing over the body. Reattach the thread and secure the glow tube at the head.

Tie in the wing by the butts. Tie in the cheek hackles. Add topping if using.

Tie in a hackle feather and wind on to form a hackle collar.

CASUAL DRESS (O)
New Zealand version

ORIGIN: ADAPTED BY MONTY WRIGHT OF DUNEDIN

HOOK: 2-14

WEIGHT: ABOUT 6 TURNS OF LEAD

TAIL: GREY AND BLACK POSSUM

BODY: POSSUM UNDER-FUR, DUBBED

COLLAR: STRAIGHT POSSUM FIBRES

HEAD: PEACOCK HERL, TWISTED

PHOTO SHOWS NZ VERSION ON LEFT AND AMERICAN RIGHT

CASUAL DRESS (O)
American version

ORIGIN: E.H. ('POLLY') ROSBOROUGH OF CHILQUIN, OREGON, USA

HOOK: 2-10

WEIGHT: NIL

TAIL: MUSKRAT BACK FUR WITH GUARD HAIRS

BODY: MUSKRAT BACK FUR WITHOUT GUARD HAIRS

COLLAR: SAME AS TAIL

HEAD: BLACK OSTRICH HERL, TWISTED

Monty was having a frustrating day failing to catch trout, which were attacking bullies in the estuary waters of the Shag River, but refusing every bully pattern he tried. That night, while looking through an American book on nymph patterns, he took a fancy to Casual Dress which was designed as a nymph.

Not having any Muskrat fur on hand, he tried a dubbing of hare's ear and possum. The hare's ear didn't look right, and through playing around with possum fur he came up with the above dressing. He first tested it on a rocky section at Lake Mahinerangi and had immediate success. The next test came at Lake Hawea. He discovered the night before that some of the local anglers were already using the original American pattern of Casual Dress. He was gratified to note that the possum version out-fished the original when he tested it the following day, and Monty's version has now become a very popular lure on all of Otago's lakes and dams when fished along rocky margins.

Weight the hook shank if local regulations permit.

Tie in a small bunch of possum fur (two colours) for the tail.

Dub on a body of possum under-fur, taking the fur back

nearly to the head.

Tie in a collar using the straight fibres from the base of the tail.

Twist together a couple of peacock herls and wind on to form the head.

CHAMBERLAIN'S LURE (O)

ORIGIN:	A.P. CHAMBERLAIN OF LAKESIDE, CHRISTCHURCH
HOOK:	NOT STATED BUT PROBABLY 2-6
TAIL:	RED WHISKS
BODY:	WHITE
RIB:	FLAT SILVER
WING:	BLACK COCK HACKLES
CHEEK:	MALE PARADISE DUCK
HACKLE:	BLACK
HEAD:	BLACK

This is one of a group of Canterbury lures developed between 1930 and 1940 to imitate the large silvery cock-a-bully and inanga prominent in Lake Ellesmere and the Selwyn and Rakaia Rivers. It was tied in the Steamer style.

It is possible that the creator of this lure is the same 'Chamberlain' who created Harts Creek.

Tie in the tail whisks. Tie in the body material and ribbing.

Wind on the body material followed by the ribbing.

Tie in the wing feathers by the butts. Tie in the Paradise duck cheeks. Tie in a hackle feather.

Wind on the hackle feather to form a hackle collar.

CHARLIE'S FAVOURITE (O)

ORIGIN:	ALAN ANDERSON OF HASTINGS
HOOK:	6-14
TAIL:	FOX TAIL
BUTT:	(OPTIONAL) RED WOOL
RIB:	COPPER WIRE
BODY:	DUBBED HARE'S FUR
HEAD:	BLACK

Of all the lures depicted in this book, I believe that this unpretentious offering is quite probably the most effective of all. As a bonus, it is also one of the easiest to tie.

Alan was fishing a Hare & Copper not far from an old Taupo angler, at Jellicoe Point. The old angler said "Why don't you put a tail on it?" The lure which the old angler was using had a possum fur tail, and the body was roughly dubbed but was not Hare & Copper.

Alan tried out a number of different materials as tails for his Hare & Copper before concluding that the best, by far, was fox tail. He also adds a butt of red wool when the fish start running up the river in winter, but otherwise leaves it off. He always fishes it on a floating line. I have used a fast sinking line with success but mostly I use a floating line. Alan uses the smallest sizes in very clear low water.

During a chance meeting with Charlie Hudson on the bank of the Tukituki River, a good-sized trout came into view. There was a brief discussion as to who should catch it. Alan pulled out this lure and gave it to Charlie and told him to go for it. With the first cast Charlie hooked, and landed, that 6lb rainbow, and a lifelong friendship developed between the two. That was in 1971. Since Alan is an Irishman, the lure became known as Paddy's Favourite. However, when I approached Alan for inclusion of this lure in this book, he requested that it be named Charlie's Favourite (which it was) in honour of his close friend who was then very ill and nearing the end of his life. When told of this, Charlie was mortified that this secret weapon was going to be "de-classified" for public consumption!

I also chanced to meet Alan on the bank of the Tukituki River, and, as he had done so many years before, he gave me a sample of this lure. It is Alan's proud claim that he has never failed to catch a trout with it! He catalogued the extensive range of rivers and lakes where he has used it. One omission was Lake Waikaremoana which, for personal tragedy reasons, he no longer visits. When I tried this lure out at Lake Waikaremoana it was an instant and enduring success. Others have tried it out at more remote locations and the verdict is always the same. It never fails! Alan has no other lure in his fly box whatsoever.

Make no mistake, this is a phenomenal daytime lure. I will even be so bold as to suggest that this might well be the most effective lure ever created. It is now my lure of first choice.

Take the thread down to the bend. Tie in the tail which should be at least equal to the length of the hook.

Tie in the red wool, if using, and wind on no more than two turns for the butt. Tie in the copper rib.

Roughly dub on a body of hare's fur. Do not trim - the rougher the better. Wind on the copper rib. Tie off.

CHINAMAN (M)

ORIGIN: RITCHIE BUCHANAN OF TAUPO
HOOK: 2-8
TAIL: RED WHISKS
BODY: YELLOW AND RED CHENILLE
RIB: OVAL SILVER
WING: YELLOW COCK HACKLES
HEAD: RED

Ritchie created this in 1990. This has proved especially effective in the area of Chinaman Creek, a small stream running into the Western Bay of Lake Taupo, and thus giving rise to its name. It is primarily a harling fly but it also works well in river fishing in daylight hours. It is at its best mid-morning to early afternoon.

Tie in the red tail whisks. Tie in the two chenille colours and the ribbing.

Wind on the two chenilles, twisted to give a harlequin or variegated effect.

Tie in the wing feather. Wind on the ribbing, tying down the wing in the Matuku style.

CHRISTIE (M)

ORIGIN: R. CHRISTIE
HOOK: 2-8
BODY: RED WOOL OR CHENILLE
RIB: SILVER TINSEL
WING: GINGER HACKLE
HACKLE: BLACK HACKLE
HEAD: BLACK

A Canterbury lure, and highly thought of at the time when Canterbury lures were developing. "An after-dusk lure, it succeeded in the lower reaches of the Canterbury streams, especially when the sea trout were running." - Keith Draper (1997).

Tie in the body material and ribbing. Secure and trim off excess.

Return the thread nearly to the head. Wind on the body material and secure. Tie in the wing feather.

Wind on the ribbing, tying down the wing in the Matuku style. Tie off and trim excess. Tie in the hackle feather and wind on to form the hackle collar.

CLAIRE'S CHARM (O)

ORIGIN: RAY PUNTER OF ROTORUA
HOOK: 2-8
TAIL: GOLDEN PHEASANT CREST
BODY: WHITE FLOSS
RIB: OVAL SILVER
WING: HAIR, PREFERABLY HUMAN - VERY BLONDE
HACKLE: HOT ORANGE TIED BEARD STYLE
CHEEKS: JUNGLE COCK
HEAD: BLACK

This is a hair fly in the manner of Blondie. It has been named after Ray's daughter, born in 1963, who had striking platinum blonde hair as a child. In 1977, Ray collected the clippings following a haircut. He tied up a lure and caught a beautiful trout the first time he tried it. The photographed example has been tied using some of those original hair cuttings gathered up in 1977.

The lure has proved to be most effective when harled in slightly murky water (clearing after rain), or in conditions of poor light, particularly at change of light in the evening. It casts reasonably well and is very durable, Ray says - more so than feathered wings.

Tie in the golden pheasant crest for the tail. Tie in the floss and ribbing.

Wind on the floss to form the body. Follow with the ribbing.

Tie in the hackle feathers under the throat. Tie in the hair wing, which should extend just beyond the end of the tail. Add Jungle Cock cheeks.

CLARET (M)

ORIGIN: POSSIBLY 'BUDGE' HINTZ OF AUCKLAND
HOOK: 4
TAIL: GOLDEN PHEASANT TIPPETS
BODY: CLARET CHENILLE
RIB: OVAL GOLD
WING: STRIP OF DARK DYED RABBIT

HACKLE: DYED CLARET COCK
HEAD: BLACK

This pattern is given by O.S. ("Budge") Hintz in his book *Fisherman's Paradise.*

It would now be regarded as little more than a (claret) red Rabbit, but in those days it probably assumed a greater significance. His dressing for Rabbit in the same publication limited the body colour to green, yellow, and orange. He claims Claret to be an excellent fly for sunset and dusk. Claret chenille was almost impossible to obtain, when I tied this, and I have used claret seal's fur in the example.

Tie in the tippets, ribbing and chenille.

Take the thread back nearly to the head and wind on the chenille to this point. Alternatively, dub on the claret body. Tie in the strip of rabbit fur.

Wind on the ribbing, tying down the rabbit strip in the Matuku style.

Tie in the hackle feather and wind on.

CLEARWATER MATUKU (M)

ORIGIN: NOT KNOWN
HOOK: 4-6
BODY: WHITE CHENILLE
RIB: OVAL SILVER
WING: PALE YELLOW COCK HACKLE
HEAD: BLACK

This appears in Keith Drapers 1997 book wherein it is described as an Australian lure, favoured in Tasmania and Victoria. It is not a pattern which I have come across commercially. Nor have I found pale yellow plumage. For this, and other Australian patterns emanating from Keith's book, you will likely have to dye your own, as I have done here. The name presumably tells you where this lure should be used.

Tie in the chenille and ribbing.

Wind on the chenille body and secure. Tie in the wing feathers by the butts.

Wind on the ribbing, tying down the wing in the Matuku style.

CLIFF'S KILLER (H)

ORIGIN: CLIFF DIXON OF WAIROA
HOOK: NOT STATED BUT PROBABLY 8-10
TAIL: BROWN SQUIRREL
BODY: ORANGE CHENILLE
HACKLE: GINGER
HEAD: BLACK

This is a very simple and very effective pattern. It featured in the Tichborne calendar of 1987. Unfortunately Cliff died a few years later. Members of Cliff's family kindly made available to me a collection of Cliff's trout flies. Among them, I found three examples of this lure, all tied on a No. 10. Essentially, it is half a Red Setter, and by all accounts just as effective. The condition of Cliff's lures certainly bore testimony to that! Older anglers may recognise this as Red Setter Pup which is indistinguishable from this lure, and which featured, somewhat strangely, in the 1988 Tichborne calendar. The example has been tied on a No. 8 hook.

Tie in the tail and the chenille.

Wind on the chenille body and secure. Tie in a hackle feather.

Wind on the hackle feather to form a hackle collar.

COACHMAN LURE (O)

ORIGIN: NOT KNOWN
HOOK: 2-8
TAIL: TIPPETS
BODY: BRONZE PEACOCK HERL
WING: WHITE SWAN, TIED LONG
HACKLE: RED COCK
HEAD: BLACK

Of this fly, Keith Draper says: "I have in my possession some old flies used by the late Mr W. Branson, an old angler who fished Taupo for years. He had several Coachmen in his box, tied long and slim with a long swept-back wing of white swan. It is a very streamlined-looking fly and without any doubt would kill fish. An angler of Branson's reputation would never have had them in his box if they weren't effective. Another successful version of the Coachman is the Bucktail. I have used this pattern myself and it will take trout as efficiently as most flies. The pattern used was livened by the addition of a red tag." (1971). The drop in popularity has no doubt been occasioned by the difficulty in obtaining white swan feathers, although the white primaries on the black swan are available to the hunter during the shooting season. In the example photographed , Garth has tied the hackle beard style. I do not know if that is historically accurate, but it conforms to the slim look, which was no doubt intended.

Tie in the tippets and the peacock herl.

Wind on the herl to form the body.

Tie in the swan feather to form the long sweeping wing. Tie in the hackle feather. (If tying the hackle beard style, tie it in before the wing.)

Wind on the hackle, secure and trim.

COCK-A-BULLY (K)

ORIGIN: TIGHT LINES (LTD) OF NAPIER

HOOK: 8-10 LONG SHANK. (SPECIFICALLY, THE STOCK PATTERN IS TIED ON KAMASAN B 830 2X)

TAIL: BROWN MARABOU

BODY: BLACK THREAD

WING: THE BROWN 'CHURCH WINDOW' COCK PHEASANT FEATHERS FROM THE TOP OF THE RUMP, TIED IN KILLER-STYLE

HEAD: BROWN CHENILLE

This is a very effective bully pattern, which enjoys success at Lake Waikaremoana fished in the shallows around the lake edge with a very slow retrieve on either a floating or sinking line. It should do equally well anywhere cock-a-bullies abound.

I have seen a commercial version tied with a tail of rabbit fur, but is otherwise identical. The example has been tied on a Kamasan B 175 No. 8 short shank hook.

Tie in a good bunch of brown marabou for the tail.

Take the thread back approximately two-thirds the length of the shank and tie in 1-2 feathers (I prefer 2) on either side of the shank in the Killer style.

Tie in the chenille. Take the thread back to the head, and then form the head with the chenille and tie off.

COMETS (O)

ORIGIN: NOT KNOWN

HOOK: 4-6

BODY: TINSEL, GOLD OR SILVER

WING: BUCKTAIL, TIED IN LONG, TRAILING WELL PAST THE BEND OF THE HOOK

HEAD: BLACK

This is recorded in Keith Draper's 1997 book. He was shown these by an American angler, Rudi, who had brought a number of these with him, which he had tied up in a vast range of colours. (Some American catalogues list Comet (singular) as commercially available stock, but they bear no resemblance to this pattern.)

They were very popular in this country for a couple of years, and they caught trout.

It is my perception that this style of lure is making something of a comeback, which pleases me greatly. I am very attracted to this style of lure.

Tie in the body tinsel. [My practise is to return the thread to the head and wind the tinsel from the head down to the bend and back to the head]

Secure and trim the tinsel after forming the body. Tie in the bucktail wing in the colour (or colour combinations) of your choice. Make sure that the tie-in point is well saturated with cement. Complete the head in the usual way.

CORONATION (O)

ORIGIN: NOT KNOWN

HOOK: NOT STATED BUT PROBABLY 2-8

TAIL: BADGER HACKLE FIBRES

BODY: THREE EQUAL PARTS - RED, WHITE, AND BLUE CHENILLE OR FLOSS

WING: BROWN TURKEY

HACKLE: BADGER HACKLES

CHEEK: JUNGLE COCK

HEAD: BLACK

This appears in *Modern Fly Dressings* by C.H. Kendrick (1946). I suspect it was named after the coronation of King George VI in 1936, and that the colouring was devised more to represent the occasion rather than to catch trout although Kendrick claims that all of the flies which he lists "have been well tried out and proved successful."

Tie in the tail fibres. Tie in the first section of body material. Wind on the body material a short distance, secure, and tie in the next body section.

Wind on the body a short distance, secure, and repeat with

the last body section.

Tie in the hackle at the throat. Tie in the turkey wing at the shoulder. Add Jungle Cock cheeks and complete the head in the usual way.

COTTEE'S SILVERY (M)

ORIGIN: A.B. COTTEE OF CHRISTCHURCH
HOOK: NOT STATED BUT PROBABLY 2-8
TAIL: RED WHISKS
BODY: WHITE
RIB: OVAL SILVER
WING: NATURAL GINGER COCK
HACKLE: GRIZZLE, THROAT ONLY
HEAD: BLACK

This was created in 1952 and appears in Bragg's book under a listing of high country lures. It is not easy to be precise about the dressing but I believe it to be as described above.

It appears to have been popular in the Waitaki River and at the mouth. Clearly, though, it would be effective wherever smelt are found.

Tie in the whisks for the tail. Tie in the body material and the ribbing.

Wind on the body material and secure. Tie in the wing feathers by the butts.

Wind on the ribbing, tying down the wing in the Matuku style.

Tie in a hackle beard under the throat.

CRAIG'S KILLER (K)

ORIGIN: CRAIG ADAMS OF PAROA, NEAR GREYMOUTH
HOOK: 4-12
TAIL: BLACK SQUIRREL
BODY: OLIVE CHENILLE
UNDERWING: (OPTIONAL) ORANGE KEA FEATHER OR SUBSTITUTE
WING: THREE OLIVE DYED MALLARD FLANK OR PARTRIDGE BREAST FEATHERS
HEAD: BLACK

This was developed as a dragonfly nymph imitation and has proved very successful on lakes in Westland and Canterbury. It is a daytime fly only, fished over weed beds and around shallow margins.

The original was tied without an underwing. The example, which appeared in the 1989 Tichborne calendar, was tied by John Morton who added his own embellishment using the orange under coverts of a kea. The example shown here has the same. The kea is a partially protected bird, and the plumage can therefore be used provided it has been legally acquired. A good substitute would be golden pheasant tippets, but while the inclusion of the underwing adds to the visual appeal, and maybe trout appeal, Craig's success has been with unadorned lures.

Tie in the tail and tie in the chenille.

Wind on the chenille to the head and tie off. Tie in the underwing if using.

Tie in three wing feathers Pukeko style sweeping back to the bend of the hook.

CRAIG'S NIGHT-TIME (P)

ORIGIN: ERIC CRAIG OF AUCKLAND
HOOK: 2-10
TAIL: A TAG OF RED WOOL
BODY: BLACK CHENILLE
RIB: OVAL SILVER TINSEL
WING: BLUE PUKEKO BREAST FEATHERS
HACKLE: BLACK
TOPPING: ONE JUNGLE COCK EYE LAID ON TOP OF THE BLUE WING
HEAD: BLACK

Widely recognised as the first fly to use Pukeko feathers. It is illegal to buy or sell Pukeko feathers, but as it is a limited game bird it is not illegal to possess the plumage or to use it. If you cannot get the real thing, commercial substitutes (blue and black dyed mallard flank) are readily available. You may find this fly dressed with á small bunch of yellow hackle fibres in place of the Jungle Cock eye, although there is a trend towards omitting that, and also the black hackle. Whichever way it is tied, it is, in the words of Hugh McDowell 'a rattling good night fly'. Tied small on a No. 10, it is a good stream or river fly, and it is also effective on a floating line fished along the edge of the current. In the larger sizes it is fished deep and slowly.

Tie in the red tag and the body material and ribbing.

Take the thread back nearly to the head. Wind on the body material and ribbing and secure. Tie in two or three Pukeko feathers.

Tie in the Jungle Cock eye to lie on top of the wing. Tie in a black hackle feather and wind on.

CRAYFISH (P)

ORIGIN: BASIL JACKSON OF ROTORUA
HOOK: 2-8
TAIL: GREY BARRED SQUIRREL
EYES: GOLDEN PHEASANT TIPPETS
BODY: RABBIT FUR TIED UNDER THE SHANK
WING: MALLARD
HEAD: BLACK THREAD (TIED BIG) OVER A SMALL TUFT OF RABBIT FUR PROTRUDING OVER THE HOOK EYE

Basil used to tie this up a long time ago to represent a koura or freshwater shrimp. Basil found one remaining sample among his collection and kindly let me have it for this book.

Undeniably, this is a good representation of a crustacean. It should be fished very slowly along the bottom, preferably around shallow sandy margins.

The photo shows the top view of the lure, rather than a side profile, to demonstrate the 'crayfish' likeness.

Regrettably, Basil died a few months after I visited him. He was a wonderful man, and by all accounts a highly regarded angler and fly-tier.

Tie in two sparse bunches of grey squirrel - one bunch on either side of the shank. Overlay with a few fibres of golden pheasant tippets on each bunch of squirrel.

Tie in a small bunch of rabbit fur under the shank, reaching back to the bend. Tie in another small bunch on top of the shank to protrude forward over the hook eye.

Lightly varnish a mallard feather and stroke it between thumb and forefinger into a cowl shape. Tie in the feather in the Pukeko style, taking care not to cover the tippet 'eyes'. Wind on a large head. Trim the crayfish 'tail' to a fan-shape.

DAINTY VEIL (H)

ORIGIN: GEOFF SANDERSON OF TURANGI
HOOK: 6-10
TAIL: BARRED GREY SQUIRREL
BODY: IN TWO SECTIONS: REAR: RED WOOL; FRONT: BLACK WOOL
HACKLE: TWO VERY PALE GRIZZLE COCK HACKLES, ONE TIED IN HALF-WAY LONG THE BODY, THE OTHER AT THE HEAD. (TWO OR THREE TURNS OF EACH)
HEAD: BLACK

This is very similar to White Veil, also by Sanderson, and I suspect that one is a refinement of the other but I do not know which came first.

Tied slim, it is said to be an effective pattern.

Tie in the squirrel tail. Tie in the first section of wool.

Take the thread back nearly to the midpoint of the shank. Wind on the wool to this point. Tie in a hackle feather.

Wind on the hackle feather. Tie in the second section of wool. Take the thread back nearly to the head.

Wind on the wool to this point. Tie in a hackle collar and wind on.

DAMSEL NYMPH No. 1 (O)

ORIGIN: ROGER SMAILES OF MASTERTON
HOOK: 4-10
THREAD: GREEN
TAIL: OLIVE MARABOU
BODY: DUBBED MARABOU STRANDS
RIB: OVAL GOLD
HACKLE: THE LONGER BACK FEATHERS OF A GREY PARTRIDGE
HEAD: GOLD BEAD

Roger calls this a Gold Bead Damsel Nymph, because of what it represents (an emerging nymph) rather than indicating a type of trout fly. It is, in fact, fished as a lure. It imitates the damselfly emerger. It is very effective in the Kourarau Dam in the Wairarapa, and is a good still-water pattern around weed beds. It is fished on a sinking line with a slow, jerky, retrieve. Roger is the proprietor of Hunting & Fishing in Masterton, and ties up this pattern for commercial sale in his shop.

This particular damsel pattern bears a striking resemblance to the gold head damsel pattern of Kevin Hart of England, but the differences are enough to warrant inclusion.

Attach the gold bead behind the hook eye. Take the thread

from behind the bead down to the bend. Tie in a bunch of marabou for the tail. Tie in the ribbing.

Strip a few marabou plumes from the stem and dub these in along the length of the shank to finish behind the gold bead.

Wind on the ribbing and secure. Tie in a hackle feather. Wind on to form the hackle collar. Tie off.

DAMSEL NYMPH No. 2 (O)

ORIGIN: BARRY KENT OF TE PUKE, BASED ON A PATTERN CREATED BY ROB LIMMER CALLED SIMPSON FLY

HOOK: 6-10 LONG SHANK

TAIL: RED MARABOU WHISKS

BODY: VARIEGATED BLACK/OLIVE CHENILLE

RIB: PEACOCK GREEN LUREX

WING: BLACK MARABOU RIBBED WITH FINE RED COPPER WIRE.

HACKLE: MALLARD BREAST OR GREY PARTRIDGE TIED IN AT THE THROAT ONLY

HEAD: BLACK

This can be tied in black or olive marabou. If tied in the olive colouring, it bears a close resemblance to Roger Smailes' pattern (see previous entry) even though both patterns evolved quite independently.

This can be fished on a floating or sinking line, and it is even good for harling. It is perhaps most successfully fished on a floating line over weed beds around lake margins.

When Barry devised this variation, he had Lake Waikaremoana in mind, and he has had a lot of success with it there. The Simpson Fly, on which it is based, includes Flashabou tinsel. Barry omitted this as it was his perception (with which I respectfully differ) that trout at Lake Waikaremoana are not so receptive to flash.

Tie in the tail whisks. Tie in peacock green lurex rib, and also the red copper wire. Tie in the chenille

Take the thread back nearly to the head. Wind on the chenille to this point and tie off. Follow with the peacock green ribbing.

Tie in a bunch of marabou at the shoulder. Wind on the red copper wire ribbing, tying down the marabou to the top of the chenille, along the length of the shank.

DANDY (O)

ORIGIN: NOT KNOWN

HOOK: NOT STATED BUT PROBABLY 6-8

TAIL: GOLDEN PHEASANT CREST

BODY: SILVER TINSEL

RIB: OVAL SILVER

WING: INNER - JUNGLE COCK. OUTER - GOLDEN PHEASANT TIPPETS

CHEEK: STRIP OF TEAL UNDER BLUE HACKLES

HACKLE: TEAL, THROAT ONLY

TOPPING: GOLDEN PHEASANT CREST

HEAD: BLACK

This is a florid Canterbury high country lure, which appears in Bragg's book. For all its flamboyance, it is in fact a 'plain' simplified version of a more elaborate early salmon fly which has at least a yellow floss tag and a peacock herl butt, and maybe other adornments, which I have not been able to ascertain.

This is a useful pattern for using up the larger Jungle Cock feathers, which are normally too big for customary dressings.

Tie in the golden pheasant crest for the tail. Tie in the body tinsel and ribbing.

Wind on the body and follow with the ribbing, finishing near the head. Tie in Jungle Cock plumes extending beyond the bend.

Tie in a bunch of golden pheasant tippets on either side of the Jungle Cock wing. Add a strip of teal as cheeks topped with blue hackle (I have used dyed mallard).

Tie in a bunch of hackle feathers under the throat.

DAPPLED DOG (H)

ORIGIN: GEOFF SANDERSON OF TURANGI

HOOK: 4-8

TAIL: GREY BARRED SQUIRREL TAIL

BODY: FLUORESCENT CHENILLE (LIME GREEN, RED, OR ORANGE)

HACKLE: GRIZZLE COCK HACKLES

HEAD: BLACK

This is an excellent pattern for fresh lake run rainbows. Keith Draper has found that "an orange dappled dog will on occasions entice the dourest of fish if it is shown to them for long enough." (1997). In the winter of 1960 Keith caught 153 trout in three months, which says it all! He also records his success with a green version in the smaller sizes. Geoff Sanderson insists on the fluorescent body. The orange version is not unlike the Red Setter, which, of course, was another Sanderson gift to anglers everywhere. This lure appeals to rainbow trout in particular.

Tie in the tail and chenille.

Take the thread part way back along the shank. Wind on the chenille to that point and secure. Tie in a hackle feather, wind on and secure.

Repeat the process with the chenille and hackle.

DELUXE HARLER (M)

ORIGIN: PAT O'KEEFE OF ROTORUA
HOOK: 2
TAIL: BUNCH OF RED OR ORANGE MARABOU
BODY: VERY LIGHT BLUE OR WHITE CHENILLE
RIB: THIN COPPER WIRE
WING: TWO LONG GRIZZLE FEATHERS
CHEEKS: TUFT OF WHITE MARABOU ON EITHER SIDE
TOPPING: SINGLE STRAND OF HOLOGRAPHIC TINSEL
EYES: JUNGLE COCK
HEAD: BLACK

This appeared in an issue of *New Zealand Fisherman*. It is really effective around the Rotorua lakes, harled early morning or late evening on the edge of weed beds. Pat recommends using a sinking level line with a long mono trace of 10-13 metres of 4 kgs breaking strain. Troll at 1 to 2 knots.

Pat also removes the bottom fibres of the wing feathers equal to the length of the shank so that the wing sits flat against the body when tying in. The marabou cheeks should cover around the head and under-section of the fly when tying in, extending back to about 2cms from the bend.

Tie in a generous (2-3cms) tuft of marabou. Tie in the chenille and the ribbing.

Wind on the chenille body. Tie in the wing feathers by the butts. The wing should extend at least 5cms beyond the bend.

Wind on the ribbing, tying down the wing in the Matuku style.

Tie in the cheeks and 'eyes' on either side of the shank. Tie in the topping.

DEMON SQUIRREL (O)

ORIGIN: NOT KNOWN
HOOK: 2-10
TAIL: GOLDEN PHEASANT TOPPING
BODY: FLAT GOLD TINSEL
WING: BROWN SQUIRREL TAIL
HACKLE: ORANGE
HEAD: BLACK

Keith Draper says: "This is a Demon with a brown hair wing and is a lure that R.K. Bragg esteems on the southern scene. This pattern is also a good Taupo river pattern." (1971).

Tie in the crest feather for the tail. Tie in the tinsel.

Wind on the tinsel to form the body. Secure and trim.

Tie in a bunch of squirrel tail fibres for the wing. Secure and trim. I would be inclined to smother the tied-off area with cement to prevent the hair fibres pulling out. Tie in the hackle feather.

Wind on the hackle, secure and trim.

DEVIL See Black and Yellow (Devil)

DEVIL DODGER (M)

ORIGIN: NOT KNOWN
HOOK: 2-8
TAIL: RED WHISKS
BODY: SILVER TINSEL
RIB: OVAL SILVER
WING: BLACK
HACKLE: BLACK
HEAD: BLACK

"This fly is dressed in a slimmer manner than the normal Canterbury lure. It is usually regarded as a sea trout fly to be used after dark, but it will sometimes take well during daylight, especially if there is colour in the water." - Keith Draper (1997).

The addition of Jungle Cock eyes would add both to its appeal and its effectiveness.

Tie in the tail whisks. Tie in the silver tinsel and ribbing. Secure and trim.

Wind on the tinsel body. Secure and trim. Tie in the wing feather.

Wind on the ribbing, tying down the wing in the Matuku style. Tie in the hackle feather.

Wind on the hackle collar. Secure and trim. Add Jungle Cock eyes if desired.

DIANNE'S KILLER (K)

ORIGIN: PETER STOREY OF AUCKLAND
HOOK: 2-14
TAIL: BUNCH OF BLACK MARABOU
BODY: DUBBED BASAL MARABOU FLUFF FROM BASE OF OLIVE DYED MALLARD PLUMAGE
WING: OLIVE DYED MALLARD BREAST FEATHERS
RIB: (OPTIONAL) PEARL MYLAR
GILL PLATES: PEARL MYLAR
HEAD: DUBBED BASAL FLUFF (AS FOR BODY)

The feathers used are those which are often sold commercially as 'Hamill's Killer' plumage. The whole of the feather is utilised in that the basal fluff is stripped from the lower part of the feather and then dubbed on to form the body and head.

This lure imitates bullies and possibly dragonfly nymphs. Tied slim, it might also be taken for smelt. It is fished over weed beds and drop-offs on anything from a floating to a fast sinking line, although it was originally designed for fishing in Lake Tarawera on a floating or medium sinking line.

The lure was named after Peter's wife.

Tie in the marabou tail. Tie in the ribbing if using.

Dub on half the basal fluff, leaving sufficient room for the head. Follow with the ribbing if using.

Tie in the wing feathers on either side of the shank in the Killer style.

Wind on pearl mylar in front of the tie off point, picking out a few stands of the mylar to give a bit of sparkle. Dub over with the second half of the basal fluff to form the head.

DIRTY HARRY (P)

ORIGIN: GARTH COGHILL OF ROTORUA
HOOK: 6-10 PARTRIDGE CODE D3ST STRAIGHT-EYED STREAMER
TAIL: GREY SQUIRREL TAIL
BODY: AURORA SKIRT
RIB: OVAL GOLD
WING: MINIMUM OF 3 MALLARD DRAKE BODY CONTOUR FEATHERS
HACKLE: YELLOW OR ORANGE DYED HEN HACKLES
HEAD: BLACK

As Garth puts it: "Come on Mr Trout – 'make my day' – and they do!"

This is best fished after dark, utilising the luminous Aurora skirt. The wings can be natural mallard feathers, or dyed either brown or green.

Tie in the tail, which should extend a full hook length beyond the bend. Tie in the body material and ribbing.

Wind on the Aurora skirt and ribbing. Secure. (At this point Garth seals the body with two coats of crystal clear nail enamel.)

Tie in the wing feathers Pukeko style. The wing should extend over the tail to the black barring, but no further. Tie in the hackle feather and wind on.

DISCO DOLL (H)

ORIGIN: NOT KNOWN
HOOK: NOT STATED, BUT PROBABLY 2-8 AS WITH MOST HACKLE FLIES
TAIL: GREY SQUIRREL TAIL OR WHITE HACKLE FIBRES
BODY: A VIOLENT SHOCKING PINK CHENILLE MARKETED AS "FLUORESCENT RED"
HACKLE: WHITE COCK HACKLES
HEAD: BLACK

This was all the rage once, but its popularity seems to have given way to the Glo-Bug varieties. Hugh McDowell gives a good account of his success with Disco Doll in his book *New Zealand Fly-Tying.*

Discerning as best I can from that account, it seems that this lure is more effective during the winter and spring months, but no doubt there is much anecdotal evidence to the contrary. It is very similar to Louie's Lure, and it would seem that it originated in America.

Tie in the tail. Tie in the chenille and secure.

Return the thread part way along the shank. Wind on the chenille to this point. Tie in a hackle feather.

Wind on the hackle, secure and trim. Take the thread back nearly to the head. Wind on the chenille to this point and tie in a hackle feather for the collar.

Wind on the hackle, to form a hackle collar.

In the larger sizes, three sets of hackles will be needed, while in the smallest sizes, just one hackle at the head is sufficient.

DOLL FLY (O)

ORIGIN: OF ENGLISH PARENTAGE, BORN AROUND 1920

HOOK: 6-8

TAG: CHARTREUSE EGG YARN OVER RED EGG YARN

BODY: AURORA SKIRT

OVERBODY: CHARTREUSE EGG YARN

HACKLE: PEARL FLASHABOU OR KRYSTAL FLASH (TIED UNDER THROAT ONLY)

EYES: YELLOW WITH BLACK PUPIL

HEAD: CHARTREUSE

This is a common and widely available lure, which can be tied up in a variety of colours and materials.

One of the more popular combinations is red and chartreuse, and that is what has been used in the example photographed. Chartreuse is a good colour for change of light early morning and evening, and the Aurora skirt means, of course, that it is more suited for night fishing but is not limited to that.

Originally, this lure was called Baby Doll, and it is still correctly called that, but is commonly known as the Doll Fly. It was popularised in New Zealand by Pat Swift of Rotorua, who was the first to use Aurora skirt for the body. In this example, Pat has used white tying thread.

Tie in the red tail material. Tie in an overlay of chartreuse egg yarn and secure. Tie in the Aurora skirt.

Take the thread back to the head. Tie in the overbody which is the same as the second tail colour (in this case, chartreuse).

Stretch the overbody material along the shank, on top of and beyond the tail. Wrap the Aurora skirt around the shank and the overbody, winding back to the head. Secure.

Pull the overbody material forward towards the eye, covering the Aurora skirt on top of the shank. Secure. Tie in a few strands of Flashabou or similar under the throat. Complete the head and add eyes for extra realism if desired.

DOROTHY (M)

ORIGIN: PHIL PARSONS OF NAPIER

HOOK: 2-8

TAIL: BUNCH OF RED DYED HACKLE FIBRES

BODY: WOOL OR CHENILLE, USUALLY YELLOW OR RED ALTHOUGH ALL THE POPULAR COLOURS CAN BE USED.

RIB: OVAL SILVER

WING: WELL-BARRED GRIZZLE

HACKLE: GRIZZLE

HEAD: BLACK

This is a popular and traditional fly although upstaged somewhat by Parsons' Glory and Taupo Tiger as a bright day fly. However Keith Draper believes that it comes into its own during evening or a change of light particularly with a red body. The silver bodied version is a superb lure (see next entry).

Phil Parsons, who, of course, created Parsons' Glory, named this fly after the wife of a close fishing companion, and who was herself an accomplished angler. Keith Draper's inferential account (1997) that the lure was named after Phil's daughter, Dorothy McGregor, is not quite accurate. Phil Parsons had a daughter, Mai, who married Lumsden McGregor and a step-daughter, Dorothy, who married one Prossor, but neither inspired the name of this lure.

Tie in the tail, chenille, and ribbing.

Wind on the chenille body. Tie in the wing feather.

Wind on the ribbing, tying down the wing in the Matuku style. Secure and trim. Tie in a hackle feather if using and wind on.

DOROTHY, SILVER (M)

ORIGIN: HALF THE POPULATION OF ROTORUA! IN FACT, THIS CAN PROPERLY BE ATTRIBUTED TO PHIL PARSONS OF NAPIER

HOOK: 2-10

TAIL: BUNCH OF RED DYED HACKLE FIBRES

BODY: FLAT SILVER TINSEL OR MYLAR

RIB: OVAL SILVER

WING: WELL-BARRED GRIZZLE

HACKLE: GRIZZLE

HEAD: BLACK

This is Hugh McDowell's favourite dressing of this

lure. He says: "In the larger sizes it is an excellent choice for harling, while tied without a hackle collar on a small No. 8 or even No. 10 hooks, it can be very effective when cast to smelting fish."

This is especially so in the Ohau Channel between lakes Rotorua and Rotoiti where this dressing using lightly marked pale grizzle feathers is the first choice of Rotorua anglers.

Tie in the tail whisks. Tie in the tinsel and ribbing.

Wind on the tinsel body. Tie in the wing feathers by the butts.

Wind on the ribbing, tying down the wing in the Matuku style. Secure and trim. Tie in a hackle feather.

Wind on the hackle feather to form a hackle collar.

DOUBLE PUFF (O)

ORIGIN: NOT KNOWN

HOOK: 4-8

TAG: FLAT SILVER

BODY: GLO-BUG YARN (FLAME) WITH FLAT SILVER TINSEL WOUND BETWEEN PUFFS

WING: WHITE MARABOU

HEAD: BLACK

This is a salmon pattern developed in Alaska and currently popular in parts of New Zealand. It is obviously yet another variation of the Glo-Bug, and by all accounts just as successful. In Alaska, it is known as Two Egg Sperm Fly. In the smaller sizes it can be used as a dropper when nymphing.

The puffs can be formed in the same manner as for a Glo-Bug, but an easier way for most tiers, I suggest, is to place the yarn in a dubbing loop and trim both ends to a tapered shape.

Tie in the tinsel tag, winding it halfway around the bend of the hook and back. Tie off.

Form a dubbing loop and dub on the glo-bug yarn into a large puff. Tie in flat silver tinsel and wind forward a short distance.

Repeat the dubbing procedure with the glo-bug yarn to make a second puff slightly larger than the first.

Tie in the (over)wing of marabou.

DRIFTER (H)

ORIGIN: KEITH DRAPER OF TAUPO

HOOK: 8-10

TAIL: GOLDEN PHEASANT TIPPETS

BODY: FLUORESCENT CHENILLE

HACKLE: SOFT GREY

HEAD: BROWN

This is an attractor lure which is tied up in a variety of fluorescent colours, normally pink, red, orange, or lime green. It is fished conventionally as a wet fly on a sinking line during daytime. It fishes well and enjoyed considerable popularity until the Glo-Bug arrived and allegiances were switched. It is still available commercially in some parts of the country.

Tie in the tippets for the tail. Tie in the chenille for the body - colour of choice.

Wind on the chenille to this point and secure.

Tie in a hackle feather at the shoulder. Wind on to form a hackle collar.

DUCHESS (K)

ORIGIN: KILWELL'S OF ROTORUA

HOOK: 2-8

TAIL: A BUNCH OF COCK PHEASANT TAIL FIBRES

BODY: YELLOW CHENILLE

RIB: OVAL SILVER

WING: THE GOLDEN BLACK-TIPPED FEATHERS FROM A COCK PHEASANT'S FLANK, TIED IN TWO A SIDE

HEAD: BLACK

Keith Draper says; "This is a pattern that has never really taken on and there is only a limited demand for the dressing. It is, however, a good Taupo fly and I know of some good bags taken on it." (1971)

It is a very attractive fly, and I have always harboured high hopes for the beautiful red and golden plumage of the ring-necked pheasant. This is a good fly for the home tier who is also a hunter.

Tie in the tail, chenille and ribbing.

Return the thread part way along the shank. Wind on the chenille and ribbing to this point. Tie in a pair of wings on either side of the shank.

Continue the thread nearly to the head and follow with the

chenille and ribbing. Secure and trim. Add another pair of wings, again in the Killer style, on either side of the shank.

The addition of Jungle Cock eyes might be worth a thought.

DUKE (K)

ORIGIN: KILWELL'S OF ROTORUA
HOOK: NOT STATED BUT PROBABLY 2-8
TAIL: BROWN SQUIRREL TAIL
BODY: PROBABLY RED
RIB: PROBABLY OVAL SILVER
WING: GOLDEN FEATHERS FROM A RING NECK PHEASANT
HEAD: BLACK

This is a stablemate to Duchess, with the only significant variation being in the tail. As with most Killer style flies, the body material and colour may be irrelevant, and ribbing would only be used for strengthening. I have omitted it. There is no reason why this should be any less effective than Duchess, although Duchess has endured and the Duke's tenure seems to have been very short.

Although created by Kilwell, they have no records of it and are unable to confirm the pattern or any other details.

Tie in the tail. Tie in the body material and ribbing if using.

Take the thread part way back along the shank. Wind on the body material and ribbing to this point.

Tie in wing feathers in the Killer style. Take the thread back nearly to the head.

Continue the body material and ribbing to this point. Tie in another set of wing feathers on either side of the shank in the Killer style.

EARLY SEASON MATUKU (M)

ORIGIN: NOT KNOWN
HOOK: 4-6
BODY: WHITE CHENILLE OR WOOL
RIB: OVAL SILVER
WING: PALE YELLOW HEN HACKLE
HACKLE: SCARLET
HEAD: BLACK

This appears in Keith Draper's 1997 book. It is of Australian origin but has found popularity in New Zealand fishing for rainbow trout. The name tells you when it is most effective.

The hen hackles give a short chunky look to this lure. I had some difficulty dyeing the feathers which should ideally be a lighter shade that I have achieved.

Tie in the body material and the ribbing.

Wind on the body material. Secure and trim. Tie in the wing feathers by the butts.

Wind on the ribbing, tying down the wing in the Matuku style. Tie in the hackle feather and wind on to form a hackle collar.

ENGLAND'S DEMON (M)

ORIGIN: PROBABLY JACK ENGLAND OF TURANGI
HOOK: NOT STATED BUT PROBABLY 2-8
BUTT: TWO TURNS OF OVAL GOLD
TAIL: ORANGE WHISKS
BODY: GOLD TINSEL
RIB: FLAT GOLD
WING: SPLIT RED PARTRIDGE TAIL
HACKLE: ORANGE
HEAD: BLACK

This was commercially tied by Kilwell's, but the name suggests that it was created by England, being a person and not a country, and the most likely candidate is Jack England who created Jack's Sprat. I venture to suggest that this was his version of Golden Demon.

Kilwell no longer have any records or memory of this lure, and the above dressing comes from the only known example in captivity, housed in Ross Marks' framed collection of Kilwell lures.

I suspect the difficulty in supply of red partridge together with the waning popularity of split wing ties caused this lure to fade from the scene.

Tie in the butt and the whisks for the tail. Tie in the body tinsel and ribbing.

Wind on the body tinsel. Tie in the split wing feathers by the butts.

Wind on the ribbing, tying down the wing in the Matuku style.

Tie in the hackle feather. Wind on to form a hackle collar.

EPOXY SPRAT (O)

ORIGIN: GARTH COGHILL OF ROTORUA

HOOK: 4-10, DOWN EYED, MODIFIED

TAIL: ANNY BLATT POYAMIDE YARN, BLANC.

FORM: ADHESIVE BACKED ALUMINIUM, CLEAR PLASTIC, OR LEAD SHEET (ZONKER TAPE)

BODY: BRAIDED PEARL MYLAR TUBING

COATING: 5 MINUTE EPOXY

EYES: HAND PAINTED OR STICK ON

TYING THREAD: WHITE 3/0 MONOBOND AND CLEAR MONFILAMENT SEWING THREAD.

Garth makes these up in the larger sizes for saltwater fishing, and smaller sizes for trout although there is no reason why you shouldn't try any size for trout. The modified hook shape keeps the fly upright in the water.

Garth has found that Mustad 9672 and Partridge JS Sea Streamer CS11 hooks are the best for bending. Most other hooks are so well hardened and tempered they break before bending. It is imperative that safety glasses be worn when shaping the hook.

To modify the hook, use round-nosed pliers, and bend slowly, a little at a time. Start behind the eye and bend the shank upwards until the eye is straight, i.e. parallel to the original plane of the shank. Gradually bend in the belly shape at a point one-third of the shank length from the eye. Correct the overall shape by bending down on the shank just above the hook point so that the eye is horizontal and in the same plane as the original shank line.

Start an even foundation of white thread behind the eye and wind down to the hook bend. Tie in a bunch of white polyamide yarn for the tail, extending about half the shank length beyond the bend. Return the thread to the eye, whip finish, and cut the thread. Apply double-sided tape to a suitable length of body form material, then fold around the hook shank with adhesive to adhesive, and squeeze together around the hook with flat-nosed pliers. Cut to fish shape with sharp scissors. If desired, colour the body form with permanent marking pens (see my comments under Zonker).

Take a piece of mylar tubing slightly longer than the shank and place it over the eye. Tie it in place just behind the eye with clear monofilament sewing thread. Seal the tie-in point. Wind the monofilament around the form to the tail with open turns, then secure with a half hitch.

Roll the tubing back towards the tail turning it inside out in the process. Pull to tighten the tubing around the form and secure in place with 4-5 turns of mono at the base of the tail. Whip finish and trim the mono. Trim the fraying ends of the mylar flush with the whipping and seal. Coat with epoxy. If using metallic eyes, place them in position before the resin sets; otherwise hand paint the eyes later.

ETHIOPIAN (M)

ORIGIN: RITCHIE BUCHANAN OF TAUPO

HOOK: 2-8

TAIL: RED WHISKS

BODY: IN TWO PARTS: REAR: RED CHENILLE; FRONT: YELLOW AND BLACK CHENILLE

RIB: OVAL SILVER

WING: BLACK COCK HACKLES

TOPPING: WHITE HACKLE WHISKS

HEAD: BLACK

Ritchie, a professional guide, created this in 1991. It is a top performing night fly with plenty of movement and bulk giving a good representation of small fish and koura when tied in the larger sizes. It is best fished at river mouths, or for harling in the early hours of the morning, during the months of February to June.

Tie in the tail whisks. Tie in the first section of chenille and the ribbing.

Take the thread part way along the shank. Wind on the red chenille to this point and secure. Tie in the two chenille colours for the second section. Wind on the two chenilles, twisted to give a harlequin or variegated effect.

Tie in the wing hackles. Wind on the ribbing, tying down the wing in the Matuku style. Tie in the topping.

EWE WASP (O) (Old Tie)

ORIGIN: NOT KNOWN, BUT THOUGHT TO BE A SCOTTISH PATTERN

HOOK: 2-8

TAIL: GOLDEN PHEASANT CREST

TAG: SILVER TINSEL

BODY: IN TWO PARTS, OF WOOL OR FLOSS. FRONT: BLACK; REAR: PORTION PALE YELLOW

RIB: OVAL SILVER TINSEL

WING: BRONZE MALLARD FLANK. THIS WAS USUALLY BOLSTERED WITH AN INSIDE WING OF TURKEY

HACKLE: BLACK

CHEEKS: JUNGLE COCK

HEAD: BLACK

Also known as Taupo Wasp. (See next entry)

Tie in the crest feather and the tinsel tag. Tie in the yellow body material and ribbing.

Take the thread part way along the shank. Wind on the body

material to this point and secure. Tie in the black wool or floss.

Take the thread back nearly to the head. Wind on the black body material and secure. Wind on the ribbing.

Tie in slips of turkey wing at the butt. Overlay the turkey wing with the bronze mallard flank, tied in the same manner.

Tie in the hackle feather and wind on. Add Jungle Cock cheeks.

EWE WASP (M) (Modern tie)

ORIGIN: SEE COMMENTS BELOW

HOOK: 2-8

TAIL: YELLOW HACKLE FIBRES

BODY: CHENILLE IN TWO PARTS. FRONT: BLACK; REAR PORTION: YELLOW

RIB: OVAL SILVER TINSEL

WING: SPLIT GROUSE TAIL

HACKLE: BLACK

HEAD: BLACK

This pattern comes from Keith Draper's 1997 book.

John Veniard, in *Reservoir and Lake Flies* , contains the same dressing except for a wing of split speckled partridge.

In his 1971 book, Keith Draper gives various versions as to the possible origin of this fly and its enigmatic name.

All has now been revealed in his 1997 book. It seems that the original was named after the River Ewe in North Scotland, and after its arrival in New Zealand it was modified by the uniquely (then) Kiwi style of tying. It is worth repeating Keith's earlier (1971) comments about this lure: "The Ewe Wasp has killed countless trout over the years, mostly at night. It is a fly favoured by some anglers on a semi-moonlit night. They feel that as it is a mixture of black and yellow it has something to offer no matter if the moon is shining or obscured by cloud. When they catch fish on it who can dispute them."

Tie in the tail, first segment of chenille, and ribbing. Take the thread part way back along the shank.

Wind the chenille on to this point and secure. Tie in the second segment of chenille. Wind on the chenille to the head.

Tie in the wing feathers by the butts. Wind on the ribbing, tying down the wing in the Matuku style.

Tie in a hackle feather and wind on to form a collar. Complete the head.

EWE WASP (BARRED) (M)

ORIGIN: BASED ON AN OLD SCOTTISH PATTERN

HOOK: 2-8

TAIL: YELLOW HACKLE FIBRES

BODY: ALTERNATE BANDS OF BLACK AND YELLOW CHENILLE

RIB: OVAL SILVER TINSEL

WING: SPLIT GROUSE TAIL

HACKLE: BLACK COCK

HEAD: BLACK

This pattern can be found in the English publication by John Veniard: *Reservoir and Lake Flies.* The most obvious variation from the other patterns given is in the way the yellow and black body is constructed, otherwise it is identical to the previous entry and the method of tying this lure is exactly as shown previously.

EXOCET (H)

ORIGIN: DAVID DANNEFAERD OF NEW PLYMOUTH

HOOK: 4,6, OR 8 LONG SHANK

TAIL: SCARLET DYED HAIR - GOAT, DEER, SQUIRREL ETC.

BODY: BRIGHT SCARLET CHENILLE OR WOOL

HACKLE: SCARLET DYED SADDLE HACKLE

HEAD: RED

David is one of Taranaki's foremost anglers. He does not recall when he first tied 'this apparition', but he carried it around for some years before he gave it its first swim. That was a memorable occasion in the lower Tongariro when the trout all seemed to have developed lockjaw. David writes: "On went this red 'thing' and bingo, an 8 fish limit in no time."

On returning to the bach, David heard the news that the British warship Sheffield had been sunk by the Argentinians in the Falklands with a guided missile - an Exocet, hence the name for a fly that "never missed".

The heady success of that first outing has not been repeated. As he says: "Like all patterns it has not always performed as it did on the fateful day that the

Exocet was 'fired' in anger."

However, at the right time and in the right circumstances it is obviously capable of triggering a frantic response.

Tie in the tail. Tie in the body material.

Wind on the chenille or wool to about the mid-point. Tie in a hackle feather and wind on.

Continue the body material nearly to the head. Tie in another hackle feather and wind on.

FERRIS (M)

ORIGIN: NOT KNOWN
HOOK: NOT STATED, BUT PROBABLY 2-8
BODY: YELLOW MOHAIR
RIB: OVAL GOLD TINSEL
WING: TWO BRIGHT RED COCK HACKLES, BACK TO BACK, AND TIED DOWN ON BODY BY WINDING RIBBING TINSEL OVER HACKLE STEM
HEAD: BLACK

This is listed in the section New Zealand Lake Patterns in John Veniard's English publication. Kilwell's of Rotorua used to tie flies for an old Englishman named Ferris, and apparently the first pattern was tied from the soft thigh feathers of a buff bantam. I have been unable to find any other reference to that original pattern, and it is unclear how this pattern evolved. Just as uncertain is whether the fly has been named by him or after him.

The lure is tied in the conventional Matuku style, and the description of the tying method given in the pattern was probably for the benefit of English readers who might otherwise be ignorant of this uniquely New Zealand style.

Tie in the body material and ribbing.

Return the thread back nearly to the head. Wind on the mohair to form the body. Tie in the hackle feathers, which will form the wing.

Tie down the wing by winding on the ribbing around the body and through the hackle fibres. Secure and trim.

FERRIS (Red & Yellow) (M)

ORIGIN: NOT KNOWN
HOOK: 2-8
BODY: RED OR YELLOW WOOL OR CHENILLE
RIB: OVAL SILVER
WING: TWO WHITE HACKLES INSIDE TWO BLACK HACKLES
HACKLE: BLACK
HEAD: BLACK

See the previous entry for comments on the 'Ferris' connections.

Keith Draper recounts his experiences with this lure on Hawkes Bay rivers and at the Waitahanui rip. There can be no doubt that it will take fish, although you are unlikely to find it in any tackle shops today. Because the photo example in both of Keith's books (1971 and 1997), has a red body, I have tied this up with a yellow body.

I can only assume that the late George Ferris either created this (and the previous) lure or has been honoured by naming the lure after him as befits an angler of his reputation.

Tie in the chenille and ribbing.

Wind on the chenille to form the body. Secure and trim. Tie in the wing feathers by the butts.

Wind on the ribbing, tying down the feathers to the shank. Secure and trim. Tie in a hackle feather. Wind on to form a hackle collar.

FERRIS VARIATION (M)

ORIGIN: SEE COMMENTS BELOW
HOOK: 4-6
TAIL: WHISKS OF DYED RED FEATHER
BODY: WHITE CHENILLE
RIB: OVAL SILVER TINSEL
WING: TWO HEN PHEASANT (MATUKU STYLE) FEATHERS, OVERLAID WITH TWO BROWN OR BLACK FEATHERS
HEAD: BLACK

Tony Orman, in his book *The Sport In Fishing*, obtained the favourite patterns of 13 experts. This variation pattern was evolved by Euan MacAlsister. No other comment is given, but if it is (or was then) the favourite pattern of this expert angler, that should be comment enough.

Unfortunately for the home tier, it is illegal to hunt

hen pheasants, so the material has to be sourced from overseas.

Tie in the tail. Tie in the chenille and ribbing.

Wind on the chenille to form the body.

Tie in the feathers to form the wings.

Wind on the ribbing, tying down the wing in the Matuku style. Secure and trim. As with the first Ferris listed, there is no head hackle.

FIREBALL (O)

ORIGIN: GARY KEMSLEY OF NAPIER

HOOK: 2-6

BODY: FLUORESCENT WOOL OR CHENILLE, RED OR ORANGE

RIB: OVAL SILVER

WING: EQUAL AMOUNTS OF ORANGE, RED, AND YELLOW MARABOU, MIXED, AND TIED IN AT THE HEAD

HEAD: BLACK OR GREY

This was created prior to 1970 during a fishing assault on the Waitahanui River. It had rained all night, and frustrated pre-dawn fishing turned to despair when daylight revealed the dirty colour of the water. Gary and his friend retired to the fishing lodge to thaw out and try and tie up something that might work in the murky conditions. Gary recalled a couple of articles he had read where this problem had been addressed and, armed with this recovered knowledge, Fireball was born. The result was a bright (trout) eye-catcher that would be visible in the dirtiest water. And it worked, if not spectacularly, at least enough to turn around what would otherwise have been a fishless day. Gary's account of this episode featured in *New Zealand Outdoor*, September 1978. He says there: "Since then I have used the fireball in dirty water on many occasions and have found that if there are fish to be caught I can usually pick up my share on this pattern."

Tie in the chenille and ribbing.

Wind on the chenille and follow with the ribbing. Secure and trim.

Select equal bunches of marabou about 25-30mm long and tie in at the head.

FRANCIS BUTCHER (O)

ORIGIN: FRANK CIOCHETTO OF AUCKLAND

HOOK: 4-14

TAIL: BLACK SQUIRREL

BODY: SILVER MYLAR TINSEL

RIB: 4 TURNS OF 1.8KG CLEAR NYLON TRACE

WING: PEACOCK SWORD -
6 STRANDS ON NO.4
5 STRANDS ON NO. 6-8
4 STRANDS ON NO. 10
3 STRANDS ON NO. 12-14

HACKLE: BRIGHT ORANGE HEN HACKLES (BEARD ONLY)

HEAD: BLACK

This was originally designed as a smelt fly, which would sink rapidly in the Tongariro River, hence the slim dressing. In sizes 4-10, the lure can be fished upstream or down on a sinking line. Sizes 12 and 14 are really small wet flies and are fished as such. For downriver fishing, let the line straighten, pause for a few seconds, and then retrieve slowly. The take will be gentle. When casting upstream (preferably to observed trout) neither floating line nor strike indicator are necessary. The strike will be vigorous. A floating line can be used to cast to smelting fish in the lake, in which case use a fast retrieve. With a sinking line in the same situation, let the lure sink to the bottom and then twitch the lure slowly back. This lure has been very successful both as a day and night fly in the southern rivers of Lake Taupo, as well as the southern end of the lake.

Tie in the tail. Tie in the tinsel and ribbing.

Wind on the tinsel body. Wind on the ribbing in four turns, going counter-wise to the body turns.

Tie in the peacock sword. Tie in the hackle fibres at the throat (like a beard).

FRUIT SALAD (P)

ORIGIN: NOT KNOWN, ALTHOUGH IT USED TO BE TIED UP BY KILWELL'S OF ROTORUA IN THE 1970's

HOOK: NOT STATED. I WOULD GUESS 2-8

TAIL: BUNCH OF DYED YELLOW COCK HACKLE FIBRES

BODY: EQUAL PORTIONS OF RED, BLACK, AND YELLOW CHENILLE

RIB: (OPTIONAL) OVAL SILVER

WING: BLUE OR BLACK PUKEKO FEATHERS

HACKLE: DYED ORANGE OR BLACK
HEAD: BLACK

This is a night fly, the success of which I have been unable to determine. It was obviously popular at one time. The original order in which the tri-coloured body is tied is shrouded in mystery but I notice that both Hugh McDowell and Kilwell's have used the colours in the order listed, starting from the rear.

Tie in the tail. Tie in the first portion of chenille and the ribbing.

Take the thread part way back along the shank. Wind on the chenille to this point and tie off. Tie in the second portion of chenille.

Take the thread further back along the shank. Wind on the second portion of chenille to this point and tie off. Repeat for the last portion of chenille.

Wind on the ribbing if using and tie off. Tie in the Pukeko feathers at the head so that the wing lies flat along the top of the body.

Tie in a hackle feather and wind on.

FURNACE SMELT (M)

ORIGIN: NOT KNOWN
HOOK: 2-8
TAIL: YELLOW HACKLE WHISKS
BODY: WHITE CHENILLE
RIB: OVAL GOLD
WING: RED/BLACK (FURNACE) HACKLES
HACKLE: AS FOR WING, TIED AS A COLLAR
HEAD: BLACK

A diligent search of the Napier Public Library will unearth a curious little publication called *58 NZ Lure Patterns* published by Daily Telegraph Print, Napier, probably in 1977. It is a collection of patterns compiled by N. Whiting for Anglers Agencies. And that is all there is to it - 58 patterns without comment, explanation, or illustration. All the standard favourites are there plus a few obscure ones I have not found elsewhere, this being one of them. As with all the popular hackles such as Badger, Grizzle, Ginger, etc, it is inevitable that Furnace would be used in the same way. Just how effective it is is anybody's guess.

Tie in the tail whisks, chenille, and ribbing.

Wind on the chenille body and secure. Tie in the wing feather.

Wind on the ribbing, tying down the wing in the Matuku style.

Tie in the hackle feather and wind on.

FURRY BARRED WASP (O)

ORIGIN: KILWELL'S OF ROTORUA
HOOK: NOT STATED BUT PROBABLY 2-8
WHISKS: GOLDEN PHEASANT TIPPETS
TAIL: GREY BARRED SQUIRREL TAIL
BODY: IN FOUR EQUAL SECTIONS - YELLOW, BLACK, YELLOW, BLACK
RIB: OVAL SILVER
WING: GREY BARRED SQUIRREL TAIL
HACKLE: SOFT NATURAL RED HEN
HEAD: BLACK

Undoubtedly, this is a hair (or fur) style version of Ewe Wasp (Barred) although the body is given a very slightly different treatment from the original. Kilwell's have no notes, records or memory of this lure but an original survivor is captured in Ross Marks' framed collection of Kilwell lures. Just as with Furry Ewe Wasp, the yellow chenille is now unquestionably white. I believe that the comments I have made with respect to Furry Ewe Wasp apply equally to this lure.

Tie in the whisks followed by the squirrel tail. Tie in the first section of chenille and the ribbing. Return the thread part way along the shank.

Wind on the first section of chenille. Tie off. Tie in the second section of chenille. Repeat, and continue with the different sections of chenille finishing with the black nearly at the head. Wind on the ribbing.

Tie in the squirrel fur wing. Tie in the hackle feather. Wind on to form a hackle collar.

FURRY BUTCHER (O)

ORIGIN: KILWELL'S OF ROTORUA (PROBABLY WARWICK WELLS)
HOOK: 2-8
TAIL: BLACK SQUIRREL
BODY: FLAT SILVER TINSEL
RIB: OVAL SILVER
WING: BLACK SQUIRREL

HACKLE: ORANGE

HEAD: BLACK

Keith Draper says: "Here is a fly that appeals to me. It has everything a good stream fly should have, slimness with a dash of brightness and colour. It is a Rotorua fly, but will kill well anywhere where the trout are prone to helping themselves to whitebait or smelt. The fly should not be overdressed and the furnishing kept a bit on the short side so that it doesn't foul the bend of the hook." (1971). I have seen an old reference to a hackle of red golden pheasant plumage but I have preferred this more modern version.

Tie in the tail. Tie in the tinsel for the body and the ribbing. Secure and trim.

Wind on the silver tinsel to form the body. Follow with the ribbing. Secure and trim.

Tie in squirrel hairs at the head to form the wing. The wing should finish about one-third along the length of the tail. Hair fibres are prone to being pulled out and it is therefore advisable to cement the area of the tie thoroughly with head varnish before proceeding.

Wind on the hackle collar.

FURRY EWE WASP (O)

ORIGIN: KILWELL'S OF ROTORUA

HOOK: NOT STATED BUT PROBABLY 2-8

WHISKS: GOLDEN PHEASANT TIPPETS

TAIL: GREY BARRED SQUIRREL TAIL

BODY: REAR: YELLOW; FRONT: BLACK

RIB: FLAT SILVER

WING: GREY BARRED SQUIRREL TAIL

HACKLE: SOFT NATURAL RED HEN

HEAD: BLACK

This was put out by Kilwell's a long time age - so long, in fact, they now have no record or memory of it. However, it did feature in a framed display of Kilwell lures sold by Kilwell's, and Ross Marks of Christchurch has two such framed collections. The problem is, the rear section of the chenille body on what is probably the sole surviving original of this lure is undeniably white. It is difficult to imagine any wasp imitation (whether on the River Ewe in Scotland or anywhere in New Zealand) having other than a black and yellow body, and no less so with a hair style version of the original. My guess is that the dye in the yellow chenille has bleached out over the years, and I am going to be bold enough to assert that the original had yellow chenille.

Tie in the whisks followed by the squirrel tail. Tie in the first section of chenille and the ribbing. Take the thread back to about the mid-point of the shank.

Wind on the chenille to this point. Tie in the second section of chenille and wind on nearly to the head. Follow with the ribbing.

Tie in the squirrel fur wing. Tie in the hackle feather. Wind on to form a hackle collar.

FURRY TAMATI (O)

ORIGIN: NOT KNOWN

HOOK: 4-8

TAIL: RED/BROWN SQUIRREL TAIL

BODY: EQUAL PORTIONS OF RED, BLACK, AND YELLOW CHENILLE

RIB: OVAL SILVER

WING: BUNCH OF RED/BROWN SQUIRREL TAIL TIED ON TOP OF HOOK AT HEAD

HACKLE: MEDIUM RED GAME COCK HACKLE WOUND AS COLLAR

HEAD: BLACK

It is not difficult to recognise this as an adaptation of what I have listed as the modern tie of Tamati. It possibly evolved to avoid the difficulties inherent in tying in a split grouse or partridge for the wing. It is listed in a funny little publication called *58 NZ Lure Patterns* (see my comments under Furnace Smelt).

Tie in the tail, first segment of chenille, and the ribbing.

Take the thread part way along the shank. Wind on the chenille to this point. Tie in the second section of chenille and repeat the process, and again with the third segment.

Wind on the ribbing to the head. Tie in a bunch of squirrel tail for the wing.

Tie in the hackle feather. Wind on to form the collar.

FUZZY BAMBI (O)

PHOTO IS ON PAGE 77

HOOK: 2-8 LONG SHANK (OPTIONAL, WEIGHTED)

TAIL: BUNCH OF MARABOU

BODY: SHORT SECTIONS OF PEARL MYLAR OR FISHSCALE

WING: SPUN DEER HAIR

HACKLE: RED DYED COCK IMMEDIATELY BEFORE SPINNING ON THE HEAD COLLAR

HEAD: SPUN AND PACKED DEER HAIR WITH OPTIONAL GOLD BEAD

The overall effect is that of a Hackle style lure but I did not feel that it could be given that designation. After tying in the tail, small short bunches of deer hair, getting progressively longer, are spun on the bare shank. The object is to trim away the butt ends of the fibres leaving just the flared tips as a series of collars. You can control the angle of the flare by the amount of pressure on the thread. Alternatively, you could stack the deer hair - one bunch under the shank and one bunch on top, holding the bunches in position. You might prefer the collars to be more vertical than sweeping back. Make sure that the tie-in area and the trimmed ends are liberally coated with cement.

The trimmed area is covered with short sections of pearl mylar or similar. You could use any material but I prefer a bit of flash to shine through. Depending on the size of the bead head (if using), you can slip the mylar tube along the shank and over the trimmed area and tie off, or you can take a couple of flat wound turns around the shank. If using the mylar as a tube, I like to pick out a short section of the fraying end nearest the hook bend.

The head is simply spun and packed in the usual way. If using a bead head, use the bead to pack the flared bunch. Because the packing needs to be done firmly, ensure the body tie-off immediately behind the head is very secure and tight. The bunch will be rammed hard against this point.

I find that the fine, soft fibres of caribou are excellent for this pattern. They lack the buoyancy of normal deer hair, and have greater movement in the water.

All the usual colour variations are available. I have a preference for olive and natural/brown.

FUZZY WUZZY (H)

ORIGIN: FRED FLETCHER OF TAUPO

HOOK: 2-8

TAIL: BLACK SQUIRREL TAIL FIBRES

BODY: RED OR BLACK CHENILLE, BUT ORANGE, YELLOW, AND GREEN ARE ALSO POPULAR

HACKLE: TWO BLACK HACKLES TIED IN ONE AT THE HEAD, THE OTHER HALFWAY ALONG THE BODY. ON A SMALL FLY, ONE HACKLE AT THE HEAD IS USED; ON AN EXTRA LARGE FLY, THREE HACKLES ARE USED.

HEAD: BLACK

This is sometimes referred to (incorrectly) as a Hairy Dog. O.S. ("Budge") Hintz in *Fisherman's Paradise*, refers to it generically as Tail and Hackle. He also referred specifically to this lure, incorrectly, as Mrs Simpson. This was originally created to simulate a freshwater crayfish (koura), and one large hackle was wound Palmerwise to represent the legs of the koura (and thus Fred came perilously close to inventing the Woolly Bugger!) Over the years the pattern has evolved to the present dressing which continues to remain a very popular fly. It is also one of the easiest style of fly to tie, and capable of infinite combinations of colours which have spawned a host of popular and effective lures.

It is generally regarded as a night lure, but it can be a very effective daytime lure as well.

Tie in the tail. Tie in the chenille. Secure and trim.

Take the thread back part way along the shank. Wind on the chenille to this point. Tie in a hackle feather.

Wind on the hackle and secure. Take the thread nearly to the head. Continue the chenille to this point and secure. Tie in another hackle feather, and wind on.

GAMELAN (M)

ORIGIN: R. (BOB) BRAGG OF CHRISTCHURCH

HOOK: NOT STATED BUT PROBABLY 2-6

TAIL: ORANGE WHISKS

BODY: RED

RIB: FLAT SILVER TINSEL

WING: BLACK COCK HACKLES

CHEEK: GUINEA FOWL DYED ORANGE

HACKLE: ORANGE

HEAD: BLACK

This was named after one of Bragg's five cats, a brown Burmese called Gamelan. I know nothing else about it except that four different dressings of this lure appear in Bragg's book which suggests that he had a great affection for the cat or the lure or both.

I have studied all the dressings closely and there seems no doubt that this is tied in the Matuku style notwithstanding the rather heavy ribbing.

Tie in the tail whisks. Tie in the body material and the ribbing.

Wind on the body material. Tie in the wing feathers by the butts.

Wind on the ribbing, tying down the wing in the Matuku style. Tie in the guinea fowl cheeks.

Tie in a hackle feather. Wind on to form a hackle collar.

GARY'S GREEN MARABOU (O)

ORIGIN:	GARY KEMSLEY OF NAPIER
HOOK:	2-10
TAIL:	TAG OF RED WOOL
BODY:	LIGHT GREEN OLIVE CHENILLE IN 2 OR 3 SECTIONS
WING:	BLACK MARABOU TIED IN 2 OR 3 BUNCHES
HEAD:	BLACK

This pattern was originally tied by Gary to represent a koura. One prototype caused mirth amongst fishing friends and was dubbed the Kemsley Crawlie. Whakaipo Bay at Taupo, and the mouth of the Mapara Stream in particular, was the proving ground for this pattern. Many colour combinations were tried before this final form was conceived and born on 26 June 1974 on the shore at Lake Taupo in cold, dark, wet conditions.

That night, Gary caught a ten fish limit fishing from 7.00pm to 9.30pm at the mouth of the Mapara Stream.

An important feature of the pattern, though simple enough, is the large red tag. The shape of the tag, says Gary, determines the water flow around the fly, which in turn activates the marabou, tied in along the back.

I have seen commercially tied examples in sports shops with a black hackle collar, but Gary insists the original has no hackle.

It was designed as a night fly, but has taken fish during the day. In fact Gary has fished around the world with this pattern and has caught many different species on it in fresh and saltwater. In a range of sizes it imitates a number of food forms from dragonfly nymphs to leeches. In larger sizes it works well as a cock-a-bully imitation. It fishes extremely well in shallow or still water with a floating line.

Tie in the red tag. Tie in the chenille. Secure and trim.

Take the thread part way along the shank.

Wind on the chenille body. Tie in a bunch of marabou.

Take the thread back to the end of the next segment or nearly to the head, depending on hook size. Wind on the chenille to this point.

Tie in another bunch of marabou. Continue the process to the head of the hook if using larger sizes.

'GEE WHIZ' KEELER (M)

ORIGIN:	NOT KNOWN
HOOK:	NOT STATED BUT PROBABLY 2-8
BODY:	PALE YELLOW CHENILLE OR WOOL
RIB:	OVAL SILVER
WING:	PALE GINGER HACKLES INSIDE DYED RED COCK HACKLES
HACKLE:	RED (SPARSE), THROAT ONLY
HEAD:	BLACK

This features in Bragg's book in a collection described as Taupo and Rotorua lures used during the period 1962-1972. It is a smelt lure, and it is very similar to Ferris. It is obviously no mere chance that the period when this lure was used coincided with a political scandal in Britain, giving rise also to Keeler (named after one of the central figures in that scandal).

Interestingly (or curiously) both lures employ a similar colouring although dressed in very different ways. In saying that, however, I have to acknowledge that the above pattern is my best guess from a small grainy photo.

Tie in the body material and the ribbing.

Wind on the body material. Tie in the wing feathers by the butts.

Wind on the ribbing, tying down the wing in the Matuku style.

Tie in a few fibres under the throat.

GILLIES LODGER (M)

ORIGIN: RITCHIE BUCHANAN OF TAUPO
HOOK: 2-8
TAIL: RED WHISKS
BODY: GREEN AND WHITE CHENILLE
RIB: OVAL SILVER
WING: WHITE COCK HACKLES
TOPPING: 3-4 STRANDS OF PEACOCK HERL
HEAD: BLACK

Ritchie designed this in 1994. It is a smelt pattern inspired by Gillies Lodge, an established Taupo fishing retreat. It is a good all-round, all-year fly, particularly deadly in stream mouths in the early morning and at night, but it can be fished at all hours of the day. It is effective both harling and river fishing.

Tie in the tail whisks. Tie in the two chenille colours and the ribbing.

Wind on the two chenilles, twisted together to give a harlequin or variegated effect. Tie in the wing feathers.

Wind on the ribbing, tying down the wing in the Matuku style. Tie in the topping.

GINGER MICK (M)

ORIGIN: KILWELL'S OF ROTORUA
HOOK: 2-8
TAIL: (OPTIONAL) BUNCH OF DYED YELLOW HACKLE FIBRES
BODY: RED CHENILLE OR WOOL
RIB: OVAL SILVER
WING: GINGER COCK
HACKLE: GINGER
HEAD: BLACK

Although similar to Parsons' Glory, confusion can be avoided by using a hackle feather which is true to the fly's name. Generally, the Parsons' Glory would be considered as having the edge, but Ginger Mick has its devotees who use it to the exclusion of all others.

While I have only ever seen it tied in red, Keith Draper lists yellow or green as available choices, and a silver body is very popular in the Rotorua district.

Another popular version with some anglers has a gold body and rib. It is highly regarded for trolling or harling whatever version is preferred.

Tie in the tail if using. Tie in the wool or chenille, and ribbing. Secure and trim.

Wind on the chenille or wool and secure. Tie in the ginger hackle feathers for the wing.

Wind on the ribbing, tying down the feathers in the Matuku style. Tie in a hackle feather at the head.

Wind on the hackle collar, secure and trim.

GINGER SMELT (O)

ORIGIN: KILWELL'S OF ROTORUA
HOOK: 2-8
TAIL: GOLDEN PHEASANT TIPPETS
BODY: WHITE CHENILLE
RIB: OVAL SILVER
WING: GINGER HACKLES TRAILING FREE AND NOT SECURED ALONG THE BODY WITH THE RIB
HEAD: BLACK

This is tied in the salmon-fly Streamer style, and is excellent for harling as it tends to avoid the problem of the trailing feathers wrapping around the bend of the hook when fly-casting.

By taking three different feather types - ginger, badger, and grizzle - Kilwell created three otherwise identical lures.

Tie in the tippets for the tail. Tie in the chenille and ribbing.

Wind on the chenille to form the body, then follow with the ribbing.

Tie in the hackle feather at the butt only to form the wing. Secure and trim.

GLACIER FLY (O)

ORIGIN: OGDEN SMITHS OF LONDON
HOOK: NOT STATED BUT PROBABLY 4-8
TAIL: GOLDEN PHEASANT CREST
BODY: SILVER TINSEL
RIB: OVAL SILVER
WING: BRONZE MALLARD
HACKLE: YELLOW, THROAT
CHEEK: JUNGLE COCK
HEAD: BLACK

This is recorded in Bragg's book. It was created in 1939, the same year that Bragg left his employ with the London tackle house of Ogden Smith Ltd, and travelled to New Zealand, presumably bringing this lure with him. It is somewhat a relic of the salmon fly style, and is very similar to a Silver Demon. I cannot be absolutely sure about the accuracy of the pattern despite powerful magnification of the tiny photos published in Bragg's book.

It is recorded as being successful in snow-fed rivers.

Tie in the golden pheasant crest for the tail. Tie in the body tinsel and ribbing.

Wind on the body followed by the ribbing. Secure and trim.

Tie in the throat hackle fibres. Tie in the wing strips of bronze mallard in the streamer style.

GLO-BUG (O)

ORIGIN: A NORTH AMERICAN STEELHEAD PATTERN DEVELOPED BY BUG SHOP OF ANDERSON, CALIFORNIA AND INTRODUCED TO NEW ZEALAND BY LOUIE (THE FISH) DE NOLFO

HOOK: 10-14

THREAD: KEVLAR OR ONE OF THE STRONGER TYING THREADS

BODY: 5-6 BRAIDS OF EGG YARN.

I pondered at length before including this 'lure', not so much because of any controversy surrounding its ethical and legal status, but because it cannot properly be described as a lure. Equally, it is not a nymph, a wet fly, or a dry fly. The undeniable popularity of this fly demanded inclusion somewhere and, rightly or wrongly, I have done so here. It is not a fly that I choose to use for reasons which are outside the scope of this work, but there is no question that it has taken some parts of the country (and many anglers) by storm. Drift-fished along the edges of rivers and lakes it has proven irresistible to trout. One technique used is called 'heave-n-leave', which gives some idea of the style of fishing and the skill level involved. It is unashamedly an imitation of fish roe, but then, I guess, so is a Red Setter.

I recall many years ago a colleague of mine, and an expert angler, telling me how he was overcome with an impulse to strip the roe from a freshly caught trout, and attach it to a bare hook "to see what all the fuss was about". He got his answer so fast that it was with a deep sense of guilt that he released his catch and he has never used roe imitation again.

Tying a Glo-Bug is relatively easy with practise, and quite fascinating, but very difficult to describe in words, and certainly not possible in the space available. A general indication can be found in the tying guide to Change of Light in Appendix 1, except that the egg yarn is held on top of the shank before tying on. If you really must use one, they are not expensive to buy.

GOLDEN DEMON (O)

ORIGIN: NOT KNOWN

HOOK: 2-10

TAIL: WHISKS OF ORANGE HACKLE

BODY: FLAT TINSEL, GOLD OR SILVER

WING: BRONZE MALLARD FLANK

HACKLE: ORANGE HACKLE

CHEEKS: JUNGLE COCK

HEAD: BLACK

This is a good bright-day fly, and was a very popular rainbow pattern once. It has evolved from an old English sea-trout pattern. In John Veniard's 1970 English publication *Reservoir and Lake Flies* he gives a dressing which has the tail of ibis, a rib of oval gold over a flat gold body, and a wing of brown mallard shoulder feather. It is undoubtedly the same fly shown here. It is sometimes listed as Demon (Gold & Silver), because a silver body can be used, or even just plain Demon, but I have only ever seen the gold version and this appears to be the more popular name. It is a very dashing and handsome fly which fortunately catches more than just anglers.

Tie in the tail whisks. Tie in the tinsel.

Wind on the tinsel body. Secure and trim. Take a large slip of bronze mallard fibres and fold over, shiny sides out. Tie in Streamer style at the shoulder using the pinch and loop method of tying. Tie in a hackle feather.

Wind on the hackle. Tie in the Jungle Cock eyes, finish the head and varnish.

GOLDEN LION (M)

ORIGIN: R.K. BRAGG OF CHRISTCHURCH

HOOK: 2-8

TAIL: GOLDEN PHEASANT TOPPING

BODY: FLAT GOLD WITH RED SEAL'S FUR AT THE

	SHOULDER
RIB:	OVAL GOLD
WING:	BLACK
HACKLE:	GALLINA (SPOTTED PLUMAGE OF GUINEA FOWL)
TOPPING:	PEACOCK SWORD
HEAD:	BLACK

Robert K. Bragg trained at Ogden Smiths of London before coming to New Zealand in 1939, where he established himself as a professional fly-tier. This lure derived from one of Ogden Smith's patterns and was introduced and styled for New Zealand fishing by Bragg.

Seal's fur is difficult to obtain. A seal's fur substitute for dubbing can be purchased. I have used seal's fur because I happen to still have some, but I doubt if the fly loses anything by tying in a shoulder of red chenille or wool.

Tie in the pheasant crest for the tail. Tie in the tinsel for the body and the ribbing. Secure and trim.

Wind on the flat gold body tinsel. Use seal dubbing fur or chenille or wool and wind in at the shoulder. Tie in the wing feather.

Wind on the ribbing, tying down the wing. Tie in the peacock topping, and then the hackle feather.

Wind on the hackle collar. Secure and trim.

GOLDEN QUEEN (M)

ORIGIN:	MATT CHRISTIANSEN OF TAUPO
HOOK:	2-8
TAIL:	RED WHISKS
BODY:	YELLOW CHENILLE
RIB:	OVAL GOLD
WING:	WHITE COCK HACKLES
TOPPING:	ORANGE WHISKS
HEAD:	BLACK

This is a smelt pattern which is popular in the Taupo region. It could be described as an Albino Parsons' Glory which more than hints that it is an effective bright daytime lure. Just as with the Parsons' Glory this lure can be harled in the larger sizes, or cast expectantly in the smaller range.

Tie in the tail whisks. Tie in the chenille and the ribbing.

Wind on the chenille to form the body. Tie in the wing feathers by the butts.

Wind on the ribbing, tying down the wing in the Matuku style.

Tie in the topping whisks. Complete the head in the usual way.

GOLDEN REAPER (M)

ORIGIN:	DEREK QUILLIAM OF CLIVE
HOOK:	2-8
BUTT:	ORANGE SYNTHETIC LIVING FIBRE
BODY:	GINGER OR GOLD SYNTHETIC LIVING FIBRE (SLF)
RIB:	OVAL GOLD
WING:	TWO YELLOW COCK HACKLES INSIDE TWO GINGER DYED GRIZZLE HACKLES
CHEEK:	YELLOW GOLDEN PHEASANT FEATHERS OVERLAID WITH JUNGLE COCK
TOPPING:	GOLDEN PHEASANT CREST
HEAD:	BLACK

With some diffidence, I add this creation of mine. While browsing through Pat O'Keefe's amazing array of materials in his Rotorua shop, I was taken by a packet of unusually dyed grizzle hackles. They were a sort of gingery-golden colour with the gold more prominent towards the base of the feather. I bought several packets and eventually came up with this dressing. Subsequent batches have been more gingery than gold so I used yellow hackles in the wing to give a more golden look. I had assumed that it would be a daytime fly.

My commitments to this book were such that I had no opportunity to try it out. However, I gave it to some expert anglers to test. One of them, Bronwyn Wilson, gave it to a friend who caught a 10.5 lb. brown at 8.00pm on Tuesday 6 January 1998. I have since used it extensively and have found it to be very efective in the evening, particularly on browns, but it has also caught rainbows.

Pat O'Keefe is a very obliging fellow. If you want some of these unusually coloured feathers, just drop him a line, or give him a ring.

Tie in the rib. Dub on the orange butt then continue with the ginger or gold SLF body, finishing nearly at the head.

Tie in the wing feathers by the butts. Wind on the ribbing, tying down the wing in the Matuku style.

Tie in the yellow golden pheasant cheeks and the Jungle Cock. Tie in the GP crest topping.

GOLDIE HAWN (O)

ORIGIN:	MAUREEN BUTLER OF ROTORUA
HOOK:	2-8
TAIL:	BROWN GRIZZLE SQUIRREL TAIL
BODY:	GOLD WOOL
RIB:	FLAT GOLD BRAID
WING:	RED FOX FUR OR SIMILAR
CHEEKS:	TWO YELLOW GOLDEN PHEASANT FEATHERS (ONE EACH SIDE)
HACKLE:	A FEW FIBRES OF THE GOLDEN PHEASANT CHEEKS PULLED DOWN AND TIED UNDER THE THROAT, BEARD STYLE
HEAD:	BLACK

Maureen has been tying this fly for more than 40 years. An old angling identity on the Ohau Channel, Ted Hunwick, had a wife who had very long blonde hair - down to her waist. When this was cut off, the tresses were kept for fly-tying, and the first Goldies were tied from it. Maureen still has a substantial amount of the original hair, but now she ties her Goldies using an old red fox stole.

It is a very attractive combination of golds and browns which fortunately attracts trout as well. It is very effective on sunny days, whether harling or casting, anywhere where trout exist.

Maureen named the fly after her favourite actress.

Tie in the squirrel tail. Tie in the wool and the ribbing.

Wind on the wool body followed by the ribbing.

Tie in the hair (fur) wing. Tie in a single golden pheasant feather on each side for the cheeks. Pick out a few fibres from each feather and pull them down under the shank at the throat and tie them in to form the beard hackle. Complete the head in the usual way.

GOTCHA (O)

ORIGIN:	VIC NOVIS OF CHEVIOT
HOOK:	4-6
TAIL:	DEER HAIR, PREFERABLY THE DARKER HAIR FOUND ALONG THE SPINE
BODY:	PALMERED BROWN HEN FEATHER (NO ADDITIONAL BODY MATERIAL NEEDED). THE BEST IS FROM AN ORDINARY BROWN FARMYARD HEN WITH A HACKLE LENGTH ABOUT 1.5 TIMES THE HOOK GAPE
RIB:	FLAT OR ROUND NARROW GOLD TINSEL
WING:	DEER HAIR, AS FOR TAIL
HEAD:	BLACK

One January night in 1964, Vic caught a 10 bag limit in Hart's Creek, North Canterbury on this lure. They were all big fish, the largest being 11 lbs., and all caught on the same lure. Over the years since, it has proved to be a deadly night fly in all parts of the Ellesmere system, and it has consistently taken fish at many other places including the Rakaia mouth.

Select a bunch of deer hair about one-third pencil thickness. Attach just behind the eye extending to form a tail about a body length beyond the bend. Bind this to the shank by winding the thread down to the bend.

Tie in the ribbing and return the thread to the head. Tie in the hackle feather by the butt.Palmer the hackle back to the bend in close, nearly touching, turns.

Secure by winding the ribbing through the hackle counter-wise to the wing. Secure and trim the ribbing and hackle butt.

Take another bunch of deer hair slightly thicker than for the tail and tie it in at the head to form a wing extending from the head to just beyond the tail. Complete the head in the usual way.

GREEN DOG (O)

ORIGIN:	DAN HARTLEY OF AUCKLAND
HOOK:	2-8
TAIL:	CREAM-COLOURED DOG HAIR
BODY:	GREEN WOOL OR SEAL'S FUR
RIB:	OVAL SILVER
WING:	CREAM-COLOURED DOG HAIR
HACKLE:	ORANGE WHISKS, BEARD STYLE
HEAD:	BLACK

Dan devised this Hairy Dog style lure using the hair from his wife's Tibetan spaniels. It featured in the 1989 Tichborne calendar and subsequent book *Angler's Paradise*. Any cream-coloured dog or other soft hair would work as well.

Dan found this lure particularly effective in April when the dwarf inanga (Gracillis) comes close inshore.

Tie in a bunch of hair for the tail. Tie in the body material and ribbing.

Wind on the body material and ribbing to the head and tie off. Tie in the throat hackles.

Tie in a generous bunch of dog hair on top of the shank. Form the head and complete in the usual way.

GREEN DRAGON (M)

ORIGIN: R.K. BRAGG OF CHRISTCHURCH
HOOK: 2-8
BODY: GREEN
RIB: OVAL SILVER
WING: BLACK WITH GREEN OVERLAY
HACKLE: BLACK
HEAD: BLACK

Superficially this can be confused with a green bodied Orbit, but clearly they are quite different flies, although their effectiveness may be equal.

This is another lure from the vice of that redoubtable fly-tier R.K. Bragg.

"It is a good night fly. As well as being a good sea trout lure, it works especially well in the slow streams which run from the Canterbury Plains into the wide, shallow, semi-brackish Lake Ellesmere." – Keith Draper (1997).

Tie in the body material and ribbing.

Wind on the body material. Secure and trim. Tie in a black hackle feather for the wing.

Tie in a green hackle feather on either side of the black one. Wind on the ribbing, tying down the wing. Tie in a hackle feather.

Wind on the hackle feather for the collar. Secure and trim.

GREEN FROG (M)

ORIGIN: RITCHIE BUCHANAN OF TAUPO
HOOK: 2-8
TAIL: RED WHISKS
BODY: GREEN AND YELLOW CHENILLE
RIB: OVAL GOLD
WING: YELLOW COCK HACKLES
HEAD: BLACK

This was created in 1989 and has proved itself a top performer ever since as a harling lure. It was tied up to resemble the green beetle and green frog, and Ritchie sometimes uses a green hackle wing inside the yellow wing feathers. It is an excellent morning fly, fishing best from mid-December through to the end of March.

Tie in the tail whisks. Tie in the two chenille colours and the ribbing.

Wind on the two chenilles, twisted to give a harlequin or variegated effect, and tie off. Tie in the wing feathers.

Wind on the ribbing, tying down the wing in the Matuku style.

GREEN MATUKA (M)

ORIGIN: NOT KNOWN
HOOK: 2-8
BODY: GREEN CHENILLE, WOOL, OR SEAL'S FUR
RIB: OVAL SILVER
WING: TWO BADGER HACKLES BACK TO BACK, TIED DOWN TO BODY BY RIBBING TINSEL
HEAD: BLACK

This pattern comes from John Veniard's English publication. The mistaken spelling, Matuka, is a geographical translation by overseas countries, most notably USA, England and Australia. (see Matuku)

Seal's fur is difficult to obtain, but a seal's fur substitute for dubbing can be purchased.

Tie in the body material and rib. Secure and trim.

Wind on the body material. Secure and trim. Tie in the wing feathers.

Wind on the ribbing, tying down the wing. Secure and trim.

GREEN MATUKU (M)

ORIGIN: NOT KNOWN
HOOK: 4-6
BODY: GREEN CHENILLE, OR DUBBED WOOL OR FUR
RIB: OVAL SILVER
WING: BADGER COCK NECK HACKLES DYED GREEN
HACKLE: AS FOR WING
HEAD: BLACK

This appears in Keith Draper's 1997 book. At first I thought it was the same as the previous entry, but there is quite a difference between natural badger and badger which has been dyed green.

However, this is described as an Australian Matuku, or long-tail lure, but the spelling of 'Matuku' is not usually found outside New Zealand. Compare the previous entry which is a New Zealand pattern but with an Australian spelling!

I feel there has to be a connection between both lures.

This lure is best fished in still water where it is taken for a tadpole, especially if tied with a plump body.

Tie in the body material and ribbing.

Wind on the body material to the head and tie off. Tie in the wing feathers by the butts.

Wind on the ribbing, tying down the wing in the Matuku style. Tie in a hackle feather and wind on to form a hackle collar.

GREEN PARSONS (M)

ORIGIN: NOT KNOWN
HOOK: NOT STATED BUT PROBABLY 2-8
TAIL: ORANGE WHISKS
BODY: OLIVE
RIB: OVAL SILVER
WING: GREEN COCK HACKLES
HACKLE: GREEN
HEAD: BLACK

This was published in the 1986 Tichborne calendar, having been copied from an old sample believed to have been tied by Frank Lord in the 1940s which indicates that this was a popular fly at least way back then, although it is still regarded as a great fish catcher today, particularly fished over weed beds. It is not too dissimilar to a Green Dragon and a Green Orbit.

The featured example *was* tied by Frank Lord, and came from a collection of lures tied by Frank and still in their original packets and proudly treasured by Allan Beamish-White of Rotorua who very kindly gave me this sample.

Tie in the tail whisks. Tie in the body material and ribbing.

Wind on the body material to this point and tie off. Tie in the wing feathers.

Wind on the ribbing, tying down the wing in the Matuku style

Tie in a hackle feather. Wind on to form a hackle collar.

GREEN PRINCE (K)

ORIGIN: NOT KNOWN
HOOK: 2-8
TAIL: COCK PHEASANT TAIL FIBRES
BODY: YELLOW WOOL
WING: COCK PHEASANT GREEN RUMP
HEAD: BLACK

This is an old pattern that was once tied up by Kilwell's of Rotorua. It comes close to being a Mrs Simpson, the popularity of which no doubt caused this pattern to fall out of favour. It differs from Awahou Special only in the tail material. Presumably it would fish, in all other respects, just as well as a Mrs Simpson.

Tie in the tail fibres and body material. Trim.

Take the thread part way back along the shank. Wind on the wool to this point. Tie in a pair of wing feathers on each side of the shank, Killer style.

Continue the thread nearly to the head. Wind on the wool to this point and tie off. Tie in another pair of wing feathers on each side of the shank. Complete the head and varnish.

GREEN SLEEVES (K)

ORIGIN: R.K. BRAGG OF CHRISTCHURCH
HOOK: 4-8
TAIL: BLACK SQUIRREL
BODY: GREEN WOOL
WING: GREY PARTRIDGE DYED GREEN AND TIED IN AT THE SIDE KILLER STYLE
HEAD: BLACK

This is a Canterbury pattern from that well-known fly-tyer, Robert Bragg. Keith Draper says that it "closely resembles a Green Hamill's Killer".

It has been suggested that Bragg in fact created Hamill's Killer with this lure, a pre-dating sample having been sent to Bill Hamill. I suspect that this lure was the source of inspiration for Hamill's famous killer, rather than a source of plagiarism. Bragg's lure did not have golden pheasant tippets and that was the only pattern difference, but Bragg used a colouring which was a cross between green, brown, and yellow - a sort of olive-yellow brown colour which I have not been able to match.

Viewed together in their original colours, they are

quite different lures although one may have influenced the other, and they were both intended to represent the same food source.

The differences may also be less apparent today because the tippets are sometimes omitted from Hamill's Killer, and the partridge or mallard feathers tend to be dyed a reasonably uniform shade of green bearing little resemblance to the original shade of either.

Tie in the tail and the body material.

Take the thread part way back along the shank. Wind on the body material to this point. Secure and trim. Tie in the wing feathers on each side of the shank.

Continue the thread nearly to the head. Wind on the body material to this point. Secure and trim. Tie in another set of wing feathers on each side of the shank. Finish the head and varnish.

GREYFRIARS (O)

ORIGIN: MAUREEN BUTLER OF ROTORUA
HOOK: 4-8
TAG: DEEP PINK WOOL, TEASED OUT
TAIL: BLACK SQUIRREL
BODY: GREY FLOSS
RIB: FLAT SILVER BRAID
WING: GREY TAHR HAIR
HACKLE: DARK PINK HACKLE, BEARD STYLE
TOPPING: FLASHABOU ACCENT
HEAD: BLACK

This is a smelt pattern best fished early morning or evening.

When using Tahr hair, which has a lot of body fur, comb some of it out, but not all, otherwise the hair wing will look lifeless.

Tie in the tag and the squirrel tail on top. Tie in the floss and the ribbing.

Wind on the floss body followed by the ribbing.

Tie in the hackle fibres at the throat to form a beard hackle. Tie in the hair wing and the Flashabou topping. Complete the head in the usual way.

GREY GHOST (M)

ORIGIN: KILWELL'S OF ROTORUA
HOOK: 2-10
TAIL: (OPTIONAL) BUNCH OF DYED RED OR GREY HACKLE FIBRES
BODY: SILVER
RIB: OVAL SILVER
WING: COCK HACKLE DYED GREY
HACKLE: GREY
HEAD: BLACK

If the home tier paints the head grey and adds a small white eye with a black centre, the resemblance to whitebait is enhanced, although Jungle Cock is very popular with this lure.

It is most effective in the smaller sizes 8's or even 10's.

Keith Draper comments: "As with other flies, the Ghost, due to popular demand, is also turned out with different coloured bodies, the most popular being the green, especially the fluorescent green which is rapidly becoming a very popular fly in the Taupo district. The home tier is well advised to drop the hackle from his fly. It isn't the least bit necessary and can give a lumpy head if not tied in correctly. The Ghost is a very effective fly for smelting fish and can also be used as a harling fly. The version with the fluorescent body is very effective on trout which have just arrived in the river from the lake." (1971)

Keith also points out that like all good flies, the Grey Ghost is simplicity itself. Hugh McDowell is the only one who refers to the optional tail, but it does appear on the stock lures available from tackle shops, along with the almost obligatory Krystal Flash or similar. One pattern I have seen calls for wings of four bright, shiny blue/grey cock hackles, and a hackle of the same colour tied in at the throat like a beard. Hugh McDowell omits the hackle collar, but he does recognise the importance of the feather colour and carries a variety ranging from almost sooty grey to nearly white.

Tie in the tail hackles if using.

Tie in the body material and rib.

Wind on the silver body.

Tie in the wing feathers. Wind on the ribbing, tying down the wing. Secure and trim. Tie in Jungle Cock eyes if using. Tie in a hackle feather (if using).

Wind on the hackle collar. Finish the head and varnish.

GRIZZLE SMELT (O)

ORIGIN: KILWELL'S OF ROTORUA
HOOK: 2-8
TAIL: GOLDEN PHEASANT TIPPETS
BODY: WHITE CHENILLE
RIB: OVAL SILVER
WING: GRIZZLE HACKLE TIED IN AT THE HEAD ONLY
HACKLE: GRIZZLE HACKLE
HEAD: BLACK

By changing the wing feather from grizzle to badger or ginger, Kilwell created three otherwise identical smelt patterns. The trailing wing, which is not tied down in the Matuku style, is better suited to harling as there would be less chance of the wing fouling the hook than is likely to be the case with fly-casting. Originally, this was dressed with a thinly-tied body of white wool.

Tie in the tail tippets. Tie in the chenille and the ribbing. Secure and trim.

Wind on the chenille, followed by the ribbing. Secure and trim.

Tie in the wing feather at the butt so that it is trailing free and not secured to the body. Tie in the hackle feather and wind on to form a hackle collar.

GRIZZLY BEAR (O)

ORIGIN: GERARD VAN WIJNBERGEN OF EGMONT VILLAGE, TARANAKI
HOOK: 6
TAIL: GREY POSSUM TAIL FUR
BODY: BLACK CHENILLE
RIB: GOLD BRAID
WING: BLACK POSSUM TAIL FUR
FLANK: EMU FEATHER TIPS
HEAD: BLACK

Another name for the possum is Tree Bear, and this gave rise to the name of this very effective lure. It was developed for late evening and night fishing in still or very slow moving water. It is fished on a slow sinking or floating line in very shallow water.

Attaching the lure to the leader with an open loop Uni-knot imparts realistic movement which no doubt has some bearing on this lure's great success rate. For reasons not known to Gerard, it is often taken by fish which are rising to midges and the like.

Take the thread down to the bend. Form a small bulge at the bend to elevate the tail and prevent the tail twisting during casting. Tie in the tail. Bind the tail butts firmly to about the mid-point of the shank. Return the thread to the bend and tie in the chenille and ribbing.

Wind on the chenille to form the body. Follow with the ribbing and tie off.

Tie in the fur wing at the shoulder and flank either side with an emu feather. Complete the head in the usual way.

GRIZZLY GREEN (H)

ORIGIN: NOT KNOWN
HOOK: 4-8
TAG: WHISKS OF DYED RED COCK HACKLE
TAIL: A PAIR OF BARRED GRIZZLE HACKLE TIPS, ABOUT 3/4 INCH (18MM) LONG AND TIED IN BY THE QUILLS ALONG THE TOP OF THE SHANK SO THAT THE HACKLE FIBRES ARE IN A VERTICAL PLANE
BODY: LIGHT GREEN WOOL IN TWO SECTIONS
BODY HACKLE: BARRED GRIZZLE WOUND ON BETWEEN THE TWO SECTIONS
HACKLE: BARRED GRIZZLE, RATHER MORE GENEROUS IN SIZE THAN THE BODY HACKLE
HEAD: RED

This appears in *Fisherman's Paradise* by O.S. ("Budge") Hintz. It was his wife's favourite fly. He describes it as a smelt fly, and a variation of the Dorothy.

Tie in the red whisks. Tie in the tail, followed by the body material.

Take the thread part way along the shank. Wind on the wool to this point and tie off. Tie in a hackle feather.

Wind on the hackle. Tie in the second segment of wool. Take the thread back nearly to the head. Wind on the wool to this point and tie off.

Tie in a hackle feather and wind on. Either use red tying thread or red head paint to create the head.

GT SMELT, Silver (M)

ORIGIN: GEOFF THOMAS OF AUCKLAND
HOOK: 6-8
TAIL: ORANGE WHISKS

BODY: WHITE WOOL

RIB: FLAT SILVER AND FINE OVAL SILVER

WING: TWO WHITE COCK HACKLES

SIDE WING: FLASHABOU PEARL (WIDE, SEAWATER)

HACKLE: (OPTIONAL) ORANGE THROAT

TOPPING: WHITE SUPREME HAIR, VERY SPARSE, PLUS A SINGLE STRAND OF LIGHT BLUE TINSEL

HEAD: BLACK

Geoff needs no introduction to angling aficionados. He devised this lure around 1993 for use in clearwater lakes. It has proved devastating in Lake Tarawera, either harling or casting.

Geoff no longer ties flies, and the above example was tied by a professional tier. Commercial ties tend to be over-dressed, and Geoff would omit the hackle ("smelt are thin fish"). The blue tinsel can be found among the myriad colours in Flashabou Bullfrog. The sparse, white, crinkly topping has defied identification but a few strands of Supreme hair scraped along the length with fingernails produces a close imitation.

Geoff also has two other smelt patterns which I have included in Appendix 2.

Tie in the tail whisks, wool, and both ribbing tinsels.

Wind on the wool body followed by the flat silver ribbing. Tie in the wing feathers by the butts.

Wind on the fine silver ribbing, tying down the wing in the Matuku style. Tie in a strip of wide pearl Flashabou on either side of the body. Tie in the throat hackle if using.

Tie in a sparse topping of Supreme hair or substitute. Tie in a single strand of light blue Flashabou. Complete the head.

GUARDSMAN (P)

ORIGIN: KEITH DRAPER OF TAUPO

HOOK: 2-8

TAG: TUFT OF RED WOOL

TAIL: BLACK SQUIRREL

BODY: BLACK CHENILLE

RIB: (OPTIONAL) OVAL SILVER

WING: RED BREAST FEATHERS OF A GOLDEN PHEASANT

HACKLE: (OPTIONAL) BLACK

HEAD: BROWN

This is a night lure created by Keith. It is an attractive looking fly, especially if cheeked with a Jungle Cock eye, and Keith says that it has proved itself on many occasions. It got its name because it reminded Keith of the Guards(man) at Buckingham Palace in red jackets and black trousers.

Tie in the tag and the tail. Trim any surplus then add the chenille and ribbing (if using).

Wind on the chenille. Secure and trim. Wind on the ribbing and tie off.

Tie in the wing feathers by the butts at the shoulder in the Pukeko style. Tie in the hackle feather (if using), and wind on to form a hackle collar.

HAEMORRHOID (O)

ORIGIN: GREG WALLS OF CROMWELL

HOOK: 2-8

TAIL: CHOCOLATE MARABOU

BODY: LEMON CHENILLE

WING: BUNCHES OF CHOCOLATE MARABOU TIED IN ALONG THE BACK FINISHING WITH A BUNCH OF RED MARABOU AT THE HEAD

HEAD: BLACK THREAD BEHIND A TUNGSTEN GOLD BEAD

Although designed by Greg, it was first used by Dick Marquand on Lake Dunstan and it is often called Dick's Haemorrhoid. Dick had a lot of success with it as a harling lure. He gave one to Monty Wright who tried it out on the Upper Manorburn Dam. A fishing friend, Rob Soulsby, was with him. After catching some very nice rainbows with it Rob asked Monty what it was called. Monty said that it didn't have a name. Rob remarked that it looked like a haemorrhoid, demonstrating either certain powers of observation, a level of personal discomfort, or a degree of biological and medical knowledge! The name stuck and it is now a popular and successful lure in most of the still waters of Otago, seemingly best suited to rainbow trout. Monty has also used it tied in smaller sizes on some rivers with success.

This can be tied up in different ways. I have described below the method preferred for tying Jock Millar Variation.

Slip on a gold bead. Take the thread down to the bend. Tie in a bunch of marabou for the tail. Tie in the chenille.

Take the thread part way back along the shank and tie in a bunch of brown marabou. Repeat at intervals along the

shank, the number depending on hook size.

Wind on the chenille, working carefully around the bunches of marabou. Secure at the head leaving space behind the gold bead.

Tie in a bunch of red marabou. Form a head of black thread behind the bead.

HAIR FLIES (O)

There is no set pattern (with two exceptions) but inclusion as a separate entry is justified by the following commentary by Keith Draper in his book *Trout Flies In New Zealand*: - "The hair fly is excellent for use on rainbow trout and sea-run browns. The only real commercial version is the Blondie, which is normally tied from human hair with a body of silver tinsel. Some shop versions are now tied with artificial hair of the synthetic material used in making dolls' wigs. Hamill's Silver Smelt, using a mixture of green and white fibre, is a tie very much favoured by some anglers.

"As a youngster I used to tie a hair fly from the tail hair of a Jersey heifer, and these did very well in Hawke's Bay, where a hair fly has always been in favour. There is no set tie, as apart from the two commercial patterns mentioned above, most are home tied. It is an easy pattern to make up so long as too many turns aren't made round the head, and the hair is well glued in with lacquer. A trout smashing around in the shallows of the river is usually responsive to a hair fly fished through his patrol. They are best tied in the smaller sizes and the hair should be tied in sparsely, in preference to a thick hank." (1971).

Keith has referred to cow's hair, human hair, and synthetic hair. There seems to be no reason why other animal fur or hair cannot be used, and I suggest that Demon Squirrel, Furry Butcher, and others, are examples of hair flies, as are Bucktails. The featured example was tied from horse-hair which was found in a local farm paddock. I tie something similar using a clipping of my own ageing greying hair, which I call Hairy Ghost. When I don't need a hair-cut I tie it from a grey fur stole I picked up in an antique shop for next to nothing. This simply demonstrates that one does not need to buy expensive materials to make effective lures. No doubt Hairy Ghosts, by whatever name, have been gracing fly boxes since Moby Dick was a tadpole. This type of lure also lends itself to the full reign of the tier's imagination. While I have dressed hair flies in fancy and purely whimsical regalia, I generally prefer to exercise restraint.

HAIRY DOG (O)

ORIGIN:	JOHN SIERPINSKI OF TAUPO
HOOK:	2-8
TAIL:	MOST COMMONLY, BLACK SQUIRREL, BUT SOME PATTERNS SUGGEST THAT SPANIEL OR GOAT HAIR, OR BLACK FISHAIR CAN BE USED
BODY:	WOOL, FUR OR CHENILLE, BLACK OR RED
RIB:	OVAL SILVER
WING:	SAME MATERIAL AS THE TAIL
HACKLE:	(UNDER THROAT ONLY) SAME AS TAIL
HEAD:	BLACK

Keith Draper gives a version of the fly's origin, based on O.S. ("Budge") Hintz's book Trout at Taupo, wherein hair was clipped from a black spaniel. Bryn Hammond, in *The New Zealand Encyclopaedia of Fly Fishing*, based on the same account, has its derivation from a pig dog. Other details differ also, but it doesn't matter. Whatever the source, this is an excellent night fly when fished deep and slowly.

Black or red are the traditionally preferred colours, but it has also been tied in yellow, green, orange, and silver and gold tinsel.

Keith Draper omits the hackle from his dressing, but the photographs in both of his books (1971 and 1997), and the majority of other references I have seen, have it included.

Tie in the tail. Tie in the chenille and ribbing.

Wind on the chenille and ribbing. Secure and trim.

Tie in a small bunch of the same material as the tail at the throat under the shank. The fibres should not extend as far as the point of the hook.

Tie in a slightly longer bunch of the same material on top of the hook. Coat liberally with glue in the area of the tie. Finish head and varnish.

HALL'S NIGHT-TIME (O)

ORIGIN: DAVID HALL OF ROTORUA

HOOK: 4-8

TAIL: BUNCH OF GRIZZLE HACKLE FIBRES DYED RED

BODY: RED AND BLACK CHENILLE TWISTED AND WOUND ALONG THE HOOK, GIVING A HARLEQUIN EFFECT

WING: PAIR OF DYED RED GRIZZLE FEATHERS TIED IN AT THE HEAD BY THE BUTTS ONLY

HACKLE: (OPTIONAL) FROM A FEATHER DYED THE SAME AS THE WINGS

HEAD: BLACK

Keith Draper's pattern gives a tail but no hackle. Hugh McDowell gives both as optional. The version tied by Kilwell's of Rotorua has both. I have followed Keith Draper's pattern in the above example, but the options are given for you to make up your own mind.

Hugh McDowell makes the bemused comment: "The continued popularity of this fly both intrigues and amazes me, because I have yet to catch a trout with one. Furthermore, I have never seen anyone else have any success with it nor indeed do I even *know* anybody who has."

On the other hand, Keith Draper says that it is well known in the Geyserland area and enjoys a good reputation with anglers who fish the mouths of Rotorua streams, but acknowledges that its popularity has not extended elsewhere. Hugh McDowell, it will be realised, lives in Rotorua.

Eddie Bosomworth of Kilwell's, Rotorua, agrees with Keith Draper. He told me he loves this lure on stream mouths.

Tie in the tail. Tie in the two chenilles.

Either wind one of the chenille colours up to the head, and spiral the other over the top, or twist the two together like a rope and wind the combination along the shank.

Place two feathers back to back and tie them in by the butts. The effect is that the wings stand clear of the body rather than lying along it (but trailing free) as, for example, in Ginger Smelt. Finish the head and varnish.

HAMILL'S KILLER (K)

ORIGIN: W. (BILL) HAMILL OF ROTORUA IN 1954

HOOK: 4-8, ALTHOUGH I HAVE HAD SUCCESS WITH THIS TIED ON A NO. 2 HOOK

TAIL: BLACK SQUIRREL TAIL FIBRES WITH A SMALL BUNCH OF GOLDEN PHEASANT TIPPETS ON TOP AND EXTENDING HALFWAY DOWN THE TAIL

BODY: WOOL OR CHENILLE, RED, GREEN OR YELLOW

WING: GREY PARTRIDGE DYED GREEN

HEAD: BLACK

This is a capital fly which enjoys a well-deserved reputation. The red body is favoured for night fishing, and the yellow for daytime. Tony Busch, in *A Trout Fishing Guide to New Zealand's South Island* says: "An effective lure at any time of the season, it excels under two conditions: on the occasion of a slight fresh with discolouration of water in a river, and in position of slow-flowing or calm water at the height of the summer when the dragonflies are hatching."

Modern dressings tend to omit the tippets, or substitute with a few orange hackle fibres. I prefer to include the tippets. They are not expensive, they enhance the appearance of the fly, and they serve to distinguish this fly from Green Sleeves.

Hamill's Killer plumage is widely available under that name, although it now generally comes in suitably dyed grey mallard flanks feathers instead of the scarce and expensive partridge. The example photographed was tied with partridge dyed the original and genuine shade of green. It is a combination of colours which is not commercially available - at least - not yet.

Take the thread down to the bend and tie in the tail fibres and tippets.

Tie in the chenille. Take the thread part way back along the shank. Wind on the chenille to this point and secure. Tie in a pair of wing feathers on each side of the shank.

Continue the chenille to the head and tie off. Tie in another pair of feathers on each side of the shank. Finish the head and varnish.

HAMILL'S SILVER SMELT (O)

ORIGIN: W. (BILL) HAMILL OF ROTORUA

HOOK: 4-8

BODY: SILVER TINSEL

WING: A BUNCH OF WHITE FIBRE, SUCH AS FISHAIR, ON TOP OF A BUNCH OF GREEN FIBRE

HEAD: BLACK

EYES: WHITE WITH A BLACK CENTRE

For comments generally on this type of lure, see the

separate entries for Blondie and Hair Flies.

This is listed in Keith Draper's books as Silver Smelt. There are numerous fibres available, all of which can be used with confidence. However, having chosen a bunch of fibres, I would caution that you then halve the quantity you have chosen. There is an immutable law of probability, which decrees near-certainty that this type of fly will be over-dressed.

My own method for forming tinsel bodies is to wind the tinsel from the eye down to the bend and back, and for me it works but you will use your own preferred method. The silver holograph tinsel is a very effective alternative.

Keith Draper claims the addition of eyes greatly enhances this lure.

Tie in the tinsel, and wind on to form the body.

Take a bunch of green FisHair or similar and tie in.

Add a bunch of white fibres on top and bind in. Finish the head in the usual way, and add eyes if desired.

HAMILL'S SMELT (O)

ORIGIN: W. (BILL) HAMILL OF ROTORUA

HOOK: 2-8

BODY: GREY CHENILLE

WING: TWO PALE GINGER HACKLES LAID OVER TWO GRIZZLE HACKLES. THESE ARE CAPPED AT THE HEAD WITH A V-CUT FROM THE GREY BREAST PLUMAGE OF A MALLARD DRAKE

HEAD: BLACK

Another lure from Bill Hamill. Keith Draper says that this fly "...though not generally known', is nevertheless an excellent fish catcher. It is a great pattern to use in the lower reaches of rivers when the rainbows and sea-run browns are feeding on smelt migrating in from the sea. I have known a yellow-bodied version to produce spectacular success when used for harling." (1997).

Tie in the chenille, and wind on the chenille to form the body. Secure and trim.

Take two grizzle hackle feathers and overlay a pale ginger hackle on each side. Tie in at the head by the butts.

Cut a v-shaped section from the grey plumage of a mallard drake.

Tie in the mallard feather so that the 'arms' of the v extend back on either side of the hackle feathers.

Finish the head and varnish.

HARLEY'S BULLY (K)

ORIGIN: CHARLES NOTT OF HAVELOCK NORTH

HOOK: 6-10

TAIL: BLACK SQUIRREL

BODY: DARK OLIVE MOHAIR

RIB: (OPTIONAL) OVAL SILVER

WING: TWO MATCHING PAIRS OF GRIZZLE (PLYMOUTH ROCK) DYED DARK OLIVE, TIED IN HALFWAY UP THE SHANK AND AT THE HEAD RESPECTIVELY; FLAT TO THE SIDE OF THE FLY IN THE KILLER STYLE

HEAD: BLACK

This pattern appears in Tony Orman's anthology. The wing feathers are tied in Killer style, two pairs on each side of the body, and the lure is fished slowly to simulate bully.

Tie in the tail. Trim off any surplus, and tie in the mohair and ribbing, if using.

Return the thread part way back along the shank. Wind on the chenille and ribbing to this point. Secure. Tie in a pair of wing feathers on each side of the body.

Take the thread back nearly to the head.

Follow with the chenille and ribbing. Tie off and trim.

Tie in another two pairs of wing feathers, one pair on either side of the body.

Finish the head and varnish.

HARRY (M)

ORIGIN: BRONWYN WILSON OF TAUPO

HOOK: 4-6

BODY: REAR THREE-QUARTERS: PEARL LUREX; FRONT QUARTER: YELLOW-ORANGE SEAL'S FUR OR SUBSTITUTE

RIB: OVAL SILVER

WING: FOUR WHITE COCK HACKLES

TOPPING: ORANGE KRYSTAL FLASH AND TWO STRANDS OF FLAT RED FLASHABOU OR SIMILAR

HACKLE: WHITE

HEAD: BLACK

Another Bronwyn creation, and named after a friend.

Sadly, Harry was tragically killed in a light plane crash near Christchurch in the latter part of 1997.

This is a smelt pattern, and as with all of Bronwyn's lures, has been well tried and tested and is a proven fish taker.

The ribbing is tied in the same manner as Albino 3 (see my comments thereunder).

Tie in the first section of body material and the ribbing.

Take the thread three-quarters of the way along the shank. Wind on the body material and ribbing to this point and tie off. Take the thread back to the head, dubbing on the seal's fur.

Tie in the wings by the butts. Take one final turn of the ribbing catching down the wings in the Matuku style. Tie in the overwing topping.

Tie in a hackle feather. Wind on to form a hackle collar. Form the head and complete in the usual way.

HART'S CREEK (M)

ORIGIN:	ONE CHAMBERLAIN (POSSIBLY IVAN) OF "CHAMBERLAIN'S FORD", LEESTON, NEAR CHRISTCHURCH
HOOK:	2-8
TAG:	RED IBIS (OR DYED SWAN)
BODY:	BLACK
RIB:	OVAL SILVER
WING:	BLACK
HACKLE:	BLACK
HEAD:	BLACK

This pattern is identical to Black Prince, by which name it is better known, Keith Draper suggests, if you live in the North Island.

The difference lies in the way in which it is dressed. Canterbury lures tend to be tied with heavy hackles and the wing tied in short, giving a chunky appearance. It is an excellent night fly, although the word from overseas, according to Hugh McDowell, is that it also fishes well during the day. Hugh believes that this fly is the red-bodied version of Black Prince, but Keith Draper makes no mention of a red body although a photo of a red-bodied version appears in his 1997 book. Early dressings, as shown in Bragg's book, had a topping of peacock herl.

Peter Hart of Christchurch tells me it was his great-great-grandfather who, while riding home from a local pub on his horse, fell while crossing a stream and drowned. The stream became known as Hart's Creek, and the lure was named after the stream.

It transpires that I am not too distantly related, by marriage, to the creator.

Tie in the tag (in the absence of ibis or swan use red hackle fibres or even wool). Tie in the chenille and ribbing.

Wind on the chenille body. Tie in the wing feathers at the head.

Wind on the ribbing, tying down the wing in the Matuku style. Tie in a hackle feather, and wind on to form a hackle collar.

HATEPE SMELT (O)

"These flies are difficult to describe except to say they are just a curl of natural sheep's wool loosely bound to a hook. They are drift-fished on a floating line along the edge of the rip, and unorthodox though they may seem, they are apparently very deadly on occasions. John Cockburn of Hinemaiaia ties them from Romney wool and I know of several reputable anglers who think very highly of them. They were designed by Mr. C. Rolleston."- Keith Draper (1971).

In a country like New Zealand there should be no difficulty in obtaining a life time's supply of material for next-to-nothing. Instructions on how to tie this type of fly seem superfluous.

Tie in a longish piece of natural sheep's wool so that a tail is formed.

Wind the remaining wool around the shank up to the head. Tie off. Form the head and complete in the usual way.

HAWK (M)

ORIGIN:	NOT KNOWN
HOOK:	NOT STATED BUT PROBABLY 2-8
BODY:	CHENILLE, COLOUR TO SUIT WITH A PREFERENCE FOR YELLOW OR ORANGE
RIB:	OVAL SILVER
WING:	FLANK FEATHERS OF A HARRIER HAWK
HEAD:	BLACK

This was a popular pattern in the 1950s and was a

good fish taker when trout were receptive.

Young hawks have darker feathers than older hawks, which have plumage becoming a pale buff. For the purposes of this fly, the paler the feathers the better, and female feathers are to be preferred over male ones.

The problem now, though, is that the hawk is a protected bird and it is illegal to buy and sell the feathers. However, John Morton has researched the point and claims to have an official acknowledgement that car strikes can be used legally. The trick then is to find an old female hawk that has been freshly killed by a car or similar, and I can assure you the search will be a long one!

Tie in the chenille and ribbing.

Wind on the chenille. Tie in the wing feather.

Wind on the ribbing, tying down the wing to the body Matuku style. Tie off and trim.

HAWK and POSSUM (O)

ORIGIN: NOT KNOWN

HOOK: 6

TAIL: CREAM TO GINGER STRIPS OF HAWK TAIL OR WING PRIMARIES

BODY: SILVER LUREX YARN

WING: BUNCH OF CREAM TO GINGER POSSUM FUR

HACKLE: GINGER HEN BREAST FEATHER TIED IN BY THE TIP

HEAD: BLACK

This is the possum version of the more common Hawk and Rabbit, but no less effective for all that. An example tied by George (Burglar) Gatchell featured in the 1986 Tichborne calendar but I do not know who created it.

It is a smelt pattern which is open to a variety of colour variations. Grey or green possum is useful, and the hackle can vary from speckled or grey partridge to brown mallard.

See my comments under Hawk as to the use of hawk feathers.

Tie in the matching strips of hawk for the tail. Tie in the body tinsel.

Wind on the body tinsel to the head and tie off.

Tie in a sparse bunch of possum fur at the head on top of the shank. Tie in a hackle feather by the tip.

Wind on a few turns to form a hackle collar. Complete the head in the usual way.

HAWK and RABBIT (O)

ORIGIN: NOT KNOWN

HOOK: 6-10

TAIL: A PALE STRIP CUT FROM THE PRIMARY FEATHER OF A HARRIER HAWK WING

BODY: WHITE OR GREEN WOOL

SHOULDER: A SMALL STRIP OR BUNCH OF RABBIT FUR. SOME TIE THIS WITH A STRIP OF SKIN ABOUT HALF THE LENGTH OF THE BODY, WHILE OTHERS PREFER A PINCH OF FUR BUNCHED ON THE SHOULDER AND TIED IN AT THE HEAD

HEAD: BLACK

"This is a Rotorua fly and is used as a smelting pattern. It is popular, although I have always felt that there are other flies which do a better job of imitating a smelt. But some anglers swear by it, and that's as good a recommendation as anyone could wish for." Keith Draper (1971).

White and green are the favoured colours, but other colours are used, including tinsel.

The same problem exists as with the previous pattern in that dealing in hawk plumage of any description is outlawed. Unless you are lucky enough to find a hawk which has met with an unfortunate mishap, a suitable substitute for this pattern might be a strip of pale cinnamon turkey tail.

Tie in the tail. Tie in the wool.

Return the thread back nearly to the head. Wind on the wool to form the body. Tie off and trim.

Tie in the rabbit fur by either of the methods described. Finish the head and varnish.

HEN PHEASANT (K)

ORIGIN: KEITH DRAPER OF TAUPO

HOOK: 2-8

TAIL: HEN PHEASANT FEATHERS

BODY: MATERIAL AND COLOUR TO SUIT (THE EXAMPLE HAS A BODY OF RED FLOSS)

WING: HEN PHEASANT FEATHERS

HEAD: BROWN

This is another effective bully pattern from Keith utilising the well-marked feathers which adorn standards such as Matuku and Leslie's Lure.

Keith has employed a slim body dressing, and then used several feathers at each tie-in stage (except at the tail) to build up a nice plump body. A single pair of feathers has been tied in at the bend, and the feathers are much longer than the body feathers. To that extent, they can be called a tail, although the overall effect is similar to a Matuku style.

Tie in a single pair of the hen pheasant feathers at the bend with the tie-in point being on top of the shank.

Tie in the body material. Take the thread a short way along the shank. Wind on the body material to this point.

Tie in two or more wing feathers on either side of the shank in the Killer style.

Continue the body material in stages nearly to the head, tying in wing feathers at each stage in the Killer style. Complete the head in the usual way.

HERB'S GLOW SMELT (O)

ORIGIN:	HERB SPANNAGL OF NEW PLYMOUTH
HOOK:	8-10 LONG SHANK
TAIL:	4-6 STRANDS OF STIFF KRYSTAL FLASH TO PREVENT TAIL WRAPPING
BODY:	AURORA SKIRT WITH A SILVER TINSEL UNDERBODY FOR ADDED REFLECTIVITY. CHANGE TO PEARL OR SILVER MYLAR FOR DAYTIME USE.
WING:	STRIP OF WHITE RABBIT. BLACK RABBIT FOR A DARK SILHOUETTE CAN ALSO BE USED
HEAD:	BLACK

This night fly is best fished near the surface to reveal the glow to fish beneath. After sunrise it is taken as an ordinary smelt fly. Tied to the trace with a Uni-Loop it dashes erratically on a fast retrieve.

The method of tying in the wing of rabbit fur is unique and was developed by Gerard van Wijnbergen of Egmont Village near New Plymouth. The strip of fur is tied in at the bend upside down and then pulled forward over the body like a wing case and tied in at the head. This avoids the need for a rib, and gives a short tail which reduces the instances of trout taking short - the rationale which led to the development of this tying style.

Tie in the Krystal Flash. Tie in the rabbit strip upside down at the bend.

Tie in the silver tinsel and Aurora skirt. Wind on the tinsel and Aurora skirt to the head.

Pull the rabbit strip forward over the body and secure under tension near the head.

If necessary, trim the rabbit strip on either side. Pluck out surplus hair until desired fly shape and bulk have been achieved. Form the head in the usual way.

HILDA (O)

ORIGIN:	WALTER WILLIS OF TE KUITI
HOOK:	2-6
TAIL:	RED TAG
BODY:	WOOL - YELLOW, RED, OR GREEN
RIB:	FLAT SILVER
WING:	A BUNCH OF FIBRES FROM THE TAIL OF A COCK PHEASANT
HEAD:	BLACK. THE CREATOR PAINTS YELLOW EYES ON THE HEAD

'This fly was named by Willis after Mrs Hilda Smallman of Turangi. It is principally a harling pattern. Mrs Smallman was one of the first to use it, being so successful that she caught a trout large enough to win her a local angling club trophy. When tying this fly great care has to be exercised in having the bend of the fibres all lying the same way, or else it looks like a tattered shaving brush. The eye gives it a good minnow appearance'.- Keith Draper (1971).

From bitter experience, I can say that Keith's description of a shaving brush is an understatement. It is important that the tail fibres at the tie-in point be saturated with cement before forming and completing the head, otherwise the fibres will tend to pull out.

Tie in the tag of red wool or similar. Tie in the body material and tinsel ribbing. Secure and trim.

Return the thread back nearly to the head. Wind on the wool and ribbing. Tie off and trim.

Tie in a bunch of pheasant tail fibres. Finish the head (including eyes if you wish) and varnish.

HOB NAILED BOOT (O)

ORIGIN:	JOHN MORTON OF CHRISTCHURCH

HOOK:	4, 3X LONG SHANK
TAIL:	LONG STRAIGHT-ISH BLACK POSSUM TAIL
BODY:	RED CHENILLE
WING:	THREE BUNCHES OF BLACK POSSUM TAIL
HEAD:	BLACK

This is winged and tailed after the style of Fuzzy Wuzzy using straight-ish black possum tail fur. John started fishing with this fly (then unnamed) one night at 11.00pm. Within 50 minutes he had caught 11 fish. All the splashing which accompanied each catch prompted another angler to call out: "Who's that thrashing around on the water? Sounds like he's got hob nailed boots on". After catching his twelfth fish John was picked up by the other anglers and thrown fully clothed into the river. Undaunted, he continued but as he was playing this thirteenth fish suggestions were loudly aired about a possible fate for his rod, so he beat a tactical retreat with the words "hob nailed boot" ringing in his mind, and hence the intriguing name.

Unlike Burglar, the clumps of possum tail fur get progressively larger, but like Burglar, the fur is pushed down with the thumb and forefinger while being tied in, causing the fur to wrap around the shank. As the above story demonstrates, it is a particularly deadly night fly.

Tie in the tail and the chenille.

Take the thread part way along the shank. Wind on the chenille to this point. Tie in a fairly thin, small bunch of possum tail fur, holding it on top of the shank and pushing down as it is tied in.

Overwrap the fur tie-in point with the chenille, then continue the thread and chenille a further third of the way along the shank. Tie in a second bunch of possum tail about half as big again as the first.

Overwrap the tied-in fur again with the chenille, and continue the thread and chenille back nearly to the head. Tie in the final bunch of possum tail, about the size of the previous two bunches combined. Finish the head and varnish.

HOPE'S DARK (O)

ORIGIN:	DAVE HOPE OF CHRISTCHURCH
HOOK:	2-8
TAIL:	TIP OF BARRED ROCK (GRIZZLE)
BODY:	WHITE
RIB:	FLAT SILVER
WING:	BLACK HACKLES
TOPPING:	GREEN PEACOCK SWORD
HEAD:	BLACK

This is very similar to the Hope's Silvery except that the wing is dark and it omits the blue 'lateral'.

This was a very popular Canterbury lure back in the 1950s for use on the Selwyn and other Canterbury rivers in the evenings.

Older dressings have a hackle collar of grizzle, but this seems to have largely disappeared.

This features widely in Bragg's book, variously tied in the loose-winged Streamer style and also the Matuku style. When tied in the latter style the rib tends to be oval rather than flat. I have preferred the pattern given in Keith Draper's books.

Tie in the tail. Tie in the body material and ribbing.

Wind on the body material to the head and secure. Follow with the ribbing unless tying in the Matuku style.

Tie in the wing feathers by the butts. Tie in the topping. Complete the head in the usual way.

HOPE'S LURE (M)

ORIGIN:	PRESUMABLY DAVE HOPE OF CHRISTCHURCH
HOOK:	2-8
TAIL:	SMALL GRIZZLE HACKLE
BODY:	RED OR BLACK WOOL OR CHENILLE
RIB:	OVAL SILVER
WING:	TWO BLACK COCK HACKLES TIED BACK TO BACK ON TOP OF HOOK BY RIB.
HACKLE:	BLACK
TOPPING:	PEACOCK SWORD
HEAD:	BLACK

This pattern was found in an odd little publication called *58 NZ Lure Patterns* (see my comments under Furnace Smelt). It appears to be a cross between Hope's Red-Silvery and Hope's Dark, with Dave Hope's fingerprints all over it, suggesting it was he who created it.

Tie in the tail, body material, and ribbing.

Wind on the body material to the head and secure. Tie in the wing feathers.

Wind on the ribbing, tying down the wing in the Matuku style. Tie in the hackle feather.

Wind on the hackle. Tie in the peacock sword topping. Complete the head in the usual way.

HOPE'S SILVERY (M)

ORIGIN: DAVE HOPE OF CHRISTCHURCH
HOOK: 2-8
TAIL: TIP OF BARRED ROCK (GRIZZLE)
BODY: WHITE
RIB: FLAT SILVER
WING: PALE BUFF OR PALEST HONEY GRIZZLE WITH A STRIP OF PALE BLUE FLOSS SILK LAID ALONG EACH SIDE AND CAUGHT UNDER THE RIBBING
TOPPING: GREEN PEACOCK SWORD
HEAD: BLACK

Best known of all the Canterbury lures. 'Silvery' is another name for smelt in some districts. The strip of floss simulates the bluish tinge along the smelt's side. It is primarily a day fly, but is considered by many to be good on a moonlit night.

Also in what might be described as the Hope's Series is Hope's Red-Silvery which is identical to Hope's Silvery except that a red body is used.

The 'flat' ribbing is a relic of the old loose-winged Streamer tie. Today, it is more likely to be found tied in the Matuku style using oval tinsel.

Tie in the tail. Tie in the wool or chenille, the ribbing, and a length of blue floss.

Take the thread and body material back nearly to the head. Take the floss up to the head on either side of the body and tie in.

Tie in the wing feathers. Wind on the ribbing tying down the wing in the Matuku style. Tie in the topping. Finish the head and varnish.

HOPKIN'S FANCY (O)

ORIGIN: NOT KNOWN
HOOK: NOT STATED BUT PROBABLY 6-8
TAIL: ORANGE WHISKS
BODY: RED
RIB: OVAL SILVER
WING: COCK PHEASANT RUMP
HACKLE: RED
HEAD: BLACK

This appears in Bragg's book along with another lure called Hopwood's Delight. The latter has orange feather tips for the tail and the hackle is tied in under the throat only, otherwise the two are indistinguishable.

This lure is a Canterbury high country and lakes pattern of the 1960s, probably used with success in Lake Coleridge.

Tie in the tail whisks. Tie in the body material and ribbing.

Wind on the body and follow with the ribbing. Secure and trim.

Tie in the wing feathers by the butts. Tie in a hackle feather and wind on to form a hackle collar.

HUGHIE'S MALLARD (O)

ORIGIN: HUGH MCDOWELL OF ROTORUA
HOOK: 6-8 (PARTRIDGE SINGLE WILSON LOW WATER)
TAIL: GOLDEN PHEASANT TIPPETS
BODY: DUBBED SEAL'S FUR OR SUBSTITUTE, YELLOW AT REAR, ORANGE AT FRONT
RIB: OVAL GOLD
WING: BRONZE MALLARD FLANK
HACKLE: SOFT RED HEN, THROAT ONLY
HEAD: BLACK

"Based on a range of old Irish patterns and from the gifted Rotorua fly-tier Hugh McDowell, who himself is based on an old Irish pattern." - Bryan Tichborne, *Anglers' Paradise*. This fly features as the eye-catching logo for Hugh's company, Angling Adventures (NZ) Ltd. Hugh has had a lot of success with this fly which is fished conventionally across and down. Depending on the size of wing required, several feathers, or pairs of feathers, may be required.

Tie in the tail tippets and the ribbing. Dub in the first section of the body to a point about halfway along the shank.

Dub in the second section of the body nearly to the eye. Wind on the ribbing and tie off. Tie in the hackle feather at the throat only.

Tie in the wing feathers which should extend back to the end of the tail tippets. Either use a slip cut from the broad side of the feather and folded, or matched pairs of slips cut from right-hand and left-hand feathers placed back to back. Finish the head in the usual way.

HYDRO HUSTLER (H)

ORIGIN: NOT KNOWN

HOOK: 2-10

TAIL: GREY SQUIRREL OR WHITE HACKLE

BODY: REAR PART: HOT ORANGE CHENILLE; FRONT PART: SHOCKING PINK CHENILLE

HACKLE: WHITE COCK HACKLE

HEAD: BLACK

This was on the New Zealand scene well before Louie's Lure, and it would appear that Louie (The Fish) DeNolfo has simply reversed the body colour segments to 'create' his lure. I believe the Hydro Hustler has its origins in North American, as a steelhead pattern. It enjoys considerable popularity as a very successful lure.

Keith Draper gives a body dressing of pale pink and intense reddish pink for the rear and front segments, and a virtually identical dressing for Louie's Lure. I respectfully have to differ from Keith on this rare occasion.

Tie in the tail. Tie in the first (orange) segment of chenille.

Take the thread part way back along the shank. Wind on the chenille to this point. Tie in a white hackle feather.

Wind on the hackle and secure. Tie in the second (pink) segment of chenille. Wind on the chenille and secure. Tie in another white hackle feather.

Wind on the hackle, secure and trim. Finish the head in the usual way.

IHI (O)

ORIGIN: NOT KNOWN

HOOK: NOT STATED, BUT PROBABLY 2-8

TAIL: TAG OF SILVER TINSEL

BODY: GREEN OR RED SEAL'S FUR OR CHENILLE

RIB: FLAT SILVER TINSEL

WING: FOUR BLACK COCK HACKLES TIED IN AS TWO PAIRS, BACK TO BACK

HACKLE: BLACK COCK

HEAD: BLACK

The comes from John Veniard's book. The Ihi has not been on the scene for a long time. You will usually find it called Ihi Green or Ihi Red, as the case may be. No doubt the green was for day fishing and the red for night.

The pattern which finds its way into Keith Draper's 1997 book has been taken from *Modern Fly Dressings* by C.H. Kendrick (1946). It implies a wing formed in the conventional way rather than two backed pairs. There is a lot of appeal in that - it makes the fly-tier's life easier - but for the example shown I have tied it as described by Veniard. It is tied in the Streamer style, i.e. with the wing trailing free.

Tie in the tinsel tag, leaving enough to use as the ribbing. Tie in the chenille.

Wind on the chenille body and follow with the ribbing.

Tie in the two pairs of wing feathers by the butts. Tie in a hackle feather and wind on to form a hackle collar.

IRISH REBEL (H)

ORIGIN: PAT O'KEEFE OF ROTORUA

HOOK: 6

TAIL: DYED RED HACKLE FIBRES OVER-TOPPED WITH BLACK SQUIRREL TAIL

BODY: DUBBED NATURAL RABBIT

HACKLE: AT MID-POINT: BLACK. AT HEAD: RED FOLLOWED BY BLACK

HEAD: BLACK

This first appeared in the 1989 Tichborne calendar, and subsequently the book *Angler's Paradise*. It is a very interesting blend of colours and materials which add up to a superb night fly, particularly at Rotorua stream mouths. Pat has only ever tied this on a No. 6 hook.

Tie in the hackle whisks. Tie in the squirrel tail fibres, overlaying the red whisks.

Dub on a section of rabbit fur to the mid-point of the shank. Tie in a black hackle feather. Wind on to form a hackle collar.

Dub on a second section of rabbit fur nearly to the head. Tie in a red hackle feather. Wind on to form a hackle collar.

Tie in a black hackle feather. Wind on to form a hackle collar, overlaying the red hackle. Complete the head in the usual way.

IRISH SETTER (H)

ORIGIN: TREVOR HALFORD OF TE ANAU

HOOK: 2-8

TAIL: BLACK SQUIRREL

BODY: REAR: ORANGE CHENILLE; FRONT: GREEN CHENILLE
WING: GINGER HACKLE WOUND AFTER EACH BODY SECTION
HEAD: BLACK

Trevor is a professional angler whose fishing 'teeth' were cut on Sanderson's Red Setter. He devised this simple variation which he found fished better than the original in the southern waters, particularly at river mouths during the winter months. The body colour combination shown here is the same as that which featured in the 1988 Tichborne calendar, although Trevor also ties it up with the colours reversed. Either way, he has found it to be attractive to rainbow and brown trout alike.

Tie in the tail. Tie in the first segment of chenille. Take the thread part way back along the shank.

Wind on the chenille to this point and tie off. Tie in a hackle feather and wind on to form a hackle 'wing'.

Tie in the second segment of chenille. Take the thread back nearly to the head. Wind on the chenille to this point and tie off. Wind on the second hackle feather. Complete the head in the ususal way.

ITALIAN STALLION (O)

ORIGIN: KARL DECKE OF KINLOCH, TAUPO
HOOK: 6
TAIL: TAG OF RED SYNTHETIC WOOL
BODY: EMERALD LUREX WITH 2-3 WRAPS OF AURORA SKIRT AT THE SHOULDER
WING: STRIP OF OLIVE GREEN RABBIT
HEAD: BLACK

Karl told me that it was "named such because of the olive green rabbit." I was already having a bad day and Edward de Bono was out. It transpires the connection is olive - olives - Italy... get the picture!

This was created in 1995 and has proved itself as a very successful lure, especially with rainbows, when fished at river mouths at night in moderately dark conditions. Karl has also taken large brown trout with this fly.

Karl usually fishes with two lures in tandem. This pattern fished with Little Green Fatale is a good combination which has worked well for Karl.

Tie in the red tag. Tie in the lurex. Return the thread back four-fifths the length of the shank.

Wind on the emerald lurex to this point and tie off. Tie in the Aurora skirt and wind on two or three wraps and tie off.

Tie in the strip of rabbit fur at the head. Complete the head in the usual way.

JACK'S SPRAT (M)

ORIGIN: JACK ENGLAND OF TURANGI
HOOK: 2-8
BODY: FLAT SILVER
RIB: OVAL SILVER
WING: BADGER COCK HACKLES
HACKLE: (OPTIONAL) BADGER
HEAD: BLACK

This is sometimes called Jack Sprat, and even Jack Spratt, but the correct name, I believe, is Jack's Sprat which is more logically to be preferred over the nursery rhyme version. As a badger version of Grey Ghost the same considerations apply with regard to the head hackle. When it is used, the preference is to tie it under the throat like a beard. Keith Draper and Hugh McDowell regard it as a smelt fly, and a "rattling good smelt fly" (Hugh). Tony Busch, in his book *A Trout Fishing Guide To New Zealand's South Island*, says this pattern "emulates the whitebait, but at a later stage of the run. It will be most effective in the mid and lower sections of all rivers during November and December". Tony's dressing calls for 4 badger hackles of a slightly golden colour. The addition of Jungle Cock cheeks makes this quite a handsome fly.

Tie in the tinsel and ribbing.

Wind on the tinsel to form the body. Tie in the wing feathers.

Wind on the ribbing, tying down the wing in the Matuku style. Add a hackle collar or beard, and cheeks, as preferred. Finish the head and varnish.

JOCK (M)

ORIGIN: POSSIBLY ADAPTED BY H. VALE OF CHRISTCHURCH
HOOK: NOT STATED BUT PROBABLY 2-8

TAIL: RED WHISKS
BODY: IN THREE SECTIONS - BLACK, YELLOW, BLACK
RIB: OVAL SILVER
WING: PALE NATURAL GINGER
TOPPING: PEACOCK SWORD
CHEEK: JUNGLE COCK
HACKLE: PROBABLY GRIZZLE, THROAT ONLY
HEAD: RED

This is an early Canterbury pattern created in 1967 and which features in Bragg's book. It is a simplified adaptation of the elaborately dressed Jock Scott - an early English salmon fly created in 1845.

I cannot be entirely certain about the accuracy of the pattern, but when dressed as I have described it the end result looks very similar to the example shown in Bragg's book.

Tie in the tail whisks. Tie in the first segment of body material and the ribbing.

Take the thread part way back along the shank. Wind on the first section of body material to this point. Repeat with the further two sections finishing near the head. Tie in the wing feathers by the butts.

Wind on the ribbing, tying down the wing in the Matuku style. Tie in the throat hackle fibres.

Tie in the topping of peacock herl and the Jungle Cock cheeks.

JOCK MILLER (O)

ORIGIN: JOHN COCKBURN OF TAUPO
HOOK: 2-8
TAIL: TWO SHORT POINTS OF GRIZZLE HACKLE
BODY: WOOL (YELLOW, ORANGE, OR RED)
WING: SEVERAL SHORT TUFTS OF RABBIT FUR TIED IN ALONG THE TOP OF THE BODY GIVING A CONTINUOUS BACK OF FUR.
HEAD: BLACK

"This pattern is unusual and while not well-known, is an excellent lure for lake-run trout, especially with an orange body." - Keith Draper (1971).

Some may consider that a 'continuous back of fur' might be more easily achieved by using a strip cut from the pelt, as with Rabbit. A possible explanation is that rabbit (or any other) fur tied in this manner gives a slimmer profile. This was Ray Punter's reasoning when he created Punter's Black Rabbit.

Tie in the tail. Tie in the wool for the body.

Take the thread a short distance back along the shank. Follow with the wool. Tie in a tuft of rabbit fur.

Take the thread a further short distance along the shank, and follow with the wool. Tie in another short tuft of rabbit fur.

Repeat the process, finishing off at the shoulder. Secure and trim.

JOCK MILLER VARIATION (O)

ORIGIN: EUAN MACALISTER
HOOK: 4-6
TAIL: PLYMOUTH ROCK (GRIZZLE) HEN FIBRES
BODY: IRISH GREEN WOOL
RIB: FLUORESCENT RED WOOL
WING: TWO TUFTS OF DARK RABBIT FUR
HEAD: BLACK

Tony Orman, in his book *The Sport in Fishing* obtained the favourite patterns of 13 experts. This pattern was Euan's contribution, about which he says: "I have had some success with this fly when used near spawning fish, as the jacks attack it madly".

Ray Punter tried several different methods of tying this lure, and the following guide describes that which gave the best result. The task is made easier, and a neater result is obtained, by using a single ply strand from the wool.

Tie in the tail fibres. Secure and trim. Tie in the two colours of wool.

Take the thread back to the mid-point along the shank. Tie in a tuft of rabbit fur.

Wind on the green wool to form the body, taking it past the rabbit fur, and tie off at the head.

Wind on the red wool ribbing, spacing it to go evenly either side of the rabbit fur. Tie off the wool at the head. Tie in another tuft of rabbit fur. Complete the head and varnish.

JOCK SCOTT (O)

ORIGIN: JOCK SCOTT OF UK (IN 1845)
HOOK: NOT STATED BUT PROBABLY 2-8
TAIL: RED WHISKS
BUTT: BLACK
BODY: YELLOW
RIB: OVAL GOLD

WING: PALE GINGER, TIED IN AT HEAD ONLY
TOPPING: PEACOCK HERL
HACKLE: TEAL, THROAT
CHEEK: JUNGLE COCK
HEAD: BLACK

This is a very simplified dressing of the original salmon fly and was popular in the Taupo and Rotorua districts during the 1950s. The pattern has been gleaned from a study of photos in Bragg's book where this fly is featured.

Tie in the tail whisks. Tie in the ribbing. Tie in the black chenille or wool and take one or two turns to form a butt. Tie in the yellow body material.

Wind on the yellow body followed by the ribbing. Tie in the wing feathers by the butts.

Tie in the hackle feather at the throat collar.

Add Jungle Cock cheeks and complete the head in the usual way.

JO JO JUGGINS (M)

ORIGIN: NIGEL BIRT OF CHRISTCHURCH
HOOK: 10-14
BODY: DUBBED HARE'S EAR MIX
RIB: THIN COPPER WIRE
WING: GRIZZLE COCK HACKLE (BADGER CAN ALSO BE USED)
HEAD: BLACK OR BROWN

This featured in the 1991 Tichborne calendar and book. Although the hook range is outside my parameter to qualify as a lure, it can nevertheless be fished as a lure. Nigel calls it a lure, and I have no doubt it would be successful tied up in larger sizes. It is very effective when used to ambush shoreline cruisers, and it is also effective in rivers and streams when fished on the swing into pools.

Nigel tells me "the JJJ was developed and evolved over four seasons of experimental lake edge fishing at Lake Brunner in the late eighties. Trout were often very selective, especially during February, when aggressively feeding on schools of spawning smelt at the lake edge. Many smelt patterns were refused, and Hare & Copper patterns looked at, yet not readily taken. Experimentation with many styles evolved the JJJ into the fly that is successfully taken by trout today - a Hare & Copper/smelt hybrid. The name developed one evening with good friends over a game of 'Dictionary', (a written version of 'Pictionary'). The word Juggins suggests that we may not be good friends, however kiwi societal norms allow you to throw stick at your good mates."

In other words, juggins (which means a person who is a bit dim-witted) has been applied to a friend in a good-natured form of banter.

Tie in the ribbing.

Dub on a body of hare's ear mix. Tie in the wing feathers by the butts.

Wind on the ribbing, tying down the wing in the Matuku style. Complete the head in the usual way.

KEELER (P)

ORIGIN: KILWELL'S OF ROTORUA (WARWICK WELLS)
HOOK: 2-8
TAIL: BROWN (RED FOX) SQUIRREL TAIL
BODY: TWO SECTIONS, THE REAR YELLOW MOHAIR, THE FRONT RED WOOL
WING: BACK TOP, YELLOW GOLDEN PHEASANT RUMP FEATHERS. FRONT TOP, RED GOLDEN PHEASANT BREAST
HEAD: BLACK

"It is no coincidence that this fly came on to the market at the time of a national political scandal in Britain. It is a pretty fly (as it should be) but while it is quite a successful lure I have found that it is more favoured in the extra large sizes and used for harling." - Keith Draper (1971).

I have tried tying this up from the red and gold feathers of our reasonably common ring-neck pheasant, but it is not the same. An older pattern I have seen describes the wing as: "Two Red and Yellow golden pheasant hackles tied in two sections as for Fuzzy Wuzzy". It might be worth a try. The example shown has been tied using seal's fur for the body - always to be preferred for those lucky enough.

Tie in the tail of squirrel fibres. Tie in the mohair for the first body section.

Take the thread part way back along the shank. Wind on the mohair to this point. Tie in the yellow rump feathers in the Pukeko style, low over the body.

Tie in the red wool for the next body section. Wind on the wool to the head. Secure and trim.

Tie in the red wing feathers in the Pukeko style, forming a canopy over the top of the body. Finish the head and varnish.

KEITH'S KRAWLIE (O)

ORIGIN: KEITH DRAPER OF TAUPO

HOOK: 2-4

CLAWS: TWO FEATHERS FROM A GROUSE TAIL WITH THE TOPS NIPPED OUT AND TRIMMED TO SHAPE. THESE ARE TIED ON TOP OF THE HOOK, AND SPREAD OUT TO SIMULATE THE PINCERS OF THE CRAYFISH

TAIL: A SHORT BUNCH OF BLACK SQUIRREL TAIL OR SHORT BUNCH OF BROWN TURKEY

FEELERS: THE STEMS OF TWO BLACK COCK NECK HACKLES STRIPPED OF THEIR FIBRES

EYES: TWO SHORT LENGTHS OF 40 KG. MONOFILAMENT, BURNT ON THE END TO FORM GLOBULES, AND TIED IN WITH THE FEELERS OVER THE SQUIRREL (OR TURKEY) WHISKERS

TOPPING: BROWN RAFFIENE OR A LONG STRIP OF BROWN TURKEY TAIL. THIS IS TIED IN FORWARD AND PULLED BACK OVER THE BODY, RIBBED ALONG THE ABDOMEN AND THEN CUT, LEAVING A SHORT SPLAYED OUT SECTION SITTING OVER THE EYE OF THE HOOK TO REPRESENT THE TAIL OF THE CRAYFISH

ABDOMEN AND THORAX: BROWN CHENILLE, THE REAR HALF (THORAX) BEING BUILT UP THEN TAPERED TOWARDS THE EYE.

LEGS: A LARGE BROWN HACKLE TIED IN BEFORE THE CHENILLE THEN WOUND AROUND THE THORAX.

RIBBING: COPPER WIRE. THIS IS WOUND OVER THE LEG HACKLE, BEING USED TO SECURE IT TO THE BODY. NEXT THE RAFFIENE (OR TURKEY) IS PULLED BACK OVER THE THORAX AND SECURED WITH THE RIB. THE COPPER RIB IS WOUND OVER THE TAIL TOWARDS THE EYE OF THE HOOK AT REGULAR INTERVALS, MAKING THE SEGMENTED TAIL OF THE CRAYFISH. THE RAFFIENE /TURKEY IS CUT TO MAKE THE TAIL FINS.

An olive-bodied version with well-marked olive grizzle hackle for the legs is a good realistic alternative. Fish with a sinking line over drop-offs, or with a floating line around lake margins after dark. The pattern, as described, incorporates the tying details. There are good drawings and tying notes on how to tie this pattern in Keith's book *Hooked of Fly-tying.*

Keith has used turkey in tying the featured example. Two long thin strips of turkey have been used for what is described in the pattern as a tail. This is quite the most realistic koura pattern I have seen.

KILWELL BLONDE (O)

ORIGIN: KILWELL'S OF ROTORUA

HOOK: NOT STATED BUT PROBABLY 4-8

TAIL: RED WHISKS UNDER A BUNCH OF LIGHT-COLOURED SIKA DEER HAIR

BODY: FLAT SILVER TINSEL

WING: BUNCH OF LIGHT-COLOURED SIKA DEER HAIR

HEAD: BLACK

This was commercially tied by Kilwell's but has passed from the scene long since. Kilwell's no longer have any records or memory of it, but its existence is known because it was once included in a framed collection now owned by Ross Marks of Christchurch.

As with all hair flies, the deer hair fibres should be well cemented in otherwise they will readily pull out. It is believed that this was originally tied using polar bear hair.

Tie in the whisks. Tie in a bunch of deer hair for the tail.

Tie in the body tinsel. Return the thread back nearly to the head. Wind on the silver tinsel body to this point and tie off. (My method is to tie the tinsel in at the head and wind it down to the bend and back to the head.)

Tie in the deer hair wing. Cement thoroughly. Complete the head in the usual way.

KILWELL BULLY (O)

ORIGIN: KILWELL'S OF ROTORUA

HOOK: NOT STATED BUT PROBABLY 4-8

TAIL: GREY BARRED SQUIRREL TAIL

BODY: SILVER TINSEL

WING: GREY BARRED SQUIRREL TAIL

HEAD: BLACK

This was put out by Kilwell, obviously, a long time ago – so long ago that they have no record or memory of it.

There is no reason I can think of why this should not

have been a successful fly except that hair flies can fall to pieces if not well glued in. While it may have fallen from grace as a commercial proposition, it is still available to the home tier.

Tie in the squirrel tail. Make sure the cut ends reach back to the hook eye to provide a level base for the tinsel body. Coat the shank with head cement.

Tie in the body tinsel or take the thread back nearly to the head and tie in the tinsel at this point depending on your preferred practice. Wind on the tinsel to form the body.

Tie in the squirrel tail wing. Coat the tie-in point liberally with head cement. Complete the head in the usual way.

KILWELL No. 1 (K)

ORIGIN: FRANK LORD OF ROTORUA, WHO ORIGINALLY CALLED IT TARAWERA KILLER. COMMERCIAL PRODUCTION WAS TAKEN OVER BY KILWELL'S OF ROTORUA AND RE-NAMED.

HOOK: 2-8

TAIL: BLACK SQUIRREL

BODY: WOOL, YELLOW OR RED

WING: STRIPED BROWN PARTRIDGE

HEAD: BLACK

All Killer style flies are a curse to tie up, and the difficulties are compounded in this instance because of the need to align the white stripe along the entire length of the fly. But one nicely tied and well balanced is not only a joy to own, but is an effective fish taker. This pattern is no exception. Although still commercially available, its future is only as certain as the supply of partridge plumage. It was once claimed by some anglers to be an old Mrs Simpson, and that name is still in vogue in the South Island.

Hugh McDowell regards it as one of the very best of the Killer patterns. As a general rule of thumb, a yellow body is used on sunny days, and a red body on dull days.

Tie in the tail fibres. Tie in the body material.

Take the thread part way back along the shank. Wind on the wool to this point. Tie in a pair of wing feathers on either side of the shank.

Take the thread back nearly to the head.

Wind on the wool and secure. Tie in another pair of wing feathers alongside the body on either side of the shank.

Finish the head and varnish.

KILWELL No. 2 (K)

ORIGIN: FRANK LORD OF ROTORUA, WHO ORIGINALLY CALLED IT ROTOITI KILLER. IT WAS TAKEN OVER COMMERCIALLY BY KILWELL'S WHO RE-NAMED IT.

HOOK: 2-8

TAIL: BLACK SQUIRREL

BODY: WOOL, YELLOW OR RED

WING: MOTTLED GROUSE PLUMAGE (ALSO DESCRIBED AS SPECKLED SEPIA AND BLACK FEATHERS FROM EUROPEAN GROUSE)

HEAD: BLACK

"Another killer pattern, this lure is not as well known as its stablemate. However, I am told it is an excellent night fly. There is no reason why it shouldn't be, as it has all the ingredients of a successful lure." - Keith Draper (1971).

Hugh McDowell claims that it is also a good day fly, especially at the change of light. He says that the fly is particularly effective at Lake Rerewhakaaitu (near Rotorua), for reasons known only to the trout there.

Difficulties in the supply of grouse plumage have limited this fly in the commercial scene, although they are still available to the home tier.

Tie in the tail fibres. Tie in the wool (or chenille). Secure and trim.

Take the thread part way back along the shank. Wind on the wool to this point. Tie in a pair of wing feathers alongside the body on either side of the shank.

Take the thread back nearly to the head.

Follow with the wool and secure. Tie in another pair of wing feathers on either side of the shank.

KIWI PARMACHENEE (M)

ORIGIN: BOB KEEN OF PALMERSTON NORTH

HOOK: 6 LONG SHANK

TAIL: SCARLET, UPON WHITE, HACKLE WHISKS

BODY: LEMON-YELLOW CHENILLE

RIB: SILVER TINSEL

WING: STRIP OF WHITE RABBIT FUR

CHEEKS: RED IBIS

HACKLE: SCARLET UPON WHITE, COCK

HEAD: BLACK

This comes from Tony Orman's anthology compilation of 1980. It is said there: "This lure was an adaptation of a famous American wet fly, the Parmacheene (sic) Belle. It has proved highly successful at Taupo for Bob Keen and his companions. *Field and Stream Magazine*, February 1967, had a very similar pattern called Parma Belle."

The original Parmachenee Belle was created prior to 1880 by Henry P Wells of USA and named after Lake Parmachenee in Maine. The only differences are that the original used mohair instead of chenille, and the wing is mixed scarlet ibis and white hackles.

In *A Dictionary of Trout Flies* by A. Courtney Williams (5th Ed. 1973), the original is described as : "Probably the most killing trout fly throughout the New World". Little wonder, therefore, why Bob and his friends had such success with their variation.

Tie in the white tail fibres. Tie in the scarlet fibres on top of the white ones. Secure and trim. Tie in the chenille and ribbing.

Wind on the chenille. Secure and trim. Tie in the strip of rabbit fur.

Wind on the ribbing, tying down the rabbit fur in the Matuku style.

Tie in the ibis (or substitute) cheeks on either side of the shank at the shoulder. Tie in the white hackle feather.

Wind on the hackle collar. Tie in the scarlet hackle feather and wind on. Secure and trim. Finish the head and varnish.

KIWI TEASER (H)

ORIGIN: ROB LIMMER OF TAURANGA
HOOK: PROBABLY 2-8
TAIL: A BUNCH OF KRYSTAL FLASH
BODY: FLUORESCENT CHENILLE
HACKLE: HACKLE FIBRES, COLOUR TO MATCH
HEAD: BLACK

Many years ago, when I was tying up Red Setters, I was struck by the notion of substituting the tail and hackles for bunches of Krystal Flash. I tied up a number in the popular fluorescent colours, mainly yellow, green, and orange. My very first experience was with a yellow version, and in nothing flat I had two nice rainbows in the bag. I cast again, and a Waikaremoana trout (presumably - unless that lake has its own version of the Loch Ness monster) hit it like a steam train. It ripped out most of my line in one sustained burst and then vanished. I still wonder about that fish!

I continued to catch trout with my "creation" and I thought I had invented an amazing fly. About three years later, I found my 'invention' rolling off the production line. My "Yellow Peril" had become a Kiwi Teaser, and I hadn't invented it after all, but I know how effective it can be in the right conditions. It was originally designed to be fished in tandem with another lure, the idea being that the brightness would attract fish which would then be tempted by the other lure. However, I find it very effective as a stand alone lure in its own right.

Tie in a bunch of Krystal Flash for the tail, colour to suit. Tie in a matching coloured chenille and wind on to the head.

Tie in a hackle feather and wind on to form a hackle collar.

KLONDIKE KATE (M)

ORIGIN: NOT KNOWN
HOOK: NOT STATED BUT PROBABLY 2-8
TAG: SILVER
TAIL: AMHERST PHEASANT WHISKS
BODY: SILVER TINSEL
RIB: OVAL SILVER
WING: BADGER
HACKLE: RED UNDER PALE GINGER
CHEEK: JUNGLE COCK
HEAD: BLACK

This appears in Bragg's book. It is contained in a section on tying New Zealand lures with no explanatory text or comment. It appears with three other lures in the same context - Silver Grey, Black Demon, and Veron Argente. It seems that it is a smelt lure principally but was also successful with salmon, which may account for the name. Gary Kemsley has successfully used this lure to take trout in the Ohau Channel.

Tie in a silver tag, taking about four turns around the shank. Tie in the Amherst pheasant whisks.

Tie in the body tinsel and ribbing.

Wind on the tinsel body. Tie in the wing feathers by the butts.

Wind on the ribbing, tying down the wing in the Matuku style.

Wind on red and ginger hackles to form a hackle collar. Tie in the Jungle Cock cheeks on either side. Complete the head in the usual way.

KOKAPU (M)

ORIGIN: KILWELL'S OF ROTORUA
HOOK: NOT STATED BUT PROBABLY 2-8
BUTT: OVAL SILVER
TAIL: ORANGE WHISKS
BODY: YELLOW
RIB: OVAL SILVER
WING: BROWN NATURAL RABBIT
CHEEK: GREY PARTRIDGE BREAST
HEAD: BLACK

This was commercially put out by Kilwell's although they no longer have any records or memory of it. The only known example is held by Ross Marks of Christchurch, in a framed collection of Kilwell lures. Fortunately, it is sufficiently moth-eaten to enable some insight into the pattern although even so it is difficult to be certain. For example, the body may have a rear section of red floss, or it may be just red tying silk showing through the decaying chenille. I have assumed the latter.

Kokopu is the name of the native trout and I suspect the name of this lure is a mis-spelling of the natural which it is intended to imitate, in much the same manner as "Matuka" developed.

Tie in the butt and the tail whisks. Tie in the body material and the ribbing.

Wind on the body material nearly to the head. Tie in the strip of rabbit fur.

Wind on the ribbing, tying down the wing in the Matuku style.

Tie in the cheek feathers on either side of the shank.

LA GIACONDA (H)

ORIGIN: JOHN GIACON OF AUCKLAND
HOOK: 8
TAIL: BROWN SQUIRREL TAIL
BODY: LIGHT OLIVE GREEN CHENILLE
RIB: TWO AND A HALF TURNS OF BROWN CHENILLE TIED SO THAT THE BUTT SECTION OF THE BODY UNDER THE TAIL IS OLIVE
HACKLE: THE OFFICIAL UMPQUA PATTERN IS FOR FURNACE TIED SO THAT THE BLACK IS NEXT TO THE HEAD WITH THE BROWN POINTS AT THE TIP END. THE ORIGINAL TIE USED GINGER, AND THAT HAS BEEN USED IN THE EXAMPLE SHOWN, ALTHOUGH JOHN HAS COME TO PREFER THE FURNACE
HEAD: BLACK

Many years ago my nephew came back from Auckland clutching one of these for an up-coming trip to Lake Waikaremoana. They were simple to tie and I produced a number for the trip. Not knowing what it was called, I irreverently dubbed it Krystnoes! Knowing a great deal less than I do now about fishing I harled away with predictable lack of success, and it was consigned to File 13.

Many years later I came across what I thought was the same fly only the squirrel tail had given way to marabou in what I assumed was the Mark II version. It was called Variegated. A year later I ascertained its correct name and pedigree. When John first used this lure, he and a friend landed 40 trout (releasing most of them). That was at Lake Rotoaira, but it has proved successful in many other lakes. It is a stillwater fly fished slowly in deep to mid-water over weed beds or along the littoral margins of the lakes. Do not harl with it!

The name, as well as being a clever play on John's family name, was also the name of the model who became better known as Leonardo da Vinci's Mona Lisa. The enigmatic qualities ascribed to that portrait mirrored the enigmatic reasons for this lure's success. John and his friends all had differing theories, but they could all agree that it worked.

John will be will known to many for his video production on tying New Zealand flies. I have now used this lure correctly and successfully. My view is that it is taken for a dragonfly nymph.

Tie in the tail. Tie in both chenille colours for the body.

Wind on the olive green chenille and tie off. Follow with the brown chenille "ribbing" ensuring a green turn of chenille at the butt.

Tie in a hackle feather. Wind on to form a hackle collar, which should be more upright than laid back.

LAMPREY (M)

ORIGIN: MONTY WRIGHT OF DUNEDIN
HOOK: 10 LONG SHANK
TAIL: FIVE OR SIX STRANDS OF KRYSTAL FLASH PEARL
BODY: SILVER TINSEL OR PEARL LURE FLASH
RIB: FINE OVAL SILVER
WING: TWO MING BLUE COCK HACKLES TIED LONG
TOPPING: FOUR STRANDS OF KRYSTAL FLASH PEARL
HEAD: GREEN

Known as Ammocoete, they are the last stage of the lamprey eel as they migrate to the sea for the next part of their life cycle. The Ammocoete is about 80-100mm in length, and brown, but as they prepare to go to sea there is a further change in their life cycle and they turn Ming blue on the back and silver on the belly. In this migratory form they are called a Macrophthalmia.

They are very common in the Otago estuaries between February and September, with the best months being July and August. Trout prey on them and heavy mono should be used as the trout will hit the lure very hard.

The most important thing when tying these is the length, especially if you intend to fish after dark. The length should be at least 70-80mm. If they are tied too small, the trout won't take them.

Tie in the Krystal Flash for the tail. Tie in the tinsel and the ribbing.

Wind on the tinsel body. Tie in the wing feathers by the butts.

Wind on the ribbing, tying down the wing in the Matuku style.

Tie in the Krystal Flash topping and complete the head in the usual way.

LESLIE'S LURE (K)

ORIGIN: LESLIE NEWDICK OF TAUPO
HOOK: NOT STATED, BUT PROBABLY 2-8
TAIL: A BUNCH OF FIBRES FROM THE TAIL FEATHER OF A COCK PHEASANT
BODY: YELLOW OR RED WOOL
WING: HEN PHEASANT BREAST FEATHERS OR THE SMALL COVERTS FROM A HEN PHEASANT WING TIED TWO TO A SIDE
HEAD: BLACK

A very long time ago, I landed a 7lb rainbow at Motuapa, Lake Taupo. The name of the lure was forever in my memory as Leslie's Lure Yellow, but the mental picture I had of that lure was a Yellow Turkey. It was not until many years later that I realised that I was confusing two very different lures. Just which one it was I will never know, but I have always retained a soft spot for Leslie's Lure. It is a good bully fly, and if it is not as popular now as it once was, this is probably because of the difficulty in obtaining the hen pheasant feathers rather than any inherent deficiency in the fly.

This was once sometimes referred to as Awahou, or according to John Veniard, an Ohahau, which is probably a corruption of Awahou (although that same English publication gives us the Awahou Special). Keith Draper is in no doubt that Newdick has first claim to this dressing.

Veniard's dressing used brown barred squirrel fibres for the tail and oval silver ribbing but is otherwise the same fly. The photo in Keith's 1997 book (as opposed to the pattern in the same book), shows this lure tied with a tail of squirrel tail. I commend this variation as an easier tie than wrestling with the pheasant tail fibres.

Tie in the tail fibres. Tie in the body material.

Wind on the body material and secure.

Tie in a pair of wing feathers alongside the body on either side of the shank. Finish the head and varnish.

LES'S FANCY (M)

ORIGIN: LESLIE HASTINGS OF PALMERSTON NORTH
HOOK: 2-8
TAG: RED WOOL
BODY: WHITE WOOL
RIB: SILVER
WING: STRIP OF WHITE RABBIT
HEAD: RED

"It has been on the Taupo scene for many years, especially in the very small sizes when it makes a capital smelt fly. In this case it is loosely referred to as a White Rabbit." - Keith Draper (1971).

Not infrequently I come across a school of thought which holds that a red tag (or tail, body, head, hackle, cheeks, whatever), is secret ingredient X. Whether that is true or not (and the pulsing effect of rabbit fur must have a bearing), there is no denying that this is an effective lure.

You may also find this sold under the name Albino Bunny.

Tie in the red tag. Tie in the wool and ribbing.

Take the thread and wool back nearly to the head. Secure the wool and trim. Tie in the strip of rabbit fur.

Wind on the ribbing, tying down the strip of rabbit fur in the Matuku style.

Finish the head. This will be red, either because red tying thread was used, or red head paint is used over some other coloured thread. Varnish.

LIGHT BROWN AND PARADISE (O)

ORIGIN:	NOT KNOWN
HOOK:	NOT STATED BUT PROBABLY 2-8
BODY:	WHITE
RIB:	FLAT SILVER
WING:	NATURAL LIGHT BROWN COCK
CHEEK:	MALE PARADISE SHELDUCK
HACKLE:	LIGHT BROWN
HEAD:	BLACK

This appears in Bragg's book. Initially, I assumed it to be Brunton No. 2 under a different name just as Brunton No.1 is sometimes referred to as Brown and Paradise (most dressings). However, I have come to the view that this is a different lure and to be included as such. It is listed as a high country lure of the period 1946 to 1972. It was tied in the loose-winged streamer style.

Tie in the body material and the ribbing.

Wind on the body material followed by the ribbing. Tie in the wing feathers by the butts.

Tie in the paradise duck cheeks on either side, extending back to the bend. Tie in a hackle feather and wind on to form a hackle collar.

LIMEY (O)

ORIGIN:	MAUREEN BUTLER OF ROTORUA
HOOK:	2-8
TAIL:	BLACK SQUIRREL
BODY:	GREEN LUREX ("MADEIRA" - SHADE 352)
WING:	THREE SHADES OF TAHR HAIR, DARK TO LIGHT
HACKLE:	DARK GREY TAHR HAIR, TIED BEARD STYLE
TOPPING:	TWO THREADS OF MADEIRA LUREX TEASED OUT
HEAD:	BLACK

This featured in the Tichborne calendar of 1991. It is a good daytime smelt fly, which is fished conventionally on a sinking line. It has been very successful in rivers, lakes and stream mouths. Comb out all of the underfur for the throat hackle, but only some for the hair wing. If it is all combed out of the wing bunches it will look lifeless. "Tahr" is more commonly spelt "Thar" but that is actually a corruption of the correct name which is Tahr.

Tie in the squirrel tail. Trim. Tie in the lurex.

Wind on the lurex to form the body. Tie off and secure. Tie in a small bunch of Tahr hair under the throat to create a beard hackle.

Tie in three bunches of Tahr hair for the wing starting with a dark shade and then successively lighter shades. Tie in the topping. Finish the head in the usual way.

LISA (H)

ORIGIN:	BRONWYN WILSON OF TAUPO
HOOK:	2-8
TAG:	RED WOOL
TAIL:	HONEY CREE COCK
BODY:	YELLOW-ORANGE SEAL'S FUR
TOPPING:	STRANDS OF ORANGE AND PEACH KRYSTAL FLASH
HACKLE:	WHITE COCK AT MID-SECTION AND HONEY CREE AT HEAD
HEAD:	BLACK

This has been named after a friend of Bronwyn, and is another successful creation from this creative tier.

An alternative body dressing is pearl lurex instead of the seal's fur (or substitute) for the rear section.

Tie in the tag. Tie in the tail.

Dub on the first section of body to about the mid-point. Tie in a white hackle feather and wind on.

Dub on the second section of body. Tie off. Tie in a honey cree feather and wind on to form a hackle collar.

Tie in the topping. Complete the head in the usual way.

LISA SIMPSON (M)

ORIGIN: SUE CRAWFORD OF TE AROHA
HOOK: 2-8
TAIL: RED WHISKS
BODY: AURORA SKIRT
RIB: OVAL SILVER
WING: OLIVE RABBIT STRIP
CHEEKS: COCK PHEASANT RUMP (TWO FEATHERS EACH SIDE)
HEAD: BLACK

This is a very effective lure on both brown and rainbow trout. The wing colouring can be either dark, medium, or gold olive to suit personal preference or requirements. It is fished in the same manner as a standard rabbit pattern, and it is also very productive as a harling lure. It has fished well on most of the Rotorua lakes and is especially good on Lakes Rerewhakaaitu, Aniwhenua, and Tarawera.

It is being tied commercially in the Tauranga area. The name comes from the popular TV series "The Simpsons" (Bart's sister, Lisa) and expands the Simpson family of lures.

Tie in the tail whisks. Tie in the Aurora skirt and ribbing.

Wind on the Aurora skirt to the head. Tie in the rabbit strip.

Wind on the ribbing, tying down the fur wing in the Matuku style.

Tie in the cheeks on either side. Complete the head in the usual way.

LITTLE GREEN FATAL (O)

ORIGIN: KARL DECKE OF KINLOCH, TAUPO
HOOK: 8
TAIL: TAG OF RED SYNTHETIC WOOL
BODY: AURORA SKIRT
OVER-BODY: FLUORESCENT LIME GREEN CHENILLE
HEAD: BLACK

This is very similar to the Doll Fly and just as effective, if not more so. It was created around 1993-94 and Karl describes it as an "absolute stock standard trout killing machine. Works all year in all conditions in virtually every kind of water."

It is a night fly which Carl fishes mostly at stream mouths on a floating line or sometimes an intermediate sinking line if the water surface is choppy. If the trout are selectively feeding on, say, smelt, then a lure change will be necessary but otherwise it is not unknown for this lure to remain firmly attached to Karl's line for up to 11 months on end. He has taken browns, but mostly he catches rainbow 'in quantity'.

It is quick and easy to tie up, and he would never be without one. For a fishing guide where success matters, he says 'this animal is a real trooper'.

Tie in the tag of red wool.

Tie in the Aurora skirt and the chenille.

Wind on the Aurora skirt. Pull the chenille over the top of the body and tie off at the head. Complete the head in the usual way.

LITTLE RAINBOW (O)

ORIGIN: PHIL STECK OF WYOMING, USA
HOOK: 2-8 LONG SHANK, WEIGHTED WITH FUSE WIRE (IF LEGAL)
TAIL: BLACK MARABOU OVER STRANDS OF FLASHABOU PEARL
BODY: CREAM YARN WITH FLASHABOU ALONG THE SIDE
WING: BLACK MARABOU
HEAD: SPUN DEER HAIR

Phil has spent a lot of his time fishing in New Zealand, and this pattern has been very successful in the Tongariro, Rangitikei, and Ngaruroro (Hawkes Bay) Rivers, whether bank casting or float fishing. It takes brown and rainbow trout alike, particularly those lying at the bottom of deep pools. It is fished with a fast sinking line and shooting head using a strip and stop retrieve once the lure has had time to get down really deep.

This lure featured in the 1989 Tichborne calendar and subsequent book. The tail and wing are formed from a single plume of marabou secured at the bend and at the head.

If permitted, pre-weight the hook. Take the thread down to the bend. Tie in several strands of Flashabou. Tie in the body yarn.

Take a plume of marabou and lay it along the shank until the right length of 'tail' is achieved. Tie in the marabou at the bend.

Take the thread two-thirds the way along the shank. Wind on the body material to this point and tie off. Take one or two strands of Flashabou and bring forward on either side of the body to the tie-off point and secure.

Tie down the marabou plume at the same point and trim. Form the collar and head from deer hair in the Muddler style.

LOGAN'S LURE (H)

ORIGIN: RICHARD LOGAN OF TIMARU
HOOK: 2-8
TAIL: DARK BROWN OR BLACK FUR
BODY: JAEGER CHENILLE
HACKLE: SOFT HEN FEATHERS OR SADDLE HACKLE, DARK OR BLACK - 2 OR 3 TURNS ONLY
HEAD: BLACK

I met Richard while we followed each other around Lake Waikaremoana trying to find a sheltered spot to fish on a very blustery day. As so often happens general chat turned to discussion of flies. He showed me his creation. It was beautifully tied, slim, and looked a very likely fish taker. He assured me it is, and he uses no other lure - day or night, rainbows or brown, any weather, North and South Islands, fished as a lure or nymph. Tied on a No. 8, it has also proved effective on Chinook salmon using a fly rod in the late evening on the Opihi River in South Canterbury.

It is at its most effective when left to lie in ambush for patrolling fish around the shoreline. Richard recommends a trace of not less that 6lbs. When the trout is very close, twitch the fly and watch. If the trout should fail to take on the first pass, twitch again and perhaps draw - slow, then very fast to excite the trout. Keep the rod tip at water level in line with the lure and when the fish is following at high speed, stop the retrieve. The trout will overrun, turn, and take the fly.

The lure can also be used as a nymph cast short over deep water around lake edges. The trick is to watch the fly as it slowly sinks, and take appropriate action if a trout appears. Place the next cast three metres along and repeat. It is also deadly deep down over weed beds, fished slow. In these circumstances, it is as well to remember that this lure tied on a No. 8 hook is about the size of a dragonfly larvae.

Is this, then, the perfect lure? The ability to reduce one's fly fishing (and fly-tying) to just one lure is a tantalising prospect, although Bloody Mary has the added ability to be fished as a dry.

I pondered anxiously about its inclusion in this book. You see, the problem is that the particular chenille, which is probably the principal ingredient in its success, is unlikely to be available. Richard's daughter managed to buy the last known ball when she was in Ireland. It may still be procurable and for those wishing to make the necessary enquiry, Jaeger Chenille is made in Ireland for Jaeger Handknitting Ltd., Darlington, U.K. It is distributed in America by Susan Bates Inc., Chester, Connecticut, 06412. The shade is 939, Lot 16. A reasonably close substitute can be created by combining black, green, and blue lurex. No doubt other ingenious solutions are possible.

In sizes 2-4, Richard uses dark squirrel for the tail. In the smaller sizes, he uses fox tail fibres cut from an old fur coat. The lure is tied in the usual Hackle style, keeping the hackle sparse and well sloped back. On No. 2 hooks, Richard ties in three body segments and larger hackle feathers. This lure on a No. 2 makes an excellent night fly.

LORD'S KILLER (K)

ORIGIN: FRANK LORD OF ROTORUA
HOOK: NOT STATED BUT PROBABLY 2-8
TAIL: BLACK SQUIRREL
BODY: YELLOW OR RED WOOL OR CHENILLE
WING: WOODCOCK PLUMAGE, PREFERABLY BROWN RATHER THAN BUFF
HEAD: BLACK

This lure was created by Frank Lord around 1940 to represent the inanga. It also presents as a good imitation of koura and cock-a-bullies. It was quite possibly the first Killer style fly created, and in Keith Draper's opinion, this is perhaps the best known of all the Killer style flies.

By inference, therefore, it is perhaps the best of all Killer flies. Lamenting the difficulty in tying in the soft feathers (as many as 16 before satisfied) Keith says: "One of these flies, well tied and nicely balanced, is a possession to be treasured." (1971)

The plumage ranges through every shade of brown from the darkest sepia to pale buff. The difficulty in obtaining any plumage at all has probably spelled the death-knell for this splendid fly. When you can get it, it will likely be buff, but be thankful for small mercies! It will still look like a bully and slay rainbows and browns alike.

Tie in the squirrel tail fibres. Tie in the chenille.

Take the thread part way back along the shank. Wind on the chenille to this point. Tie in a pair (or more) of wing feathers on either side of the shank to lie along the body in the Killer style.

Take the thread back nearly to the head.

Wind on the chenille. Secure and trim. Tie in a further set of feathers on either side of the shank. Finish the head and varnish.

LOUIE'S LURE (H)

ORIGIN: LOUIE DeNOLFO OF ROTORUA
HOOK: 4-8
TAIL: GREY SQUIRREL TAIL OR WHITE HACKLE FIBRES
BODY: REAR PART: SHOCKING PINK CHENILLE; FRONT PART: HOT ORANGE CHENILLE
HACKLE: WHITE COCK HACKLES
HEAD: BLACK

This is a Hydro Hustler with the body segment colours reversed and cleverly marketed by the well-known and flamboyant fishing guide, Louie The Fish (DeNolfo). Its popularity seemed to give way with the arrival of the Glo-Bug, but it has been, and can be, a spectacularly successful lure.

I am told that Louie The Fish now lives permanently in Samoa.

Hydro Hustler, Disco Doll, Louie's Lure and Pink Lady are all variations on a theme, with Hydro Hustler the likely progenitor. It was certainly in New Zealand before Louie's Lure.

Respectfully, I have to disagree with Keith Draper's pattern for this lure and that of Hydro Hustler as being made up of two shades of pink. (See Hydro Hustler.)

Tie in the tail. Tie in the first (pink) segment of chenille.

Take the thread part way back along the shank. Wind on the chenille to this point. Tie in a white hackle feather.

Wind on the hackle and secure. Tie in the second (orange) segment of chenille. Wind on the chenille and secure. Tie in another white hackle feather.

Wind on the hackle, secure and trim.

LOU'S GREEN PARROT (M)

ORIGIN: ROB LIMMER OF TAURANGA
HOOK: 2-8
TAIL: RED WHISKS
BODY: LIME GREEN CHENILLE
RIB: OVAL SILVER
WING: CHARTREUSE HACKLE
HACKLE: FLUORESCENT ORANGE
TOPPING: ORANGE KRYSTAL FLASH
HEAD: FLUORESCENT ORANGE

Lou Jordain came into the tackle shop and asked Mike Limmer for a Green Parrot lure. He had read about it in a fishing magazine and it was harling well in the Rotorua lakes and he wanted some. Mike had never heard of it. He made some enquiries and found that there had been a misprint. Green Parrot should have read Green Rabbit. However, Mike went and purchased a small green soft toy Budgie and inserted a hook into a place that would have startled a live bird and gave it to Lou as a Green Parrot fly! The joke was appreciated, and at about this time Mike's dad got involved and subsequently this lure evolved. The colouring is based on the Indian Ring-Neck Parrot which Rob used to breed.

What started out as a joke ended up with a successful lure, now tied professionally, which took rainbow trout, in particular, both harling and casting.

Tie in the tail whisks. Tie in the chenille and ribbing.

Wind on the chenille. Tie in the wing feathers by the butts.

Wind on the ribbing, tying down the wing in the Matuku

style. Tie in the topping. Tie in a hackle feather and wind on to form a hackle collar.

MALLARD (1) (K)

ORIGIN: GEOFF SANDERSON OF TURANGI
HOOK: 2-8
TAIL: BLACK OR GREY BARRED SQUIRREL
BODY: CHENILLE OR WOOL, RED OR YELLOW.
WING: THE GREY BREAST FEATHERS OF A MALLARD DRAKE
HEAD: BLACK

This is a very effective lure on lake-run trout. The choice of tail is a matter of personal preference. Some prefer to use the same wing feathers for the tail (see next entry), while others are adamant that the tail must be of squirrel. Those who fancy squirrel are divided again as to whether it should be black or grey. Most prefer black, and that is the dressing you will likely see in the commercially tied lures.

Keith Draper, on the other hand, is one of those who prefers the barred grey squirrel, and that's good enough for me.

It is difficult to form any view as to body colour because the body material is hidden by the wings when tied in the Killer style. John Veniard gives a dressing of yellow chenille and the old name of Mallard and Yellow. It is clearly the same fly which is described here and now called Mallard.

Tie in the tail. Tie in the body material.

Take the thread part way back along the shank. Wind on the chenille or wool to this point. Tie in a pair of wing feathers on either side of the shank.

Continue the thread and chenille or wool nearly to the head. Secure and trim the chenille or wool. Tie in another pair of wing feathers on either side of the shank to lie along the hook.

Finish the head and varnish.

MALLARD (2) (K)

ORIGIN: GEOFF SANDERSON OF TURANGI
HOOK: 2-8
TAIL: TWO GOOD GREY HACKLES LAID BACK TO BACK
BODY: CHENILLE OR WOOL, RED OR YELLOW
WING: THE GREY BREAST FEATHERS OF A MALLARD DRAKE
HEAD: BLACK

This is a variation of the standard Mallard (see previous entry) preferred by many in that the grey hackle tail gives a more or less uniformity of colour. The overall effect is of a lure which is sufficiently different in appearance from the standard pattern that separate inclusion seemed warranted.

Keith Draper notes yet another variation tied by a Mrs Val Galley who uses a cock pheasant tail which she calls a Grey Drake - which seems logical enough!

Tie in the hackles for the tail. Tie in the body material.

Take the thread back part way along the shank. Wind on the body material.Tie in a pair of mallard flank feathers on either side of the shank.

Take the thread back nearly to the head.

Wind on the body material to this point. Secure and trim.

Tie in another pair of mallard feathers on either side of the shank to lie flat along the body. Finish the head and varnish.

MALLARD and BLACK (P)

ORIGIN: EDDIE BOSOMWORTH OF ROTORUA
HOOK: 6-8
TAIL: GOLDEN PHEASANT TIPPETS OR BRIGHT ORANGE FIBRES
BODY: BLACK WOOL TEASED OUT TO LOOK A LITTLE ON THE SCRAGGY SIDE
RIB: OVAL SILVER
WING: SEVERAL GREY MALLARD FEATHERS LAID ON TOP AND TIED IN SO THAT THE EDGES PULL NICELY DOWN THE SIDE
HEAD: BLACK

"This fly is the creation of Eddie Bosomworth, the New Zealand champion flycaster. It is a night fly which fishes well on more moonlit nights: Bosomworth tells me it fishes well at the Rotorua stream mouths when used in conjunction with a floating line." - Keith Draper (1971)

This is listed in both of Keith Draper's books (1971 and 1997), as Mallard Black, but Eddie tells me the correct name is as I have given it. He says that this is a variation of an early 19th century Irish lure called Connamara Black, after Connamara County, and which is still popular today. He claims it is particularly deadly on brown trout near stream mouths.

Tie in the orange tips sparsely. Tie in the wool and ribbing. Secure and trim.

Wind on the wool and then overlay with the ribbing. Secure at the shoulder and trim.

Tie in the wing feathers at the butt in the Pukeko style so that the wing forms a low canopy over the top of the body and pulled down at the sides.

Finish the head and varnish.

MALLARD and CLARET (O)

ORIGIN:	NOT KNOWN
HOOK:	2-8
TAIL:	GOLDEN PHEASANT TIPPETS
BODY:	CLARET SEAL'S FUR OR CLARET CHENILLE
RIB:	GOLD OVAL TINSEL
WING:	BRONZE MALLARD
HACKLE:	CLARET, TIED UNDER THE THROAT ONLY, LIKE A BEARD
HEAD:	BLACK

In older publications you may see this called a Claret Mallard. For some reason this name has come to be preferred. It is an excellent night fly, and is one of the few older patterns to survive virtually unchanged.

Tie in the tippets for the tail. Tie in the body material and ribbing. Secure and trim.

Wind on the body material and ribbing to the head and tie off. Trim.

Tie in the hackle at the throat, under the hook shank. Keep the fibres short enough so that they do not wrap around the bend of the hook. Tie in a slip cut from the broad side of the feather and folded, or matched pairs of slips.

MALLARD HEN (K)

ORIGIN:	KEITH DRAPER OF TAUPO
HOOK:	2-8
TAIL:	TWO NICELY MARKED GRIZZLE HACKLES LAID OVER THE TOP OF TWO GINGER HACKLES. THIS GIVES THE TAIL A MOTTLED COLOUR IN KEEPING WITH THE SIDE FEATHERS
BODY:	YELLOW OR RED
RIB:	OVAL SILVER
WING:	BREAST FEATHERS FROM A MALLARD HEN
HEAD:	BLACK

"This is a little-known but very effective lure. It is tied in exactly the same manner as Sanderson's Mallard lure, except that the body feathers are those from a mallard hen. This fly has a colouration very close to the natural bully, and is a good fly for either lake or river fishing." - Keith Draper (1971).

This is also called Mother Duck (great name!) and is a lure which I find very appealing. This is an instance where the presence of a body is important as the colour clearly shows through the single wing feather on each side (see the chapter Tying Killer Lures).

Tie in the tail. Tie in the chenille using the colour of choice and the ribbing. Secure and trim.

Wind on the body material and follow with the ribbing.

Tie in a wing feather on either side of the shank to lie along the body. Secure and trim. Complete the head in the usual way.

MALLARD SMELT (O)

ORIGIN:	A.V. (BRUNO) KEMBALL OF HATEPE, LAKE TAUPO
HOOK:	6-10
TAIL:	A NARROW STRIP OF MALLARD DRAKE FLANK
BODY:	WHITE FLOSS
RIB:	SILVER
HACKLE:	WHITE (TIED SPARSELY)
HEAD:	BLACK

"The Mallard Smelt is an extremely effective fly and is tied with a variation of body colours, green being almost as popular as the white. If white nylon wool is used for dressing the hook, and red or green tying silk used, the colour shows through when the fly is wet; just as the colour of the plankton the smelt feed on shows through the thin walls of their stomachs." - Keith Draper (1971).

I have seen variations tied with a silver body and a green head, and variations with bodies of green, red, or grey are now popular.

Tie in the strip of mallard cut from the flank feather of a mallard drake.

Tie in the body material and the ribbing.

Wind on the body material followed by the ribbing. Tie in a hackle feather at the head and wind on sparsely.

MAORI ALL BLACK (H)

ORIGIN: MARU MANIOPOTU OF TE RANGIITA, LAKE TAUPO
HOOK: 2-8
TAIL: BUNCH OF BLACK MARABOU
BODY: BLACK CHENILLE
HACKLE: HONEY GRIZZLE WOUND PALMER-WISE ALONG THE BODY
HEAD: BLACK

This appeared in Nancy Tichborne's 1987 calendar. Maru noticed that trout fed on koura during the day at the mouths of rivers and streams entering Lake Taupo, particularly the Tauranga-Taupo. He tied up this lure to emulate the koura, basing it on a pattern he saw in an American magazine. Using a slow retrieve, the lure proved very effective as a day fly (despite its colour), especially bright sunny days, although it will take fish at night.

It is *almost* a Woolly Bugger, the only distinction being the omission of the Flashabou, and the Palmered hackle facing forward, which Maru believes gives more realistic movement on the retrieve. Maru also insists that the tail must be long - longer than for the Woolly Bugger, and at least two inches (50mm).

Part of the reason behind the name of this lure is Maru's view that no other colour variations are possible.

Tie in a good-sized bunch of marabou for the tail. Tie in the body chenille and the hackle feather by the tip, with the dull side of the feather facing forward towards the hook eye.

Wind on the chenille for the body.

Wind the hackle feather Palmer-wise forward along the shank to the eye. Form a small head and complete in the usual way.

MAORI CHIEF (O)

ORIGIN: NOT KNOWN
HOOK: 2-8
TAG: THE END OF A RED HEN'S NECK HACKLE
BODY: RED SILK OR MOHAIR
RIB: OVAL GOLD
WING: BUNCHED FIBRES FROM THE TAIL OF A COCK PHEASANT
HACKLE: RED COCK
HEAD: BLACK

"This is an old Taupo fly that has gone out of fashion. It was one of the transitory patterns that bridged the evolution between the salmon fly and the Taupo fly as we know it today." - Keith Draper (1971).

Tie in the tag. Tie in the body material and ribbing.

Wind on the body material followed by the ribbing. Secure and trim.

Tie in the pheasant tail fibres taking care to align the fibres in the same direction otherwise they will splay out in an unseemly mess. Tie in the hackle feather and wind on to form a hackle collar.

MARABOU KING (O)

ORIGIN: GEOFF SANDERSON OF TURANGI
HOOK: 2-8
TAIL: SHORT BLACK SQUIRREL
BODY: BLACK CHENILLE
RIB: GOLD DFM WOOL
THORAX: GINGER WISPS
HACKLE: BUNCH OF ORANGE MARABOU ON TOP, TIED IN AT THE HEAD, THEREFORE FORMING A WING ALSO
HEAD: BLACK

This highly effective lure is another Geoff Sanderson invention and is recorded in Tony Orman's book *The Sport in Fishing*, in which he obtained the favourite patterns of 13 experts, which Geoff Sanderson undoubtedly was. Sadly, he is now longer with us, and doubly sad because I have been unable to find anyone who has ever heard of "DFM" wool, far less describe it. Whether DFM wool has any particular property which makes anything else inappropriate I can not say, but I imagine any gold ribbing would suffice. For the photographed example I have used two strands of DMC embroidery yarn, shade 783.

Tie in the tail. Tie in the chenille and the ribbing. Secure and trim.

Wind on the chenille and ribbing to the head. Tie in a ginger hackle feather and wind on with one or two turns for a sparse hackle to emulate the thorax. (This is my interpretation of "thorax wisps".)

Tie in the bunch of marabou at the head on top of the shank so that it streams back to form a wing.

MARABOU KING VARIATION (O)

ORIGIN: ROB LIMMER OF TAURANGA
HOOK: 2-8
TAIL: BLACK SQUIRREL
BODY: YELLOW FLOSS OR FINE WOOL AND BLACK CHENILLE
WING: BUNCH OF ORANGE MARABOU WITH A FEW STRANDS OF ORANGE KRYSTAL FLASH OR SIMILAR
HACKLE: (OPTIONAL) BLACK
HEAD: BLACK

As a 17 year old teenager struggling to catch trout at the Waimarino Stream mouth (Taupo), Rob had the good fortune to receive sympathetic assistance from Geoff Sanderson who gave him a Marabou King to use. He then proceeded to catch seven trout with it before he lost it. Over the years, Rob played around with the original design, finally settling on this pattern.

This lure is extremely popular in the Rotorua region as a harling lure on No.2 hooks. Although not so well known in the smaller sizes, it does in fact fish particularly well at Lake Rotoma for the shore-based angler after fish cruising the shallows with spawning in mind, and over drop-offs with a sinking line. Rob has also had success at Lake Otamangakau, especially when the large orange dragonflies are hovering over the surface.

Tie in the tail. Tie in both body colours.

Wind on the black chenille to the head and stripe over with the yellow floss or wool.

Tie in a few strands of orange Krystal Flash and then a bunch of marabou on top. Tie in a hackle collar if using.

MARABOU KOURA (P)

ORIGIN: MAUREEN BUTLER OF ROTORUA
HOOK: 2-8
TAIL: FIBRES FROM A MALLARD DRAKE BREAST FEATHER
BODY: FLAT OR OVAL SILVER BRAID
THROAT: RED WOOL, TEASED OUT
UNDERWING: A FEW HERLS OF BLACK, WHITE, ORANGE, AND OLIVE MARABOU
OVERWING: MALLARD BREAST FEATHER TIED PUKEKO STYLE AND LIGHTLY COATED WITH CLEAR LACQUER TO STIFFEN
HEAD: BLACK

This is a Koura pattern, with the marabou representing legs. It is bottom fished, preferably on sandy margins. The lure is retrieved by giving a couple of twitches and then letting it sink before repeating. Locally, this is known as "scratching". It has proved very successfull at Lake Rotoiti in particular, but elsewhere as well.

Tie in the mallard fibres for the tail. Tie in the silver braid for the body.

Wind on the silver body and tie off. Tie in the wool at the throat.

Tie in the small bunches of marabou for the underwing. Tie in two mallard breast feathers in the Pukeko style for the overwing. Form the head in the usual way.

MATUKU (M)

ORIGIN: NOT KNOWN
HOOK: 2-8
BODY: WOOL OR CHENILLE, COLOUR TO LIKING
RIB: OVAL TINSEL
WING: TWO SOFT HEN PHEASANT FLANK FEATHERS TIED IN BACK TO BACK AND SECURED TO THE BODY BY TINSEL RIBBING TAKEN THROUGH THE WINGS
HEAD: BLACK

"Matuku" is the Maori name for the bittern, the feathers of which were used in the original tie, particularly the yellowy breast feathers and the pale cream under-rump feathers. The bittern is now totally protected and use of its plumage is illegal.

"Reluctant to lose these wonderful flies, anglers found a substitute in the soft flank feathers of a hen pheasant. Since they were used as a substitute for the Matuku, any fly tied with them in this manner is now called a Matuku. They are good flies and have stood me in good stead over the years... I would think that the two favoured colours would be yellow and orange although they are tied in many colours. For some reason the Matuku is not used by many anglers these days." Keith Draper (1971).

The word "Matuku" is now more applied to the method of tying, rather than the fly itself. That method was unique to New Zealand, but was quickly adopted overseas, particularly in Australia, England, and America where a transliteration of the Maori Matuku has universally become "matuka".

According to John Veniard, jungle cock feathers are sometimes added, and "matukas" (ie. any Matuku style lure) tied with this addition are known as "Imperials".

Tie in the body material and ribbing. Return the thread and body material back nearly to the head. Tie in the wing feathers.

Wind on the ribbing, tying down the wing to the top of the body.

Finish the head and varnish.

MATUKU MUDDLER (O)

ORIGIN:	HUGH MCDOWELL OF ROTORUA
HOOK:	2-6, LONG SHANK IN THE SMALLER SIZES
TAIL:	RED OR ORANGE FEATHER FIBRES
BODY:	YELLOW CHENILLE
RIB:	OVAL GOLD OR SILVER
WING:	HONEY GRIZZLE OR CREE
HEAD:	DEER HAIR (RED OR WHITETAIL). SPINNING DEER HAIR REQUIRES VERY STRONG THREAD. USE KEVLAR WHICH IS EXCEPTIONALLY STRONG. IT WILL CUT YOUR FINGER BEFORE IT BREAKS

Basically, this is a Parsons' Glory with a Muddler Minnow head. While the Parsons' Glory base has been used here, in fact any Matuku pattern can be used, although Hugh has found the Parsons' Glory version to be the most effective.

The deer hair is very buoyant and if fished deep, it requires a very fast sinking line to drag it down. Hugh also fishes it on a floating line, across and down, for big browns at dusk. With floatant applied, smaller sizes can be cast upstream as a dry fly during summer when cicadas are about.

Hugh's best experiences have been with the lure tied on a No. 2 where he felt it had just the right colours and proportions, although the example photographed is on a No. 4, and Hugh has added some optional Flashabou. Hugh cautions that "some of the takes I have had with the Matuku Muddler have been among the most violent and savage I have ever experienced...so I don't mess around with dainty 6 or 7 lb. tippets any more!"

Tie up a Parsons' Glory or any other Matuku pattern but finish it two thirds of the way up the hook shank. In his fly-tying book, Hugh included a hackle collar, but dispensed with it in his article on the same fly in Fish & Game New Zealand, *Issue 13, 1996. It has been omitted here, also.*

Cut a bunch of deer hair about halfway down to the base. Hold the deer hair along the top of the bare shank. Tie one turn of Kevlar around the middle of the bunch and pull down. The hair will spin around the shank, flaring out. Take successive turns pulling tighter each time.

Push the bunch away from the eye (I use an empty ball-point barrel) and repeat the process until the shank is covered. Tie off, then shape head with scissors.

MELLOW YELLOW (M)

ORIGIN:	JOHN MORTON OF CHRISTCHURCH
HOOK:	2
TAIL:	PEARL KRYSTAL FLASH
BODY:	YELLOW CHENILLE
RIB:	SILVER TINSEL (FLAT OR OVAL)
WING:	ONE PAIR OF GIZZLE HACKLES FLANKED BY TWO PAIRS OF DYED YELLOW HACKLES, ALL FACING BACK TO BACK.
CHEEKS:	ONE PAIR OF MALLARD FLANK FEATHERS DYED YELLOW.
HACKLE:	SOFT GRIZZLE, BEARDED STYLE.
TOPPING:	PEACOCK SWORD
HEAD:	BLACK

This was designed for the very murky waters of Lake Forsythe in Canterbury, and has also proved itself in the tannin coloured lakes such as Lake Mapourika. It can be fished on either a long trace on a floating line in shallow weedy lake edges or deeply on a medium or slow sinking line. A fast sinking line would be useful if harling. Retrieve in short quick jerks to imitate the frightened darting action of a whitebait.

Tie in the tail, chenille, and ribbing.

Wind on the chenille and tie off. Tie in a pair of grizzle feathers.

Take two pairs of dyed yellow hackle feathers, each pair being back to back. Tie in each pair, one on either side of the grizzle feathers.

Wind on the ribbing, tying down the wing in the Matuku style. Tie in the cheek feathers on either side of the head.

Tie in a beard hackle under the throat. Tie in the peacock sword topping. Finish the head and varnish.

MICHELLE'S MAGIC (H)

ORIGIN: MICHELLE BATSON OF WELLINGTON

HOOK: 6-8

TAIL: BLACK SQUIRREL

BODY: REAR TWO-THIRDS: BROWN CHENILLE; FRONT THIRD: OLIVE CHENILLE

WING: BLACK HACKLE COLLAR AT HEAD

HEAD: BLACK

This featured in the 1991 Tichborne calendar and subsequent book. It is a very good lake fly having proved itself on Lakes Aniwhenua and Waikaremoana, to name but two. It is fished in a similar manner to (and has the general colouring of) La Giaconda.

It is not really suitable as a harling or fast river fly, being best tied in the smaller sizes and fished deep and quickly over weed beds and shallow margins or on the edge of rips.

Tie in the squirrel tail and the first section of chenille.

Return the thread two-thirds the way along the shank. Wind on the brown chenille to this point and tie off. Tie in the olive chenille.

Continue the thread back nearly to the head. Wind on the olive chenille to this point and tie off. Tie in a black hackle feather and wind on to form a hackle collar.

MIDNIGHT (M)

ORIGIN: NOT KNOWN

HOOK: NOT STATED BUT PROBABLY 2-8

TAIL: RED WHISKS

BODY: RED CHENILLE

RIB: OVAL GOLD

WING: FURNACE (NOT TOO LONG)

HACKLE: BLACK

HEAD: BLACK

This is a Canterbury pattern which can be found in Robert Bragg's *New Zealand Fishing Flies*. I have not come across it anywhere else.

The name should probably not be taken literally but as indication that this is a night lure. It should be remembered that in some parts of New Zealand (I believe only in the North Island) trout fishing is not permitted after midnight (until 5.00 am).

I read somewhere of an overseas angler enquiring why it was that fishing was not permitted beyond midnight. The answer he received was that "around here, if we didn't have to stop at midnight, every married man in town would be divorced!"

Tie in the tail whisks. Tie in the chenille and ribbing.

Wind on the chenille body and tie off. Tie in the wing feathers by the butts.

Wind on the ribbing, tying down the wing in the Matuku style.

Tie in a hackle feather and wind on to form a hackle collar.

MISSIONARY (O)

ORIGIN: CAPT. J. J. DUNN OF ENGLAND

HOOK: 4-8

TAIL: WHITE COCK FIBRES

BODY: WHITE WOOL OR CHENILLE

RIB: OVAL SILVER

WING: STRIPS OF TURKEY TAIL CHEEKED WITH DARK TEAL ON THE OUTSIDE

HACKLE: WHITE, ORANGE, OR RED GAME HACKLE, BEARDED STYLE

HEAD: BLACK

This appeared in a small publication called *58 NZ Lure Patterns* (see my comments under Furnace Smelt). In the absence of teal plumage, and for New Zealand waters, I would be inclined to use mallard feathers rather than the more recognised substitute of dark mottled breast feathers from a male paradise duck.

A long time ago a Mr C.G. Heywood used this lure with an orange hackle on the Tongariro River. He took seven trout averaging 12lbs, the two largest each weighing 16lbs.

The official dressing given also appears in A. Courtney Williams *A Dictionary of Trout Flies.*

I have seen another dressing which uses scarlet dyed cock hackles for the tail and head hackle, and whole mallard breast feathers for the wing, tied Pukeko style.

When tied with the turkey tail dressing (as illustrated),

the wing should sweep back well beyond the bend.

Tie in the tail whisks, chenille, and ribbing. Secure and trim.

Take the thread back nearly to the head. Wind on the chenille and ribbing and tie off. Tie in the strips of turkey wing.

Tie in the teal cheeks. Tie in the hackle feather at the throat, beard style.

MIZOOLIAN SPOOK (O)

ORIGIN: NOT KNOWN
HOOK: 2-6, LONG SHANK
TAIL: SCARLET IBIS OR LIGHT BROWN TURKEY
BUTT: RED CHENILLE
BODY: WHITE CHENILLE
RIB: FLAT SILVER TINSEL
WING: GREY SQUIRREL TAIL TOPPED WITH LIGHT BROWN TURKEY
HACKLE: BROWN DEER HAIR, SPUN
HEAD: FLARED DEER HAIR, SPUN AND CLIPPED TO SHAPE
THREAD: SPINNING DEER HAIR ONTO THE SHANK REQUIRES VERY STRONG THREAD. USE KEVLAR OR SIMILAR

This is a variation of the famous Muddler Minnow, although in choosing which version of the Muddler to follow I have gone for the original one (see Muddler Minnow). The Spook version appeared in Tony Orman's book *The Sport in Fishing*. The dressing there called for a wing of brown impala hair but I have been unable to obtain that anywhere.

Start the thread one third the way down the shank. Tie in the ibis whisks. Tie in the red chenille and take one or two turns to create the butt. Tie off and tie in the white chenille and ribbing.

Take the thread, chenille and ribbing back two-thirds along the shank. Tie in the underwing of squirrel tail and then the turkey wing at the butt only.

Take a bunch of deer hair and place it along the bare shank. Take one turn with the Kevlar and pull. This will cause the deer hair to flare around the shank. Push the flared ball of hair back towards the wing. This will form the hackle.

Repeat the deer hair spinning process progressively towards the head until the shank is full. Tie off. Trim the head to shape with sharp pointed scissors.

MOHAKA No.1 (O)

ORIGIN: BARRY KENT OF TE PUKE
HOOK: 4-8
TAIL: BLACK SQUIRREL WITH 2 STRIPS OF GOLD FLASHABOU OR SIMILAR
TAG: RED MARABOU
BODY: BLACK CHENILLE
RIB: FLAT GOLD
HACKLE: BLACK COCK HACKLE WOUND PALMERWISE ALONG THE SHANK AND ALSO AS A HACKLE COLLAR AT THE HEAD
WING: TUFT OF RED MARABOU
HEAD: BLACK

Most lures are tied up to represent or mimic food forms of one type or another which trout feed on, be they nymphs, smelt, whitebait, snails, koura, cock-a-bullies, or any of a multitude of creatures which swim in, on, or fall into, the water. Others, of course, bear no known resemblance whatever to anything edible, relying on the trout's inherent trait of snapping at anything which has glint, glitter, flash, movement or colour.

In this instance, however, the lure has been created to emulate a black and gold Toby spinner which has proved very effective on the Mohaka River in Hawkes Bay. Curiously (given its colouring), this lure is an excellent day fly.

Tie in one strand of gold Flashabou. Tie in the red tag on top. Next, tie in the squirrel tail and the second strand of Flashabou on top. Secure and trim.

Tie in the chenille, ribbing, and a hackle feather by the tip.

Wind on the chenille. Secure and trim. Palmer the hackle along the body (spiral the feather up to the head). Wind on the ribbing.

Tie in the tuft of red marabou at the shoulder.

MOHAKA SPECIAL (H)

ORIGIN: BARRY KENT OF TE PUKE
HOOK: 4-8
TAIL: BLACK MARABOU WITH 2 STRANDS OF GOLD FLASHABOU OR SIMILAR
TAG: RED MARABOU
BODY: GOLD ICE-CHENILLE
HACKLE: BLACK
HEAD: BLACK

This evolved at the same time as the Mohaka No.1 with the same colours but handled in a different way to give the fly more dash. It has proved to be a very effective bright day, clear water, fly - not just on the Mohaka River but (as I have found), on other rivers also.

Tie in, first, one strand of gold Flashabou. Tie in the red tag on top. Then tie in the marabou tail. Finally, tie in the second strand of gold Flashabou on top of the tail.

Tie in the ice-chenille. Take the thread part way back along the shank. Follow with the chenille to that point. Tie in a hackle feather.

Wind on the hackle, tying it down so that it slopes nicely backwards at about 45 degrees.

Continue the thread and chenille back nearly to the head. Tie in another hackle feather and wind on. Finish the head and varnish.

MOLINEAUX'S SILVERY (M)

ORIGIN: PAUL MOLINEAUX OF CHRISTCHURCH
HOOK: NOT STATED BUT PROBABLY 2-8
BODY: WHITE
RIB: OVAL SILVER
WING: GREY COCK HACKLE
CHEEK: A SMALL STRIP OF LIGHT BLUE WOOL, TEASED OUT, OR SUITABLY DYED HACKLES
HACKLE: GREY
HEAD: BROWN

This, plus one of indeterminate dressing, appears in Bragg's book. Apparently created in 1962, Molineaux regarded both as two of the best for the Rakaia River.

I cannot be absolutely certain about some aspects of the pattern or its dressing, but tied as shown here gives a very close imitation.

Tie in the body material and ribbing.

Wind on the body material to the head. Tie in the wing feathers.

Wind on the ribbing, tying down the wing in the Matuku style.

Tie in the light blue 'laterals' on either side. Tie in a hackle feather and wind on to form a hackle collar.

MONSUM'S BULLY (O)

ORIGIN: MONTY WRIGHT OF DUNEDIN
HOOK: 10-16, BUT I WOULD HAVE NO HESITATION IN TYING THIS UP IN LARGER SIZES
WEIGHT: A SMALL AMOUNT OF LEAD
TAIL: SOFT GREY MARABOU CUT SQUARE
BODY: BUNCHES OF POSSUM FUR IN ALTERNATING COLOURS, LAID ON USING A WAXED THREAD, THEN TRIMMED TO SHAPE

Every winter the storage water at Lake Hawea is drawn off to augment the flows from Lakes Wanaka and Wakatipu for electricity generation. The lake edge bullies lose their home and sit out in the open where they are easy prey for brown trout that have returned from spawning.

On one such winter's day, Monty had been fishing the lake edge with his version of Casual Dress designed for that purpose and was not having any luck. While he was observing the movement of bullies he noticed that because they had to sit out in the open they had taken on a very mottled appearance. Later that same day, while taking the boat out of the water, he found a dead possum beside the ramp. He cut off some of the fur and, while his friends commiserated at the pub, tied up three lures, ending with the version shown here. The fishing next day was spectacularly successful, landing 22 trout. This lure is now used in all the lakes and dams wherever there is some rock shelving. While Monty prefers possum fur, he acknowledges that any fur would probably do the job. That would also extend, I suggest, to include synthetic craft fur as in, for example, Paddle Tail. 'Monsum' is an amalgamation of Monty and possum.

Tie in the marabou tail and trim square to produce a fan-shaped tail.

Lay small bunches of fur onto waxed thread and wind on to form the body. Use alternating colours - light, dark, and in-between.

Trim to shape as you do with deer's hair, with the head being larger than the rear.

MOONSHINE (M)

ORIGIN: NOT KNOWN
HOOK: 2-8
TAG: BRIGHT RED WOOL WITH STRANDS OF PEACOCK SWORD
BODY: FLAT SILVER TINSEL
RIB: OVAL SILVER
WING: BLACK SADDLE HACKLE
HACKLE: SOFT BLACK HEN HACKLE
TOPPING: PEACOCK SWORD TAIL THREE-QUARTERS THE

	LENGTH OF THE TAIL
HEAD:	BLACK

This was an early pattern put out by Kilwell's of Rotorua. It is visually similar to the old English lure called Butcher, and is not too far removed from a Black Prince or Devil Dodger. It is a night fly, and the name suggests that it performs best on moonlit nights.

Over time, the peacock sword tended to be omitted, and the example on display in the Kilwell museum is without it.

Tie in the red tag. Tie in the body tinsel and ribbing. Trim.

Wind on the silver tinsel for the body and tie off. Tie in the wing hackle feather.

Wind on the ribbing, tying the wing down in the Matuku style. Tie in the hackle collar feather.

Wind on the hackle collar. Add peacock sword if using.

MORTON'S SMELT (M)

ORIGIN:	JOHN MORTON OF CHRISTCHURCH
HOOK:	10, LONG SHANK
BODY:	PEARSALLS GREEN FLOSS SILK
RIB:	SILVER MYLAR TINSEL
WING:	BLUE DUN
HEAD:	BLACK

Although a Morton's Smelt featured in the 1986 Tichborne calendar, it bears little resemblance to the latest model to bear the name. Originally, the wing was Cree feathers photo dyed using the same chemicals and methods that you would use to develop a black and white film. The example shown here was done in that original manner but the home tier will probably prefer to use blue dun. The wing should be one third longer than the hook for proportion.

As might be expected from someone of John's calibre and expertise, here is an effective and proven smelt pattern.

Tie in the floss and the tinsel.

Wind on the floss silk body and tie off. Tie in two pairs of wing feathers, two on each side, with the concave sides facing inwards.

Wind on the ribbing, tying down the wing in the Matuku style.

MOTHER SUPERIOR (M)

ORIGIN:	NOT KNOWN, BUT BELIEVED TO BE GEOFF SANDERSON OF TURANGI
HOOK:	2-8
BODY:	ORANGE CHENILLE
RIB:	OVAL GOLD OR SILVER TINSEL
WING:	WHITE RABBIT FUR
HACKLE:	HONEY OR WHITE HACKLE
HEAD:	BLACK

Among the 13 experts who supplied their favourite patterns to Tony Orman for his book *The Sport in Fishing*, this one came from Pedro Burney who rated the Mother Superior as his favourite lure, which is recommendation enough for anyone! He first came across it in Jack Neill's tackle store at Motuoapa, Taupo, but was unable to ascertain its origin although it is believed to have come from Geoff Sanderson.

The colouring suggests it is a smelt fly.

Tie in the chenille and ribbing.

Wind on the chenille to the head. Tie in the strip of rabbit fur.

Wind on the ribbing, tying down the rabbit strip in the Matuku style. Secure and trim. Tie in a hackle feather and wind on with just a few turns to effect a sparse hackle collar.

MR SIMPSON (K)

ORIGIN:	PAT SWIFT OF ROTORUA
HOOK:	4-10
TAIL:	BLACK SQUIRREL TAIL
WING:	GREY PARTRIDGE DYED GREEN, OVERLAID WITH PHEASANT RUMP FEATHERS
HEAD:	BLACK

This is a clever combination of Hamill's Killer and Mrs Simpson. Both are such renowned fish takers that it will come as no surprise to learn that this marriage of the two is every bit as effective as the individual components.

Pat Swift is one of a growing number of tiers who omit the body from Killer patterns (see the chapter Tying Killer Lures and The South Island Way).

Two feathers are tied in on either side of the shank at each stage.

In the photo example the partridge feathers have been dyed a shade of green which is very close to the original Hamill's Killer. You can buy mallard plumage dyed a shade of green which comes close, or you could use mallard feathers which are an olive colour and sold as Hamill's Killer feathers.

Tie in the squirrel tail. Take the thread to the mid-point of the shank.

Tie in the partridge feathers in the Killer style. Take the thread back nearly to the head.

Tie in the pheasant rump feathers in the Killer style. Complete the head in the usual way.

MRS SIMPSON (K)

ORIGIN:	NOT KNOWN
HOOK:	2-8
TAIL:	BLACK SQUIRREL TAIL
BODY:	YELLOW OR RED WOOL OR CHENILLE
WING:	THE GREENY SHORT RUMP FEATHERS OF A COCK PHEASANT
HEAD:	BLACK

This is one of the most effective and best-known lures in New Zealand. It can probably claim more "origins" than any other fly and the truth will forever be shrouded in mystery. If the original dressing was ever pheasant rump (as claimed by Hugh McDowell, but about which there has been some dispute) then certainly it was the greenish fringed feathers. Today it is not uncommon to see it tied with the chocolate and cream "church-window" feathers found higher up the back. Either way it is a superb fly for both day and night fishing.

Variations abound. One, using a gold bead head and a black tail of different fur from the squirrel, rejoices under the unlikely name of National Bank. Another differs only in that the tail is also of pheasant rump, and plays on the name of Bart Simpson. In reality, it is a remake of the Awahou Special, and I had to break the news to the 'creator' that he was at least 25 years too late. I have not thought them sufficiently innovative to warrant separate inclusion.

Tie in the tail. Tie in the chenille, conventionally yellow for day, red for night, although green has been used.

Take the thread and chenille part way back along the shank.

Tie in a pair of wing feathers on either side of the shank in the Killer style.

Continue the thread and chenille nearly to the head. Tie in a further pair of feathers on either side of the shank. The feathers do not tie in easily, and you may need more than two per side, and I sometimes find it easier to use a judicious dab of cement to hold things in place. Finish the head and varnish.

MUDDLER MINNOW (O)

ORIGIN:	THE ORIGINAL MUDDLER WAS CREATED BY AN AMERICAN, DON GAPEN, OF MINNESOTA, IN THE 1950's
HOOK:	2-6, LONG SHANK
TAIL:	MOTTLED TURKEY FEATHER
BODY:	GOLD DIAMOND BRAID OR FLAT GOLD TINSEL
WINGS:	GREY SQUIRREL TAIL TOPPED WITH MOTTLED TURKEY
HACKLE:	BROWN DEER HAIR
HEAD:	FLARED DEER HAIR, CLIPPED TO SHAPE. USE VERY STRONG THREAD SUCH AS KEVLAR

It has been said that this is possibly the single most effective lure ever created, and if one was ever limited to just one lure then this would be first choice. There are many variations. O.S. ('Budge') Hintz, in *Fisherman's Paradise*, describes the wing as containing a small bunch of reddish-brown calf hair, with a smaller bunch of white calf hair on top and brown mottled turkey over that. The pattern which appeared in Tony Orman's book *The Sport in Fishing* called for light brown turkey and brown impala hair instead of grey squirrel. The body was of thin gold tinsel. That pattern was the favourite of Jim Ring of Nelson who rated the Muddler as his most successful lure. The text records: "It has proved exceptional at Taupo and elsewhere and doubles as a good cicada dry fly pattern. Variations can be done to suit availability of materials. I have used brown or dark brown opossum fur instead of the impala hair." I have yet to locate impala hair. It probably imitates a cock-a-bully or tadpole which, at night, can be taken by big trout. Fished dry during summer it is probably taken for a cicada.

Use very strong thread and start one third of the way along the shank (from the eye). Tie in the tail. Tie in the body tinsel.

Take the thread and tinsel back to the starting point. Tie in the squirrel underwing, followed by the turkey wing on top.

Take a bunch of deer hair and place it along the bare shank. Take one turn with the thread and pull down so that the deer hair flares. Take further turns, pulling harder each time. Push the ball of hair away from the eye and repeat the process until the shank is full. Clip to shape with sharp scissors.

MURPHY (O)

ORIGIN: I BELIEVE THIS CAN BE ASCRIBED TO JOHN WADHAM OF ENGLAND
HOOK: PROBABLY 6-10, LONG SHANK
TAIL: ORANGE MARABOU
BODY: ORANGE CHENILLE
WING: SEVERAL BUNCHES OF ORANGE MARABOU, DEPENDING ON HOOK SIZE
HEAD: BLACK

This appeared in the 1988 Tichborne calendar, and subsequent book *Anglers' Paradise*. In reality, it seems to be to be an orange Poodle. I have seen this tied up in every colour imaginable, and sporting a variety of names. Since the advent of marabou, this has become a very popular style of lure, and with good reason, but I believe they should all be regarded as Poodles, whatever the colour (see Poodle).

Tie in a bunch of marabou for the tail. Tie in the chenille.

Take the thread part way along the shank. Wind on the chenille to this point and secure. Tie in another bunch of marabou on top of the shank.

Repeat the procedure until the hook is full, leaving room for the head. Complete the head in the usual way.

MUSKRAT (1) (M)

ORIGIN: GRAEME HUGHES OF KUROW
HOOK: 2-4
TAIL: BROWN SQUIRREL TO MATCH HACKLE, MIXED WITH A FEW FIBRES OF CLARET OR RED DYED FEATHER
BODY: CLARET SEAL'S FUR TIED HEAVY RATHER THAN SLIM
RIB: OVAL GOLD (3 TURNS)
WING: A NARROW STRIP OF MUSKRAT
HACKLE: GRIZZLE
HEAD: BLACK

This is fished slow and deep on a sinking line, or on a floating line at night in shallow water around lake margins. Graeme finds it effective while harling with Muskrat tied on a short dropper about 600mm above a spinbait or wobbler.

The muskrat strip should be nicely tapered at each end, with plenty of long guard hairs to give movement. The strip should not be too long or the end will foul to the hook (not usually a problem when harling).

When Muskrat was conceived, Graeme had in mind the Upland Bully (Gobiomorphus Greviceps) hence the deep, slow fishing, but he is unsure what the trout in fact perceive it to be. When it catches trout, who cares!

Tie in the tail. Trim. Tie in the ribbing.

Dub on the seal's fur body up to the head.

Tie in the strip of muskrat. Wind on the ribbing, tying down the fur strip in the Matuku style.

Tie in the hackle feather and wind on (Graeme suggests several turns for bulk). Tie off and form the head in the usual way.

MUSKRAT (2) (M)

ORIGIN: ROB LIMMER OF TAURANGA
HOOK: 6-10
TAIL: RED KRYSTAL FLASH OVERLAID WITH BLACK MARABOU
BODY: ORANGE MICRO-ULTRA CHENILLE
RIB: FINE RED COPPER WIRE
WING: MUSKRAT STRIP
HACKLE: BLACK
HEAD: BLACK

This has been a spectacularly successful creation for Rob, fished anywhere, but particularly at Lakes Rerewhakaaitu, Aniwhenua, and Tarawera. It will take rainbows and browns alike, but it is especially deadly on browns when fished with a floating line over weed beds around lake margins.

Colour variations include red, yellow, claret wine, purple, fluro lime, and caddis green bodies, and also black with a purple hackle. The orange-bodied version will fish from late afternoon through until midnight, especially on moonlit nights.

Tie in the strands of Krystal Flash. Tie in an overlay of marabou.

Tie in the chenille and ribbing. Wind on the chenille to the head and tie off. Tie in the muskrat strip.

Wind on the ribbing, tying down the fur in the Matuku style.

Tie in a hackle feather. Wind on to form a hackle collar.

NAILER (O)

ORIGIN: R. NAYLOR OF TAUPO
HOOK: 2-8
TAIL: GOLDEN PHEASANT TIPPETS
TAG: SILVER
BODY: CHENILLE IN FOUR SEGMENTS OF ALTERNATE BLACK AND YELLOW
WING: TURKEY
HACKLE: BLACK COCK
CHEEKS: THE LESSER COVETS OF A HEN PHEASANT WING
HEAD: BLACK

"I believe that this fly should really be called the Naylor after its inventor Mr R. Naylor, who was an angler on the Taupo scene for many years. After he had tied the original it was lost in the jaws of a trout which was caught several days later by another angler. The fly was sent to Kelly's in Rotorua and appears in one of their old pattern sheets. This fly is not to be found in the shops today, but I include its dressing because of its historical significance". - Keith Draper (1971).

For the same reason, I include it also.

Tie in the tag, tippets, and the first segment of chenille. Secure and trim.

Take the thread part way along the shank. Wind on the chenille to this point and tie off. Tie in the next segment of chenille. Continue the process with each segment of chenille almost to the head.

Tie in the turkey wing at the butt. Tie in the cheeks on either side of the shank. Tie in a hackle feather.

Wind on the hackle to form a collar. Finish the head in the usual way and varnish.

NIGHT-TIME (K)

ORIGIN: NOT KNOWN
HOOK: NOT STATED BUT PROBABLY 2-8
TAIL: BROWN SQUIRREL
BODY: NOT KNOWN, POSSIBLY RED
WING: GUINEA FOWL DYED GREEN
HEAD: BLACK

A photo of this lure appears in Bragg's book but no other details are recorded. It is not possible to determine the body colour but the name gives a clue. Obviously, it is a night fly and I would guess that the body colour (if it has a body at all) is either black, red, or - given the colour of the wings - green. I have chosen red wool for the above example.

Tie in the squirrel tail. Tie in the body material.

Take the thread part way back along the shank, or all the way depending on hook and feather size. The wing shown in Bragg's book appears to be tied in at the head only, as I have done.

Tie in the wing feathers in the Killer style. Complete the head in the usual way.

NORTHERN RABBIT (M)

ORIGIN: BARRY BIRCHALL OF KAIKOHE
HOOK: 2-8
TAG: RED HACKLE FIBRES
BODY: ORANGE CHENILLE
RIB: OVAL SILVER
WING: STRIP OF NATURAL BLACK RABBIT
HACKLE: RED
TOPPING: 2-3 STRANDS EACH OF PEARL FLASHABOU AND YELLOW KRYSTAL FLASH TIED EITHER SIDE OF THE WING
HEAD: BLACK

This is Barry's favourite rabbit pattern which he fishes regularly in the Northern streams. It has also been successful in the Taupo and Rotorua regions. In particular, it fishes well in slightly discoloured waters (some of the Northland streams are 'tea' coloured) and as rivers are clearing after rain.

Natural black rabbit fur is really dark tipped grey or blue/grey fur. It fishes better during the day than dyed black rabbit fur.

Barry says that this lure is a good imitation of the dark bullies found in many of the Northland streams and rivers. In the above example, Barry has added his trademark 'eyes'.

Tie in the tail whisks, chenille, and ribbing.

Wind on the chenille body. Tie in the rabbit strip.

Wind on the ribbing, tying down the rabbit strip in the Matuku style.

Tie in the topping and a hackle feather. Wind on the hackle to form a collar.

O'KEEFE'S KILLER (K)

ORIGIN: PAT O'KEEFE OF ROTORUA
HOOK: 6-8
TAIL: BLACK SQUIRREL
WING: SECONDARY FEATHERS FROM A JUNGLE COCK CAPE
HEAD: BLACK

This is a very effective fly for night or day fishing. Pat has enjoyed a lot of success with it on the Rotorua lakes. Pat has employed the technique of omitting a body in the tying of this Killer style lure, (see the chapter Tying Killer Lures and The South Island Way).

Not all Jungle Cock capes offered for sale have the secondary feathers attached. You may have to hunt around a bit, but it is possible you could purchase the secondaries without incurring the horrible cost of taking the Jungle Cock 'eyes' as well.

Tie in the squirrel tail.

Tie in the secondary feathers at the head in the Killer style. Overlay the wing with the yellow strip which is also found amongst the secondaries. Complete the head in the usual way.

O'KEEFE'S SMELT (O)

ORIGIN: PAT O'KEEFE OF ROTORUA
HOOK: 6-8
TAIL: SMALL BUNCH OF NATURAL RABBIT
BODY: DUBBED NATURAL RABBIT
OVERBODY: 3 MM STRIP OF MOTHER-OF-PEARL AURORA SKIRT
HACKLE: NATURAL RABBIT
HEAD: BLACK

Pat has had a lot of success with this pattern, particularly in the weedy margins around lake edges. It is fished on a slow to intermediate sinking line or a floating line with a sink tip. Pat's method is to give three or four quick retrieves and then pause before repeating.

The Aurora skirt is not the strips of luminous material with which most will be familiar. The material used in this pattern comes in sheet form in a variety of lustrous colours, none of them, to my knowledge, being luminous.

Tie in a small tuft of rabbit fur for the tail. Take a strip of Aurora skirt. Snip the corners off one end of the strip. Lay this part over the first half of the tail and tie in at the bend.

The balance of the Aurora strip (which will extend beyond the hook eye) is pulled up and retained out of the way. Dub on a body of rabbit fur.

Pull the Aurora strip over the rabbit body and tie off at the head. Tie in a small bunch of rabbit fur at the head to wrap around the shank like a hackle collar. Complete the head in the usual way.

OLD JACK (M)

ORIGIN: JACK MCNEILL OF CHRISTCHURCH
HOOK: NOT STATED BUT PROBABLY 2-8
TAIL: RED WHISKS
BODY: BLACK
RIB: OVAL SILVER
WING: FURNACE
TOPPING: TURKEY STRIPS
HACKLE: PROBABLY FURNACE, THROAT ONLY
HEAD: BLACK

This was created in 1950 and is another example of a Canterbury high country lure which comes from Bob Bragg's book. I know nothing else about it.

Tie in the tail whisks. Tie in the body material and ribbing.

Wind on the body material. Tie in the wing feathers by the butts.

Wind on the ribbing, tying down the wing in the Matuku style.

Tie in the throat hackle. Tie in the turkey strips (i.e. without quill) as a wing topping. Complete the head in the usual way.

OLD NICK No.1 (O)

ORIGIN: NOT KNOWN
HOOK: 6-8
TAIL: GOLDEN PHEASANT TIPPETS
BODY: DARK CLARET MOHAIR OR SEAL'S FUR
RIB: OVAL GOLD TINSEL
WING: BLACK-BROWN BARRED SKUNK OR SQUIRREL TAIL FIBRES

HACKLE: RED GAME COCK

CHEEK: JUNGLE COCK
HEAD: BLACK

This pattern appears in John Veniard's book. It is in the same mould as Demon Squirrel and Squirrel Nutkin without the same degree of slimness. There is no reason why it should not be effective.

Tie in the tippets, body material, and ribbing.

Wind on the body material, then follow with the ribbing. Tie off and trim. Tie in the hair wing at the shoulder. Saturate the area tied with cement to stop the fibres pulling out.

Add the Jungle Cock cheeks. Tie in the hackle feather and wind on to form a hackle collar.

OLD NICK No.2 (O)

ORIGIN: NOT KNOWN
HOOK: NOT STATED BUT PROBABLY 6-10
TAIL: IBIS OR SUBSTITUTE
BODY: RED WOOL
RIB: OVAL GOLD TINSEL
WING: UNDER: RED GOOSE OR IBIS
OVER: SPECKLED PARTRIDGE TAIL
HACKLE: MEDIUM RED
HEAD: BLACK

This also is from John Veniard's book. The same comments made with reference to Old Nick No.1 can be made here. Obviously, both flies have long since disappeared from the scene, and I have never come across any other reference to them. That does not mean that they were ineffective flies. Their inclusion in John Veniard's book suggests they enjoyed a degree of popularity once.

The example has been tied on a No.10 hook. The length of the partridge tail fibres determines the length of the hook when not using the split tail method

Tie in the tail, body material, and ribbing.

Wind on the wool for the body, followed by the ribbing.

Tie in the underwing of goose or ibis at the shoulder. Tie in the speckled partridge tail over the top of the underwing, tying it in at the butt. Tie in a hackle feather and wind on.

OLIVE SMELT (M)

ORIGIN: NOT KNOWN
HOOK: 4-8
BODY: OLIVE WOOL, TIED SLIM
RIB: OVAL GOLD
WING: SLIM COCK HACKLES DYED OLIVE
HACKLE: OLIVE
HEAD: BLACK

This appears in Keith Draper's 1997 book. It is described as a great smelting pattern whether fished on the cast or trolled. A variation has a flat gold tinsel body for added dash (see Bruno Kemball's dressing, Appendix 3).

Tie in the wool and the ribbing.

Wind on the wool body. Tie in the wing feathers by the butts.

Wind on the ribbing, tying down the wing in the Matuku style.

Tie in a hackle feather. and wind on to form a hackle collar.

O'NEIL'S SPECIAL (M)

ORIGIN: NOT KNOWN
HOOK: NOT STATED BUT PROBABLY 2-8
BODY: WHITE CHENILLE
RIB: OVAL SILVER
WING: INNER: BARRED ROCK
OUTER: BUFF *CAUGHT* FLAT TINSEL
HACKLE: BUFF
HEAD: BLACK

This appears in Bragg's book as a listed pattern but with no other commentary or photo. I have assumed a black head otherwise the pattern is as set out in Bragg's book. The photo example is my interpretation of that pattern. See Pulley Lure.

Tie in the chenille and the ribbing.

Wind on the chenille to the head. Tie in the wing feathers by the butts.

Wind on the ribbing, tying down the wing in the Matuku style.

Tie in a hackle feather and wind on to form a hackle collar.

OPOSSUM LURE (M)

ORIGIN: NOT KNOWN

HOOK: 2-8
WHISKS: RED (DYED)
BODY: YELLOW CHENILLE
RIB: OVAL SILVER
WING: A STRIP OF YELLOW OPOSSUM BELLY WITH FUR ATTACHED
HEAD: BLACK

This is not a fly you are likely to come across anymore, but this used to have its devotees. It was popular on Lake Tarawera, especially at the outlets. It is claimed to be extremely effective tied up in the very small sizes. The words 'opossum' and 'possum' are interchangeable and refer, in the context of this book, to the Australian phalanger known as the Brushtail (o)possum or Trichosurus Vulpecula, which was introduced to New Zealand. It is the only species to be found in New Zealand, whereas Australia has 28 species. None of them are to be confused with the American opossum which is very different although faintly from the same family. It is only the American species which 'play possum'. Unfortunately, American opossum is not available here. The sight of its fur is enough to make the pulse quicken.

The lure depicted here is essentially a Rabbit but with possum fur, and in that regard it is very similar to Urchin.

Tie in the red hackle whisks and the chenille and ribbing.

Wind on the chenille and tie off. Tie in the strip of possum fur.

Wind on the ribbing, tying down the fur strip in the Matuku style.

ORANGE HAWK (M)

ORIGIN: NOT KNOWN
HOOK: NOT STATED, BUT PROBABLY 2-8
BODY: ORANGE CHENILLE
RIB: OVAL SILVER TINSEL
WING: TWO CREAM WITH BROWN CENTRE HEN HAWK LEG HACKLES, BACK TO BACK, AND TIED ON "MATUKA" STYLE
HEAD: BLACK

This comes from John Veniard's book, hence the mis-spelt "Matuka".

This differs from Hawk in that the gingery flank feathers give way to the cream and brown feathers found further down the body. The best examples are to be found on older female hawks. In reality, this is an orange-bodied version of Willy's Wonder - or perhaps the other way around. Just how the distinction came about, and which came first, is not known.

Hawks are protected birds. See my comment under Hawk as to the use of these feathers. A possible substitute would be hen badger feathers.

Tie in the chenille and ribbing.

Wind on the chenille and tie off. Tie in the wing feathers.

Wind on the ribbing, tying down the wing feathers in the Matuku style.

ORANGE LONGTAIL (M)

ORIGIN: PROBABLY KEITH DRAPER OF TAUPO
HOOK: 2-8
BODY: HOT ORANGE CHENILLE
RIB: OVAL GOLD
WING: ORANGE COCK
HACKLE: ORANGE
HEAD: BLACK

This comes from Keith Draper's 1997 book. Although he describes it there as an Australian pattern ("longtail" is an Australian term), it transpires that it is identical to a pattern which Keith and a friend devised many years ago. The angling friend had noticed that in places where ornamental carp abound, the trout seemed to take a particular liking to the small golden variety which made up a small percentage of the total carp population.

The lure was a success although it became forgotten over the years until the sight of the Australian lure brought the memories back. While it is still likely to succeed in carp-filled dams and lakes (Lake Aniwhenua would be a good choice), it may also work in the manner of Orange Roughie.

Tie in the chenille and ribbing.

Take the thread and chenille back nearly to the head. Tie in the wing feathers by the butts.

Wind on the ribbing, tying down the wing in the Matuku style.

Tie in a hackle feather. Wind on to form a hackle collar.

Complete the head in the usual way.

ORANGE RABBIT (M)

ORIGIN: GEOFF OF ORUATUA, LAKE TAUPO
HOOK: NOT STATED BUT PROBABLY 2-8
TAIL: YELLOW WHISKS
BODY: CHENILLE IN TWO PARTS - REAR: ORANGE; FRONT: YELLOW
RIB: OVAL GOLD
WING: STRIP OF NATURAL BROWN RABBIT
HACKLE: WHITE
HEAD: BLACK

This is featured in the Tichborne calendar of 1987. The commentary, by Bryan Tichborne, records that it should be retrieved slowly, with the occasional quick movement. It is not easy to discern from Nancy Tichborne's painting what the exact colour of the head hackle is (being printed against a white background). It seems to me to be white but it could be light grey or some other pale colour.

Geoff was a very reticent fellow who shunned any form of publicity, and "Geoff of Oruatua" was as much information as the Tichborne's could get from him. He died many years ago.

Tie in the tail. Tie in the first section of chenille, and the ribbing.

Take the chenille part way back along the shank. Tie off. Tie in the second section of chenille.

Take the chenille back nearly to the head. Tie in a strip of rabbit fur.

Wind on the ribbing, tying down the rabbit strip to the top of the body. Tie in a hackle feather and wind on the hackle collar.

ORANGE ROUGHIE (M)

ORIGIN: RITCHIE BUCHANAN OF TAUPO
HOOK: 2-8
TAIL: RED WHISKS
BODY: ORANGE AND BLACK CHENILLE
RIB: OVAL SILVER
WING: ORANGE COCK HACKLES
HEAD: BLACK

Ritchie, a professional guide, created this lure in 1990 and it has been a consistent performer for him and his clients ever since. He acknowledges that the colouring is deliberately representative of fish roe and irresistible during spawning. It is a top performer in river mouths and in deep pools of major rivers, and best from April through to August, which, of course, covers the spawning season.

Tie in the tail whisks. Tie in the two chenille colours and ribbing.

Wind on the chenilles, twisted to give a harlequin or variegated effect, and secure. Tie in the wing feathers.

Wind on the ribbing, tying down the wing to the top of the body.

ORANGE WITCH (K)

ORIGIN: PETER LAING OF CHRISTCHURCH
HOOK: 4-8
TAIL: BLACK SQUIRREL
BODY: ORANGE CHENILLE
WING: BARRED FLANKS FROM CHUKOR
HEAD: BLACK

This is an attractive, albeit unusual-coloured, fly. It does not represent any form of aquatic life known to me, but it can attract trout as Keith Draper recounts: "... this fly is effective in the early part of the season but for some reason it loses its appeal after Christmas. It is an early morning or night fly. In 1966 one Ellesmere angler took 49 trout in six trips. He fished with two flies, one always a Witch, and used about 20 other patterns for the second fly, alternating tail or dropper. The Witch accounted for 48 of the trout taken" (1997).

The plumage is readily available from tackle shops, where it is likely to be sold as French Partridge.

Although a pair of feathers could be tied in at the mid-point in the usual Killer style, I believe that it is more commonly tied with two pairs of feathers on either side of the shank at the head only, and that is how I have tied the example. It might be worth trying a single feather tied each side at the head as this allows the body colour to show through.

Tie in the tail. Tie in the chenille.

Wind on the chenille body and tie off.

Tie in a pair of feathers on each side of the shank in the Killer style.

ORBIT (M)

ORIGIN: WILFRED BEAUMONT-ORR
HOOK: 2-8
BODY: GREEN WOOL, FUR, OR CHENILLE
RIB: OVAL GOLD
WING: GRIZZLE HACKLE DYED GREEN
HACKLE: GRIZZLE HACKLE DYED GREEN
HEAD: BLACK.

"This fly was the design of the late Wilfred Beaumont-Orr, a fly-tier and tackle retailer who operated in Taupo before the Second World War. The name of the fly is a play on the surname of the originator.

The Green Orbit is a good fly, especially at night, but in the smaller sizes it will often kill well during daylight hours. In the summer you will often find fish with a fair amount of green weed in their stomachs and some anglers claim that this is why the trout prefer the Orbit. I have yet to be fully convinced as I have yet to see a piece of weed swimming upstream against the current, but there can be no denying it is a good fly.

The dyeing of the grizzle feathers often covers a wide range of tints from deep emerald green to a lime-hued colour, but whatever the shade of green they are still an Orbit.

Not so well known as the Green Orbit but equally as effective are the Red Orbit and the Yellow. They are tied with grizzle feathers dyed to the correct colour, the body material being the same colour as the feather.

The Yellow Orbit is an excellent trolling fly and the red is favoured by some anglers as a night fly. I have noticed some Orange Orbits in one or two tackle shops but I think this is a later development. No doubt colour changes could be made until every shade of the rainbow was employed." -Keith Draper (1971).

Commercially tied stock I have come across have red whisks at the tail, and silver ribbing, neither of which conforms to the original pattern. There is a modern trend, particularly by commercial tiers, to add little extras, and the red whisks might be seen as an available option.

Tie in the body material and ribbing.

Wind on body material nearly to the head. Tie in the wing.

Wind on the ribbing, tying down the wing to the top of the body. Tie in a hackle feather and wind on.

ORSIM (M)

ORIGIN: PAT SWIFT OF ROTORUA
HOOK: 4-10
TAG: RED HACKLE FIBRES
BODY: OLIVE DUBBING
RIB: FINE OVAL GOLD
WING: 4 OLIVE GRIZZLE COCK FEATHERS
CHEEK: PHEASANT RUMP FEATHERS
HEAD: BLACK

This is part green Orbit and part Mrs Simpson, thus giving rise to the clever name which, phonetically, also describes this lure's effectiveness.

It is fished conventionally, but it is probably best around weed beds, close to the bottom on a sinking line.

Tie in the tail fibres and the ribbing.

Dub on an olive body by whatever method you prefer. Tie in the wing feathers at the head.

Wind on the ribbing, tying down the wing to the top of the body.

Tie in the pheasant rump cheeks on either side of the shank.

PADDLE TAIL (O)

ORIGIN: GARTH COGHILL OF ROTORUA
HOOK: 4-8 STRAIGHT-EYED, MODIFIED
TAIL: FOUR MATCHED HEN HACKLES (COLOUR TO SUIT) TIED BACK TO BACK EXTENDING A MINIMUM OF ONE SHANK LENGTH BEYOND THE BEND
BODY: ACRYLIC CRAFT FUR OF DESIRED COLOUR, DUBBED
EYES: 4MM MOTHER OF PEARL OR CLEAR 'PEARLS-BY-THE- YARD'
DUBBING LOOP: LIGHT COLOURED KEVLAR

This is yet another work of art from the vice of this very skilled and creative fly-tier. It is most effective fished deep and slow, with frequent pauses. Realistic barred or mottled bodies can be made by arranging very short lengths of different coloured fur strips within the dubbing loop.

Perhaps the best way to create the eyes is to buy 'pearls-by-the-yard' which are continuously connected somewhat like a necklace. Snip off a connected pair and file the outer facing surfaces flat. Stick or paint on 'eyes' to each filed surface.

The hook is modified by bending a small upward curve (approximately 15 degrees) at a point one-third of the shank length from the eye . Take great care and wear safety glasses. Test the hook for damage by 'twanging' it in the vice. A dull sound with no ring indicates damage.

Take the thread down to the hook bend. Tie in the tail. Secure a 150mm (approx.) long kevlar dubbing loop at the bend just ahead of the tail. Wind a tight foundation of tying thread forward to just behind the eye and then return to the new upward bend.

Tie in the eyes with a figure of eight tie over a dot of 5-minute Araldite or epoxy. Wind the thread forward to just behind the hook eye, whip finish, and cut free. Coat the eyes and tie-in point with clear Araldite or similar and set aside for 2 hours to harden.

Replace hook in vice and restart tying thread just behind hook eye. Cut a strip of acrylic fur along the lie of the fur. The strip should be 6-8 mm wide by 100-150mm long for a No.6 hook. Position the fur strip inside the dubbing loop. Use a 'Y' shaped dubbing whirl to secure the fur in the loop. Cut off the 'skin' backing. Twist the loop while applying downward tension until the fur fibres are tightly twisted inside the loop, rather like a dense oversized dubbing brush.

The body is tightly wound with this 'brush' with each turn tightly packed against the previous turn. As each turn is made, carefully pull back the fur fibres so they don't get trapped by the next turn. Make sure the fur is densely packed around and between the eyes.

Tie off just behind the hook eye and seal. Keep the tie-off point as small as possible.

Trim to desired shape with sharp scissors in much the same way as with Muddler-style deer hair heads.

PALAMINO (O)

ORIGIN: RON DOUGLAS OF TAUPO
HOOK: 2-8
TAG: RED EGG (GLO-BUG) YARN
BODY: YELLOW CHENILLE
THROAT: OVAL SILVER
WING: STRIP OF WHITE RABBIT
HEAD: RED

This is a successful smelt pattern which evolved as a response to another commercial pattern sold in the Taupo region called Black Beauty. In reality, and quite unwittingly, Ron has come up with a yellow bodied Streamer version of Les's Fancy which just goes to demonstrate that the only thing new in fly-tying is the materials.

It is principally a summer morning daytime fly, tied mainly for river fishing.

Tie in the tag. Tie in the chenille.

Wind on the chenille, stopping short to allow the ribbed throat.

Tie in the silver ribbing and wind on several close turns to form the throat.

Tie in a strip of rabbit fur at the head. Complete the head in the usual way.

PARADISE KILLER (K)

ORIGIN: HERB SPANNAGL OF NEW PLYMOUTH
HOOK: 6-8
TAIL: SQUIRREL OR DARK CAT
WING: THREE PAIRS OF LAYERED BODY FEATHERS FROM A PARADISE DUCK
HACKLE: BUNCH OF DARK RABBIT FUR
HEAD: BLACK

This featured in the 1988 Tichborne calendar. The version shown here uses the brown body feathers of the female Paradise duck. The same feathers from the drake will produce a darker fly.

The fur head suggests the gills and dorsal fins of the small native Kokopu, but would no doubt be taken for any kind of bully anywhere.

This is another example of a Killer style pattern which omits the body (see Tying Killer Lures and The South Island Way).

It is a lake fly which should be fished deep with a variable retrieve.

Tie in a generous bunch of fur for the tail. Take the thread about one-third of the way along the shank.

Tie in a pair of matching body feathers on either side of the shank. Wind the thread forward a bit.

Tie in another pair of feathers on either side of the shank.

Repeat with another set of wing feathers.

Take a bunch of rabbit fur and place it on the hook shank with the tips extending 10-15mm forward of the eye.

Place a loose turn of thread around the fur and tighten slowly to drag the fur around the shank like a hackle. Fold tips back along the body and tie off. Form a head in the usual way.

PARADISE WRIGGLER (M)

ORIGIN:	NOT KNOWN, BUT ADAPTED BY ROB LIMMER OF TAURANGA
HOOK:	6-10, BUT IT CAN BE TIED UP IN LARGER SIZES FOR HARLING
TAIL:	RED KRYSTAL FLASH OVERLAID WITH OLIVE MARABOU
BODY:	OLIVE
RIB:	OVAL SILVER TINSEL
WING:	STRIP OF OLIVE RABBIT FUR
HACKLE:	GRIZZLE
HEAD:	BLACK

Rob first came across this in Auckland at a time when he was employed by Tightlines. He was asked to tie up a few which he did after slimming down the body and adding the marabou tail. He also tied up a version with a fluorescent fire orange body. It is fished in exactly the same way as Rob's Muskrat (2). The olive bodied version is equally effective on brown and rainbow trout, while the fire orange body attracts mainly rainbows. Rob's preference is for a wing of medium to light olive, and tied on a No. 8 hook. It has proved very productive in murky, even dirty, water.

Tie in the strands of Krystal Flash and a small bunch of marabou. Tie in the ribbing and body material.

Wind on the body material and tie off. Tie on a short strip of rabbit fur.

Wind on the ribbing, tying down the wing to the top of the back.

Tie in a grizzle hackle and wind on to form a sparse collar.

PARSONS' GLORY (M)
(Old Tie)

ORIGIN:	PHIL PARSONS OF NAPIER
HOOK:	2-10
TAIL:	GOLDEN PHEASANT TIPPETS
BODY:	YELLOW MOHAIR
RIB:	GOLD TINSEL
WING:	4 HONEY GRIZZLE COCK FEATHERS
TOPPING:	GOLDEN PHEASANT CREST
HACKLE:	HONEY GRIZZLE, BEARD STYLE
CHEEK:	JUNGLE COCK
HEAD:	BLACK

This was created in 1924 and named in 1929 when it became a commercial reality.

Such is the heritage of this lure in New Zealand's angling history it seemed only right that it should grace the cover of this book. The changes which have led to the modern dressing were dictated by economic and commercial considerations. The essential character and quality of the lure has, however, remained undiminished. While it may not be the biggest selling fly in New Zealand, it is certainly the most enduring and best known of all New Zealand lures.

Tie in the golden pheasant tippets. Tie in the mohair and the ribbing.

Wind on the mohair body. Tie in the wing feathers.

Wind on the ribbing, tying down the wing to the top of the body.Tie in the beard hackle fibres. Tie in the pheasant crest topping. Add Jungle Cock cheeks.

PARSONS' GLORY (M)
(Modern Tie)

ORIGIN:	PHIL PARSONS OF NAPIER
HOOK:	2-10
TAIL:	RED OR ORANGE WHISKS
BODY:	YELLOW CHENILLE OR WOOL
RIB:	OVAL GOLD BUT SILVER IS COMMONLY PREFERRED
WING:	HONEY GRIZZLE NECK HACKLE
HACKLE:	HONEY GRIZZLE NECK HACKLES
HEAD:	BLACK

This fly was the brainchild of Phil Parsons who farmed at Meeanee near Napier. You will often see it called Parson's Glory, but the creator's name dictates that the correct spelling is Parsons' Glory. The dressing has undergone a number of changes over time, although the home tier might well wish to retain the Jungle Cock cheeks. Even with the modern dressing it is as Hugh McDowell puts it: "...still a masterpiece in skilfully blended shades of buff, ginger, yellow and gold."

Keith Draper's classic description should be immortalised: "... I think that as long as trout swim in New Zealand his memory will be perpetuated by this fly. It is the golden fly, both in colour and quality, and there can be no doubt that it is the most favoured of all lures for daylight fishing."(1971). Keith goes on to claim that it is deadliest when tied on the smaller sizes, even as small as No. 10.

This fly continues to remain an enduring legend among the aristocracy of New Zealand trout lures.

Tie in the tail whisks. Tie in the chenille and ribbing.

Wind on the chenille nearly to the head. Tie in the wing feathers.

Wind on the ribbing, tying down the wing to the top of the body. Tie in the hackle feather and wind on to form a hackle collar

PARSONS' GLORY VARIATION (M)

ORIGIN: BARRY BIRCHALL OF KAIKOHE

HOOK: 2-8

TAIL: ORANGE HACKLE TOPPED WITH A LITTLE RED MARABOU

BODY: YELLOW CHENILLE

RIB: OVAL SILVER

WING: BROWN MARABOU

OVERWING: A FEW STRANDS OF GREEN FLASHABOU AND KRYSTAL FLASH

HACKLE: ORANGE

HEAD: BLACK

Nancy Tichborne took a liking to this fly for inclusion in her calendar. It had no name at the time, and I believe it was Nancy who dubbed it Parsons' Glory Variation on the spot. While the logic is faintly discernible, it is really quite distinct from Parsons' Glory and probably deserves a better name.

The process of binding the marabou wing to the body creates an effect which is not unlike that of hackle feathers, as can be seen from the photograph.

While it may be inherently different from a Parsons' Glory, it is fished in exactly the same way. Over the years, Barry has had a lot of success with it.

Tie in the tail fibres and marabou topping. Tie in the chenille and ribbing.

Wind on the chenille and tie off. Tie in the marabou wing.

Wind on the ribbing, tying down the marabou to the top of the body. Tie in the hackle feather and wind on.

PARSONS' SUNSET (M)

ORIGIN: HUGH MCDOWELL OF ROTORUA

HOOK: 6

TAIL: ORANGE WHISKS

BODY: DUBBED SEAL'S FUR OR SUBSTITUTE, YELLOW AT REAR, ORANGE AT FRONT.

RIB: OVAL GOLD

WING: THIN "DRY FLY" HONEY GRIZZLE WITH A FEW STRANDS OF GOLD FLASHABOU

HACKLE: NATURAL RED COCK

CHEEK: JUNGLE COCK

HEAD: BLACK

Hugh was tying up an order for Hughie's Mallard, making up the dubbed bodies first, and then adding the hackle and wing after. However, he ran out of bronze mallard feathers before he could complete the order and he put the unfinished flies away in a box. Some time later, while tying up some Parsons' Glories, he came across the unfinished flies and, on impulse, added honey grizzle wings. Flashabou had just arrived on the scene (this was in late 1970's or early 1980's), so Hugh added some strands of that and completed the lure with Jungle Cock cheeks. It was an instant success, and caught 18 trout on its first outing!

Subsequently, Hugh changed to the 'skinny' wing version, and now never uses any other fly when harling. "Curiously", he says, "I have never had much luck with it as a casting fly though, for reasons best known to the trout."

Because it incorporated the sunset colours of yellow and orange with feathers used for Parsons' Glory, he thought Parsons' Sunset seemed appropriate and so that is what it became.

Tie in the tail whisks, and ribbing.

Dub on the yellow section of the body to the mid-point. Repeat for the orange section of the body.

Tie in the long thin wings. Wind on the ribbing, tying down the wings to the top of the body.

Add a few strands of gold Flashabou. Tie in a hackle feather

and wind on. Add Jungle Cock cheeks and complete the head in the usual way.

PEPPERMINT TWIST (O)

ORIGIN: MAUREEN BUTLER OF ROTORUA
HOOK: 4-8
TAIL: DEEP PINK WOOL
BODY: WHITE RABBIT WOOL (3-PLY SPLIT TO 2- PLY), TEASED OR BRUSHED
RIB: THIN STRIPS OF ADHESIVE-BACKED SILVER PRISM TAPE
WING: WHITE FUR (NOT RABBIT)
TOPPING: PINK PART OF MULTI-COLOURED FLASH SKIRT (FOUND WITH SEA LURES) OR FLASHABOU
HACKLE: PINK HACKLE FIBRES UNDER THE THROAT, BEARD STYLE
HEAD: BLACK

This is a smelt pattern which has proved very successful at river mouths and on the Tongariro River at times of changing light. It is fished conventionally on a sinking line.

Maureen insists that rabbit fur is not suitable for the wing. The material needs to be fairly stiff so that it holds its shape and angle. In the example photographed, polar bear fur has been used, but white arctic fox could be a useful substitute.

Rabbit wool was, and may still be, available from knitting and craft shops. Any white furry wool such as mohair could be used, or even dubbed rabbit fur.

Tie in the wool tail. Tie in the body material and the ribbing.

Wind on the body material and follow with the ribbing. Tie off.

Tie in the throat hackle. Tie in a bunch of fur for the wing then tie in the topping.

PETERKEN'S POACHER (O)

ORIGIN: SYD PETERKEN OF WAIPUKURAU
HOOK: 4-8
TAIL: POLAR BEAR FUR OR OTHER LIGHTISH HAIR
TAG: A FEW FIBRES OF RED IBIS OR SIMILAR OVERLAID ON THE TAIL
BODY: PALEST WATERY GREEN
RIB: ABOUT FOUR TURNS OF SILVER TINSEL
WING: POLAR BEAR HAIR CUT FROM SKIN, WITH UNDER-FUR REMOVED. TIE THIS AROUND THE SHANK AT THE HEAD AND FIX TEMPORARILY WITH TWO HALF HITCHES. TAKE A BLACK AND WHITE FEATHER FROM AN AMHERST PHEASANT, CUT OFF ABOUT 15 FIBRES AND OVERLAY THESE ON THE BEAR HAIR. TIE IN AND WHIP FINISH.
HEAD: BLACK

This appeared in Tony Orman's book *The Sport in Fishing*. The general effect when finished and held up against the light should be one of transparency. The fly was invented by Syd, but named by some anglers who tried it. In Syd's words: "It was evolved after a lot of thought for the Tauranga-Taupo River. I tried to achieve several things, movement, transparency, water tint and a bully-like appearance in the water. A few years ago, I asked Tom Ward of Waipukurau, to try it out at Taupo. It was miles ahead of any other fly used and Tom has used it since with consistent success."

Sadly, Syd has been dead long since. I was once privileged to meet this redoubtable angler at his home where he tied up for me a nymph which he called Peterken's Red which unfortunately I no longer possess courtesy of a burglar.

A common substitute for polar bear fur is white calf hair although polar bear fur has been used in the example photographed.

Depending on the material used, this could be regarded as a Bucktail or Hair Fly version.

Tie in the tail and tag. Tie in the body material and rib.

Take the thread, body material, and rib back nearly to the head. Tie in the hair wing and the feather overlay (substitute if necessary). Finish the head and varnish.

PETERKEN'S POSSUM (O)

ORIGIN: SYD PETERKEN OF WAIPUKURAU
HOOK: 4-8
TAIL: RUSSIAN SQUIRREL OR SUBSTITUTE
TAG: A FEW STRANDS OF RED IBIS OR SIMILAR FEATHER, OVERLAID ON TOP OF THE SQUIRREL
BODY: RED, GREEN, YELLOW, OR GOLD WOOL OR CHENILLE
RIB: A FEW TURNS OF SILVER TINSEL
WING: DYED POSSUM FUR, USUALLY GREEN. CUT THE REQUIRED AMOUNT OF FUR FROM THE SKIN, HOLD TIGHTLY BETWEEN FINGER AND THUMB AND REMOVE SURPLUS SHORT UNDER-FUR. LAY THE BALANCE COMPLETELY AROUND THE

	SHANK AND TIE IN. A RED OR GOLD TOPPING MAY BE ADDED IF DESIRED. DO NOT OVERDO THE VOLUME OF FUR USED. TRY TO ACHIEVE A REASONABLE AMOUNT OF TRANSPARENCY AND 'MOVEMENT' IN THE FLY.
HEAD:	BLACK

Another pattern from one of 13 experts who submitted their favourite patterns in Tony Orman's book, and another by renowned Hawkes Bay trout fisherman, the late Syd Peterken. It has proved itself on the Tongariro and Hawkes Bay rivers, and at one stage the green version upstaged Hamill's Killer. Syd advises the fly "requires a winter skin with fur of good length; thoroughly washed in a detergent, and dyed a dark green with a Veniard's dye. The volume of dye needed is far in excess of that which you would need for feathers and the dyeing period is much longer in order to achieve the depth required."

Tie in the tail and whisks in the usual way. Add in the chenille and ribbing.

Return the thread, chenille, and ribbing back nearly to the head.

Tie in the possum fur at the shoulder, wrapping it completely around the shank. Finish the head and varnish.

PHANTOM BURGLAR (O)

ORIGIN:	GEORGE GATCHELL OF HAVELOCK, MARLBOROUGH SOUNDS
HOOK:	4-6
TAG:	RED WOOL, DOUBLED OVER FOR THICKNESS AND WELL TEASED
TAIL:	SQUIRREL TAIL OR 2-4 HACKLE FEATHERS IN PAIRS
BODY:	FUR, USUALLY POSSUM BUT ALSO RABBIT, TIED IN BUNCHES PROGRESSIVELY ALONG THE SHANK
TOPPING:	BLUE PUKEKO FEATHERS
CHEEKS:	(OPTIONAL) JUNGLE COCK EYES
HEAD:	BLACK

In the course of gathering material for this book, I was privileged to meet George who accorded me the honour of demonstrating the tying of this fly, and explained the rationale behind the Pukeko topping. Possum fur, like rabbit fur, flares and pulses in the water in an enticing manner. Possum fur is 'springier' than rabbit fur and does not close up like rabbit fur. This is not a problem in faster waters, but George found that in calmer water the fur tended to stay puffed out, giving a rather bulky appearance. While it still caught trout, George conceived the idea of topping the Burglar with Pukeko in a manner not unlike Black Phantom - hence the name. However, the Pukeko feathers are not tied in at the sides, Killer style, and they are not tied in on top Pukeko style. They are tied somewhere in between. Then George ties a final pair on top Pukeko style, somewhat like the capping ridge on a roof. The end result is a conventional Burglar with a canopy over the top which stops the fur puffing out. Scraggy bits of fur protrude from the underside of the body representing legs, and giving movement. George claims that this is an absolutely deadly night fly.

Tie up a Burglar in the conventional way - the basic pattern never varies. Don't complete the head at this stage.

Tie in a pair of blue Pukeko feathers (or dyed Mallard substitute) to lie alongside the body on either side, sloping at an angle out towards the side.

Tie in a pair of Pukeko feathers on top so that the upper part of the body is encased in a cocoon.

Tie in Jungle Cock eyes if using. Finish the head and varnish.

PINK AND GREY (H)

ORIGIN:	HERB SPANNAGL OF NEW PLYMOUTH
HOOK:	6-8 MEDIUM, 8-10 LONG SHANK
TAIL:	BUNCH OF LONG, SOFT GREY HACKLE FIBRES
BODY:	PINK SPARKLE CHENILLE
HACKLE:	SOFT, GREY HACKLE, PALMERED
HEAD:	BLACK

In the same manner as Herb's Starling, Herb has employed the Palmered hackle technique to create the attractor pattern with smelt grey trimmings.

It is a good daytime fly for spawning run rainbows in fast water.

Crushing the hackle feathers by rolling the body between the fingers will get the hackles lying back nicely.

Tie in the tail. Tie in a hackle feather at the bend by the butt, making sure that several fibres are tied in to supplement the tail.

Tie in the chenille. Take the thread back nearly to the head. Wind on the chenille to this point and tie off.

Palmer the hackle forward to the eye. Give a few additional turns to bulk up near the head. Complete the head in the usual way.

PINK DAWN (M)

ORIGIN: RON DOUGLAS OF TAUPO
HOOK: 4-8
TAIL: BLACK HACKLE FIBRES
BODY: GREY CHENILLE
RIB: OVAL SILVER
WING: PINK HACKLE FEATHERS
HACKLE: LIGHT GREY
HEAD: BLACK

This was tied up one early morning to match the pink colourful sunrise through breaking grey clouds. It was immediately successful. It is fished on a sinking line with a slow retrieve. Ron also created Grey Dawn, which reverses the colouring. It has a pink chenille body and grey wings. Both versions are sold commercially, with Grey Dawn proving more popular than its pink counterpart. Pink sunrises are less common than grey mornings, but the notion of sky colouring affecting trout preferences is an interesting one.

I know of one angler who matches the body colour to the seasonal foliage - light green for spring (cf. Kakahi Queen), dark green for summer, orange and yellow for autumn, and drab colours for winter. It is common to prefer yellow for bright sunny days, and red for dull days and change of light. Perhaps it is not silly to consider the effect of sunrises and sunsets. It has certainly worked for Ron, and his lures sell well.

Tie in the tail fibres. Tie in the chenille and ribbing.

Wind on the chenille body and tie off. Tie in the wing feathers.

Wind on the ribbing, tying down the wings in the Matuku style. Tie in a hackle feather and wind on.

PINK LADY (H)

ORIGIN: GEOFF OF ORUATUA, LAKE TAUPO (SEE MY COMMENTS UNDER ORANGE RABBIT)
HOOK: NOT STATED BUT PROBABLY 6-10
TAIL: WHITE WHISKS
BODY: FLUORESCENT PINK CHENILLE
HACKLE: WHITE
HEAD: BLACK

This appeared in the Tichborne calendar of 1987. It is identical to Disco Doll if Disco Doll is tied using the alternative tail dressing given for that pattern.

Tie in the tail hackle fibres and the first section of chenille.

Take the thread part way back along the shank. Wind on the chenille to this point and tie off. Tie in a hackle feather and wind on. Tie in the second section of chenille.

Wind on the chenille to the head and tie off. Tie in a hackle feather.

Wind on the hackle feather to form a collar.

PLUTO (M) & (K)

ORIGIN: GARTH COGHILL OF ROTORUA
HOOK: 6-8
BODY: REAR TWO-THIRDS: DOUBLE WOUND FLAT SILVER MYLAR TINSEL, SIZE 10
RIB: REAR TWO-THIRDS: OVAL SILVER
REAR WING/TAIL: TWO MATCHING PAIRS OF MALE PARADISE DUCK BODY CONTOUR FEATHERS TIED IN PLACE, BACK TO BACK, MATUKU STYLE, AND EXTENDING A MINIMUM OF HALF THE SHANK LENGTH BEYOND THE BEND.
VEILING: TWO MATCHING PAIRS OF MALE PARADISE DUCK BODY CONTOUR FEATHERS TIED IN PLACE EITHER SIDE OF THE REAR WING KILLER STYLE TO COVER THE HOOK BEND AND BLEND WITH THE REAR WING.
SIDE WING: MATCHING PAIRS OF MALE PARADISE DUCK BREAST FEATHERS TIED KILLER STYLE TO OVERLAP THE VEILING FEATHERS. TIE IN MATCHING PAIRS ALONG THE SHANK FINISHING AT THE HEAD. EACH PAIR SHOULD SLIGHTLY OVERLAP THE PREVIOUS PAIR, BLENDING IN, AND GET PROGRESSIVELY SMALLER AS YOU WORK TOWARDS THE HEAD. AS MANY AS 8 PAIRS MAY BE NECESSARY TO BUILD UP A PLUMP BODY
CHEEK: JUNGLE COCK (OPTIONAL)
HEAD: BLACK

This is a superb example of Garth's exquisite fly-tying skills, which are internationally renowned. Those familiar with the Pluto depicted in Nancy Tichborne's 1986 calendar will notice that it has undergone minor surgery to remove the squirrel tail. It fishes well at all times but Garth claims that it is at its best in changes of light, fished slowly around lake margins and inshore weed beds. He has found that a take can be 'induced' by allowing the fly to sink to the lake floor. A sudden fast twitch to lift the fly from the bottom, sending up a small cloud of disturbed sand, etc., will attract trout. Pause a moment before knitting the retrieve. This trick works well at stream mouths where there is little weed.

Tie in the mylar and ribbing. Return the thread two-thirds the way back along the shank. Wind on the mylar to this point and tie off.

Tie in two pairs of feathers. Wind on the ribbing, tying down the feathers to the top of the shank in the Matuku style. Trim.

At the same point, tie in two pairs of feathers, one pair on either side of the shank in the Killer style.

Continue tying in matching pairs of breast feathers in the Killer style, inching forward (towards the eye), a millimetre or so at a time until the head is reached. Form the head in the usual way.

POLECAT SMELT (M)

ORIGIN: DEREK QUILLIAM OF CLIVE
HOOK: 6-12
TAIL: GOLDEN PHEASANT TIPPETS
RIB: OVAL SILVER
BODY: BLUE PEARL MIRROR FLASH
WING: STRIP OF WHITE POLECAT
HACKLE: DARK RED
HEAD: BLACK

Seen underwater, the predominant feature of smelt is the thin black backbone seen through a virtually transparent body. For that reason, I like to use polecat fur which has long dark guardhairs. Polecat fur has more mobility than rabbit or possum fur, and this pattern is very effective as a smelt imitation, and also when whitebait are running in early summer, particularly in the smaller sizes.

The Golden Pheasant Tippets are probably not the least bit necessary, but I had included them when I first devised this pattern and as it was so successful I was loathe to change a winning team. Mirror Flash is now sold as Angel Hair.

The example has been tied on a number 8 hook.

Take the thread down to the bend. Tie in the Golden Pheasant Tippets and the ribbing.

Dub on the mirror flash body. Tie in the strip of polecat fur.

Wind on the ribbing, tying down the fur wing to the top of the body in the Matuku style.

Tie in the hackle feather. Wind on to form a hackle collar. Complete the head in the usual way.

POODLE (O)

ORIGIN: JOHN WADHAM OF ENGLAND
HOOK: 6-10, LONG SHANK
TAIL: BLACK MARABOU
BODY: BLACK CHENILLE
WING: THREE OR FOUR BUNCHES OF BLACK MARABOU, DEPENDING ON THE SIZE OF HOOK USED
HEAD: BLACK

Although originating in England, I have seen this commercially available in New Zealand. It can be tied up in a variety of colours, with olive seeming to win the preference stakes. I have kept to the original pattern here, which is obviously for night fishing. The 'movement', colour, and shape of the marabou would give this fly similar properties and effectiveness of Gary's Green Marabou, whether fished day or night (see also Murphy).

Tie in a generous bunch of marabou for the tail. At the same point, tie in the chenille.

Take the thread part way back along the shank. Wind on the chenille to this point. Tie in another bunch of marabou.

Repeat the procedure until the hook is full, leaving a turn of chenille free at the head. Finish the head and varnish.

POSSUM (see Opossum)

POTT'S PET (O)

ORIGIN: SEE COMMENTS BELOW
HOOK: 2-6
TAG: ORANGE
BODY: YELLOW WOOL
RIB: OVAL GOLD TINSEL
WING: BRONZE PEACOCK HERL
CHEEKS: LESSER COVERTS FROM A HEN PHEASANT WING
HEAD: BLACK

Gwynne Potts was the Taupo district ranger for many years and was well known as an angler and game law enforcer. Whether he invented the fly, or it was named after him, I am unable to say.

The fly has passed from the scene today, but had its adherents fifty or more years ago. There is no reason why a fly which was effective then should be any less effective today.

The pattern does not give a tail of golden pheasant tippets, and it may be that this has given way to the orange tag. However, they are included in the photo in Keith Draper's first (1971) book and I have done so here. So far as I can tell from that same photo, there appears to be an orange butt (tag?) and so I have included that also. I doubt if it makes one iota of difference to performance, but it may do to historical accuracy.

Tie in the tippets and/or tag (or butt). Tie in the body material and ribbing.

Wind on the chenille and ribbing. Tie in a bunch of bronze peacock herl by the butts at the shoulder.

Tie in the cheeks on each side of the shank. Finish the head and varnish.

PRETTY PRETTY (O)

ORIGIN: NOT KNOWN

HOOK: NOT STATED BUT PROBABLY 4-8

TAIL: GOLDEN PHEASANT TOPPING UNDER FLOSS SILK

TAG: SILVER TINSEL

BODY: PEACOCK HERL GREEN OSTRICH TWISTED TOGETHER

RIB: SILVER OVAL TINSEL

WING: GOAT HAIR DYED ORANGE OR YELLOW

HACKLE: TWO TURNS GREEN HEN

HEAD: BLACK

This appears in Bragg's book as a listed pattern but with no other commentary or photo. I have assumed a black head, and that it is the ostrich which is green, and for the purposes of the tying guide and the photographed example, I have ignored the reference to the floss silk under-body.

The example was tied on a Mustad 3666 No.8 hook.

I suggest that this was a transitional salmon fly. It is not too difficult to conjure up a scenario in which the creator shows this lure to a friend who then makes a comment, sarcastically or otherwise, by which the lure gets its name!

Tie in the tinsel for the tag and wind on a few turns. Tie in the golden pheasant topping, peacock herl and ostrich, and the ribbing.

Wind on the peacock and ostrich herl body. Follow with the ribbing.

Tie in the goat hair wing at the shoulder. Tie in the hackle feather and wind on two turns.

PROSPECTOR (O)

ORIGIN: GARTH COGHILL OF ROTORUA

HOOK: 4-10, STRAIGHT-EYED

THREAD: APPROPRIATE TO MATCH COLOUR OF FUR USED FOR BODY

BODY: ANGORA RABBIT FUR IN SELECTED COLOURS

EYES: STICK-ON OR PAINTED

HEAD: COLOUR OF THREAD USED, SEALED WITH 5-MINUTE CRYSTAL ARALDITE

Garth has had a lot of success with this, 'prospecting' the many stream mouths around Rotoura. The right retrieval speed is important to activate the fur in a tantalising way.

The whole lure is built up from bulky sections of fur, of desired colours, either natural, dyed, or a combination of both. The belly colour should be lighter than the back, with optional narrower bright red or orange lateral lines to complete the deception. Also optionally, a few strands of orange or red Krystal Flash can be mixed with the laterals, but use sparingly.

Take the thread to a point just around the bend. Leave a small head-space gap behind the eye so that the shank is clear. Tie in a bulky section of lighter coloured belly fur just around the bend to extend at least one and a half times the shank length. Next, tie in thinner sections of red or orange fur (one per side). Then tie in a bulky section of darker coloured fur above the laterals, matching the other fur for length.

Take the thread back to a point just ahead of the tail section and repeat the process, this time tying in the belly fur under the shank. The length should be such that the fur fibres overlap and blend in with the previous section.

Repeat with two or three more sections along the shank finishing at the clear head-space behind the eye.

Tie in the final bunches at the clear head-space but with the

fur fibre tips pointing forward over the hook eye. Taper trim the butts, whip finish, trim and seal. When dry, carefully gather all the forward pointing fibres together and firmly draw them back over themselves evenly around the hook and just behind the eye. The firmer the pull, the smaller the head. Seal the head. When dry, flatten the sides of the head with pliers to form a base for the eyes. Paint or stick on eyes. Seal again.

PULLEY LURE (O)

ORIGIN: NOT KNOWN
HOOK: NOT STATED BUT PROBABLY 2-8
TAIL: SHORT BUNCH SOFT SCARLET HACKLE
BODY: RED SEAL'S FUR
RIB: FLAT SILVER
WING: INNER - CREAM; OUTER - BLACK NOT CAUGHT
HACKLE: SOFT BLACK SHORT
HEAD: BLACK

This appears in Bragg's book as a listed pattern but with no other commentary or photo. I have assumed a black head, otherwise the pattern is as set out in Bragg's book. Compare the wing description with that of O'Neil's Special. I have assumed from the wording that one is tied in the Matuku style, and one (this one) in the loose-winged Streamer style.

This is very similar to a red Ferris (Red and Yellow).

Tie in the tail whisks and the ribbing.

Dub on the seal's fur (or substitute) body, stopping near the head. Wind on the ribbing.

Tie in the wing feathers by the butts. Tie in the hackle feather or fibres (it may well be that it is a throat hackle only). Complete the head in the usual way.

PUNTER'S BLACK RABBIT (O)

ORIGIN: RAY PUNTER OF ROTORUA
HOOK: 2-8
BODY: BLACK TYING THREAD
WING: BLACK RABBIT FUR CUT FROM A STRIP OF RABBIT PELT APPROXIMATELY 4MM IN WIDTH
HEAD: BLACK

This is a night fly designed for use at stream mouths when trout are taking smelt. Tufts of fur are tied in by the tying thread progressively along the hook shank. This method of tying - i.e. without the skin attached - makes for a slimmer lure yet still retains the attractive movement of the fur. The method is similar to Jock Miller, only in this case the bunches follow one after the other. On a size 6 hook, ten or so small bunches of fur are used. There is no reason why different coloured fur and tying thread can't be used for daytime variations. To differentiate, this fly has been renamed from the Punter's Rabbit which featured in the 1986 Tichborne calendar.

Take a strip of black rabbit pelt as for a conventional Rabbit lure. Using a dubbing needle, pick out a small section of fur from the front of the strip. Snip off close to the skin and place it in position on top of the shank close to the bend and tie this in.

Repeat the process so that a series of bunches are closely tied in whilst progressing towards the head. Form the head and complete in the usual way.

PURPLE MARABOU PRINCE (O)

ORIGIN: ROB LIMMER OF TAURANGA
HOOK: 4-8
TAIL: RED WOOL OR EGG YARN TAG
BODY: BLACK, OVERWOUND WITH AURORA SKIRT
WING: BUNCH OF PURPLE MARABOU OVER A FEW STRANDS OF LAVENDER ACCENT FLASH
HEAD: BLACK

This is a further variation of Marabou King. Rob is of the view that purple is the most under-rated colour that can be used on trout lures, followed closely by pink - a view with which I entirely agree. Rob points to the popularity of purple and pink Tasmanian Devil spinners which are very successful, and I point to the fact that blue is the most visible colour at depth, all of the other colours, especially red, being progressively filtered out when the sunlight passes through the water.

This lure works very well as a day or night fly and has taken good browns as well as rainbows. Rob feels that on some nights in very shallow, calm water, a full glow body can scare off trout, but a softer glow from a glow stripe or rib can often do the trick.

This lure is very successful in Lake McLaren in the Tauranga district.

Tie in the tag. Tie in the body material and Aurora skirt.

Wind on the body material followed by the Aurora skirt.

Tie in a few strands of lavender accent flash under a bunch of marabou.

PURPLE PARSONS' GLORY (M)

ORIGIN:	ROB LIMMER OF TAURANGA
HOOK:	2-8
TAIL:	RED WHISKS
BODY:	PURPLE CHENILLE
RIB:	OVAL SILVER
WING:	HONEY GRIZZLE HACKLE
HACKLE:	HONEY GRIZZLE
TOPPING:	(OPTIONAL) FLASHABOU PEARL
HEAD:	BLACK

Rob has been tying this for over ten years. He says that it is truly an excellent lake fly. He finds that it excels about an hour before dark. He has taken many large trout in Lake Tarawera, and has been broken off on the strike more times than he cares to admit ('they hit it hard'). Rob catches more trout with this dressing than he does with the yellow-bodied standard.

Apparently this lure took a limit bag of eight in the Ohau Channel on opening day, 1 October 1997. It is now being tied commercially.

Tie in the tail whisks. Tie in the chenille and ribbing.

Wind on the chenille to the head. Tie in the wing feathers by the butts.

Wind on the ribbing, tying down the wing to the top of the body. Tie in a hackle feather.

Wind on the hackle to form a collar. Tie in the topping if using.

QUAIL (K)

ORIGIN:	A.V. (BRUNO) KEMBALL OF HATEPE, TAUPO
HOOK:	6-10
TAIL:	BLACK SQUIRREL
BODY:	FINE WOOL, GREEN, RED, OR YELLOW
WINGS:	FOUR PAIRED FLANK FEATHERS OF A BROWN QUAIL
HEAD:	BLACK

Frank Harwood, of Turangi, recalls the occasion in the mid 1960s when Bruno first started fishing with this fly. You will not be able to buy the feathers commercially, but if you are a hunter, or know someone who is, you should be able to obtain the feathers.

The fly is tied in the Killer style with pairs of plumage tied in each side of the shank. The end result should be something close to a Kilwell No. 1, in both appearance and effectiveness. This pattern was printed in an Auckland Angler's Club news letter and found its way into Tony Orman's *Angling Anthology*.

The plumage takes dye well, and a nice barred green pattern can be achieved if desired.

In the smaller sizes, the wing feathers would be tied in at the head only.

Tie in the tail. Trim. Tie in the body wool.

Take the wool part way back along the shank and secure. Tie in a pair of flank feathers on either side of the shank. Secure and trim.

Continue the thread and wool almost to the head and repeat the process with the flank feathers. (With most Killer flies, I like to tie each feather in separately and cement them in place when I am satisfied with the result.)

RABBIT (M)

ORIGIN:	JUST ABOUT ANYONE WHO HAS TIED A FLY, BUT ACCORDING TO KEITH DRAPER, THE OLDEST SUPPORTED CLAIM HE KNOWS OF IS THAT OF ALAN DUNCUM OF NAPIER
HOOK:	2-10
TAG:	A FEW WHISKS OF DYED COCK HACKLE, RED OR YELLOW. HUGH MCDOWELL ADDS ORANGE TO THAT LIST
BODY:	WOOL OR CHENILLE, COLOUR TO SUIT
RIB:	OVAL TINSEL, USUALLY SILVER BUT GOLD ON A BLACK-BODIED VERSION
WING:	A STRIP OF RABBIT PELT
HACKLE:	TO SUIT, BUT USUALLY TIED TO MATCH THE BODY COLOUR. FOR YELLOW AND ORANGE-BODIED FLIES A PALE HACKLE IS USED, WHEREAS FOR NIGHT PATTERNS A BLACK OR CLARET HACKLE LOOKS WELL
HEAD:	BLACK, ALTHOUGH THE PATTERN IN JOHN VENIARD'S BOOK CALLS FOR A RED HEAD WITH GREEN-BODIED FLIES

"Here perhaps is the best fly of its type in this country...I myself consider the Rabbit Fly to be the best lure of its type when fishing for lake-run trout.

The soft fur works and ripples with every nuance of current and the skin soon softens in the water". - Keith Draper (1971)

Tied in the smaller sizes it makes a good smelt fly, while the larger sizes probably imitate a bully, particularly if two cheeks of hen pheasant feathers are added. I have fished the Rabbit for many years and caught countless trout with it. The pulsing, writhing, flaring fur as it is retrieved is unquestionably the secret to its enormous success, but do allow time for the water to soften the stiff, dry skin (or soak it to soften before attaching it to the line).

Adding cheeks of pheasant rump, female Paradise duck, partridge, grouse, mallard, etc. undoubtedly enhances this lure - see for example the next entry.

Tie in the tail whisks. Tie in the chenille and ribbing.

Take the thread and the chenille back nearly to the head. Tie in a strip of rabbit. Tapering the ends of the cut pelt makes for a neater tie.

Wind on the ribbing, tying down the rabbit strip in the Matuku style. Wind on a hackle collar, finish the head and varnish.

RABBIT BULLY (M)

ORIGIN: KEITH DRAPER OF TAUPO
HOOK: 2-8
BODY: CHENILLE, COLOUR TO SUIT
RIB: OVAL SILVER
WING: STRIP OF RABBIT FUR
CHEEK: FEMALE PARADISE DUCK FEATHERS
HEAD: BLACK

By taking the standard Rabbit lure and adding cheeks, a very effective bully imitation will result. A variety of cheek feathers can be used, and this is Keith's version. The Kokapu, which probably pre-dates this lure, used cheeks of grey partridge breast feathers.

The extent to which the cheek feathers veil the body can vary in accordance with personal preference. In the example, the cheek feathers enclose the entire body, (olive chenille in this case), with the result that the lure is a combination of Matuku and Killer styles.

Tie in the chenille and ribbing.

Wind on the chenille and tie off. Tie in the strip of rabbit fur.

Wind on the ribbing, tying down the fur wing to the top of the body in the Matuku style.

Tie in the cheek feathers on either side and complete the head in the usual way.

RABBIT MUDDLER 1 (M)

ORIGIN: NOT KNOWN, BUT PROBABLY CLIFF DIXON OF WAIROA
HOOK: 2-8
BODY: OLIVE GREEN
RIB: OVAL GOLD
WING: STRIP OF NATURAL BROWN RABBIT
HACKLE: DEER HAIR
HEAD: DEER HAIR, MUDDLER STYLE

This appeared in the Tichborne calendar of 1987. Bryan Tichborne's commentary states that smaller versions tied on a No. 8 hook are especially good for brown trout, cruising the shallow margins of lakes and rivers. It is suggested that it could represent a bully or even a tadpole.

Start the thread one-third of the way along the shank. Tie in the body material and ribbing.

Take the thread two-thirds of the way back along the shank. Wind on the body material to this point and tie off. Tie in a strip of rabbit fur.

Wind on the ribbing, tying down the rabbit fur to the top of the body in the Matuku style. Tie off the thread and attach strong thread such as Kevlar.

Place a bunch of deer hair on the bare shank. Take a couple of loose turns of the thread around the bunch then pull down tightly causing the deer hair to spin around the shank and flare out. Continue pulling tighter with each successive turn. Push the flared hair away from the hook eye, and repeat with another bunch of deer hair. Continue to repeat until the shank is full. Clip the deer hair to shape, leaving a hackle collar of deer hair.

RABBIT MUDDLER 2 (O)

ORIGIN: NOT KNOWN, BUT PROBABLY CLIFF DIXON OF WAIROA
HOOK: 2-8
TAIL: BLACK SQUIRREL
BODY: TUFTS OF BROWN RABBIT TIED BURGLAR STYLE
HACKLE: DEER HAIR
HEAD: DEER HAIR, MUDDLER STYLE

This appeared (along with Rabbit Muddler 1) in the 1987 Tichborne calendar. When I was sorting through a collection of Cliff Dixon's flies (see Cliff's Killer), I came across a number of Rabbit Muddlers (both 1 and 2), obviously tied up by Cliff. The rabbit fur tufts were tied in sparingly along the shank. Judging by the condition of Cliff's examples, trout obviously like this lure.

Start the thread one-third of the way along the shank. Tie in the tail. Tie in a small tuft of rabbit fur, pushing down with thumb and forefinger so that the fur wraps right around the shank.

Continue to tie in tufts of rabbit fur along the shank until the bare section of shank is reached.

Tie the muddler head with deer hair in the same manner as the previous entry.

RAINBOW TROUT (M)

ORIGIN: RITCHIE BUCHANAN OF TAUPO

HOOK: 2-8

TAIL: RED WHISKS

BODY: WHITE CHENILLE WITH A RED BLOOD-LINE OF DMC EMBROIDERY YARN CAUGHT UNDER THE RIBBING

RIB: OVAL SILVER

WING: OLIVE COCK HACKLE

HEAD: BLACK

This is a good summer smelting lure, especially harling from early morning to midday. It will take fish throughout the year, but the red lateral line emulates the blood-line which appears on smelt during the summer months and which accounts for its greater success during that period.

Tie in the tail whisks, chenille, ribbing, and red embroidery yarn on either side of the shank.

Wind on the chenille and secure. Draw up the blood-line yarn to lie along both sides of the body. Tie off at the head.

Tie in the wing feathers. Wind on the ribbing, tying down the wing to the top of the body.

RASTAFARIAN (M)

ORIGIN: RITCHIE BUCHANAN OF TAUPO

HOOK: 2-8

TAIL: RED FLUFF (MARABOU) FROM BASE OF HACKLE FEATHER

BODY: IN THREE PARTS: RED/BLACK, YELLOW/ BLACK, AND GREEN/BLACK, ALL CHENILLE, STARTING FROM THE REAR

RIB: OVAL SILVER

WING: OLIVE-DYED COCK HACKLE

HEAD: BLACK

Ritchie, a professional guide, created this in 1989. It was his first 'designer' fly, and was an instant sensation, although it was at first a secret known only to his clients. Now it is an open secret, and is a demand lure by other local guides and charter operators all year round. It is deadly for both river and lake fishing.

As his first commercial success, it is his 'pet' lure, although its effectiveness may have induced that endearment in any event. Other tiers have produced their own commercial versions of the Rasta; as the saying goes - imitation is the sincerest form of flattery!

Tie in the marabou tail. Tie in the first section of body chenille and the ribbing.

Take the thread a short way back along the shank. Wind on the red and black chenille to this point and tie off. Continue the thread a further short distance and wind on the second section of the body. Repeat for the final body segment.

Tie in the wing feathers. Wind on the ribbing, tying down the wing to the top of the body.

RECKLESS WILLIAM (K)

ORIGIN: CAPTAIN J. J. DUNN OF ENGLAND

HOOK: 8

TAG: ROUND GOLD, FOUR TURNS

BODY: ONE-THIRD FLAT SILVER, FOLLOWED BY FOUR TURNS FLAT GOLD AND THEN WHITE FLOSS

WING: PHEASANT TAIL DYED DARK OLIVE

HACKLE: ORANGE

TOPPING: DARK GREEN SWAN UNDER GOLDEN PHEASANT CREST

HEAD: GREEN

Captain Dunn also created Missionary which, like this lure, has proved very successful for large lake trout in England and also in the Tongariro River and other New Zealand rivers. The slim dressing suggests that it was designed to sink fast, particularly in our fast rivers.

This pattern appears in *A Dictionary of Trout Flies* by

A. Courtney Williams (first published in 1949). It is a very attractive and likely looking lure, but the pheasant tail fibres are brittle making it both difficult to tie, and subject to the ravages of trout attack.

The wing is constructed from matching slips of tail fibres, i.e. without the quill.

Tie in the tag and the tinsel.

Wind on the silver tinsel for one-third of the shank. Tie off. Tie in the gold tinsel and wind on four turns.

Complete the body with the white floss. Tie in the orange hackle feather and form a hackle collar.

Tie in the pheasant tail wing feathers in the Killer style. Add the toppings and complete the head in the usual way.

RECKLESS WILLIAM'S MATE (K)

ORIGIN:	CAPTAIN JJ DUNN OF ENGLAND
HOOK:	8
TAG:	OVAL GOLD
TAIL:	GOLDEN PHEASANT CREST
BODY:	ONE THIRD EACH OF FLAT SILVER, FLAT GOLD, AND WHITE FLOSS
HACKLE:	ORANGE
WING:	SILVER AMHERST PHEASANT DYED LIGHT OLIVE WITH A STRIP OF YELLOW SWAN UNDER
HEAD:	GREEN

This is a slight variation of the previous entry, being overall lighter in colour and containing more yellow than its stablemate. This also appears in A Dictionary of Trout Flies, by A Courtney Williams and the same comments made in respect of Reckless William apply to this lure.

The wing is constructed from the long central tail of the male Amherst pheasant.

No doubt there is a fascinating tale behind the name but research has failed to uncover it.

Tie in gold tinsel and form a tag. Tie in the golden pheasant crest. Tie in the tinsel for the body and return the thread part way back along the shank.

Wind on the silver tinsel for one-third of the shank. Complete the body in the same manner as for Reckless William.

Tie in the orange hackle feather and wind on to form a hackle collar.

Tie in the strip of yellow swan. Overlay with matching slips of tail fibres in the Killer style.

RED and BLACK MATUKA (M)

ORIGIN:	NOT KNOWN
HOOK:	2-8
BODY:	RED CHENILLE OR WOOL
RIB:	OVAL GOLD TINSEL
WING:	TWO BLACK HEN HACKLES BACK TO BACK, AND TIED DOWN ON TOP OF BODY WITH RIBBING TINSEL
HEAD:	BLACK

This comes from John Veniard's book, hence the mis-spelt "Matuka". Apart from very minor cosmetic differences, this is in fact a Black Prince or Hart's Creek. It would be considered a night fly in this country, but overseas it is well regarded as a daytime fly also.

The use of hen hackles instead of cock feathers, and Hugh McDowell's description of "too-short wings", hints that this is tied in the Canterbury style.

The example has been tied on a No. 8 hook.

Tie in the chenille and ribbing.

Wind on the chenille and tie off. Trim. Tie in the wing feathers.

Wind on the ribbing, tying down the wing to the top of the body.

REDFIN MATUKU (M)

ORIGIN:	NOT KNOWN
HOOK:	2-6
TAIL:	TUFT OF SCARLET HACKLE FIBRES
BODY:	WHITE CHENILLE
RIB:	OVAL GOLD
WING:	GRIZZLE HACKLES DYED OLIVE
HACKLE:	SCARLET HACKLE FIBRES (THROAT ONLY)
HEAD:	BLACK

This appears in Keith Draper's 1997 book. It is an Australian pattern "designed to imitate the fry of the redfin perch. Large trout are not averse to a meal of any small fish. This fly should have a good application on waters where perch are common."

Tie in the tail fibres. Tie in the chenille and ribbing.

Wind on the chenille to the head. Tie in the wing feathers by the butts.

Wind on the ribbing, tying down the wing to the top of the body.

Tie in the throat hackle.

RED SETTER (H) (Old Tie)

ORIGIN: GEOFF SANDERSON OF TURANGI

HOOK: 2-8

TAIL: RUSSIAN RED FOX SQUIRREL TAIL

BODY: MID-TONED ORANGE WOOL

HACKLE: GINGER

HEAD: BLACK

Bronwyn Wilson of Taupo had a close association with Geoff Sanderson over many years. She was familiar with the original tie and believes she has recreated the original very accurately in the photographed example.

In a letter which Geoff wrote to Hugh McDowell, he claimed that the tail change from brown to black came about because the black fished better. Keith Draper tells it differently, and with greater logic.

In Russia, the red fox squirrel tail is brown in summer turning black in winter. The thicker winter pelt was preferred. With some squirrels, the brown colouring lingered into the winter and were harvested along with the black. Accordingly, both colours were available, but black predominated. The shortage of brown tails led anglers to change to the black.

It is perhaps a moot point whether black fished better. No doubt there were a great many more black tailed lures being used than the brown. It should be remembered that the brown red fox squirrel is a different colour and texture than the gingery-brown squirrel tail which is so widely available today. If you compare this original tie with Brown Bomber, some authority is given to Ivan Bodley's account of a rusted Red Setter giving rise to his creation. The sober orange wool lent itself to the muted rusty brown colour the elements (and Ivan) created. The hot orange chenille so common today was never intended or envisaged by its creator.

RED SETTER (H) (Modern tie)

ORIGIN: GEOFF SANDERSON OF TURANGI

HOOK: 2-8

TAIL: BLACK OR BROWN SQUIRREL TAIL

BODY: ORANGE CHENILLE OR WOOL

HACKLE: USUALLY TIED WITH TWO LARGE GINGER HACKLES, ONE AT THE HEAD, THE OTHER TIED IN HALFWAY ALONG THE BODY. IN THE SMALLEST SIZES ONE HACKLE CAN BE USED WHILE ON THE EXTRA LARGE HOOKS THREE, OR EVEN FOUR, ARE SOMETIMES TIED IN

HEAD: BLACK

Geoff Sanderson has given us many fine flies (Dappled Dog, Mallard lures, Marabou King, etc), but surely his greatest contribution to the New Zealand angler has been the Red Setter. Not only is it one of the very best for taking lake-run trout, but at the time Hugh McDowell wrote his classic guide to fly-tying, according to Kelly's of Rotorua the Red Setter was the most popular fly in the country - fractionally ahead of Parsons' Glory, which was just ahead of Hamill's Killer. It is interesting to note that three of the four main tying methods are featured in the top three. Indeed, at the time of writing this, I believe that the Woolly Bugger has taken over the top spot. It cannot be said that any one style of fly has a mortgage on effectiveness. But effective this fly is. One of these tied up huge on a No. 2 long shank looks oddly disproportionate, but I have enjoyed great success with them at Lake Waikaremoana.

It is not well known that this lure is also an effective night-time pattern.

Tie in the tail. At the same point tie in a length of chenille.

Take the thread part way back along the shank. Wind on the chenille to this point. Tie in a hackle feather. Wind on the hackle and tie off.

Repeat the process once again, or more often depending on the size of the hook. Finish with a hackle collar at the head.

RED SHADOW (M)

ORIGIN: R.K. (ROBERT) BRAGG OF CHRISTCHURCH

HOOK: 2-8

BODY: WHITE CHENILLE

RIB: OVAL SILVER

WING: TWO DYED RED HACKLES LAID OVER BLACK HACKLES
HACKLE: BLACK
HEAD: BLACK

"Here is a Canterbury pattern that enjoys a great deal of popularity in Rotorua. It is a night fly at its best and while I have never used it, I have met some anglers who are prepared to swear by it."- Keith Draper (1971).

In his 1997 publication, Keith recounts how he was cleaned out by a friend who used this lure in the middle of the day, fishing the mouth of the Tauranga-Taupo, notwithstanding its reputation as a night fly.

Tie in the chenille and ribbing.

Wind on the chenille to the head. Take two black hackle feathers and place a red hackle feather on each side so that the black feathers are enclosed. Tie in the total of four feathers by the butts at the shoulder.

Wind on the ribbing, tying down the feathers to the top of the body. Tie in a black hackle feather and wind on to form a hackle collar.

RED TERROR (M)

ORIGIN: NOT KNOWN
HOOK: 2-8
BODY: RED
RIB: SILVER
WING: DYED RED COCK HACKLE
HACKLE: DYED RED COCK HACKLE
OVERLAY: GREEN PEACOCK
CHEEKS: JUNGLE COCK
HEAD: BLACK

This is a Canterbury lure regarded as a night fly. Essentially , it is a Cardinal with trimmings and has been known to perform just as effectively.

Tie in the body material and ribbing.

Wind on the body material the head. Tie in the wing feathers by the butt at the shoulder.

Wind on the ribbing, tying down the wing to the top of the body.

Tie in the peacock herl at the shoulder so that it sweeps back over the wing. Tie in the Jungle Cock cheeks, one on either side of the shank.

ROTODYERAN SPECIAL (H)

ORIGIN: HUGH MCDOWELL OF ROTORUA
HOOK: NOT STATED, BUT PRESUMABLY 4-8 AS WITH DAPPLED DOG
TAIL: BLACK SQUIRREL TAIL
BODY: FLUORESCENT LIME CHENILLE
HACKLES: DYED YELLOW AND GRIZZLE COCK HACKLES
HEAD: BLACK

This whimsical creation by Hugh occurred when he started to tie up a Red Setter. The black tail went on, then he discovered he was out of hot orange chenille. He decided to change to a Dapple Dog notwithstanding the tail colour, and tied on a segment of lime chenille. A yellow feather caught his eye and, on impulse, wound it on in the Hackle style. The colour combination was too garish so he added a grizzle hackle on top to soften the effect. Hugh tried the pattern out many times without success and the fly ended up stuck in his cap. Some years later, on a fishing trip with an American friend, the American spotted the fly and decided to use it, everything else at that stage having failed.

By now the sun and the elements had faded the dye-leached materials to a golden-grey effect with a greenish tinge from the lime body. It worked a treat and he recalls "that special day we once had on Rotoaira using the fly on which the 'dye ran' - hence the corny name".

The moral seems to be to give the fly a good wetting, leave it out in the weather for ages, and then who knows! It has worked spectacularly in the past.

Tie in the tail and the first segment of chenille.

Take the thread and chenille part way back along the shank. Tie in the two hackle feathers and wind on. Secure and trim.

Repeat the process, finishing at the head with a hackle collar. Finish the head in the usual way and varnish.

ROTOITI (see Albino 2)

ROYAL COACHMAN LURE (O)

ORIGIN: ADAPTED BY PAT O'KEEFE OF ROTORUA
HOOK: 6-8
TAIL: GOLDEN PHEASANT TIPPETS
BUTT: PEACOCK HERL
BODY: RED FLOSS
WING: STRAIGHTENED CALF TAIL
HACKLE: SOFT BROWN HEN, BEARD STYLE
HEAD: BLACK

This is a hair-wing version of the better known dry or small wet fly of the same name. The calf hair is straightened by washing it in detergent and drying it with a blow-dryer.

This is a daytime lure which Pat likes to work in rips and currents using a slow to intermediate sinking line or a floating line with a sink tip

Tie in the tail tippets. Tie in a strand of peacock herl.

Wind on about three turns of the peacock herl to form the butt. Tie in the floss. Take the thread nearly to the head. Wind on the floss to this point and tie off.

Tie in the throat hackle. Tie in the hair wing. Complete the head in the usual way.

ROYAL TAN (M)

ORIGIN: R.K. (ROBERT) BRAGG OF CHRISTCHURCH
HOOK: 2-8
TAIL: RED WHISKS
BODY: YELLOW CHENILLE
RIB: OVAL SILVER
WING: GRIZZLE HACKLES DYED DEEP GOLDEN YELLOW
HACKLE: GRIZZLE HACKLES DYED DEEP GOLDEN YELLOW
HEAD: BLACK

"This pattern is a variation of the Parsons' Glory, although it should really be classed as a version of the Yellow Orbit. When W. Beaumont-Orr designed his Orbits the yellow never reached the popularity of its green brother, so it is understandable how Bragg came to evolve his dressing.

"The Royal Tan sold quite well on the Rotorua scene, as Bragg used to dress the flies for one of that town's retailers." Keith Draper (1971).

Tie in the tail whisks. Tie in the chenille and the ribbing. Secure and trim.

Wind on the chenille and tie off. Tie in the wing feathers by the butt at the shoulder.

Wind on the ribbing, tying down the wing to the top of the body. Tie in a further hackle feather at the shoulder.

Wind on the hackle collar. Secure and trim.

RUSTLER (M) & (K)

ORIGIN: GARTH COGHILL OF ROTORUA
HOOK: 6-8
BODY: REAR TWO-THIRDS: DOUBLE WOUND FLAT GOLD MYLAR TINSEL, SIZE 10
RIB: REAR TWO-THIRDS: OVAL GOLD
REAR WING/TAIL: TWO MATCHING PAIRS OF RUSTY BROWN , LONG-FIBRED, UPPER TAIL COVERTS FROM A COCK PHEASANT OR THE IRIDESCENT GREEN RUMP ("MRS SIMPSON") FEATHERS
VEILING: TWO MATCHING PAIRS OF GREEN OR RUSTY BROWN RUMP COCK PHEASANT FEATHERS
SIDE WING: COCK PHEASANT FEATHERS AS DESCRIBED ABOVE
CHEEK: JUNGLE COCK (OPTIONAL)
HEAD: BLACK

This is tied in exactly the same manner as Pluto . The rear wing/tail is tied in the Matuku style, extending a minimum full hook length beyond the bend. The veiling feathers are tied Killer style and of sufficient length to completely cover the hook bend. The side wings are tied Killer style, each succeeding pair of feathers overlapping and blending with the previous pair. Each matched pair should be progressively smaller than the previous pair.

Garth says this is a summer fly, at its best in the early morning in the shallows but is also an effective night-time fly if given luminous "glow in the dark" eyes.

Peter Hart (see Hart's Creek) caught a limit bag in thirty minutes using this lure.

Tie in the mylar and ribbing. Return the thread two-thirds the way back along the shank. Wind on the mylar to this point and tie off.

Tie in two pairs of feathers. Wind on the ribbing, tying down the feathers to the top of the shank in the Matuku style. Trim.

At the same point, tie in two pairs of feathers, one pair on either side of the shank in the Killer style.

Continue tying in matching pairs of feathers in the Killer style, inching forward (towards the eye) a millimetre or so at a time until the head is reached. Form the head in the usual way.

SCOTCH POACHER (P)

ORIGIN: JOCK KIRKPATRICK OF ROTORUA
HOOK: 2-8
TAIL: BLACK SQUIRREL
BODY: HOT ORANGE CHENILLE
RIB: OVAL GOLD
WING: BLUE PUKEKO FEATHERS
HACKLE: ORANGE
HEAD: BLACK

Apparently, Bill Hamill (of Hamill's Killer fame) used to refer, jokingly, to Jock Kirkpatrick as "an old Scotch poacher". When his creation became a commercial reality, the name was a foregone conclusion. Any good dour Scotsman will tell ye tha' unless Hamill meant tha' Jock, aye, was stealin' whisky, the fly should be called a "Scots Poacher". Grammatical considerations apart, the fly is an excellent night fly which few night-time anglers would be without.

Tie in the tail. Tie in the chenille and ribbing.

Wind on the chenille then follow with the ribbing. Tie off.

Tie in a couple of blue Pukeko feathers by the butt at the shoulder so that the wing forms a neat canopy over the body. Tie in a hackle feather and wind on.

SIERPINSKI (O)

ORIGIN: JOHN SIERPINSKI OF TAUPO
HOOK: NOT STATED, BUT PROBABLY 2-8
TAIL: BLACK SQUIRREL (SPARSE)
BODY: EQUAL SECTIONS OF FLAME ORANGE AND BLACK
WING: GREY POSSUM (SPARSE)
HEAD: BLACK

I have taken this from a very old original which John gave to Bronwyn Wilson. It is so old, there is virtually nothing left but the body.

I have used DMC embroidery yarns for the body. The flame orange is shade 606 and is very close to the original, albeit of a different and unknown material.

John Sierpinski was known to have fished for all 365 days of at least one year around Taupo. I came upon this pattern late in my research, and I have recounted further details about John in the next entry.

Tie in the squirrel tail.

Tie in, and wind on, a short section of flame orange and then black body material. Tie in a sparse bunch of possum on top of the shank.

Repeat the double body sections, tying in the possum fur after each black section. Finish at the head with a black section and a final tuft of fur. Complete the head in the usual way.

SIERPINSKI DOG (O)

ORIGIN: JOHN SIERPINSKI OF TAUPO
HOOK: 4-8
TAIL: DOG OR GOAT HAIR
BODY: WOOL
WING AND HACKLE: POSSUM FUR HALFWAY ALONG THE BODY, OTHER AT HEAD, AROUND WHOLE DIAMETER OF HOOK, AND TIED SPARSELY
HEAD: BLACK

This pattern appeared in Tony Orman's book *The Sport in Fishing* which set out the favourite patterns of 13 experts. The expert who submitted this pattern was John Henderson who rated this highly as a day or night fly, especially at Taupo.

John Sierpinski was a colourful angling legend around Taupo, and author of *Taupo Fishing Guide*. In that book, he recounts the occasion when he hooked a trout in the Tongariro and, after a moment of frustration when he 'gave it the butt', lost it without ever once setting eyes on his quarry. He had then been playing the fish for five hours!

Colours are not given in this pattern, and they are probably matters of choice. Red and black was a favoured combination for Serpinski and that is what I have chosen, along with goat hair. This lure provided the inspiration for Margaret Orman's Wisp which is also included alphabetically herein.

It is only proper that the Sierpinski name should be perpetuated even if his creation is not well known.

Tie in the tail and the wool for the body.

Take the wool part way back along the shank. Tie in the

possum fur so as to sparsely encircle the shank.

Continue the wool back nearly to the head. Tie in the possum fur in the same manner as before. Finish the head and varnish.

SIERPINSKI RED (O)

ORIGIN: JOHN SIERPINSKI OF TAUPO
HOOK: NOT STATED BUT PROBABLY 6-10
TAIL: BUNCH OF POSSUM TAIL FUR
BODY: RED
WING: BUNCHES OF POSSUM TAIL FUR TIED IN AT INTERVALS ALONG THE TOP OF THE BODY AND ALSO AT THE HEAD
HEAD: BLACK

There are obvious similarities between all the Sierpinski lures recorded here, but it is this lure which has endured to become an established commercial proposition selling well in the Taupo area. Sierpinski most likely fished this during the day, but it would be a very effective night lure bearing, as it does, a close resemblance to Hob Nailed Boot, although created well before the Boot.

I do not know if Sierpinski was the first to popularise the use of possum fur (George Gatchell would also be a contender), but it has certainly caught on. I had to reject a number of submissions offered for inclusion in this book because they were too similar or identical to other patterns which took precedence. I have no doubt that in all cases the creator thought he or she had invented an original.

The size of the hook will be determined by the length of the fur, which should be tied in, getting progressively longer as you work towards the head.

Tie in a bunch of possum tail fur for the tail. Tie in the body material.

Take the thread a short way back along the shank. Wind on the body material to this point and secure. Tie in a tuft of possum tail fur on top of the shank.

Repeat the process, tying in bunches of fur along the shank, the number depending on the size of the hook. Finish with a bunch at the head. Complete the head in the usual way.

SILVER DOCTOR (O)

ORIGIN: NOT KNOWN
HOOK: 2-8
TAIL: GOLDEN PHEASANT TIPPETS
BODY: FLAT SILVER TINSEL
RIB: FINE OVAL SILVER
WING: GREY MALLARD FLANK
HACKLE: PALE BLUE
HEAD: BLACK

"This fly is a relic from the days of the salmon fly. It is still used to good effect in many parts of the country and is to be considered as a good early-season fly. There can be little doubt that it is taken by trout as some small form of fry. The pattern used today is a simplification of the more colourful original. The salmon fly dressed in full regalia uses a wing of strips of goose dyed red, yellow and green then overlaid with grey mallard flank. All the fancy petticoats have been dropped and our modern version has a wing of grey mallard only. I suspect that it is none the worse for it." - Keith Draper (1971).

The original, from England, with the married strips of different coloured feathers is a work of art beyond the capability of most home tiers, I would suggest. It is, however, still very popular in England.

Tie in the tippets. Tie in the tinsel body material and ribbing. Secure and trim.

Wind on the tinsel and ribbing. Secure and trim. Tie in the wing feathers by the butt.

Tie in the hackle feather. Wind on the hackle collar. Finish the head and varnish.

SILVER GREY (M)

ORIGIN: NOT KNOWN
HOOK: 4-6, LONG SHANK
TAIL: GOLDEN PHEASANT CREST OVER WHISKS OF AMHERST PHEASANT
BODY: SILVER TINSEL
RIB: OVAL SILVER
WING: GREY COCK HACKLES
SIDE WING: AMHERST PHEASANT TAIL FIBRES
HACKLE: BADGER, THROAT ONLY
CHEEK: JUNGLE COCK
HEAD: BLACK

This appears in Bragg's book (see my comments under Klondike Kate). It is a smelt pattern which seems to have been successful with salmon also. I cannot be entirely certain that I have accurately ascertained the pattern.

Tie in the Amherst pheasant whisks. Tie in the Golden Pheasant crest. Tie in the body tinsel and the ribbing.

Wind on the body tinsel. Tie in the wing feathers by the butts.

Wind on the ribbing, tying down the wing to the top of the body.

Tie in the side wing of Amherst pheasant tail fibres. Tie in the beard hackle. Add Jungle Cock cheeks and complete the head in the usual way.

SILVER FITCH (M)

ORIGIN:	JIM KOLLER OF LAKE ROTOEHU, ROTORUA DISTRICT
HOOK:	8, LONG SHANK
TAIL:	TUFT OF RED WOOL
BODY:	WHITE ICE CHENILLE OR SILVER BRAID OR TINSEL
RIB:	OVAL SILVER
WING:	STRIP OF CREAMY-WHITE FITCH WITH BROWN OR DARKER GUARD HAIRS, ABOUT TWICE THE LENGTH OF THE SHANK
THROAT:	TUFT OF RED WOOL
TOPPING:	2-4 STRANDS OF FLASHABOU PEARL
EYES:	JUNGLE COCK
HEAD:	BLACK

This is best fished beside or over weed beds and in shallow water over rocks. Although principally a smelt pattern, Jim believes the black shine to the head and the general shape is similar to the prolific small snails found in Lake Rotehu. He covers his options "If the trout aren't full of smelt, they will be full of snails - so I give them both".

Jim fishes this in tandem with his Silver Possum, either harling or casting to seen fish from an anchored or drifting boat. When casting, he uses a floating or slow sinking line. This lure has been very successful for Jim, having no equal when trout are smelting.

Although the white ice chenille version is shown here, Jim is just as likely to use the silver-bodied model with equal expectations for success.

Tie in the wool tail. Tie in the body material and ribbing. Wind on the body material nearly to the head.

Tie in the strip of fitch fur. Wind on the ribbing, tying down the fur wing in the Matuku style.

Tie in the wool throat, the topping, and the Jungle Cock eyes. Complete the head in the usual way.

SILVER POSSUM (M)

ORIGIN:	JIM KOLLER OF LAKE ROTOEHU, ROTORUA DISTRICT
HOOK:	8, LONG SHANK
TAIL:	TUFT OF RED WOOL
BODY:	SILVER TINSELLED WOOL
RIB:	OVAL SILVER
WING:	STRIP OF SILVERY-GREY POSSUM, ABOUT TWICE THE LENGTH OF THE SHANK
THROAT:	TUFT OF RED WOOL
TOPPING:	2-4 STRANDS OF FLASHABOU PEARL
EYES:	JUNGLE COCK
HEAD:	BLACK

This is the possum version of Jim's Silver Fitch. It has a very good appearance in the water, and Jim says it out-fishes everything except the Fitch when the trout are smelting. It is fished in exactly the same way as the Fitch. Jim writes: "Depending on water conditions, time of the year, and all the other variables, I fish these 2 flies (Fitch and Possum) with floating or slow sinking lines when casting , and a sinking line when fish are deep. When harling to my best fishing spots, I tie the possum on a dropper some 4 feet above the fitch. The catch rate on both flies is about the same. In sighted fish' situations, casting with this 2-fly trace is also very successful."

Trimming and tapering the ends of the fur strip makes it easier to tie in, and gives better movement in the water.

Tie in the wool tail. Tie in the tinsel wool and ribbing. Wind on the tinsel wool body.

Tie in a strip of possum fur. Wind on the ribbing, tying down the fur wing to the top of the body.

Tie in the wool throat, the topping, and the Jungle Cock eyes. Complete the head in the usual way.

SILVERY (M)

ORIGIN:	NOT KNOWN
HOOK:	NOT STATED BUT PROBABLY 2-8
BODY:	WHITE

RIB: OVAL SILVER
WING: PALE GRIZZLE
HACKLE: PALE GRIZZLE
HEAD: BLACK

This is a Canterbury high country lure of unknown origin which was probably fished in Lake Ellesmere. It is very similar to Barred Rock, and should catch trout almost anywhere.

This lure appears in Bragg's book and I have come across a 'live' one in an old collection which I could look at but not keep. The grizzle feathers should be quite pale in contrast to those used in Barred Rock.

Tie in the body material and ribbing.

Wind on the body material. Tie in the wing feathers by the butts.

Wind on the ribbing, tying down the wing to the top of the body. Tie in a hackle feather and wind on.

SILVERY RED BODY (M)

ORIGIN: W. WOOSTER OF CHRISTCHURCH
HOOK: NOT STATED BUT PROBABLY 2-8
BODY: RED CHENILLE OR MOHAIR
RIB: OVAL GOLD
WING: LIGHT FURNACE
HACKLE: BARRED ROCK (GRIZZLE); DO NOT OVER-HACKLE
TOPPING: LIGHT MALLARD
HEAD: BLACK

This appears in Bragg's book as a high country Canterbury smelt pattern popular during the period 1946-1954. Both the pattern (as above) and photos serve to confirm the dressing although light furnace is not easy to come by. In reality, the colour has the appearance of natural ginger and that is what I have used.

Tie in the chenille or mohair and the ribbing.

Wind on the body material. Tie in the wing feathers by the butts.

Wind on the ribbing, tying down the wing in the Matuku style.

Tie in the hackle fibres under the throat. Tie in the topping and complete the head in the usual way.

SIMPKIN (M)

ORIGIN: BOB BRAGG OF CHRISTCHURCH
HOOK: NOT STATED BUT PROBABLY 2-8
TAIL: BLACK SQUIRREL
BODY: WHITE CHENILLE
RIB: OVAL SILVER
WING: GRIZZLE
CHEEK: MALE PARADISE SHELDUCK
HACKLE: GRIZZLE
HEAD: BLACK

This was named after one of Bragg's five cats variously owned and loved over a 30 year period from 1944.

Aspects of the Barred Rock and Brunton series of lures and Dorothy, are evident, whether or not influenced by any of them.

Tie in the bunch of squirrel. Tie in the chenille and ribbing.

Wind on the chenille. Tie in the wing feathers by the butts.

Wind on the ribbing, tying down the wing in the Matuku style.

Tie in the paradise duck cheeks on either side. Tie in the hackle feather and wind on to form a hackle collar.

SIMPLE SALMON (O)

ORIGIN: MAUREEN BUTLER OF ROTORUA
HOOK: 4-8
TAG: FLAT SILVER BRAID FOLLOWED BY A SHORT SECTION OF YELLOW FLOSS
TAIL: GOLDEN PHEASANT CREST
BUTT: THREE TURNS OF PEACOCK HERL
BODY: OLIVE FLOSS
RIB: FLAT SILVER
WING: STRIPS OF MALLARD BREAST FEATHER
HACKLE: MALLARD BREAST FIBRES, BEARD STYLE
TOPPING: GOLDEN PHEASANT CREST
HEAD: BLACK

This is a simplified version of the salmon-style flies of old, hence the name. As might be expected, it is effective on salmon as well as trout. Maureen has had a lot of success with this lure at Lake Waikaremoana and elsewhere. It is effective as a harling lure or for casting, using either a floating line with a sinking tip, or a sinking line.

The particular braid which Maureen uses is "Verna" brand. While it can properly be described as "flat" it is quite narrow and more closely resembles medium oval tinsel.

This lure featured in Nancy Tichborne's calendar of 1991.

Tie in the silver braid and take three turns around the shank. Tie in the crest feather for the tail. Add a short section of yellow floss followed by three turns of peacock herl.

Tie in the floss and the ribbing. Wind on the floss body followed by the ribbing. Tie off.

Tie in a few hackle fibres under the throat. Tie in the hackle wing and the golden pheasant topping. Complete the head and varnish.

SIMPSON FLY (O)

ORIGIN: ROB LIMMER OF TAURANGA
HOOK: 6-10 LONG SHANK
BODY: OLIVE ICE CHENILLE
RIB: PEACOCK LUREX (NO. 085) AND RED COPPER WIRE
TAIL: OLIVE MARABOU OVER A FEW STRANDS OF GREEN FLASHABOU
HACKLE: (THROAT ONLY) MALLARD OR PARTRIDGE
HEAD: BLACK

This has been adapted from a South African pattern which has ended up, Rob says, as basically a cross between Woolly Bugger and Doll Fly.

Rob also ties this up in brown, the only difference being brown ice chenille, brown marabou, and gold Flashabou.

This has proved very effective at Lakes Aniwhenua, Rerewhakaatu, and Tarawera. Rob also says that it "seems to work well from float tubes, don't ask me why, probably coincidence."

It is best fished as close to the bottom as possible with a slow to medium strip and stop retrieve.

Tie in the Flashabou, lurex and copper wire ribbing, and ice chenille.

Wind on the chenille and tie off. Follow with the peacock lurex ribbing. Tie in a bunch of marabou at the shoulder.

Wind on the copper wire rib (in the opposite direction from the lurex rib) tying down the marabou and thus forming the tail. Tie off the ribbing. Tie in a throat hackle, trim, and complete the head in the usual way.

SINGLE PUFF (O)

ORIGIN: SKIP JOHNSON OF ALASKA
HOOK: 6-10
BODY: GLO-BUG YARN (DARK ROE) FOLLOWED BY SILVER TINSEL OR YARN
WING: WHITE MARABOU
TOPPING: TWO STRANDS OF PEACOCK SWORD
THROAT: ORANGE MARABOU OR FLUFF FROM BASE OF ORANGE DYED GRIZZLE HACKLE
HEAD: BLACK, IF NOT USING EYES
EYES: SILVER DUMB-BELL

This is a salmon pattern developed in Alaska and currently popular in parts of New Zealand. It is unashamedly another variation of a roe imitation. It works well as a nymph with the eyes incorporated from sizes 10 and smaller. Without the eyes, it can be used as a streamer up to size 6. The puff is formed in the same manner as Double Puff.

Take the thread down to the bend.

Form a dubbing loop and wind on a tapered bunch of glo-bug yarn.

Tie in the silver tinsel. Return the thread back nearly to the head. Wind on the silver tinsel to this point and tie off.

Tie in the marabou at the throat. Tie in the marabou wing and peacock sword topping.

If using eyes, attach with a small drop of super-glue and thread binding. If not using eyes, form a small neat head and tie off.

SKINNY MAC (M)

ORIGIN: NOT KNOWN
HOOK: NOT STATED BUT PROBABLY 6-10
TAIL: YELLOW WHISKS
BODY: RED
RIB: OVAL SILVER
WING: SLENDER GINGER 'DRY FLY' HACKLE
HACKLE: GINGER
HEAD: BLACK

Dave McLellan, now of Auckland, had been in New Zealand only a matter of days (35 years ago) and was fishing the Ohau Channel at Rotorua. A Maori angler a short distance away was hauling them in while Dave could catch nothing. Eventually, the unknown Maori turned towards Dave and asked him to hold his arm out, which he did. The Maori then expertly cast a lure to catch on Dave's sleeve. 'Bite that off and use that' said the stranger. Dave obliged, and immediately caught a trout. The lure turned out to be a skinny version of Ginger Mick. Dave tied up many of these and one day happened to show them to Hugh McDowell. Hugh was inspired by this slender concept to tie up a whole range of 'standards' in this slim style - Parsons' Glory, Dorothy, Jack's Sprat, and Bishop's Blessing.

He enjoyed considerable success with these streamlined models, sometimes better than with the original. They came into their own in the summer months fished at the cooler stream mouths. Indirectly, this svelte style had some influence in the creation of Hugh's Parsons' Sunset.

When Nancy Tichborne was looking for flies for her 1989 calendar, she took a particular liking to this lure and asked Hugh what it was called. As far as Hugh was concerned, it didn't have a name and so he called it Skinny Mac after Dave "who was decidedly skinny himself back in those days!"

It is, of course, a Ginger Mick, but this particular dressing gives it a different profile. The whole concept, and the way in which it can be applied to any number of Matuku style patterns, justifies its separate inclusion.

The tying sequence is exactly the same as for Ginger Mick.

SNAIL FLY (P)

ORIGIN: FRANK LORD OF ROTORUA
HOOK: 8-10
BODY: BLACK
WING: PUKEKO
TOPPING: A GOOD CURL OF GREEN PEACOCK SWORD HERL
HEAD: BLACK

This fly is intended to copy more or less the shape of a freshwater snail, probably the pulmonate type which have to surface occasionally to fill their single lung. It is very effective fished slowly on a floating line. Anyone who has ever examined the contents of a trout's stomach will know the importance of these molluscs in the trout diet.

I had the good fortune and privilege to met with Frank in October 1996. I had wanted to discuss his famous Lord's Killer, but it was this lure which he reminisced and enthused over, recounting many marvellous fishing stories where the Snail had reigned supreme.

It is a night fly, and Frank appeared to hold it in higher regard than his better known Killer creation.

Tie in the body material. Secure and trim.

Wind on the body material to the head. Tie in a Pukeko feather by the butt so that it forms a small canopy over the body.

Tie in the peacock sword topping.

SNOW QUEEN (O)

ORIGIN: NOT KNOWN
HOOK: PROBABLY 6-10
TAIL: WHITE MARABOU
BODY: WHITE CHENILLE OR WOOL
WING: TUFT OF WHITE MARABOU AT SHOULDER WITH A SHORTER TUFT AT THE THROAT
HEAD: BLACK

This is a very old pattern - so old, in fact, it has not survived in any New Zealand literature. In its day it was regarded as a good smelt pattern and no doubt would be today. Way back then, the marabou used was the basal fluff from the base of the quill. It was not pure white, the overall effect being a greyish-white. Peter Hart of Christchurch can recall seeing one of these tied up by a very old angler using the down from feathers plucked from a very live and indignant chook!

I have attempted to tie this up as close as possible to how I imagine the original would have been tied, although today I expect pure white marabou in greater profusion would be preferred.

Peter is clear in his recollection that the dressing uses no rib or head hackle.

Tie in a bunch of downy fluff for the tail. Tie in the chenille or wool.

Wind on the body material and tie off.

Tie in a short tuft of down under the throat. Tie in a longer tuft on top. Complete the head in the usual way.

SORCERER (P)

ORIGIN: NOT KNOWN
HOOK: NOT STATED BUT PROBABLY 2-8
TAIL: NONE APPARENT
BODY: PROBABLY BLACK
RIB: POSSIBLY
WING: RED FEATHERS FROM A GOLDEN PHEASANT
THROAT: A TUFT OF RED MARABOU
HEAD: BLACK

This appears in Bragg's book and is reminiscent of Guardsman. It is recorded as a Canterbury pattern used in the 1960s. My guess is that it is a night lure.

It is not easy to make out the exact dressing from the photo in Bragg's book but I feel confident that the pattern is as I have tied it. If it differs from the original, the differences will be marginal.

Tie in the body material. Tie in ribbing if you wish.

Wind the body material back nearly to the head. Tie in the wing feathers by the butts in the Pukeko or Cowl style.

Tie in the marabou tuft at the throat. Complete the head in the usual way.

SOUTHERNER'S COMFORT (P)

ORIGIN: JOHN MORTON OF CHRISTCHURCH
HOOK: 6
TAIL: PHEASANT TAIL FIBRES OVERLAID WITH DEER TAIL HAIR DYED RED
BODY: OLIVE CHENILLE
RIB: OVAL SILVER
WING: THREE SETS MALLARD FLANK FEATHERS DYED HAMILL'S KILLER GREEN
HACKLE: TUFT OF SPICULES FROM THE BLUE NECK FEATHERS OF A PEACOCK, TIED BEARD STYLE
HEAD: BLACK

This is an attractor-type fly imitating the large olive green Anisoptera Dragonfly nymph. The wings are mounted on top of the hook in the same manner as for Craig's Night-time.

According to John, this fly is very effective at night, and an excellent all-season pattern. It can be fished on either a floating or sinking line depending on water depth. It is best fished near the bottom and very slowly, on the edge of lake or river weed beds. A very effective strategy is to use it as an assault fly sunk to the bottom on a sandy delta of a stream entering a lake, twitching it to approaching trout with a slight lift of the rod tip. The trout will charge this fly down, and hit hard.

Tie in the pheasant tail fibres and deer tail overlay. The deer tail is set to half the length of the pheasant tail beneath it. Tie in the chenille and ribbing.

Wind on the chenille followed by the ribbing. Tie in the beard hackle (peacock feathers).

Tie in the pairs of mallard flank feathers as one, set on top of each other in the Pukeko style. Form the head and complete in the usual way.

SPA SPECIAL (K)

ORIGIN: LESLIE NEWDICK OF TAUPO
HOOK: 2-8
TAIL: A BUNCH OF FIBRES FROM A GREY TURKEY FEATHER
BODY: YELLOW MOHAIR
RIB: OVAL SILVER
WING: GREY PARTRIDGE TIED IN EACH SIDE
HEAD: BLACK

The Spa Special is a stablemate of Leslie's Lure by the same creator. It is tied up in the Killer style and will kill fish just as effectively as it did fifty years ago. Keith Draper can vouch for it, knowing "personally what a great lure it can be."

I have used brown turkey. It appears to be the same colour as the one in the photo in Keith's 1971 book and it matches the wing colour. I have tied in the wings in the same splayed manner as depicted in Keith's book and I have to assume that it has been tied in that way deliberately. The feathers (which come from the lower flank), are an absolute curse to tie in. If I were tying this for myself I would tie them conventionally as for a Kilwell No. 1, which bears some resemblance with the stripe.

Tie in the tail of turkey feathers. Tie in the body material and ribbing.Take the thread back nearly to the head.

Wind on the body material and ribbing and tie off. Tie in a pair of wing feathers on either side of the shank. Finish the head and varnish.

SPLIT PARTRIDGE (M)

ORIGIN: NOT KNOWN
HOOK: 2-8
TAIL: YELLOW HACKLE FIBRES
BODY: ORANGE CHENILLE
RIB: OVAL SILVER TINSEL
WING: SPLIT PARTRIDGE TAIL
HACKLE: NATURAL RED COCK HACKLE
HEAD: BLACK

I have given here the dressing which appears in John Veniard's book under the name Orange Partridge, but which is undoubtedly the Split Partridge of Keith Draper's publications. Keith does not nominate a colour. However, John Veniard points out that the body colours can be varied whereby it becomes a Yellow Partridge, Green Partridge, etc. Whatever colour is used, it is a great fly, and as Keith points out, Barney Northcroft of Waitahanui, widely known for his ability with a fly rod, claims that for rip fishing in the lake there is no better fly.

Tie in the tail whisks. Tie in the chenille and ribbing.

Wind the chenille back nearly to the head. Split a partridge tail feather in half down the spine. This provides two matching sides which are then tied in at the butt.

Wind on the ribbing, tying down the wing to the top of the body. Tie in the hackle feather, and wind on to form a hackle collar.

SPLIT TURKEY (O)

ORIGIN: NOT KNOWN
HOOK: 2-8
TAIL: GOLDEN PHEASANT TIPPETS
BODY: CLARET CHENILLE
RIB: OVAL GOLD TINSEL
WING: SPLIT MOTTLED BROWN TURKEY TAIL
CHEEK: JUNGLE COCK
HACKLE: CLARET - WOUND IN FRONT OF WING
HEAD: BLACK

This comes from John Veniard's book. The three Turkey lures listed in this book are all variations on a theme, but there are sufficient differences to warrant separate inclusion. Like the Split Partridge, once upon a time no self-respecting angler would be caught in the open without one of these flies. Both the fly, and the method of tying it, have fallen out of fashion over the years, but that does not lessen its value or reputation.

Tie in the tippets. Tie in the chenille and ribbing. Secure and trim.

Wind on the chenille and tie off. Tie in matching halves of a split turkey tail.

Wind on the ribbing, tying down the wing to the top of the body.

Tie in a hackle feather and wind on.

Add Jungle Cock cheeks. Finish the head and varnish.

SPOTTY GOLD (M)

ORIGIN: RITCHIE BUCHANAN OF TAUPO
HOOK: 2-8
TAIL: RED WHISKS
BODY: BLACK CHENILLE AND YELLOW ICE CHENILLE
RIB: OVAL SILVER
WING: RED COCK HACKLES INSIDE YELLOW COCK HACKLES
TOPPING: RED DMC EMBROIDERY THREAD OR FLOSS REACHING BACK TO THE END OF THE WING
HEAD: BLACK

This was created in 1990, based on the Australian Spotty Gold Cobra lure. It is primarily designed for harling, but the bright colours perform well for river fishing in murkier waters. It performs best from August/September through to the end of December.

Ritchie also uses an alternative dressing which omits the red wing hackle, using ordinary yellow chenille instead of ice chenille, and has a red head.

Tie in the red tail whisks. Tie in the two chenille colours and the ribbing.

Wind on the two chenille colours to the head and tie off. Tie in the wing feathers, with or without the red hackles as desired.

Wind on the ribbing, tying down the wing in the Matuku style. Tie in the topping which should reach back to the end of the wing. Complete the head in the usual way, either black or red as the case may be.

SQUIRREL NUTKIN (O)

ORIGIN: ROBERT K. BRAGG OF CHRISTCHURCH
HOOK: 2-8

TAIL: BROWN HACKLE POINTS
BODY: FLAT GOLD TINSEL
WING: BROWN SQUIRREL
HACKLE: BROWN
HEAD: BLACK

"This is Bob Bragg's variation of the Demon, which has a wing of brown mallard and a hackle of orange...The Squirrel Nutkin is a smelt fly, developed on the faster Canterbury rivers. It is a great fly for catching sea trout as they splash in the ripples chasing silveries, as the Cantabrians call the smelt." - Keith Draper (1997).

Slim hair style flies have always been popular, and they are a particular favourite of Maureen Butler who has a number of her creations featured in this book. The slimness of the dressing allows the fly to sink quickly, a desirable feature when fishing big, fast mountain rivers.

Tie in the tail. Tie in the tinsel for the body. Secure and trim.

Wind on the tinsel body.

Tie in the squirrel hair at the shoulder so that it sweeps back over the body. Saturate the tied area with cement to prevent the hairs being pulled out. Tie in a hackle feather.

Wind on the hackle collar. Finish the head and varnish.

STARLING (H)

ORIGIN: HERB SPANNAGL OF NEW PLYMOUTH
HOOK: 6-8 MEDIUM, 8-10 LONG SHANK
TAIL: BUNCH OF LONG, SOFT BLACK HACKLE FIBRES WITH (OPTIONAL) 2-4 STRANDS KRYSTAL FLASH, OR TEASE OUT THE RIB FIBRES
BODY: BLACK CHENILLE
RIB: RAINBOW FLASHABOU
HACKLE: BLACK HACKLE (SHORTER THAN THAT USED FOR THE TAIL)
HEAD: BLACK

The effect is that of Hackle style lures, and I have designated it as such, although the hackle wing is Palmered, which is a faster way of tying these up than the more conventional Fuzzy Wuzzy style. Any Hackle style fly could be tied in this manner, and indeed, the Starling evolved after originally tying up Red Setters in this way. The black version got its name because the combination of black and the Rainbow Flashabou caused it to glitter like the plumage of a starling.

It fishes well in fast water, coloured water, and during changes of light.

The Palmered hackle can be made to slope back by rolling the body between the fingers, crushing the hackles. The hackle can be made sparser, if desired, by stripping one side of the feather.

Tie in the tail fibres and the Krystal Flash.

Tie in a trimmed hackle feather butt first. Make sure that some hackle fibres are tied in to supplement the tail. Tie in the chenille and ribbing.

Wind on the chenille. Counter wind with the ribbing. Tie off and trim.

Palmer the hackle to the eye. Give a few additional turns to bulk up near the head. Tie off, trim, and form the head in the usual way.

STOAT (M)

ORIGIN: NOT KNOWN
HOOK: NOT STATED BUT PROBABLY 4-8
TAIL: RED WHISKS
BODY: PALE YELLOW
RIB: OVAL SILVER
WING: STRIP OF STOAT WITH DARK GUARD HAIRS
HACKLE: PALE GINGER OR BUFF
HEAD: BLACK

This appears in Bragg's book as a Taupo and Rotorua districts lure used in the 1960s. Again, I can not be certain about the accuracy of the pattern, but dressed as above gives a very close result.

I would expect this to be an excellent smelt lure. The only other lure I know of which uses stoat fur, or fitch, is Jim Koller's Silver Fitch which he uses to great effect.

Tie in the tail whisks. Tie in the body material and the ribbing.

Wind on the body material. Tie in a strip of stoat fur on the skin.

Wind on the ribbing, tying down the wing to the top of the body.

Tie in a hackle feather. Wind on to form a hackle collar.

STRING FLY (O)

ORIGIN: NOT KNOWN
HOOK: 8-10
TAIL: PIECE OF WHITE STRING OR JUTE FROM A SUGAR BAG
BODY: WHITE WOOL
RIB: SILVER
HEAD: BLACK

"This pattern is so simple many anglers would consider it to be an insult to a trout's intelligence. Be that as it may, the string fly is extremely effective when trout are smelting. Mr Tom Hope, a Taupo angler of repute, is well known as an exponent of the pattern and has taken countless trout on it over the years.

"Taxi Kapua, Borough Councillor and Maori elder, tells me that the pattern is especially effective where the hot Waipahihi stream flows into Lake Taupo. The smelt sometimes swim into the hot water and are cooked, turning white. Kapua claims that a white string fly drifted along the edge of the current is deadly when a school of trout are in the bay."- Keith Draper (1971).

Tie in the piece of string. Tie in the wool and ribbing.

Wind on the wool to the head, then follow with the ribbing and tie off. Finish the head and varnish.

As a variation, you could try using red thread and white nylon 'wool' to create the effect described under Mallard Smelt.

SUCCESS (M)

ORIGIN: BRONWYN WILSON OF TAUPO
HOOK: 2-6
TAG: RED WOOL OR HACKLE WHISKS
BODY: GREEN BARBIE DOLL MATERIAL
RIB: OVAL SILVER FOR THREE-QUARTERS OF BODY, THEN ONE TURN AT HEAD TO HOLD WING DOWN
WING: TWO WHITE FEATHERS INSIDE TWO GREEN GRIZZLE FEATHERS
HACKLE: GREEN GRIZZLE
TOPPING: GREEN FLASHABOU OR GREEN HOLOGRAPHIC TINSEL
HEAD: RED

So named for obvious reasons, Bronwyn and others have had a lot of success with this lure harling at Lake Taupo. It is also makes a good night fly if tied with a glow tube body, in which case the rib is omitted and the wing is tied in by the butts only.

Barbie Doll material is a luminescent fabric available from drapers in a variety of colours. It has narrow lines running through it, a bit like a timber grain. Cutting a thin strip along the 'grain' produces a strip of stretchy material which will naturally roll into a flexible braid-like cord, not unlike mylar, which makes effective bodies.

See my comments under Albino 3, with regard to the ribbing.

Tie in the tag. Tie in a thin strip of body material and the ribbing.

Return the thread back three-quarters of the way along the shank. Wind on the Barbie Doll material and ribbing to this point and secure.

Continue the thread nearly to the head. Wind on the body material to this point and tie off. Tie in the wing feathers by the butts. Make one final turn with the ribbing catching the wing down to the top of the shank and tie off.

Tie in the topping. Tie in a hackle feather. Wind on to form a hackle collar.

SUNSET FLY (H)

ORIGIN: GRAHAM ANDREWS OF ROTORUA
HOOK: 4-6
TAIL: BLACK SQUIRREL
BODY: THREE EQUAL SEGMENTS OF DANVILLE RED, TRUE ORANGE, AND BLACK, CHENILLE
HACKLE: MATCHING COLOUR BETWEEN EACH SEGMENT, INCREASING IN SIZE SO THAT ALL HACKLES LAY BACK TO THE BASE OF THE TAIL WHEN WET
CHEEK: (OPTIONAL) JUNGLE COCK
HEAD: BLACK

This is a Fuzzy Wuzzy style night fly first tied on 2 February 1978, on which date it caught 6 rainbows in 2 $^1/_2$ hours. It is fished on a floating or sink-tip line in shallow stream mouths, or with a sinking line in faster deeper water. Use a medium retrieve. It is particularly effective on rainbow, and the takes are invariably savage.

Tie in the squirrel tail. Tie in the first (red) segment of chenille.

Take the thread a short distance along the shank. Wind on the chenille to this point and tie off. Tie in a red hackle feather and wind on.

Repeat the process with the orange chenille, orange hackle, then the black chenille and finishing with a black hackle at the head.

SUNSET RABBIT (M)

ORIGIN: GARY KEMSLEY OF NAPIER
HOOK: 2-8
TAIL: BLACK OR RED WHISKS
BODY: RED CHENILLE
RIB: OVAL SILVER
WING: STRIP OF BLACK RABBIT FUR
HACKLE: BLACK
HEAD: BLACK

This simple but highly effective lure was developed during the summer of 1974. Gary was fishing the mouth of the Waitahanui River and wanted a fly that would catch fish during the usually unresponsive change of light period. This lure proved to be the answer, catching many big browns during morning and evening change of light. It has also proved over the years to be deadly in discoloured water. In those conditions, Gary has had great fishing in the Tongariro, Tukituki, and Hutt Rivers. It is worth noting that the very similar Claret appeared at about the same time with similar success during sunset hours. Gary's Sunset Rabbit is now tied commercially.

Tie in the tail whisks. Tie in the chenille and ribbing.

Wind on the chenille. Tie in the strip of rabbit fur.

Wind on the ribbing, tying down the wing to the top of the body.

Tie in a hackle feather and wind on to form a hackle collar.

SWAGGER (M)

ORIGIN: DAVE HOPE OF CHRISTCHURCH
HOOK: 2-8
TAIL: BARRED ROCK (GRIZZLE)
BODY: WHITE
RIB: FLAT EMBOSSED SILVER TINSEL
WING: BLACK ORPINTON
HACKLE: BARRED ROCK (GRIZZLE)
CHEEKS: CHEST FEATHERS FROM A MALE PARADISE DUCK
HEAD: BLACK

"This is a variation of the Hope's Dark, with the addition of the paradise duck cheeks. Another very successful Canterbury lure, this fly is an example of the fly-tier's economy. The hackle tips used in the tail would come from the same feathers used for the head hackle." - Keith Draper (1997).

Orpinton is a breed of hen. It is unlikely that you will come across orpinton feathers through commercial outlets, but any black hackle could be substituted.

Tie in the tail. Tie in the body material and the ribbing. Secure and trim.

Wind on the body material. Tie in the wing at the shoulder.

Wind on the ribbing, tying down the wing to the top of the body. Tie in the cheeks on either side of the shank.

Tie in the hackle and wind on.

SWEEP (M)

ORIGIN: R.K. BRAGG OF CHRISTCHURCH
HOOK: 2-8
TAIL: RED HACKLE WHISKS
BODY: BLACK CHENILLE
RIB: OVAL GOLD TINSEL
WING: BLACK ORPINTON WITH SIDE FEATHERS OF WHITE HEN DYED KINGFISHER BLUE
HACKLE: BLACK
HEAD: BLACK

This is another Robert Bragg creation, first designed in 1949. As with Swagger, it incorporates black orpinton, which is a breed of poultry. Again, any black feather could be substituted.

While this entry appears in both of Keith Draper's books, the photo appears only in the 1971 publication. That photo shows a tail of red whisks but the pattern omits it. I have assumed that the omission is an error, particularly as the example photographed was tied by its creator.

Tie in the tail whisks, body material and ribbing. Secure and trim.

Wind on the chenille and tie off. Tie in the wing feathers at the shoulder.

Wind on the ribbing, tying down the wing to the top of the body. Tie in the side feathers. Secure and trim.

Tie in the hackle feather and wind on.

SYD'S GINGER (M)

ORIGIN: NOT KNOWN
HOOK: NOT STATED, BUT PROBABLY 2-8
BODY: YELLOW MOHAIR OR FLOSS
RIB: OVAL GOLD TINSEL
WING: FOUR GINGER COCK HACKLES
HEAD: BLACK

This comes from John Veniard's book. It appears to be a variation of Ginger Mick (or vice versa), and no doubt performed - and will continue to perform in the same manner. The origin is not given, but I know of only one angler named Syd, with that spelling, and that is Syd Peterken of Waipukurau. If he was indeed the creator, then you can be assured of this fly's pedigree. If he was the creator he would have been quite young at the time because a similar dressing is given in Kendrick's 1946 book *Modern Fly Dressings.*

Tie in the body material and ribbing. Secure and trim.

Wind on the body material. Tie in the four wing feathers at the shoulder.

Wind on the ribbing, tying down the wing to the top of the body.

Tie off and trim.

TADPOLE (M)

ORIGIN: BARRY KENT OF TE PUKE
HOOK: LONG-SHANK 10 2X
TAIL: GOLDEN PHEASANT TIPPETS
BODY: YELLOW FLOSS
RIB: FINE COPPER WIRE
WING: STRIP OF OLIVE RABBIT
EYES: MONO-FILAMENT
HEAD: VARIEGATED CHENILLE

This pattern was created by Barry Kent, once a professional fly-tier of Napier but now residing in Te Puke. He also ties a black version which differs only in that it has red marabou whisks instead of golden pheasant tippets, black rabbit fur, gold or brown floss, and a black chenille head.

As the name suggests, it is intended to imitate a tadpole. It can be fished on a floating or sinking line, and should be cast over weed beds and retrieved very slowly.

Monofilament eyes can be created easily by taking a short length of nylon fishing line, say 40 lbs. breaking strain, and burning the ends with a flame.

Tie in the tippets. Tie in the floss and ribbing.

Take the thread back nearly to the head, leaving enough room for 2-3 turns of chenille to form the head. Wind on the floss body to this point. Tie in the strip of rabbit fur.

Wind on the copper wire ribbing, tying down the rabbit fur to the top of the body. Tie in the chenille for the head.

Purchase or create the filament eyes. Tied up in the size given in this pattern, the distance between the eyes should be about 5mm. Fasten the eyes to the shank with the thread using a figure of eight tie. Wind on the chenille head and tie off.

TAGARTI (O)

ORIGIN: JACK MURRAY OF TAURANGA
HOOK: 6-10
TAIL: BUFF-COLOURED PHEASANT RUMP FEATHER. STROKE THE FIBRES TO LIE CLOSE ALONGSIDE THE SPINE AND THEN ROLL TO FORM A TUBE. ONCE SECURED, CUT CLEANLY ACROSS TO GIVE A STRAIGHT EDGE CROSS SECTION AT HALF THE BODY LENGTH.
BODY: BROWN CHENILLE WITH A DARK OLIVE HACKLE PALMERED ALONG THE LENGTH, THE FIBRES FACING FORWARDS TOWARDS THE EYE
RIB: (OPTIONAL) OVAL GOLD
HACKLE: DARK OLIVE (SAME AS THE BODY HACKLE) BUILT UP AT THE HEAD WITH FIVE OR SIX TURNS
TOPPING: PEACOCK SWORD
HEAD: BLACK
EYES: YELLOW WITH RED PUPIL

The name is a union of the Zulu 'Inthagati' for Witchcraft, and Joe Taggerty, an American friend and angler from California who helped trial the lure at Lake Aniwhenua.

Jack is adamant that the tail fibres must be cut off square as this is an important factor in its effectiveness. Jack does not use a rib. He points out that he has taken nine trout on one fly without the Palmered hackle breaking or unwinding, and therefore sees no need for one.

However, Rob Limmer is going to tie this up commercially and intends using a rib. Jack's preference is to fish this lure with a fast, short, jerky retrieve. However, he says, at times a slow jerky retrieve with a sink and draw pause in between can be effective, especially at night.

Tie in the tail fibres and trim square. Tie in the chenille and a hackle feather by the butt with the inside facing forward (and ribbing if using).

Wind on the chenille. Palmer the hackle along the body and secure. Wind on the ribbing if using.

Tie in a hackle feather and wind on to form a hackle collar. Tie in the peacock sword topping. Complete the head in the normal way and add eyes.

TAIHAPE TICKLER (P) (Old Tie)

ORIGIN: FRANK LORD OF ROTORUA
HOOK: 2-8
BODY: CLARET CHENILLE
WING: BLUE PUKEKO FEATHERS
HACKLE: CLARET COCK
HEAD: BLACK

This is a night fly created by Frank Lord (of Lord's Killer fame). He set out to combine features of two well known and proven night flies - Craig's Night-time and Mallard and Claret. The end result incorporated the body and hackle of the Mallard and Claret and the Pukeko wing used in Craig's Night-time and tied in the same way. The result was a limit bag the first night it was used, and the name, Keith Draper tells us, came from a Taihape angler, Bert Jensen, who was curious to see this fly which had been causing so much havoc, and upon examining it commented, "by crikey, that's a real Taihape Tickler".

Obviously, the original dressing worked a treat, but for some reason has evolved into the dressing which is described on the following entry. The pattern above comes from Keith Draper.

Tie in the chenille for the body.

Wind on the chenille to form the body and tie off. Tie in the Pukeko feathers to form a canopy over the body.

Tie in the hackle feather and wind on the hackle collar.

TAIHAPE TICKLER (P)
(Modern Tie)

ORIGIN: FRANK LORD OF ROTORUA
HOOK: 2-8
TAIL: SMALL TAG OF RED WOOL
BODY: RED CHENILLE
RIB: OVAL SILVER
WING: BLUE PUKEKO FEATHERS
HACKLE: DYED ORANGE HACKLES
HEAD: BLACK

Hugh McDowell says "the Taihape Tickler is now almost exclusively dressed as shown above. When or why it changed remains a mystery." To add to the mystery, John Veniard in 1970, a year before Keith Draper's first book, gave this dressing except that the Pukeko wing had a topping of yellow hackle fibres, and a throat hackle only of red cock. That seems to have been the preferred dressing for Kilwell in the early 1970s.

John Veniard notes that the Taihape Tickler was also known as Deadly Dick, a reference I have not seen elsewhere. It does not square with Keith Draper's account of how the Tickler got its name, but it might conceivably have something to do with the changed dressing. Veniard also lists a Pukeko and Red which is a Taihape Tickler (his dressing), without the topping of yellow hackle fibres.

Whichever way it is tied, it is unquestionably an impressive fish taker.

Tie in the wool tag. Tie in the chenille and ribbing.

Wind on the chenille and ribbing and tie off. Tie in the Pukeko feathers.

Tie in the hackle feathers. Wind on to form a collar.

TAIL-LIGHT (H)

ORIGIN: KEITH DRAPER OF TAUPO
HOOK: 2-8
TAIL: A LARGE TAG OF BRIGHT RED WOOL
BODY: BLACK CHENILLE IN TWO SECTIONS
HACKLE: TWO LARGE BLACK HACKLES, ONE TIED INTO THE BODY, THE OTHER AT THE HEAD
HEAD: BLACK

This is a truncated Fuzzy Wuzzy, designed to catch fish that are taking short, particularly brown trout at night. We have all experienced those frustrating times when fish strike but never seem to get hooked.

"If the problem persists" says Keith, "go down to the smallest pattern." (1997). 'Tail-light' is a clever play on the imagery of the red tag as a car tail-light, and the literal absence of the tail, unlike most hackle-style flies.

Tie in the wool tag. Tie in the chenille for the body.

Take the thread part way back along the shank. Wind on the chenille to this point and secure. Tie in the first hackle feather.

Wind on the hackle. Wind on the chenille to the head and tie off. Tie in the second hackle feather.

Wind on the hackle as before. Finish the head and varnish.

TAMATI (O) (Old Tie)

ORIGIN:	TAMATI? OR L.F ELSBY?
HOOK:	1/0-8
TAG:	(KEITH DRAPER) FLAT SILVER TINSEL (JOHN VENIARD) SILVER TINSEL AND RED FLOSS
TAIL:	GOLDEN PHEASANT TIPPETS
BODY:	(KEITH DRAPER) BLACK AND YELLOW IN FOUR SEGMENTS, WITH NATURAL RED HACKLE WOUND BETWEEN EACH SEGMENT
	(JOHN VENIARD) IN SECTIONS - RED, YELLOW, BLACK, YELLOW CHENILLE WITH EACH SECTION BUTTED WITH NATURAL RED GAME HACKLE
WING:	DARK MOTTLED TURKEY TAIL, TIED IN SALMON-FLY STYLE, I.E. IN STRIPS WITHOUT THE QUILL
HACKLE:	NATURAL RED, TIED UNDER THE THROAT
CHEEKS:	JUNGLE COCK
HEAD:	BLACK

"Tamati was an old Maori who lived at Waipahihi, Taupo. The bay now known as Two Mile Bay was once called Tamati's Bay. There he kept a boat for hire, with himself as boatman. It is said that when devising this fly he used the ragwort moth for inspiration....It hardly looks like a ragwort moth, especially as it was usually tied on a No. 2 or 1/0 hook, but it did catch trout. That was the original dressing and it disappeared from the scene about twenty years ago. The fly sold under the name today bears little resemblance to Tamati's creation, but those old-timers who personally knew the old Maori are pleased that at least his name is perpetuated; he was a great old fisherman." - Keith Draper (1971).

For further comment on the history of this lure, see the next entry.

John Veniard's spelling of this fly is "Tamiti", but there is no doubt it is the same fly. The following brief guide is based on Draper's pattern.

Tie in the tag and tippets. Tie in the first section of body material.

Take the thread a short distance along the shank. Wind on the body material to this point. Tie in a hackle feather and wind on. Repeat the process with each segment finishing nearly at the head.

Tie in the wing, cheeks, and throat hackle. Finish the head and varnish.

TAMATI (M) (Modern Tie)

ORIGIN:	TAMATI? OR L.F. ELSBY?
HOOK:	2-8
TAIL:	YELLOW HACKLE WHISKS
BODY:	(DRAPER) THREE SEGMENTS OF RED, BLACK, AND YELLOW CHENILLE (VENIARD) FOUR SECTIONS OF RED, YELLOW, BLACK, YELLOW CHENILLE
RIB:	OVAL SILVER
WING:	SPLIT GROUSE OR PARTRIDGE
HACKLE:	NATURAL RED (VENIARD - AT THROAT ONLY)
HEAD:	BLACK

The probable origin of the original Tamati and its creator are detailed in the previous entry. However, in *Fish & Game New Zealand* (issue 12, 1996), there is an article which recounts the exploits of one L.F. Elsby of Wellington. Interest in Mr Elsby was aroused when the author of the article stumbled upon notes and memorabilia that belonged to him and which provided some insight into fishing Tongariro back in the '20s and '30s. The article quotes what purports to be an extract from his diary which says that he was using "a 40 yard heavy tapered line and a *fly of my own make* which Barlow and I called Tamati, tied on a long shank No.1 hook with a piece of peacock herl." (Emphasis added)

An accompanying photo of a trout lure proclaims it to be "The Tamati fly." It is difficult to tell from a black and white photo but it appears to be dressed in the old tie with the addition of a peacock herl topping.

Whether the old Maori Tamati actually created the fly, or was simply the inspiration for its name will perhaps now be shrouded in doubt as a result of that diary entry. I have to say that I rather doubt Mr Elsby's account. It is difficult to imagine a gentleman from Wellington creating a fly and plucking 'Tamati' out of the air as a suitable name.

Whatever the truth is, Mr Elsby's diary records are further proof that the Tamati is a celebrated fish catcher.

The modern dressing is tied up in the Matuku style, in the same manner as, for example, the Split partridge. It should be fished slow and deep.

TAUPO TIGER (M)

ORIGIN: JAMES ROSS OF NAPIER
HOOK: 2-8
TAIL: (OPTIONAL) RED HACKLE WHISKS
BODY: YELLOW
RIB: OVAL SILVER
WING: BADGER HACKLES, WITH A GOOD BLACK CENTRE
HACKLE: BADGER
HEAD: RED

This was designed around 1930 by James Ross of Napier, who ran a tobacco and tackle business. It was originally called Tiger Ross but when it became a commercial proposition the name was changed to Taupo Tiger. Hugh McDowell sheds light (or confusion) with the thought that the Tiger Ross is actually a red-bodied version with the colouring being close to that of a very popular Scottish wet fly called Peter Ross. The version tied by Kilwell in the early 1970's had a red body but was called Taupo Tiger. John Veniard's dressing is the same as Keith Draper's (but includes Jungle Cock cheeks), and that is the dressing I have preferred.

Tie in the tail whisks. Tie in the chenille and ribbing.

Wind on the chenille and tie off. Tie in the wing feathers.

Wind on the ribbing, tying down the wing to the top of the body. Tie in the hackle feather and wind on to form a hackle collar.

TAUPO WASP (See Ewe Wasp)

TEAL (O)

ORIGIN: NOT KNOWN
HOOK: 8-14
TAIL: GOLDEN PHEASANT TIPPETS, OR NATURAL RED COCK FIBRES
BODY: RED FLOSS OR WOOL
RIB: OVAL SILVER
WING: TEAL FLANK (OR SUBSTITUTE MALE PARADISE SHELDUCK)
HACKLE: NATURAL RED COCK OR HEN, AT THROAT
HEAD: BLACK

This is an older series of small wet flies from the U.K. which became very popular in New Zealand, but which have largely disappeared from the scene. They were tied in a variety of colours giving rise to Teal and Red (this pattern), Teal and Black, Teal and Green, etc.

Tied in the larger size it can be fished as a lure, and it features in Bragg's book as a Canterbury lure pattern of the 1960s. Keith Draper recalls successful outings using this and also a Teal and Orange on the Hawkes Bay rivers in the 1950s.

Notwithstanding the hook range given, the featured example has been tied on a No. 6 hook.

Tie in the tippets for the tail. Tie in the floss and the ribbing.

Wind on the floss body followed by the ribbing.

Tie in the hackle beard under the throat. Tie in the wing by the butts. Complete the head in the usual way.

TE TAUIWHA (O)

ORIGIN: NOT KNOWN
HOOK: NO. 1, LONG-SHANKED
BODY: PALE LEMON CHENILLE
WING: PALE GREY MOHAIR TIED IN AT INTERVALS ALONG THE BODY AND EXTENDING BEYOND THE END OF THE HOOK
HACKLE: BADGER COCK
HEAD: BROWN

Now here is one you are unlikely to have heard of! It comes from John Veniard's book, but how it came by the name, or any other details, is not recorded. It is described as a whitebait fly, and the colouring matches that description, but I doubt whether it was ever intended to be limited to one hook which is better suited for catching sharks!

Pale lemon chenille must be as old as this pattern, for I have never seen any. Wool is just as good, and that is what I have used.

The example has been tied on a Kamasan B800 No. 6 long shank hook.

Tie in the chenille for the body. Secure and trim.

Take the thread part way along the shank. Wind on the chenille to this point. Tie in a bunch of mohair which extends back past the bend of the hook.

Continue the process along the hook shank. Each subsequent tie of mohair should reach back to the end of the preceding bunch. Once the head is reached, tie in the hackle feather and wind on.

THAT PURPLY-BLUE THING (H)

ORIGIN: ROB LIMMER OF TAURANGA
HOOK: 4-8
TAIL: PURPLE SQUIRREL TAIL
BODY: SOLDIER BLUE CHENILLE IN TWO SECTIONS
HACKLE: CLARET AT MID-SECTION AND HEAD
HEAD: BLACK

This is a very effective lure, particularly with brown trout although it will catch rainbows as well. Rob has fished with this widely in the Rotorua and Tauranga areas. It is good on dull overcast days, change of light, and dark nights. It should be fished on a slow to medium retrieve unless harling in the larger size. It is now being tied commercially.

Tie in the tail. Tie in the chenille.

Take the thread part way back along the shank. Wind on the chenille to this point and tie off. Tie in a claret hackle.

Wind on the hackle and tie off. Take the thread and the chenille back nearly to the head and tie in another hackle feather.

Wind on to form a hackle collar.

THE BOSS (H)

ORIGIN: THIS IS A NORTH AMERICAN STEELHEAD PATTERN
HOOK: 2-8
BUTT: ORANGE FLOSS
TAIL: BLACK SQUIRREL
BODY: BLACK CHENILLE
RIB: OVAL SILVER
HACKLE: ORANGE
HEAD: BLACK

Roger Smailes, of Masterton, came across this pattern in an American magazine. He was attracted to the colouring and felt that it would do well in the New Zealand scene. He tied up a few for himself and some friends, and found that trout were indeed attracted to the colour combination. It fishes very well in the Tongariro River, and is a good change of light pattern. It is fished on a sinking line in the usual way. Roger now ties these commercially for his shop, whereby I can (just) justify its inclusion in this book.

The differences between this and the Umpqua (USA) pattern called simply Boss are very slight, and I suspect they are one and the same pattern.

Tie in the orange floss and wind on to form the butt. Tie in the tail. Secure. Tie in the chenille and ribbing.

Wind on the chenille and ribbing and tie off.

Tie in a hackle feather. Wind on to form a hackle collar..

THE SMELT FLY (M)

ORIGIN: HUGH MCDOWELL OF ROTORUA
HOOK: 2-10
TAIL: PINCH OF RED OR ORANGE HACKLE FIBRES
BODY: SILVER OR PEARL MYLAR FLAT TINSEL WOUND OVER WHITE WOOL
RIB: OVAL SILVER
WING: PAIR OF PALE FEATHERS (BADGER OR SIMILAR)
HACKLE: (OPTIONAL) TO MATCH WING
HEAD: BLACK, SILVER-GREY, OR RED

This is, obviously enough, a smelt pattern which works best in the smaller sizes unless harling, when No.4 or even No. 2 hooks are favoured.

This pattern lends itself to many variations. Some may prefer to omit the hackle, or use diamond braid or even fluorescent lime wool instead of mylar. However, neither of these two body options require a white wool underbody. White or yellow eyes with a black pupil are other options. Hugh says that it fishes well after dark if tied with a luminous body. A more detailed explanation and tying guide can be found in *Fish & Game New Zealand*, Issue 7, 1995.

Hugh has added Jungle Cock eyes in the above example. It is a matter of personal choice but many lures can be enhanced by this addition.

Tie in the tail fibres, wool, ribbing, and mylar.

Wind on the white wool, followed by the mylar which is spiralled over the wool. Secure and trim. Tie in the wing feathers.

Wind on the ribbing, tying down the wing to the top of the body.

If using, tie in a matching hackle feather and wind on to form the hackle collar.

THUNDER & LIGHTNING (O)

ORIGIN:	NOT KNOWN
HOOK:	NOT STATED BUT PROBABLY 2-8
BODY:	PROBABLY SILVER TINSEL
RIB:	PROBABLY OVAL SILVER
WING:	FURNACE, TIED IN AT HEAD ONLY
HACKLE:	ORANGE, THROAT ONLY
CHEEK:	JUNGLE COCK
HEAD:	BLACK

The text in Bragg's book is so inaccurate that it should not be thought that this lure was devised by James Wright around 1930. James Wright is the famous Tweedside (England) fly-tier who tied (not created) the very first Greenwells Glory in 1854. James Wright did create a salmon fly called Thunder and Lightening but the pattern is so dissimilar I do not think it can be said that this is a simplified version of that original, although the identical and unusual name indicates otherwise. Both versions appear in Bragg's book.

It is described as a dark fly which is good in discoloured water. The photo in Bragg's book shows the hackle as yellow, but reference to other lures which are known to have orange, and which appear the same shade as this one, suggests that it is a trick of the photographic reproduction process.

As with many of the examples shown in Bragg's book, I have had to employ some intuition in determining the pattern.

Tie in the tinsel and ribbing.

Wind on the body tinsel followed by the ribbing. Secure and trim.

Tie in the wing feathers by the butts. Tie in the hackle fibres under the throat.

Add Jungle Cock cheeks, and form the head in the usual way.

TIGER ROSS (see Taupo Tiger)

TINOPAI (O)

ORIGIN:	NOT KNOWN
HOOK:	NOT STATED, BUT PROBABLY 2-8
TAG:	ROUND SILVER TINSEL
TAIL:	RED IBIS OR SUBSTITUTE
BODY:	TWO EQUAL PARTS OF YELLOW AND RED MOHAIR OR CHENILLE
RIB:	OVAL GOLD TINSEL
WING:	BROWN MOTTLED TURKEY FEATHER WITH A STRIP OF RED GOOSE OVER
HACKLE:	BROWN PARTRIDGE BACK FEATHER
HEAD:	BLACK

This comes from John Veniard and is another pattern that has fallen into obscurity for one reason or another, probably the difficulty in obtaining partridge feathers. I know nothing else about this fly except that it is obviously one of the turkey series which were then very popular and successful.

The small settlement of Tinopai on the Kaipara Harbour is a possible (even if curious) origin for the name.

Tie in the tag and tail whisks. Trim. Tie in the first segment of body material and the ribbing.

Take the thread halfway along the shank. Wind on the chenille to this point and tie off. Tie in the second segment of body material. Take both the thread and chenille back nearly to the head. Follow with the ribbing and tie off.

Tie in the turkey wing in the streamer style followed by the strip of goose which should form a topping over the turkey.

Tie in the hackle feather and wind on to form a hackle collar.

TIPPET RED (O)

ORIGIN: NOT KNOWN

HOOK: NOT STATED BUT IN THE SMALLER SIZES, PROBABLY 6-10

TAIL: RED WHISKS UNDER GOLDEN PHEASANT CREST

BODY: RED SEAL'S FUR OR SUBSTITUTE

RIB: OVAL SILVER

WING: GOLDEN PHEASANT TIPPETS

TOPPING: RED HACKLE FEATHER, GOLDEN PHEASANT CREST, AND JUNGLE COCK

HACKLE: TEAL, THROAT

HEAD: BLACK

This is one of a number of patterns that takes its name from the body colour, hence Tippet (and) Black, Silver, etc. These are favoured throughout Scotland and Ireland for low water sea trout and lake fishing. They found their way to New Zealand where they enjoyed a degree of popularity.

The pattern varies depending on the source of information. The above pattern is based on the example shown in Bragg's book in which it is listed as a Canterbury pattern of the 1960s, which can only mean that it was popular there at that time. It originated a very long time before, half a world away.

Tie in the tail whisks and the golden pheasant crest. Tie in the body material and the ribbing.

Wind on the body material and follow with the ribbing. Tie in the golden pheasant tippet wings.

Tie in a hackle feather beard style.

Tie in the topping. Form the head in the usual way.

TOMMO (H)

ORIGIN: ALI THOMPSON OF ROTORUA

HOOK: NOT STATED BUT PROBABLY 4-8

TAIL: BROWN SQUIRREL

BODY: CHENILLE IN THREE PARTS - RED, BLACK, YELLOW, STARTING FROM THE REAR

RIB: OVAL SILVER

HACKLE: GINGER

HEAD: BLACK

This appeared in Nancy Tichborne's 1987 calendar. It is said to be very effective fished around the weed beds of Lakes Otamangakau, near Turangi and Aniwhenua in the Bay of Plenty. It is fished on a floating line with a slow retrieve.

The body colouring is reminiscent of Tamati, which has acquired a well earned reputation as a fish taker.

Tie in the tail. Tie in the first segment of chenille and the ribbing.

Take the thread a short way back along the shank. Wind on the chenille to this point and tie off. Tie in the second segment of chenille.

Take the thread a further short distance along the shank. Wind on the black chenille to this point and tie off. Repeat with the third segment of chenille.

Wind on the ribbing. Tie in a hackle feather and wind on to form a hackle collar.

TONGARIRO QUEEN (O)

ORIGIN: NOT KNOWN

HOOK: 2-8

TAG: SILVER TINSEL

TAIL: GOLDEN PHEASANT TOPPING

BODY: FOUR SEGMENTS OF CHENILLE IN ALTERNATE RED AND YELLOW WITH A GINGER HACKLE BETWEEN EACH SEGMENT AND AT THE THROAT

WING: TURKEY

HEAD: BLACK

There are many aspects about this fly which are reminiscent of the original dressing for Tamati. It was perhaps inevitable that a fly would be named after the mighty Tongariro but like so many others of this style, it has disappeared with the passage of time.

The above dressing comes from Keith Draper's 1997 book.

I have a suspicion bordering on certainty that if this lure was re-introduced to the Tongariro River trout, it would do very nicely.

Tie in the tag and topping. Trim. Tie in the first segment of chenille.

Take the thread a short way along the shank. Wind on the chenille to this point and tie off. Tie in a hackle feather and wind on. Trim. Tie in the second segment of chenille.

Repeat the process until all four segments have been tied in, with a hackle wound between each. Tie in some hackles at the throat. Tie in the turkey wing in the salmon-fly style, i.e. in strips without the quill.

TURKEY (M) (Modern Tie)

ORIGIN: NOT KNOWN
HOOK: 2-6
TAIL: RED GAME HACKLE FIBRES
BODY: COLOUR AND MATERIAL OF CHOICE
RIB: OVAL SILVER TINSEL
WING: SPLIT MOTTLED BROWN TURKEY TAIL
HACKLE: RED GAME HACKLE COLLAR
HEAD: BLACK

This comes from John Veniard's book which gave a green body dressing and was called Turkey and Green. The body colour would determine the name, hence Turkey and Red, Turkey and Yellow etc. It is tied in the split-wing style which Keith Draper refers to as a later development of the (then) traditional or orthodox salmon style, i.e. without the quill. Both this pattern and the next can be tied either way, and the two photos show the difference in tying methods. Tied either way, the Turkey lures were very effective. I have an idea that it may have been a Turkey and Yellow tied as above, which accounted for a 7lb trout at Taupo when no one else was catching anything (see Leslie's Lure).

This pattern differs only marginally from Split Turkey.

Tie in the tail whisks. Tie in the chenille and ribbing.

Wind on the chenille body. Tie in the matching split turkey tail wing.

Wind on the ribbing, tying down the wing in the Matuku style. Tie in the hackle feather and wind on.

TURKEY (Yellow & Red) (O) (Old Tie)

ORIGIN: NOT KNOWN
HOOK: 2-6
TAIL: A BUNCH OF BROWN TURKEY, THE TAIL ENDING UNDER THE LONG WING TIP
BODY: THICK WOOL OR MOHAIR, USUALLY YELLOW OR RED
RIB: OVAL SILVER
WING: BROWN TURKEY, TIED LONG AND SWEPT BACK
HACKLE: LONG SOFT RED COCK
HEAD: BLACK

"Once upon a time no respectable Taupo angler would be without his Turkeys, be they reds or yellows. These large flies were one of the most popular styles for many years and their reputation was justly deserved. Somewhere along the way they fell out of favour, relics of the transitory stage of fly development after the salmon fly had passed on. The old ties were large and had a rough look. This appearance was a carefully cultivated one, and to tie a bunch of consistently rough-looking flies takes more skill than is generally credited. Thick-tufted bodies of wool or mohair were normally used.

"A later development of the Turkey was the split tie and in most cases the feather used was split grouse tail, but this mode of tying has also nearly disappeared."- Keith Draper (1971)

Bragg's book features a lure called Taupo Turkey which conforms to the pattern given here but which is tied in a chunkier, more compact way.

Tie in the tail feathers. Tie in the body material.

Take the thread and body material back nearly to the head. Tie in the turkey tail fibres for the wing.

Tie in the hackle feather and wind on. Finish the head and varnish.

URCHIN (M)

ORIGIN: GARTH COGHILL OF ROTORUA
HOOK: 2-8
TAIL: RED WOOL OR SPARKLE YARN
BODY: FLAT GOLD OR SILVER TINSEL
RIB: OVAL GOLD OR SILVER
WING: STRIP OF POSSUM FUR
HACKLE: HEN HACKLES
EYES: JUNGLE COCK
HEAD: BLACK

This is a possum version of Rabbit which performs just as effectively. The fur is well brushed out using a cat flea comb or similar. The above version has been dyed green, but Garth also ties it up using natural possum fur and silver tinsel and ribbing.

Possum fur does not absorb water as readily as rabbit. The lure should be thoroughly soaked before using, or left for some time after casting before retrieving.

Tie in the tail. Tie in the body tinsel and ribbing.

Wind on the tinsel body and tie off. Tie in the possum strip.

Wind on the ribbing, tying down the fur wing to the top of the body.

Tie in a hackle feather. Wind on to form a hackle collar. Add Jungle Cock eyes.

VERON ARGENTE (M)

ORIGIN: NOT KNOWN
HOOK: 4-6, LONG SHANK
TAG: SILVER
TAIL: GOLDEN PHEASANT TIPPETS
BODY: SILVER TINSEL
RIB: OVAL SILVER
WING: ORANGE INSIDE BADGER
HACKLE: ORANGE
CHEEK: JUNGLE COCK
HEAD: BLACK

This appears in Bragg's book under a section relating to tying New Zealand lures (see my comments under Klondike Kate). Again, it is difficult to be exact about the pattern from the photograph provided. 'Argent', in heraldry, means white or silver-white and that part of the name reflects the body colour. I had hoped that 'Veron' would lead me to confirm the rest of the pattern, but it was not to be. I have no idea what the name signifies.

Tie in the tag. Tie in the tippets for the tail. Tie in the body tinsel and the ribbing.

Wind on the tinsel body. Tie in the wing feathers by the butts.

Wind on the ribbing, tying down the wing to the top of the body.

Tie in the hackle feather and wind on to form a hackle collar. Tie in the Jungle Cock cheeks.

WAIHORA (O)

ORIGIN: TOM RICKIT OF TAUPO
HOOK: 2-6
TAIL: RED WHISKS
BODY: BLACK WOOL OR CHENILLE
RIB: FLAT SILVER
WING: TURKEY
HACKLE: BLACK
HEAD: BLACK

"This fly was the design of Tom Rickit of Taupo, who many years ago served as a guide to Zane Grey on some of his fishing trips to New Zealand. It is a night fly and while not much in evidence today still has its adherents." - Keith Draper (1971).

Waihora Bay is in the Western Bays area of Lake Taupo. Presumably the fly was named after it, or in honour of its success in that area.

The addition of Jungle Cock is always an embellishment worth considering. The head hackle is tied under the throat, beard style.

Tie in the red whisks and the body material and ribbing.

Wind on the body material and ribbing to the head and tie off.

Tie in the hackle fibres under the throat, beard style, sweeping back to the point of the hook.

Tie in the turkey wing so that it sweeps back over the body. Tie in Jungle Cock cheeks if using.

WARDEN'S WORRY (K)

ORIGIN: KILWELL'S OF ROTORUA
HOOK: 2-8
TAIL: BROWN SQUIRREL TAIL
BODY: WOOL, YELLOW OR RED, SOMETIMES GREEN
RIB: SILVER TINSEL
WING: THE LONG RUSTY RUMP FEATHERS OF A COCK PHEASANT (TAIL END)
TOPPING: GREEN PEACOCK SWORD
HEAD: BLACK

"A Rotorua fly that has on occasions lived up to its title. It is my experience that in the Taupo area at least it is more favoured as a trolling fly." - Keith Draper (1971).

Although this is a Killer pattern, the wings are tied in at the head only. For all but the largest hooks the feathers are too long to tie in along the shank in the usual way. You may need to tie in three or four feathers on each side. The ribbing is not the least bit necessary and could be omitted. In his updated 1997 book, Keith expands on his earlier comment:

"It is a perfect fly for fishing in slow, dark, weedy waters where the trout cruise looking for victims. Tied shortish, and in the smaller sizes, it is more than a passable suggestion of a dragonfly larvae, especially if it is tied with a green body."

Tie in the tail. Tie in the wool and ribbing. Secure and trim.

Take the thread back to the head. Follow with the wool and ribbing and tie off. Tie in a pair or more of rump feathers on either side of the shank.

Tie in the peacock sword topping. Finish the head and varnish.

WATER RAT (O)

ORIGIN: PAT O'KEEFE OF ROTORUA
HOOK: 6-10
TAIL: BUNCH OF NATURAL RABBIT
BODY: DUBBED NATURAL RABBIT
HEAD: BLACK

Artie McAdam of Melbourne was an Australian fly-casting champion who loved fishing in New Zealand so much he made 128 fishing trips to this country. He used to use a Water Rat of his own creation using the fur from the genuine article - the Australian Water Rat, but which is now fully protected. This is Pat's version of that original Rat. It is very similar to O'Keefe's Smelt, and is fished in the same way over weed beds with a series of quick retrieves and a pause. Pat has had a lot of success with this lure and describes it as an excellent smelt fly.

In the example shown, Pat has added a very short strip of mother-of-pearl Aurora skirt as a kind of overwing, tied in at the head and extending back about quarter of an inch (6mm). Details of this material are more fully discussed under O'Keefe's Smelt.

Take the thread down to the bend. Tie in a small bunch of rabbit fur for the tail.

Dub on a body of rabbit fur by whichever method of dubbing is preferred. Tie off and complete the head in the usual way.

WATSON'S FANCY (O)

ORIGIN: NOT KNOWN
HOOK: NOT STATED BUT PROBABLY 4-8
TAIL: TIPPET FIBRES OR IBIS
BODY: HALF RED AND HALF BLACK FLOSS OR DUBBING
RIB: SILVER TINSEL
WING: BLACK CROW WINGS
HACKLE: BLACK
CHEEK: JUNGLE COCK
HEAD: BLACK

This pattern comes from Kendrick's book *Modern Fly Dressings* (1946). A photo of this lure, dressed as above, appears in Bragg's book.

In the absence of the crow's wings, I have substituted feathers taken from the wing of a Pukeko. Visually, the appearance is very similar to that shown in Bragg's book.

It is tied in a loose-winged streamer style, and the hackle is tied in under the throat only. I have also seen it dressed with a golden pheasant crest for the tail, and no ribbing.

I presume it is a night fly. The example has been tied on a No. 8 hook.

Tie in the tippets or ibis for the tail. Tie in the first section of body material and the ribbing.

Take the thread back to the mid-point. Wind on the body material to that point and tie off. Tie in the second section of body material. Take the thread and body material back nearly to the head. Follow with the ribbing.

Tie in the throat hackle. Tie in the wing feathers by the butts. Add Jungle Cock cheeks and complete the head in the usual way.

WHANGANUI SMELT (M)

ORIGIN: RITCHIE BUCHANAN OF TAUPO
HOOK: 2-8
TAIL: RED WHISKS
BODY: RED AND BLACK CHENILLE
RIB: OVAL SILVER
WING: RED COCK HACKLES
TOPPING: GREY HACKLE WHISKS
HEAD: BLACK

This is a good all-round fly, but as might be expected with a colouring similar to Hall's Night-time, it comes into its own at night. It was originally tied up with Lake Rotoaira in mind because Ritchie believes that trout in that lake respond well to this colour combination. However, it proved itself to be particularly effective in Whanganui Bay in the Western Bays of Lake Taupo, hence the name.

However, it also harls well anywhere in Lake Taupo, especially from mid-afternoon to early evening.

Tie in the tail whisks. Tie in the two chenille colours and the ribbing.

Wind on the two chenilles, twisted or overlapped to give a harlequin or variegated effect. Tie in the wing feathers.

Wind on the ribbing, tying down the wing to the top of the body. Tie in the topping.

WHITEBAIT SERIES

There are numerous example of whitebait or smelt flies listed, and a representative collation of regional smelt patterns are contained in the Appendices. Most anglers will have their personal favourites.

John Veniard, in his English publication *Reservoir and Lake Flies* (1970), includes a section of New Zealand lake patterns. In it, he lists a series of whitebait fly patterns (eight in all) which obviously were in vogue at the time.

A similar compilation of whitebait and 'smolt' patterns appears in *Modern Fly Dressings* (1946) by C.H. Kendrick. Most of those appearing in Veniard's book also appear in Kendrick's list, but numbers 9-14 are contained only in Kendrick's book.

The following selection are included for historical reasons, but the home tier may wish to build up a collection of this series. Presumably they have proven themselves in the past, and there is no reason why they should not do so at any time.

With some, it is difficult to see the resemblance to whitebait but that is the classification given and so it stands.

I have given the tying style designation (M, O, etc.) but no guidelines on how to tie them. The accompanying photographs, together with the method described for any other patterns throughout this book with the same designation will provide all the clues the fly-tier needs.

In respect of all 14 of the following patterns, the origin in each case is not known, and the hook size range is not stated although it might be presumed to be in the smaller sizes, say 6-10. All 14 patterns photographed have been tied on size 6 hooks.

WHITEBAIT No. 1 (O)

TAIL: WHITE OSTRICH HERL

BODY: FLAT SILVER TINSEL

WING: WHITE MOHAIR EXTENDING TO END OF TAIL

HACKLE: WHITE, TIED UNDERNEATH ONLY, SALMON-FLY STYLE

HEAD: BLACK

WHITEBAIT No. 2 (M)

BODY: YELLOW MOHAIR

RIB: FLAT GOLD TINSEL

WING: BADGER HACKLES IN ANY OF THE LIGHT COLOURS, RANGING FROM PURE WHITE TO DEEP CREAM, AND TIED ON "MATUKA" STYLE

HEAD: BLACK

WHITEBAIT No. 3 (O)

TAIL: WHITE AND GREEN MOHAIR

BODY: FLAT SILVER TINSEL

WING: IN THREE LAYERS - WHITE, GREEN, WHITE MOHAIR

HEAD: BLACK

WHITEBAIT No. 4 (O)

TAIL: RED MOHAIR

BODY: FLAT GOLD TINSEL

WING: WHITE OR CREAM MOHAIR

HEAD: BROWN

WHITEBAIT No.5 (M)

BODY: GREY SEAL'S FUR OR WOOL

RIB: OVAL SILVER TINSEL

WING: TWO GRIZZLE (PLYMOUTH ROCK) COCK HACKLES, TIED ON "MATUKA" STYLE

THROAT: A SHORT TUFT OF RED WOOL

HEAD: BLACK

WHITEBAIT No. 6 (M)

BODY: FLAT SILVER TINSEL

RIB: OVAL SILVER TINSEL

WING: TWO GRIZZLE COCK HACKLES DYED ORANGE,

AND TIED ON "MATUKA" STYLE

HACKLE: RED COCK, WOUND AS A COLLAR (DYED BRIGHT RED)

HEAD: BLACK

WHITEBAIT No. 7 (M)

BODY: FLAT GOLD TINSEL

RIB: OVAL GOLD TINSEL

WING: TWO GRIZZLE COCK HACKLES DYED ORANGE, TIED ON "MATUKA" STYLE

HACKLE: RED COCK, WOUND AS A COLLAR (DYED BRIGHT RED)

HEAD: BLACK

This is a gold-bodied version of Whitebait No. 6

WHITEBAIT No. 8 (M)

BODY: ORANGE FLOSS SILK

RIB: OVAL GOLD TINSEL

WING: TWO BADGER COCK HACKLES DYED BRIGHT YELLOW, AND TIED ON "MATUKA" STYLE

HACKLE: DYED BRIGHT RED COCK, WOUND AS A COLLAR

HEAD: RED

WHITEBAIT No. 9 (O)

TAIL: HUMAN HAIR, BLONDE

BODY: SILVER OR GOLD TINSEL

WING: HUMAN HAIR, BLONDE

HEAD: BROWN

WHITEBAIT No. 10 (O)

TAG: SILVER TINSEL

BODY: ORANGE SILK OR MOHAIR

WING: HONEY GRIZZLE

HEAD: BLACK

WHITEBAIT No. 11 (O)

TAIL: YELLOW MOHAIR

BODY: GOLD TINSEL

WING: WHITE MOHAIR

HEAD: BROWN

WHITEBAIT No. 12 (O)

BODY: GOLD TINSEL

WING: YELLOW MOHAIR

HEAD: BROWN

WHITEBAIT No. 13 (O)

TAIL: HUMAN HAIR, BLONDE

BODY: YELLOW MOHAIR

RIB: SILVER TINSEL

WING: HUMAN HAIR, BLONDE

HEAD: BROWN

WHITEBAIT No.14 (O)

TAIL: TIPS OF TWO HONEY GRIZZLE HACKLES

BODY: YELLOW MOHAIR

WING: HONEY GRIZZLE HACKLES

HEAD: BLACK

WHITE VEIL (H)

ORIGIN: GEOFF SANDERSON OF TURANGI

HOOK: 2-8

TAIL: RUSSIAN SQUIRREL

BODY: RED DFM BUTT THEN BLACK CHENILLE

HACKLE: WHITE

HEAD: BLACK

This is another Geoff Sanderson pattern which appears in Tony Orman's book *The Sport in Fishing*, in which he collated the favourite lures of 13 experts. It appears to be a variation of Dainty Veil.

As with another Sanderson creation, the Marabou King, he uses DFM wool. I have yet to find anyone who has ever heard of it, far less describe it. I imagine that any red wool, yarn, floss or chenille would suffice.

The name suggests that the white hackle collar should be long and tied well back at the back at an angle of about 45 degrees so that it covers the body like a veil.

Russian Squirrel' is black squirrel.

Tie in the tail. Tie in the red material for the butt.

Wind on the material to create the red butt. Tie in the chenille.

Wind on the chenille to form the body. Tie in the hackle feather at the shoulder. (In the larger sizes, two or more hackles could be wound in along the length of the hook.)

Wind on the hackle collar. Finish the head and varnish.

WILLIS SMELT (M)

ORIGIN: WALTER WILLIS OF TE KUITI

HOOK: 4-8

TAIL: RED HACKLE WHISKS

BODY: FLAT SILVER TINSEL

RIB: OVAL SILVER

WING: A PAIR OF SMALL WHITE SATINS FROM THE UNDERSIDE OF A WILD DUCK'S WING

EYES: YELLOW WITH A BLACK CENTRE

HEAD: BLACK

The only criticism Keith Draper has of this otherwise simple pattern is that the particular feathers involved are a little on the stiff side. However, Mr Willis responds that they have the distinct advantage of never wrapping around the hook (while casting) as softer feathers are inclined to do.

The small white satins are found under the wings of most game birds, and are readily available to game hunters.

Tie in the tail wisks, body tinsel, and ribbing.

Wind on the tinsel for the body and tie off. Tie in the wing feathers at the shoulder.

Wind on the ribbing, tying down the wing to the top of the body.

Paint on eyes for added realism.

WILLY'S WONDER (M)

ORIGIN: NOT KNOWN

HOOK: 2-8

BODY: RED MOHAIR

RIB: OVAL SILVER

WING: HAWK FEATHERS, DARK BROWN CENTRE AND CREAM OUTER (TWO ONLY, BACK TO BACK)

HEAD: BLACK

Kilwell's of Rotorua have a collection of old lures, suitably framed, named and hanging in a piscatorial equivalent of a Rogues' Gallery. This was among them. Eddie Bosomworth (creator of Mallard and Black) kindly and enthusiastically took me on a tour of this interesting museum. The difficulty in obtaining hawk feathers, let alone those from an old female hawk, is no doubt the reason for its status as a relic in a museum.

This was once used by many of the commercial (boat) anglers at Taupo. A green-bodied version was very popular, and deadly. See my comments under Hawk as to the use of hawk feathers, which are otherwise prohibited.

Tie in the mohair and ribbing. Trim.

Wind on the mohair for the body and tie off. Tie in the wing feathers.

Wind on the ribbing, tying down the wings to the top of the body. Tie off and trim.

WILSON'S WUNDER (H)

ORIGIN: ERIC WILSON OF TURANGI

HOOK: 6-12

TAG: (OPTIONAL) RED

TAIL: WHITE-TIPPED SQUIRREL TAIL

BODY: OLIVE GREEN CHENILLE

RIB: THIN OVAL GOLD

HACKLE: NATURAL RED COCK

HEAD: BLACK

Eric tends to think of this as a green Red Setter, albeit without a mid-section hackle. It was a friend, Brian Batson of Waikohe, who gave it the above name, under which it appears in the Tichorne calendar and book. It is fished in the same manner as Red Setter on a sinking line, and has proved very successful in the Tongariro, Waiau, and Ruakituri Rivers, and Lakes Otamangakau and Rotoaira. Eric took an 11 lb. trout from Lake Otamangakau in early December 1996, and three 5 lb. trout in 30 minutes at Kowhai Flat on the Tongariro River on the last day that it snowed in Turangi that same year, demonstrating that this is a lure for all seasons.

Eric learned lure fishing using a Red Setter. Subsequent experimentation convinced him that green was a better colour for catching fish, and he used the Red Setter as his model. The addition of the red tag does not seem to make any appreciable difference, and he usually omits it.

Tie in the tag and squirrel tail.

Tie in the chenille and ribbing. Wind on the chenille and ribbing and tie off.

Tie in a hackle feather. Wind on to form the hackle collar. Complete the head in the usual way.

WISP (O)

ORIGIN: MARGARET ORMAN OF NELSON

HOOK: 4-8

TAIL: BROWN SQUIRREL TAIL

BODY: CHENILLE OR WOOL

RIB: OVAL SILVER

HACKLE: POSSUM FUR AROUND WHOLE OF BODY, HALFWAY ALONG BODY AND AT HEAD, TIED SPARINGLY SO THAT IT STREAMS BACK

HEAD: BLACK

This comes from Tony Orman's book The Sport in Fishing, in which he collated the favourite patterns of 13 experts. This particular lure was the favourite of Pedro Burney, who rated this pattern highly. It is a pattern evolved by Margaret Orman based on John Sierpinski's creation Sierpinski Dog. Green dyed possum fur with an orange body is claimed to be the most effective combination, and its success has been good not only in New Zealand, but even as far afield as California.

Margaret tells me that it is an excellent daytime fly. She used green dyed possum fur to emulate the colours of Hamill's Killer.

Tie in the tail. Tie in the chenille and ribbing.

Take the thread part way along the shank. Wind on the chenille and ribbing to this point and tie off. Tie in the first section of possum fur.

Wrap the possum fur around the shank and secure. Tie in the chenille and ribbing for the next section.

Take the thread, chenille, and ribbing back nearly to the head and tie off. Tie in the possum fur collar as before. Finish the head and varnish.

WOOLLY BUGGER (H)

ORIGIN: RUSSELL BLESSING OF PENNSYLVANIA, USA

HOOK: 2-10, LONG SHANK

TAIL: MARABOU AND 2-3 STRIPS FLASHABOU OR SIMILAR

BODY: CHENILLE OR WOOL

RIB: (OPTIONAL) FINE COPPER WIRE

HACKLE: COCK HACKLE, USUALLY GRIZZLE DYED TO SUIT, TIED PALMERWISE

HEAD: BLACK

Now here is a fly! It has been described as one of the most consistent fish takers known. For night fishing I seldom use anything else.

I am often asked: "If you were restricted to just one lure, which would you choose?" This begs a number of questions as to where and when we are fishing, but I have decided that if I were limited to just one lure (but not necessarily colour), I would probably reach for this lure.

It can be tied up in a variety of colours, the most effective being black, brown, olive, and white, although an orange or yellow pattern can be particularly effective in murky water conditions. For night fishing, my preference is for a body colour which is different from the tail colour and the combination I nearly always turn to is that shown in the photo (which I believe was also the original dressing), although a red body is also good. Commercial variations abound, and a gold bead head is popular. At the end of the day, however, I find myself always coming back to this original model. I have had such stunning fishing with it I follow the American adage "if it ain't broke, don't fix it!"

The example has been tied as the 'purist' might tie it, but I believe it is more effective when given a 'woollier' dressing of long soft hackles and a chunkier tail.

For casting, as opposed to harling, I secure the Palmered hackle with the thin copper ribbing. I have had the Palmered hackle break on me while casting, but never when harling.

Tie in a generous bunch of marabou. Tie in the Flashabou on either side of the marabou. Tie in the chenille and the tip of the hackle feather. Tie in the ribbing if using.

Take the thread back nearly to the head. Follow with the chenille and tie off. Palmer the hackle along the body to the head and tie off. Follow with the ribbing if using. Finish the head and varnish.

WOOLLY WORM (H)

ORIGIN: NOT KNOWN

HOOK: 2-8

TAIL: USUALLY JUST THE TIP OF A HACKLE FEATHER

BODY: CHENILLE, COLOUR TO SUIT. FAVOURED SHADES ARE ORANGE AND GREEN

RIB: OVAL SILVER

HACKLE: USUALLY GRIZZLE, TIED PALMERWISE

HEAD: BLACK

Keith Draper says that this is a style of fly generally tied on a large hook and fished in the northern lake area. It has been my practice to tie this on a No. 2 hook, orange body, because that is how the trout like them at Lake Waikaremoana. The example photographed is tied on a No. 6 hook. I have used orange, green, and brown bodied versions with success.

I believe this lure originated in America. In some parts of America, "woolly worm" is the name given to certain caterpillars which is what I believe this lure is intended to imitate.

Tie in the tail. Tie in the chenille, ribbing, and the tip of the hackle feather. Trim.

Wind on the chenille and the ribbing to the head and tie off.

Wind on the hackle feather Palmerwise along the length of the shank to the head. Secure and trim.

WOOSTER'S SILVERY (M)
(Modern Tie)

ORIGIN: W. (BILL) WOOSTER OF CANTERBURY

HOOK: 2-8

BODY: WHITE

RIB: OVAL SILVER

WING: GINGER COCK HACKLE WITH GREY MALLARD OVERLAY

HACKLE: GINGER COCK

HEAD: BLACK

This is of South Island origin where flies tend to be dressed in a heavy chunky style, see e.g. Barred Rock. The above example has been tied up in the slimmer style of dressing which is more effective when cast to trout that are feeding on smelt or whitebait.

A variation called Wooster's Silvery Red is exactly as above but with a red body.

In some South Island districts, smelt are known as 'silvery' - hence the name. (See the next entry for the original tie of this highly regarded lure).

Tie in the body material and ribbing. Trim.

Wind on the body material to the head and tie off. Tie in the wing feather.

Wind on the ribbing, tying down the wing to the top of the body. Tie in the wing overlay. Tie in the hackle feather.

Wind on the hackle collar. Trim. Finish the head and varnish.

WOOSTER'S SILVERY (O)
(Old Tie)

ORIGIN: W. (BILL) WOOSTER OF CANTERBURY

HOOK: NOT STATED BUT PROBABLY 2-6

TAIL: GINGER HACKLE TIPS

BODY: WHITE WOOL

RIB: FLAT SILVER

WING: TWO WHITE HACKLES INSIDE TWO GINGER HACKLES TIED IN AT THE HEAD

TOPPING: TEASED OUT STRANDS OF LIGHT BLUE RAYON FLOSS WITH PALE WATERY GREENY-BLUE RAYON FLOSS OVER

HACKLE: GINGER

HEAD: BLACK

Vic Novis from Cheviot purchased these lures from Bill Wooster more than fifty years ago. He kindly gave me this original sample which he is 95% certain would have been tied by Wooster himself. Vic is an avid devotee of this lure which he says "probably accounted for more trout than any other lure used in the South Island."

How, or why, the dressing changed to the modern form is not known.

Rayon was widely available after WW2 but it might be difficult to match the exact colour now, even allowing for some fading which is likely to have occurred over the years. Use a brand of soft rayon such as DMC.

Tie in the hackle tips for the tail. Tie in the wool and the ribbing.

Wind on the wool to the head. Follow with the ribbing and tie off. Trim.

Tie in the wing feathers by the butts. Tie in the topping.

Tie in a hackle feather and wind on to form a hackle collar.

YELLOW FUZZ (O)

ORIGIN: JOHN MORTON OF CHRISTCHURCH

HOOK: 4, 3X LONG SHANK
TAIL: LONG STRAIGHT-ISH BLACK POSSUM TAIL
BODY: YELLOW CHENILLE WITH A SMALL MASKING TUFT OF POSSUM TAIL AT THE CENTRE OF THE BODY
WING: BUNCH OF BLACK POSSUM TAIL AT THE HEAD WRAPPED RIGHT AROUND THE SHANK
HEAD: BLACK

John refers to this as a variation of The Hob Nailed Boot, but I believe it is sufficiently different that it can be regarded as a separate creation, although no less effective. John claims that it is a very deadly fly the hour before and just after dark. He says:"It is extraordinarily good on Rainbow trout and has been the downfall of many fish in the little, man made lake of Otamangakau, over the hill from Turangi in the central North Island. It is a fly I just wouldn't be without."

Tie in the tail and chenille. Take the thread back to the mid-point of the shank.

Wind on the chenille to this point and tie off. Tie in a small bunch of possum tail fur. Tie in the chenille again.

Take the thread back nearly to the head.

Wind on the chenille to this point. Tie in a bunch of possum fur at the shoulder, pushing down with thumb and forefinger as it is tied in. This will cause it to wrap right around the shank. Form the head and complete in the usual way.

YELLOW LADY (M)

ORIGIN: BRAD BOCKETT OF TAUPO
HOOK: 2-8
TAIL: RED HACKLE WHISKS
BODY: YELLOW CHENILLE
RIB: OVAL GOLD
WING: YELLOW COCK HACKLE
HACKLE: YELLOW
TOPPING: KRYSTAL FLASH OR SIMILAR
HEAD: RED

There is a saying at Lake Waikaremoana that when the buttercups appear (November) use yellow.

There is certainly some truth in it, and this lure – which is as yellow as you can get - is one of the lures which knowledgeable anglers turn to, particularly harling in the larger sizes. It was originally designed as a harling pattern, and is very popular at Lake Taupo.

Tie in the tail whisks. Tie in the chenille and the ribbing. Trim. Wind on the chenille to the head and tie off. Tie in the wing feathers.

Wind on the ribbing, tying down the wing to the top of the body.

Tie in about ten strands of Krystal Flash or similar. Tie in the hackle feather and wind on to form a fairly sparse collar. Finish the head and varnish.

YELLOW RUDDEL (M)

ORIGIN: BARRY BIRCHALL OF KAIKOHE
HOOK: 2-8
UNDERTAIL: FLAT GOLD TINSEL WRAPPED AROUND BEND OF HOOK
TAIL: ORANGE HACKLE WHISKS
BODY: YELLOW CHENILLE
RIB: OVAL SILVER
WING: BROWN MARABOU
OVERWING: A FEW STRANDS OF GREEN FLASHABOU AND KRYSTAL FLASH
HACKLE: ORANGE
HEAD: BROWN

This was named after Warren Ruddel, an expert Northland fly fisherman who gave Barry his first yellow bodied Matuku fly for use on the Kai Iwi Lakes.

The lure is very similar to - and tied in the same manner as - Barry's Parsons' Glory Variant but in Barry's view, this is a better fly. It is an excellent Kai Iwi Lake fly, imitating the pale bullies in the lake.

Barry has taken trout with it by trolling, harling, jigging, and traditional casting. Barry has added eyes to this original for added realism.

Take the thread to halfway around the bend. Tie in the tinsel. Wind the tinsel back to the top of the shank. Tie in the tail whisks, chenille, and ribbing.

Wind on the chenille and tie off. Tie in the marabou wing.

Wind on the ribbing, tying down the marabou to the top of the body along the length of the shank.

Tie in a few strands of Flashabou and Krystal Flash. Tie in the hackle and wind on. Finish the head in the usual way.

YELLOW TERROR (M)

ORIGIN: ROBERT BRAGG OF CHRISTCHURCH
HOOK: 2-8
BUTT: A TURN OF FLUORESCENT RED CHENILLE

BODY: SILVER TINSEL WITH A YELLOW HACKLE WOUND PALMERWISE ALONG THE BODY
RIB: OVAL SILVER
WING: DYED YELLOW COCK HACKLES

HACKLE: YELLOW
HEAD: BLACK

This is a bright Canterbury lure from the vice of the ever creative R.K. Bragg. It is considered by some to be a good pattern for coloured water. A slightly unusual feature is the combination of a Palmered hackle with a Matuku tied wing.

Tie in the ribbing and the red chenille for the butt. Take one turn of the chenille and tie off. Tie in the body tinsel and the tip of the hackle feather.

Wind on the tinsel for the body and tie off. Palmer the hackle feather along the body to the head and tie off. Tie in the wing feathers.

Wind on the ribbing, tying down the wing to the top of the body. Tie in the hackle collar feather and wind on.

ZONKER (O)

ORIGIN: DAN BYFORD OF COLORADO, USA
HOOK: 4-8 LONG SHANK
UNDERBODY: ZONKER STRIP AND (OPTIONAL) PRISM TAPE
BODY: SILVER MYLAR TUBE
WING: A STRIP OF RABBIT FUR ON THE SKIN
HACKLE: (OPTIONAL) GRIZZLE COCK
HEAD: BLACK

This is an American variation of the New Zealand designed Rabbit fly - if you like a Rabbit with bells and whistles. The close association of this pattern to our Rabbit, and its wide-spread popularity in this country justifies its inclusion.

I rate this fly highly, and in my experience, it is no less effective than the Rabbit. The original Zonker had a red head, but I have only ever seen it with a black head in this country.

I tie these up on No. 6 long shank hooks with my own embellishment. After attaching the zonker strip to the hook, I add self-adhesive prism tape to the zonker strip. This comes in a variety of colours which flash appealingly through the (pearl) mylar body. Using natural rabbit fur, you can have a variety of body colours - red, yellow, green, blue, silver. Alternatively, you can match the colour of the fur to the body; for example, olive green fur with a green prism tape body. Prism tape is used to create spinners, and is available from any fishing tackle shop. There are, however, a wide variety of colours of mylar now available and these obviate the prism tape option. I have given below the standard method of tying this lure. However, another method (which I believe is the original way, and which may commend itself) is to glue the rabbit strip to the top of the body with epoxy or similar.

Secure a length of red thread at the bend of the hook. Cut a piece of zonker strip to length and fold it over the hook shank. Add prism tape if desired. Cut the zonker strip to shape.

Slip a length of mylar tubing over the strip. Secure at the bend with the thread left there for that purpose. Do not trim the frayed end. Secure black thread at the head and secure the mylar at that point. Trim the frayed end at the head.

Place a strip of rabbit fur on top of the hook. Tie it on with the thread at the head and also at the tail with the thread left there for that purpose.

Tie in a grizzle feather at the head. Wind on to form a hackle collar. Form the head and complete in the usual way.

ZULU (M)

ORIGIN: NOT KNOWN
HOOK: NOT STATED BUT PROBABLY 2-8
BODY: BLACK
RIB: OVAL SILVER
WING: BLACK INSIDE RED COCK HACKLES
HACKLE: BLACK
HEAD: BLACK

This is described in Bragg's book as a lure of the Taupo and Rotorua Districts during the period 1950s to 1962. It is very similar in many respects to Red Shadow, a Bragg creation which was a very popular evening lure in the Canterbury district in the 1950s.

The ribbing is either gold or silver, it is impossible to discern from the photo in Bragg's book, and my guess is silver.

Tie in the body material and the ribbing.

Return the thread back nearly to the head. Wind on the body material. Tie in the wing feathers by the butts.

Wind on the ribbing, tying down the wing to the top of the body.

Tie in a hackle feather. Wind on to form a hackle collar.

BRONWYN WILSON'S SERIES

Bronwyn Wilson is a consumate fly-tier living in Taupo. Her exciting rabbit patterns caught my attention following publication of some of them in the Tichborne Calendars and subsequently in *Anglers' Paradise* by Nancy and Bryan Tichborne.

I spent a memorable 24 hours in Taupo where Bronwyn introduced me to some of the finer points of fly-tying and demonstrated the dressing of a number of her creations. The vast quantity of fly-tying material which she has amassed, particularly from overseas, is truly astonishing. One of Bronwyn's particular skills is an ability to re-create an original pattern, however obscure. Between them, Bronwyn and her equally resourceful mother came up with the very close substitute for the body material used in Logan's Lure.

Bronwyn has tied flies professionally for a number of angling identities, including George Gatchell and Eddie Bosomworth, and had a close association with the late Geoff Sanderson who was a close friend of Bronwyn's grandfather. There are, of course, a great number of very expert fly-tiers in New Zealand and I am conscious that by including this substantial selection of Bronwyn's patterns I may be accused of trying to elevate Bronwyn into a state of elitism that reflects unfairly on many other experts. This is not my intention at all, but Bronwyn's creativity has produced a number of effective patterns which could not be ignored.

While I recognise that some patterns are merely variations in dressing, the end result nevertheless is a lure which I felt was sufficiently distinctive to warrant inclusion. To have included, say, Bronwyn's Rabbit in the alphabetical section as her sole (albeit representative) contribution would have been misleading. The problem became one of what to leave out, and my unequal struggle with that issue was resolved by including them all.

I have chosen Change of Light as the principal entry, complete with tying guide. Thereafter, the patterns and photo suffice. The method of tying will be either very similar, or will be in accordance with other examples to be found throughout this book.

The common denominator of all of Bronwyn's patterns shown here is that, as one would expect with Rabbit style lures, they are effective and can be fished with confidence.

All examples photographed were tied by Bronwyn Wilson herself.

CHANGE OF LIGHT (M)

ORIGIN: BRONWYN WILSON OF TAUPO
HOOK: 2-8
BODY: GREEN LUREX THREAD
RIB: OVAL SILVER
THROAT: GLO-BUG YARN (BURNT ORANGE)
WING: NATURAL GREY RABBIT STRIP
CHEEKS: JUNGLE COCK
TOPPING: 6 STRANDS COPPER FLASHABOU AND 2

STRANDS OF GREEN FLASHABOU
HACKLE: BRIGHT ORANGE COCK
HEAD: BLACK

This fly is good in change of light situations (hence its name) and in deep holes in rivers. The throat puff acts as an attractor. The first time I used this fly I caught a trout with my first cast, the first time that has happened to me. It went on to catch many more fish in short order, both casting and harling. It is a very very effective fly.

Lurex can be purchased from sewing and craft shops, although it is not easy to get balls of the thicker type which is preferable. You will often find it described as metallic embroidery thread.

Tie in the lurex body material and the ribbing.

Take the thread back about two-thirds of the way along the shank (you will need to leave enough room for the puff and the head). Wind on the lurex to this point and tie off.

Take a short length of glo-bug yarn (about 12mm), and hold it horizontally against the hanging thread under the shank. Take 4 or 5 turns of the thread around the middle of the yarn.

Maintaining a tight grip, pull the front part of the yarn down and take about three turns of thread around the shank immediately in front of the yarn. Do exactly the same with the rear part of the yarn. Then pull down both the front and rear parts of the yarn and wind the thread horizontally about three times around just under the shank. Take another couple of turns vertically around the shank to secure. Pull both ends of yarn down firmly and snip the yarn horizontally.

Tie in the rabbit strip, wind on the ribbing, and add the other features in the normal way.

BRONWYN'S RABBIT (M)

HOOK: 2-6
UNDER-BODY: WOOL OR FLOSS
BODY: ORANGE BI-COLOUR MYLAR TUBING
THROAT: GLO-BUG YARN (DARK ROE OR FLAME)
WING: NATURAL LIGHT BROWN RABBIT STRIP
HACKLE: WHITE COCK
HEAD: BLACK

Featured in the Tichborne calendars and book. Excellent around the Tongariro River Delta and other rivers also.

BRONWYN'S ZONKER (O)

HOOK: 2-10
UNDER-BODY: WOOL OR FLOSS
BODY: PEARL MYLAR TUBING
THREAD: (TAG END) WHITE - FOR TYING DOWN THE RABBIT STRIP INSTEAD OF RIBBING
THROAT: GLO-BUG YARN (BRIGHT PINK CHERISE)
WING: CHINCHILLA OR WHITE RABBIT STRIP
HACKLE: WHITE
HEAD: BLACK

COMMANDER (M)

HOOK: 2-8
BODY: OLIVE GREEN CHENILLE
RIB: OVAL SILVER
WING: BLACK RABBIT STRIP
HACKLE: OLIVE OR BLACK
HEAD: BLACK

EARLY DAWN (M)

HOOK: 2-8
BODY: GOLD/BLACK LUREX YARN
RIB: OVAL GOLD OR SILVER
THROAT: GLO-BUG YARN (OREGON CHEESE OR GOLDEN NUGGET)
WING: NATURAL GREY RABBIT
CHEEKS: JUNGLE COCK
TOPPING: GOLD FLASHABOU OR KRYSTAL FLASH
HACKLE: DYED GOLD OR YELLOW COCK
HEAD: BLACK

The name says it all, and works in the same situations as Change of Light.

ELF (M)

HOOK: 2-8
BODY: FLUORESCENT GREEN GLO-BUG YARN (MOSS)
RIB: OVAL SILVER
THROAT: GLO-BUG YARN (RED OR FLAME ORANGE)
WING: GREY CHINCHILLA RABBIT STRIP
HACKLE: WHITE
HEAD: BLACK

EXTINGUISHER (M)

HOOK: 2-10
TAG: YELLOW
BODY: IN TWO PARTS - REAR HALF: CREAM OR WHITE WOOL OR SEAL'S FUR; FRONT HALF: WINE WOOL OR SEAL'S FUR
RIB: OVAL SILVER
WING: LIGHT BROWN NATURAL RABBIT STRIP
HACKLE: WINE OR RED COCK
HEAD: BLACK

FERNIE FLASH (M)

HOOK: 2-6
BODY: OLIVE SPARKLE YARN
RIB: OVAL SILVER
THROAT: GLO-BUG YARN (DARK ROE)
WING: BLACK RABBIT STRIP
HACKLE: ORANGE
HEAD: BLACK

FIRST LIGHT (O)

HOOK: 2-6
TAIL: BLACK SQUIRREL
BODY: IN TWO PARTS - REAR HALF: GLO-BUG YARN (FLAME); FRONT HALF: GLO-BUG YARN (DARK ROE)
HACKLE: RED COCK TIED IN AFTER THE FIRST SECTION OF BODY, BRIGHT ORANGE COCK TIED IN AFTER THE SECOND SECTION OF BODY
WING: TUFT OF BLACK RABBIT FUR TIED IN AFTER EACH SECTION OF BODY AND HACKLE
CHEEK: JUNGLE COCK (OPTIONAL)
TOPPING: BRONZE, COPPER, OR CRYSTAL FLASHABOU
HEAD: BLACK

Bronwyn says this fly is a must for fishing morning, evening, dirty water, and also in moonlight. It got its name after fishing with great success at first light on the little stream at Kaiapo.

FUZZY WUZZY RABBIT (H)

HOOK: 2-4
BODY: RED OR WINE SEAL'S FUR OR SUBSTITUTE
HACKLE: BLACK RABBIT FUR SPUN AROUND THE SHANK AT THE MID-SECTION AND AGAIN AT THE SHOULDER.
HEAD: BLACK

The method of spinning the rabbit fur is the same as that used for possum fur - see the tying guide comments under Burglar, or dubbing using the loop method.

GALAH (M)

HOOK: 2-8
BODY: PINK GLO-BUG YARN (SALMON EGG)
RIB: OVAL SILVER
THROAT: GLO-BUG YARN (DEEP DARK RED)
WING: GREY CHINCHILLA RABBIT STRIP
HACKLE: WHITE
HEAD: BLACK

This is a good daytime lure

MARABOU SCOTCH POACHER (P)

HOOK: 2-4
BODY: ORANGE SEAL'S FUR OR SUBSTITUTE
RIB: OVAL SILVER
UNDERWING: A STRIP OF THE BASE DOWNY MARABOU FROM AN ORANGE COCK HACKLE. THIS IS LAID ALONG THE SHANK WITH THE END OVERHANGING TO FORM A TAIL, AND TIED DOWN WITH THE RIBBING
WING: A BUNCH OF BLACK MARABOU TIED IN AT THE HEAD
TOPPING: A SMALL BUNCH OF BLUE MARABOU
HACKLE: BRIGHT ORANGE
CHEEKS: JUNGLE COCK
HEAD: BLACK

This is a good night fly, best fished at river mouths and lake edges. Bronwyn would not be without it.

MARSHMALLOW (M)

HOOK: 2-8
BODY: SILVER LUREX YARN
RIB: OVAL SILVER
THROAT: GLO-BUG YARN (SALMON EGG OR APRICOT SUPREME)
WING: WHITE RABBIT STRIP

CHEEK: JUNGLE COCK (OPTIONAL)
HACKLE: WHITE
HEAD: BLACK

This is a good daytime fly around river mouths and in low lies of river pools

MONARCH (M)

HOOK: 2-8
BODY: ORANGE SEAL'S FUR OR SUBSTITUTE
RIB: OVAL SILVER
WING: BLACK RABBIT STRIP
HACKLE: ORANGE COCK
HEAD: BLACK

A good night fly and also early morning.

MOODY BLUE (P)

HOOK: 6-8
TAG: RED SPARKLE YARN
BODY: BLUE LUREX YARN
RIB: OVAL SILVER
WING: BLACK MARABOU
TOPPING: BLUE FLASHABOU
CHEEK: JUNGLE COCK (OPTIONAL)
HACKLE: BLACK COCK
HEAD: BLACK

This, together with Marabou Scotch Poacher, is a fly Bronwyn would not be without. It is fished in the same manner as Marabou Scotch Poacher.

MOODY RABBIT (M)

HOOK: 2-8
TAG: RED SPARKLE YARN
BODY: BLUE LUREX YARN
RIB: OVAL SILVER
WING: BLACK RABBIT STRIP
TOPPING: BLUE OR CRYSTAL FLASHABOU
HACKLE: BLACK COCK
CHEEKS: JUNGLE COCK
HEAD: BLACK

This is a good night and early morning fly, and especially in moonlight conditions.

MOTHER'S CHOICE (M)

HOOK: 4-8
BODY: CLARET OR WINE CHENILLE OR SEAL'S FUR
RIB: OVAL SILVER
THROAT: PINK GLO-BUG YARN (PINK LADY OR SALMON EGG)
WING: BLACK RABBIT STRIP
HACKLE: CLARET COCK
HEAD: BLACK

A fly for night-time and early morning.

NIGHT RIDER (M)

HOOK: 4-8
TAG: OLIVE SPARKLE YARN
BODY: CLARET CHENILLE
RIB: OVAL SILVER
WING: BLACK RABBIT STRIP
HACKLE: DARK RED OR WINE
HEAD: BLACK

A good fly for night-time and early morning.

PINK DUSK (O)

HOOK: 2-6
TAIL: BLACK OR GREY SQUIRREL
BODY: BRIGHT PINK GLO-BUG YARN (CHERISE)
HACKLE: BLACK AND WHITE GRIZZLE AT MID-SECTION; BLACK COCK AT HEAD
WING: TUFTS OF CHINCHILLA RABBIT TIED ON TOP AT MID-SECTION AND AT HEAD
TOPPING: SILVER OR CRYSTAL FLASHABOU OR HOLOGRAPHIC TINSEL
HEAD: BLACK

PURPLE SPLENDOUR (M)

HOOK: 2-8
BODY: PURPLE LUREX YARN
RIB: OVAL SILVER
THROAT: GLO-BUG YARN (CHERISE)
WING: NATURAL GREY RABBIT STRIP
TOPPING: 6 STRANDS PURPLE FLASHABOU, 2 STRANDS PINK FLASHABOU OR KRYSTAL FLASH
HACKLE: BRIGHT PINK
HEAD: BLACK

Good for morning, evening, change of light, and changing water conditions.

RUFUS (M)

HOOK: 4-8
BODY: FLUORESCENT GREEN GLO-BUG YARN
RIB: OVAL SILVER
WING: WHITE RABBIT
TOPPING: OLIVE MARABOU
HACKLE: LIGHT LIME GREEN
HEAD: BLACK

An effective fly named after Bronwyn's mother who likes the colour green. Bronwyn adds eyes for greater realism.

TANGELO

HOOK: 2-8
BODY: GLO-BUG YARN (OREGAN CHEESE)
RIB: OVAL SILVER
THROAT: GLO-BUG YARN (BURNT ORANGE OR LIGHT ROE)
WING: BROWN HONEY RABBIT STRIP
HACKLE: COCK HONEY GRIZZLE OR HEN NATURAL RED
HEAD: BLACK

A good fly when fish are running up rivers

TARAWERA CHIEF (M)

HOOK: 4-8
TAG: RED WOOL OR SPARKLE YARN
BODY: FLUORESCENT GREEN WOOL OR GLO-BUG YARN (CHARTREUSE)
RIB: OVAL SILVER
WING: CHINCHILLA RABBIT STRIP
HACKLE: WHITE
HEAD: BLACK

This is a good smelt imitation first used with great success on Lake Tarawera, and later on Lake Taupo from November to March. Bronwyn adds eyes for realism.

TARAWERA PRINCESS (M)

HOOK: 4-8
TAG: RED WOOL OR SPARKLE YARN
BODY: FLUORESCENT GREEN WOOL OR GLO-BUG YARN (CHARTREUSE)
RIB: OVAL SILVER
WING: WHITE RABBIT STRIP
HACKLE: WHITE
HEAD: BLACK

THREE-IN-ONE (H)
(FUZZY WUZZY VERSION)

HOOK: 2-6
TAG: RED (OPTIONAL)
TAIL: BLACK SQUIRREL
BODY: FIRST SECTION - RED WOOL
SECOND SECTION - ORANGE CHENILLE
THIRD SECTION - BLACK OR BROWN CHENILLE
HACKLE: RED, ORANGE, AND BLACK, AFTER EACH SECTION. PROGRESSIVELY INCREASE THE NUMBER OF HACKLE TURNS AT EACH SECTION
HEAD: BLACK

THREE-IN-ONE (M)
(RABBIT VERSION)

HOOK: 2-6
TAG: RED (OPTIONAL)
TAIL: BLACK SQUIRREL
BODY: SAME AS FOR FUZZY WUZZY VERSION ABOVE
HACKLE: SAME AS FOR FUZZY WUZZY VERSION ABOVE
RIB: OVAL SILVER TINSEL TIED IN AT THE START OF SECOND SECTION
WING: STRIP OF BLACK RABBIT CUT TO LENGTH OF SHANK ONLY, AND RIBBED DOWN, THROUGH, AND OVER BODY AND HACKLES
CHEEK & TOPPING: (OPT) JUNGLE COCK AND FLASHABOU
HEAD: BLACK

UNCLE HARRY (M)

HOOK: 2-8
TAG: RED WOOL
BODY: BLACK AND SILVER LUREX YARN
RIB: OVAL SILVER
WING: BLACK RABBIT STRIP
TOPPING: 6 STRANDS BLUE FLASHABOU AND 2 STRANDS SILVER CRYSTAL FLASHABOU
CHEEKS: JUNGLE COCK

HACKLE: BLACK COCK
HEAD: BLACK

Named after, and dedicated to, Harry Tanfield, a popular former Senior Wildlife Officer. This fly proved itself as a great fish taker at the Te Wairoa Stream mouth.

WHITE RABBIT (M)

HOOK: 2-10
BODY: 50/50 MIX OF YELLOW AND ORANGE SEAL'S FUR, DUBBED ON AND SLIGHTLY TAPERED
RIB: OVAL SILVER
WING: WHITE RABBIT
HACKLE: GINGER HEN HACKLE
HEAD: BLACK

This is one fly Bronwyn says she would not be without. It is a good smelt pattern, and also when trout are spawning. It is good at night and morning, and also in dirty water. Locals refer to it as her "bread and butter" fly. It is also effective tied with a pearl body.

ROTORUA REGIONAL PATTERNS

The following selection of patterns have (with two exceptions) been supplied by Pat Swift and Pat O'Keefe, both of Rotorua. These lures, which in many cases are adaptations of old standards, have proved very successful in the Rotorua region, performing better than the original. They will, of course, fish just as successfully anywhere.

Pat Swift is a very expert fly-tier and angler and has been involved in the trout fishing industry since the late 1970s, tying professionally both overseas and in New Zealand. He currently has a number of patterns - mostly nymphs - which Umpqua tie commercially.

In Eruera Street Rotorua, is O'Keefe's Fishing Specialists, run by Pat and Helen O'Keefe. Pat is a supreme angler. In 1997 he was the Oceania Champion and also New Zealand Champion trout angler. He was also a member of the New Zealand Fly Fishing Team that same year. Pat is also a professional fishing guide.

Both Pats are well-qualified to judge which patterns, or variations of patterns, work best in the myraid of opportunities which abound in this lake-studded region. If a pearl mylar bodied Grey Ghost works better than the original, then that becomes the vogue.

Both contributors, quite independently, felt they could come up with 80 or so patterns of local smelt lures, although it was acknowledged that a number would be 'one-season-wonders' - fanciful whimsies which come and go. The following selection is but a sample, hopefully representative, of local patterns and variations of originals which work, and can be fished with confidence anywhere. Neither Pat Swift nor Pat O'Keefe would use them if it were not so. They have been tied by the respective creators.

There were also a number submitted to me which I felt were deserving of greater focus and were therefore included in the alphabetical section. Those patterns are Mr Simpson, Orsim, Bully Fly, Bum Fly Variations 2 and 3, O'Keefe's Smelt, Royal Coachman Lure, and Water Rat.

The two exceptions, the final two listed, come from Geoff Thomas who will be well known to anglers everywhere. For the trout hunter, he wrote *Trout Secrets* (published 1994). He has also written five other books on sea fishing, and the recently released (1997) *Complete Book of New Zealand Fishing* which covers all things piscatorial, including trout. He writes a weekly column in The New Zealand Herald, appears on Newstalk ZB and has produced at least 30 videos on fishing, and has been involved in five television series on fishing.

In addition to all that, Geoff was a professional trout guide for about 15 years in the 1970s and early 80s. He has fished smelt patterns for the past 40 years, and fished extensively in the Rotorua and Taupo districts. His smelt patterns have evolved after careful study of the smelt in the different lakes and their particular colouration. When Geoff says his smelt patterns catch fish, you can believe it! The two patterns shown here featured in the 1986 Tichborne calendar. Both have been tied by the author.

EPOXY SMELT (O)

ORIGIN: PAT SWIFT
HOOK: 4-10
BODY: PEARL MYLAR TUBING WOUND AROUND SHANK
RIB: FLAT SILVER TINSEL
WING: GREY ULTRA HAIR WITH ONE STRAND OF HOLOGRAPHIC TINSEL TIED ON EITHER SIDE
EYES: STICK-ON HOLOGRAPHIC EYES
HEAD: GREY

The body and head are covered in 5-minute epoxy glue which makes it a very durable fly. It is good for deeper water because it sinks very quickly.

GREY GHOST PEARL (M)

ORIGIN: ADAPTED BY PAT SWIFT
HOOK: 2-10
TAG: RED HACKLE FIBRES
BODY: SMALL PEARL MYLAR TUBING WOUND AROUND SHANK
RIB: FINE OVAL SILVER
WING: 4 GREY COCK FEATHERS
TOPPING: 4 STRANDS PEARL FLASHABOU
EYES: BLACK
HEAD: GREY

A popular and very effective version of the Grey Ghost which fishes particularly well in the smaller sizes.

HELEN'S SMELT (M)

ORIGIN: HELEN O'KEEFE OF ROTORUA
HOOK: 4-8
TAIL: RED COCK HACKLE FIBRES
BODY: MOTHER-OF-PEARL UNI-GLOW
RIB: OVAL SILVER
WING: ENGLISH SUFFOLK OR BADGER COCK HACKLES
THROAT: WHITE OR RED MARABOU
TOPPING: 3 STRANDS PEARL KRYSTAL FLASH
HEAD: BLACK

This featured in the 1989 Tichborne calendar and subsequent book. English Suffolk feathers are preferred because the plumage is whiter and cleaner than badger, but they are very difficult to obtain. The example shown here has a badger wing. In reality, it is a variation of Jack's Sprat.

JACK'S SPRAT PEARL (M)

ORIGIN: ADAPTED BY PAT SWIFT
HOOK: 2-10
TAG: RED HACKLE FIBRES
BODY: SMALL PEARL MYLAR TUBING WOUND AROUND SHANK
RIB: FINE OVAL SILVER
WING: 4 BADGER COCK FEATHERS
TOPPING: 4 STRANDS PEARL FLASHABOU
EYES: BLACK
HEAD: GREY

Pat Swift's variation of Jack's Sprat. This is a very effective variation of the original

JAFFABOU (O)

ORIGIN: PAT SWIFT
THREAD: WHITE
HOOK: 4-8
TAIL: ORANGE MARABOU
BODY: LUMO FLASHABOU, ORANGE OR GREEN - 5 OR 6 STRANDS
WING: ORANGE MARABOU AT MID-BODY; BLACK MARABOU AT HEAD
HEAD: FLUORESCENT PINK NAIL POLISH

This is a particularly effective night fly on moonlit nights.

KELLY GREEN DOLL FLY (O)

ORIGIN: FIRST SHOWN TO PAT SWIFT BY JOHN (BUGSY) WILSON OF ROTORUA WHO IS BELIEVED TO BE THE CREATOR
HOOK: 6-8
THREAD: WHITE
TAG: KELLY GREEN POLY YARN OVER RED EGG YARN
BODY: AURORA SKIRT
OVERBODY: KELLY GREEN POLYPROP YARN
THROAT: PEARL FLASHABOU OR KRYSTAL FLASH
EYES: YELLOW WITH BLACK PUPIL
HEAD: GREEN

Another colour variation of the popular Doll Fly, which has been enjoying a lot of success. It was originally designed for Lake Tarawera but has been successful everywhere.

L.B. FUZZY WUZZY (H)

ORIGIN: PAT SWIFT

HOOK: 6 LONG SHANK

TAIL: SQUIRREL TAIL - ORANGE, WHITE, RED, BLUE-GREEN, OR BLUE

BODY: AURORA SKIRT IN TWO SECTIONS

HACKLE: RED AFTER FIRST BODY SECTION. BLACK AFTER SECOND SECTION (AT HEAD)

HEAD: FIRE ORANGE THREAD BEHIND AN AURORA LUMO BEAD

EYES: YELLOW WITH BLACK PUPIL

This interesting variation of the original fishes best in deeper water. It is a night fly.

LUMO ALEX (O)

ORIGIN: NOT KNOWN

HOOK: 6-10

TAG: RED WOOL OR EGG YARN

BODY: AURORA SKIRT

WING: PEACOCK SWORD

CHEEK: (OPTIONAL) JUNGLE COCK

HEAD: BLACK

Based on the English fly, Alexandra, but given this different, and luminous, treatment by an unknown Australian and subsequently shown to Pat Swift who was quick to utilise it in New Zealand waters. It is a night fly.

LUMO BLACK MARABOU (O)

ORIGIN: PAT SWIFT

HOOK: 4-10

TAG: RED WOOL OR EGG YARN

BODY: AURORA SKIRT

WING: BLACK MARABOU

CHEEK: (OPTIONAL) JUNGLE COCK

HEAD: BLACK

A very effective and popular night fly. The wing is tied in several bunches along the shank as the body is wound on, one at the tail, one at the mid-body, and one at the head. It should be fished slowly to allow the marabou to pulse.

LUMO CRAIG'S NIGHT-TIME (P)

ORIGIN: ADAPTED BY PAT SWIFT

HOOK: 4-10

TAG: RED WOOL OR EGG YARN

BODY: AURORA SKIRT

WING: BLUE PUKEKO

HACKLE: BLACK

CHEEK: (OPTIONAL) JUNGLE COCK

HEAD: BLACK

I have seen a very likely variation using Mirror Flash for the body. Pat Swift has had a lot of success with this luminous version, which is a night fly.

MALLARD SMELT PEARL (O)

ORIGIN: ADAPTED BY PAT SWIFT

HOOK: 4-10

TAIL: MALLARD BREAST FEATHERS

BODY: PEARL MYLAR TUBING

TOPPING: 4 STRANDS PEARL FLASHABOU

HACKLE: GREY

EYES: YELLOW WITH BLACK PUPIL

HEAD: WHITE

Another variation of Bruno Kemball's original.

MARA DOLL CHARTREUSE (O)

ORIGIN: ADAPTED BY PAT SWIFT

HOOK: 6-8

THREAD: WHITE

TAG: RED EGG YARN

TAIL: WHITE MARABOU

BODY: AURORA SKIRT

OVERBODY: CHARTREUSE EGG YARN TIED IN AT THE BEND AND PULLED FORWARD OVER THE LUMO BODY

THROAT: PEARL FLASHABOU

EYES: YELLOW WITH BLACK PUPIL

HEAD: CHARTREUSE

This is a variation of the popular Doll Fly, given enhanced life and movement by the addition of marabou.

MARA DOLL GREEN (O)

ORIGIN: ADAPTED BY PAT SWIFT
HOOK: 6-8
THREAD: GREY
TAG: RED EGG YARN
TAIL: GREEN MARABOU
BODY: AURORA SKIRT
OVERBODY: GREEN POLY YARN TIED IN AT THE TAIL AND PULLED FORWARD OVER THE LUMO BODY
THROAT: PEARL FLASHABOU
EYES: YELLOW WITH BLACK PUPIL
HEAD: GREY

Another variation of the Doll Fly.

ROTOITI RABBIT (M)

ORIGIN: PAT O'KEEFE OF ROTORUA
HOOK: 6
TAIL: ORANGE WHISKS
BODY: FLUORESCENT ORANGE CHENILLE
RIB: OVAL SILVER
WING: STRIP OF WHITE RABBIT FUR
THROAT: A FEW STRANDS OF RABBIT FUR PULLED DOWN AND TIED UNDERNEATH THE SHANK
HEAD: BLACK

Although effective during the day, this is particularly effective on moonlit nights.

SCOTCH POACHER VARIATION (P)

ORIGIN: ADAPTED BY PAT SWIFT
HOOK: 2-10
TAIL: BLACK MARABOU
BODY: ORANGE CHENILLE
RIB: OVAL GOLD
WING: ORANGE MARABOU
OVERWING: BLUE PUKEKO
CHEEK: (OPTIONAL) JUNGLE COCK
HEAD: BLACK

Pat Swift has imbued the original with lively animation with his use of marabou while still retaining the essential character of Kirkpatrick's creation. A deadly night fly. Retrieve very very slowly.

TARAWERA RABBIT (M)

ORIGIN: PAT O'KEEFE OF ROTORUA
HOOK: 6
TAIL: GREEN WHISKS
BODY: CHARTREUSE CHENILLE
RIB: OVAL SILVER
WING: STRIP OF WHITE RABBIT FUR
THROAT: A FEW STRANDS OF RABBIT FUR PULLED DOWN AND TIED IN UNDER THE SHANK
HEAD: BLACK

The same comments relating to Rotoiti Rabbit apply to this lure. Despite their names, the success of either is not confined to those lakes.

WEEDLESS LUMO WALLABY (O)

ORIGIN: PAT SWIFT
HOOK: 6-10
THREAD: WHITE
TAIL: PEARL KRYSTAL FLASH
BODY: PEARL FLASHABOU OVERWOUND WITH AURORA SKIRT
WING: STRIP OF WALLABY FUR. PIERCE THE SKIN WITH THE HOOK POINT, PULL AROUND THE BEND, AND TIE OFF AT THE HEAD
EYES: YELLOW WITH BLACK PUPIL
HEAD: WHITE

This is a very effective night fly utilising the luminous body. Wallaby fur is available commercially, but in limited supplies. Rabbit is not a suitable substitute because of the way it absorbs water, but possum might be an option.

GT SMELT, Green (M)

ORIGIN: GEOFF THOMAS
HOOK: 6-8
TAIL: RED WHISKS
BODY: GREEN WOOL (UNRAVEL TWO-PLY WOOL, AND REVERSE THE TWO STRANDS TO WIND ONTO THE HOOK SHANK SO THAT THE BODY IS CRINKLY AND UNEVEN)
RIB: THIN SILVER
WING: FOUR FEATHERS OF DARK GREY GRIZZLE. THEY MUST BE LONG AND THIN (FROM THE END OF THE HACKLE FEATHER)

TOPPING: OVERLAY OF WISP OF MALLARD AT HEAD

HEAD: BLACK

This is used over dark, weedy bottom areas, and in lakes where the smelt are dark in colour such as Lake Rotorua.

GT SMELT, Yellow (M)

ORIGIN: GEOFF THOMAS

TAIL: RED WHISKS

BODY: YELLOW 2-PLY WOOL UNRAVELLED (SEE PREVIOUS ENTRY)

RIB: THIN SILVER

WING: FOUR FEATHERS - TWO OF DARK GREY GRIZZLE INSIDE ONE HONEY GRIZZLE ON EACH SIDE. THEY MUST BE LONG AND THIN

TOPPING: OVERLAY OF WISP OF MALLARD AT HEAD

HEAD: BLACK

A smelt pattern for use over light sandy areas.

TAUPO REGIONAL SMELT PATTERNS

For a district in which smelt plays such an important part in both the trout's diet, and the angler's fishing strategy, I found a curious absence of localised patterns which might have reflected this. It seemed to me that a possible explanation was that standard patterns work so well, and have done so for so long, that there was a reluctance to change.

It is true that some patterns such as Albino (2), Golden Queen, Palamino, many of Bronwyn Wilson's patterns in Appendix 1, and elsewhere, and Ritchie Buchanan's patterns have a localised following and perhaps could have been included in this section rather than in the main body of this book. My reasons for not doing so are difficult to articulate but have something to do with the changing structure of this book as it progressed at a time when this, and other appendices, were not in contemplation.

The following selections are in two parts: Bronwyn Wilson has again come to the fore and supplied a selection of useful and effective smelt patterns which have stood her in good stead over the years. I have no doubt that the style of Bronwyn's patterns has been influenced to some degree by Bruno Kemball's lures, which make up the second part of this selection.

Bruno Kemball was a very well-known, highly respected angling identity. For some time prior to his death he was the proprietor of the Red Spinner tackle shop at Hatepe, Lake Taupo. While Bruno's patterns attracted widespread interest and popularity, it was well known that close inspection was possible only with the aid of tweezers supplied, and woe betide anyone foolish enough to manhandle his precious works of art with bare hands.

A number of Bruno's patterns have been taken from a collection stored in Taupo which are so housed that they cannot be removed for the purposes of photographing them. Bronwyn Wilson has re-created those patterns including Bruno's trademark use of salmon hooks with an up-turned eye. I have indicated which of Bruno's patterns have been tied by him, and those which have been tied by Bronwyn.

BRONWYN WILSON'S SMELT PATTERNS

EDDIE'S MALLARD SMELT (O)

HOOK: 6-10

TAIL: MALLARD FLANK TIED SHORT

BODY: SILVER LUREX YARN (REAR) AND INSECT GREEN WOOL (FRONT)

WING: MALLARD FLANK FEATHERS

HACKLE: GRIZZLE

HEAD: BLACK

Originally tied for Eddie Bosomworth but Bronwyn made a mistake with the pattern. However it turned out to be a great fish catcher around river mouths and lake edges.

GOLDEN PHEASANT SMELT (O)

HOOK: 6-10
TAIL: GOLDEN PHEASANT TAIL FIBRES
BODY: MULTI-COLOURED SOCK WOOL
HACKLE: BROWN SPECKLED PARTRIDGE
HEAD: BLACK

HAWK and POSSUM (PEARL) (O)

HOOK: 6-10
TAIL: HAWK TAIL OR WING PRIMARY FIBRES
BODY: PEARL LUREX YARN
WING: TUFT OF POSSUM FUR
HACKLE: BROWN PARTRIDGE
HEAD: BLACK

The colour of the hackle can be varied to match the colour of the possum fur.

MADEIRA SMELT (BLUE) (O)

HOOK: 6-10, LONG SHANK
TAIL AND BACK: WHITE MARABOU EXTENDING OVER BODY LIKE A WING CASE
BODY: BLUE MADEIRA METALLIC THREAD
HACKLE: WHITE COCK
HEAD: WHITE

MADEIRA SMELT (GREEN) (O)

HOOK: 6-10, LONG SHANK
TAIL AND BACK: WHITE MARABOU EXTENDING OVER BODY TO HEAD
BODY: GREEN MADEIRA METALLIC THREAD
HACKLE: LIGHT GREEN COCK
HEAD: BLACK

MADEIRA SMELT (PINK) (O)

HOOK: 6-10, LONG SHANK
TAIL AND BACK: DUSK PINK MARABOU EXTENDING OVER THE BODY TO HEAD
BODY: MULTI-MIXED MADEIRA
HACKLE: GREY COCK, FOLLOWED WITH A BLACK HEAD

MALLARD SMELT (O)

HOOK: 6-10
TAIL: MALLARD FLANK FEATHERS
BODY: FLUORESCENT GREEN WOOL
HACKLE: WHITE COCK
HEAD: BLACK

Deadly in a rip, lake margins, and lower reaches of rivers. Use a slow sinking or floating line with a slow retrieve.

SALMON SMELT (O)

HOOK: 6-10, LONG SHANK
TAIL AND BACK: WHITE MARABOU EXTENDING OVER BODY LIKE A WING CASE
BODY: SALMON ANTRON YARN
RIB: WHITE ANTRON FIBRES SPUN ON A THREAD
HACKLE: WHITE BASAL MARABOU FLUFF FROM BASE OF HACKLE
HEAD: BLACK

BRUNO KEMBALL'S PATTERNS -Tied by Kemball

GOLDEN PHEASANT SMELT (O)

HOOK: 6-10 UPTURNED EYE
TAIL: GOLDEN PHEASANT TAIL FIBRES
BODY: OLIVE GREEN WOOL
RIB: FINE OVAL GOLD
HACKLE: BROWN SPECKLED PARTRIDGE
HEAD: BLACK

GOLD-OLIVE SMELT (O)

HOOK: 8-10 UPTURNED EYE
TAIL: TWO DYED GOLD-OLIVE COCK FEATHERS
BODY: OLIVE GREEN WOOL
RIB: FINE OVAL GOLD
HACKLE: DYED GOLD-OLIVE COCK
HEAD: OLIVE GREEN

GREEN ORBIT SMELT (O)

HOOK: 6-10 UPTURNED EYE
TAIL: TWO DYED GREEN GRIZZLE FEATHERS
BODY: OLIVE GREEN CHENILLE
RIB: FINE OVAL GOLD
HACKLE: DYED GREEN GRIZZLE
HEAD: BLACK

GREY GHOST SMELT (O)

HOOK: 6-10, UPTURNED EYE
TAIL: GREY OR WHITE HAWK (FROM TAIL OR FLIGHT FEATHERS)
BODY: LIGHT LIME GREEN WOOL
RIB: FINE OVAL GOLD
HACKLE: GREY
HEAD: BLACK

MALLARD SMELT (O)

HOOK: 4-8, UPTURNED EYE
TAIL: DARK MALLARD FLANK
BODY: GREEN WOOL
RIB: FINE OVAL GOLD
HACKLE: GRIZZLE COCK
HEAD: BLACK

OLIVE SMELT (O)

HOOK: 8-10, UPTURNED EYE
TAIL: TWO DYED LIGHT OLIVE COCK FEATHERS
BODY: FLAT GOLD TINSEL
HACKLE: DYED LIGHT OLIVE COCK
HEAD: BLACK

This is Bruno's treatment of Olive Smelt where the soft head hackle takes the place of the Matuku style wing (see Alphabetical section)

SQUIRREL SMELT (O)

HOOK: 6-8, UPTURNED EYE
TAIL: BARRED WHITE-TIPPED GREY SQUIRREL TAIL
BODY: FLAT SILVER TINSEL
HACKLE: GREY SPECKLED PARTRIDGE
HEAD: BLACK

TURKEY SMELT (O)

HOOK: 6-10, UPTURNED EYE
TAIL: SPECKLED TURKEY FEATHERS
BODY: WHITE WOOL
RIB: OVAL SILVER
HEAD: BLACK

The following patterns are of Kemball's framed collection kept in the Taupo Fishing Club rooms, recreated here and tied by Bronwyn Wilson. No hook size is given, but all are probably in the same size range as those shown above.

BLACK DEMON SMELT (O)

TAIL: TWO BLACK COCK FEATHERS
BODY: RED WOOL
RIB: FINE OVAL SILVER
HACKLE: BLACK
HEAD: BLACK

GOLD SMELT (O)

TAIL: LIGHT GINGER FURNACE COCK
BODY: FLAT GOLD TINSEL
HACKLE: LIGHT GINGER FURNACE COCK
HEAD: BLACK

PARTRIDGE BULLY (K)

TAIL: BROWN SQUIRREL TAIL
BODY: YELLOW WOOL
WING: TWO SPECKLED PARTRIDGE BREAST FEATHERS TIED IN EACH SIDE AT THE HEAD, KILLER STYLE
HEAD: BLACK

SILVER SMELT (O)

TAIL: TWO LIGHT BADGER FEATHERS WITH FINE DARK CENTRE LINE
BODY: FLAT SILVER TINSEL
HACKLE: LIGHT BADGER
HEAD: BLACK

TIGER ROSS SMELT (O)

TAIL:	TWO BADGER COCK FEATHERS
BODY:	YELLOW WOOL
RIB:	OVAL SILVER
HACKLE:	BADGER
HEAD:	BLACK

A BEVY OF BURGLARS

George Gatchell created the Burglar in 1974, which took the angling world by storm and went on to develop a virtual cottage industry of framed collections of Burglar lures. I have described elsewhere the essential elements in the construction of the Burglar lure. Provided those elements are present, it will be a Burglar regardless of the variation in materials and colour. Hence, George was able to tie up a wide variety of Burglars, and the famed collections adorning the walls of the Crystal Brook Tackle Shop at Waitahanui, Taupo were a major drawcard.

The collection which is shown here was kindly loaned to me by Bronwyn Wilson of Taupo who professionally tied Burglars for George in response to the heavy demand for those popular lures.

George is no longer the proprietor of the Crystal Brook. He has retired to the Marlborough Sounds. Sadly, he became disillusioned with the declining ethics of some anglers on the Waitahanui River and elsewhere - a trend which has become one of increasing concern. He has packed away his fishing and fly-tying equipment.

BOTTLE-TOPS AND BIROS

Many years ago, a colleague of mine from Feilding was holidaying in America. He told me of a discussion between two (American) flatmates who argued about the respective merits of correct fly presentation versus realism in imitation. It was the contention of one that trout will take anything if it is presented right. He was challenged to come up with an effective lure using only what he could find in the sparsely furnished kitchen. He duly fashioned lures using such items as foil milk-bottle tops, rubber bands, and cigarette butts (I seriously doubt that part, although I am aware that cigarette butts have been found in trout stomachs!). The point is, he did create lures out of throw-away rubbish and caught trout.

While clever imitations will fool trout (and swell the egos of fly-tiers), not all effective lures can be regarded as imitations of anything. Rainbow trout, in particular, seem to have a penchant for snapping at anything which flashes, or glitters. I recall an occasion fishing the Mohaka River without success. Another angler, working the same stretch advised 'give 'em plenty of dash'. This was many years before Mohaka Special was created. That particular lure imitates a spinner which does not imitate anything known to me, and both are excellent fish takers.

There is a school of thought that trout react to a stimulus which has been termed a 'supernormal releaser'. The theory is that trout respond to a general shape, feature, or splash of colour, and the more that characteristic is caricatured or exaggerated, even to the point of distortion, the greater will be the response. Other research, however, suggests that since trout stop feeding once they are replete, the attack on a lure is an act of instinctive aggression out of territorial protection. An interesting discussion on this topic can be found in *The New Zealand Encyclopaedia of Fly Fishing*, by Bryn Hammond (1988). For either, or possibly both, of those reasons, the American caught trout on his foil milk-bottle top lure.

Once a year, I join a team of enthusiastic fishermen and other liars for a four day assault on the trout at Lake Waikaremoana. There are two boats and thereby two opposing groups. The competition is for the heaviest fish and the rivalry is intense. Traditional lures are paraded and swum with confidence and a lot of fish are caught, the majority of which are released. It is not how many, but how big - a target which has largely eluded the opposition year after year! In some measure of frustration, I suspect, one of the better anglers in the other camp, Detective Sergeant Rick Graham, of Napier, fashioned a lure out of a beer bottle top. I can't imagine how he managed to find such an item on their boat, but having done so the resulting lure proved to be effective at catching trout, albeit that it has not yet caught the winning big fish. That is beside the point. Trout were induced to snap at a crude spinning beer bottle top.

Without wishing to be accused of trying to promote any particular brand of beer, Rick claims that the 'shape' of the name on the bottle top is important. A long black name such as that shown in the photo gives a lateral rib effect when spinning. The name should therefore be aligned in the same direction as the leader, rather than at right angles to it.

Another member of that group caught a 2.4kg brown on the last day of November 1997 using nothing more than a tab from a tear-top can of food, twisted to make it spin, and with a small white lure attached.

At the same lake is a local identity, Tim Warren, known to everyone simply as Tim. Chronicling his experiences would be a fascinating venture in itself, but outside the scope of this book. Tim spends much of his time sailing around the lake on his sizeable yacht. Yachts are not ideally suited to trout fishing. They cannot skirt the shoreline. The boat still has to be manoeuvred while playing a trout. You cannot just switch off a trolling motor. The transom is high out of the water which makes landing a trout difficult. But Tim catches a lot of trout. One of his favoured lures, and one of the most effective, is fashioned out of the transparent lower barrel of an ordinary biro pen.

The lure is made by cutting off the clear plastic barrel. Two notches are cut into the edge of the cut section, opposite each other. This causes the plastic tube to spin. A single hook is attached to a nylon leader which is inserted through the narrow end of the tube. The leader should be attached to a swivel. That is all there is to it. Tim insists that nothing else should be added. As the biro spins through the water, it appears white and probably imitates a smelt. It is most effective in March.

Obviously, in order to impart a continuous spin to the lure, it is really only suited to harling or trolling. Whether trout are triggered by a supernormal releaser or are being territorial (Tim fishes right out in the middle of the lake) is open to discussion - but not here. The significance is that, to catch trout, it is not necessary to own hideously expensive Metz capes or boxes and boxes of tinsel, chenille, fur, dubbing materials, and costly gizmos. Good old-fashioned Kiwi ingenuity can create a device, limited only by one's imagination, which will catch trout.

SHAPING UP

WORKING WITH DEER HAIR

Sometime back in the 1950s, American Don Gapen created the famous Muddler Minnow. It was designed to imitate the nocturnal, flat-head cockatush minnow, a bullhead fish not unlike our cock-a-bully. The importance of this lure - apart from the fact that it will catch practically anything, anywhere, at any time - is that it was the first time that the art of spinning deer hair was used, albeit in a rather scraggly, sparsely-dressed way. Once the art of spinning deer hair was appreciated and understood, variations were unleashed and Muddler-type heads underwent many changes and styles with elongated cylindrical heads, bullet-shaped heads, small round balls, broad flattened bullheads and sculpins, and so on.

Deer hair fibres are hollow and very buoyant, a property which has lent itself to numerous dry fly patterns. It can, however, be fished deep on a sinking line using the natural buoyancy to cause the lure to rise after wriggling downwards on the retrieve, giving the appearance of a disabled fish or one which is struggling to reach the shelter of the bottom. Well, that is one theory. In the August 1996 English magazine, *Trout and Salmon*, Charles Jardine propounds another thought: "Deer hair is hollow and, when trimmed, becomes a tiny hollow tube, which must produce some sort of sound wave when drawn through the water. I feel sure that this sound is picked up by the trout via their lateral line".

Whether or not the deer hair lure looks like an injured or escaping fish, or is a piscatorial dinner gong, or simply a clever imitation of the original, there is no doubt that lures utilising deer hair can be highly effective.

American fly-tiers such as Dave Whitlock, Larry Dahlberg, Jim Stewart, and Jimmy Nix (to name but a few), have elevated deer hair tying to an art form. From their vices have come realistic replicas of cock-a-bullies, mice, crabs, frogs, rats, field crickets, hoppers, and water snakes. But the list certainly does not stop there. Anyone interested in this form of fly-tying, and the endless range of possibilities, should purchase *Fly Patterns of Umpqua Feather Merchants* (1995)

In New Zealand, we are limited in the range and type of deer hair available, but that which is available is generally suitable for spinning and stacking. I use either fine or medium hair with a preference for medium. If you can get it, caribou and yearling elk are excellent, while antelope is the ultimate for spinning.

One of the fascinations of deer hair tying is observing the way different hairs react to differing thread pressures and the different effects which can be achieved. Do not be afraid to experiment.

Spinning Deer Hair

By the time you come to tie in the deer hair, you will

likely have completed the tail, body, and wing in whatever style or combination you have in mind. I recommend that you use a long shank hook. To use a No. 6 hook as an example, the long shank incorporates a normal No. 6 plus some extra shank length. If you were tying a Rabbit with a Muddler style head, you would tie the Rabbit lure just as you would on a No. 6 hook. The extra hook length is then available for the head. This head space should be bare and thread-free. Having completed the body, wing ,etc. using whatever tying thread you consider appropriate, I strongly suggest that you secure thoroughly, tie off, and cement your work at this stage. If you make a mess of the head subsequently, you can cut it away and start again without having to re-do the whole lure.

Okay, you now have a section of bare shank, about one-third or one-quarter the total length of the shank. Attach a strong thread such as Kevlar at the last tie-off point. You can, if you wish, use single strand floss, or even ordinary tying thread, provided you use a great deal of care and caution. Quite a lot of force is used in spinning deer hair and it can be exasperating to have the thread snap when you are almost finished. (If you have not noticed it before, you will soon discover that tying thread breaks only towards the end of the job, never at the start!).

Take a smallish bunch of deer hair. Deer hair fibres are quite long and my practice is to cut a bunch from the top half of the fibre lengths. Place this bunch directly on top of the shank with the fine pointed tips facing the tail. Those tips will form the deer hackle collar in the same way that a feather hackle does, so try and gauge the length of the bunch of hairs you cut and whereabouts on the shank you want to tie it in. Ideally, the mid-point of the deer hair bunch should be close to the last tie-off point.

Take one turn of the thread around the bunch. Tighten with direct downward pressure. This will cause the deer hair to flare and spin around the bare shank. Take another turn and pull tighter. Take a third turn, the tightest of all. You may need to support the hook eye with a free hand to counter the downwards pressure. By now the deer hair should be flared and encircling the shank. Advance the tying thread to the bare shank in front of the deer hair.

The deer hair now needs to be packed by pushing the whole flared bunch firmly back towards the rear. This can be done with the fingers, but a far better arrangement is to use the tapered end of an empty ball-point barrel, cut back so that the hole will fit over the hook eye. Once the bunch is packed back as tightly as possible, take a couple of turns with the thread immediately in front of the bunch to hold it in position.

Repeat the same procedure of spinning and packing until the shank is full. For the second and subsequent bunches, I tend to use (where possible) the bottom half of the previously cut bunch used for the collar. This is the part which will be trimmed to shape, and it doesn't matter if it has fine tips or not, but it is important, I believe, for the collar to come from the tip hairs.

Packing the deer hair back firmly is very important. This determines the density and evenness of the finished head and also its buoyancy by creating air pockets. If it is not done right, the finished head will suffer from uneven gaps and visible thread. Make sure that the final packing clears the eye then tie off. You will now have a rather unsightly mess that looks like a well-worn bottle brush.

Trimming to shape is very much a matter of practice, 'feel', and experimentation. Start from the eye and take small snips at the angle you want the finished head, whether conical, round, broad or whatever. I tend to rotate around the eye before moving up and repeating. I have seen it suggested that you should use curved scissors. That is an individual matter, but whatever scissors are used, they must be sharp and I believe they must be serrated. Serrated-edged blades catch the fibres and are excellent for trimming deer hair. Once the head has been shaped to your satisfaction you can, if you wish, give the whole thing a final trim with a sharp razor blade or scalpel. I also think it is a good idea to hold the lure upright and put a few drops of head cement on the tie-off point, letting the cement run down into the base of the fibres.

Eyes can be created by using a waterproof felt-tip pen, or you can stick on artificial eyes using epoxy. I put a blob or two of epoxy on either side of the head and work it down into the fibres with a pin. Capillary action will take the epoxy down to the base of the fibres and provide a good foundation for the eyes, which I stick in place before the epoxy sets. Once firmly in place, I give a final coating over the eyes with gloss coat or head varnish.

Stacking Deer Hair

Dave Whitlock added a new dimension to deer hair tying with his technique of stacking deer hair. Now it was possible to build in defined bands of colour combinations for greater effect. The procedure is relatively simple but some care is needed. When creating his famous sculpin patterns, Dave Whitlock arranged his colours so that light colours were at the bottom and dark colours were at the top. Without having studied, in depth, the trout's swimming diet of bullies and such like, I suspect the same consideration would apply in New Zealand - think of the tadpole for instance.

The first step in stacking is exactly as for spinning deer hair. Lay a bunch of light coloured deer hair on the bare shank, tips pointing towards the bend of the hook. Attach with two or three loose turns of the thread. Tighten the thread very slowly. The hair will start to flare and roll under the shank. When the bunch is underneath the shank, hold it there so that it cannot rotate any further and wrap another two or three turns of thread tightly.

Now, take a second bunch of deer hair (with tips). It may be the same colour, or a different colour depending on the effect you are seeking. Hold it directly over the shank at the point where the first bunch was originally placed. Take two or three loose wraps or thread (which will encompass the first bunch underneath the shank) while at the same time holding the second bunch so that it will not rotate. Tighten the thread so that the deer hair flares but stays in its position on top of the shank.

Take a third bunch of hair and place it directly over the second bunch. You might want this bunch to be slightly longer than the others if you want the tips to simulate a dorsal fin. Follow the same procedure as for the second bunch, trying to ensure that the different colours do not mix. Take the thread forward to the bare shank in front of the head and pack the flared bunch back firmly as described in the previous section. Secure with a few tight turns of thread.

Repeat this stacking procedure until the shank is full, varying the colours to suit. The first lot of stacked bunches will form the collar and part of the head, and subsequent stacked bunches will form the head. Generally, the top bunch in each case will provide the widest band and determine the overall dominant colour. The second bunch will show up as different coloured strips on either side of that dominant colour. The first colour gives the under-belly colour.

After the last bunch has been stacked and packed, whip-finish at the eye and tie off. Trimming will be determined by the result you are seeking to achieve. In the case of sculpin type lures, the hair under the shank is cut flat and wide, leaving a few hair tips extending back to the body.

Dave Whitlock recommends coating the underside, top of the head, and the thread wrap at the eye with thin rod varnish. This makes the lure more durable and retains the shape while fishing.

The Patterns

The first is Runna Muk Muddler, which I tie up in six different colour variations. The photo and pattern features the olive version. That, and brown, are my preferred choices but other colours which work are yellow, white, orange and black. I tie these only on a No. 6 long shank and thus far I have only ever harled with them. And no, the trout do not run amok when these enter the water, but they do catch trout.

I have then added a Fuzzy Wuzzy version of my own to demonstrate further possibilities using deer hair. After that is my Brer Muddler followed by Keith Draper's Bully Muddler. The last pattern, Puddler, demonstrates exciting possibilities using the innovative technique of Palmering strips of deer hair. It has been tied on a No. 2 long shank.

With the exception of Puddler, all of the patterns are home grown although with a strong American flavour in the case of my own patterns. I readily acknowledge the inspiration and enormous influence which Dave Whitlock, in particular, has had on me. It might be said that 'Runna Muk' aptly describes the elaborate dressing, and I would be slow to disagree. However, they are not difficult to tie and the omission of a few ingredients is unlikely to make any difference if you do not have all the materials. Provided it is legal, I am not above using as much (or as little) of any materials of any description which are available, if the end result is a lure which takes trout.

The Brer Muddler is nearly always tied on a No. 2 long shank, and the example photographed is no exception. Again, this can be tied up in a number of colour variations.

I have suggested weighting as an option with my own patterns because I think it is a desirable feature if you wish to fish these lures deep, and the law may one day change. Weighting is permitted in some districts.

Pectoral fins add a degree of realism, particularly if they project out. This is achieved by tying them in with the 'good' side facing the body. However, they do not take kindly to being whipped through the air at high speed while casting. I usually tie them to jut out only when I am harling, otherwise they are tied a la Mrs Simpson.

I have varied the style of head to show how individual preferences can be accommodated. The inclusion of eyes does make a difference, I believe, but that is a personal choice and I do not specify eyes in the patterns.

I have not given a tying guide. The focus of these lures is the use of deer hair, and the method of tying deer hair heads has been set out in detail above.

RUNNA MUK MUDDLER (O)

HOOK: 6, LONG SHANK (OPTONAL WEIGHTED)

BODY: PEARL MYLAR WOUND FLAT

WING: (IN ORDER OF TYING FROM THE BOTTOM UP)
CHARTREUSE MARABOU
KRYSTAL FLASH RED
OLIVE MARABOU
FLASHABOU PEARL

THROAT: RED MARABOU

COLLAR GREY OR NATURAL CARABOU, SPUN

HEAD: SPUN DEER HAIR, OLIVE CADDIS BROWN, AND GREY

BRER MUDDLER (O)

HOOK: 2-6, LONG SHANK (OPTIONAL WEIGHTED)

BODY: GOLD OR SILVER HOLOGRAPHIC TINSEL

RIB: OVAL GOLD OR SILVER

WING: STRIP OF RABBIT FUR

SIDE WING: TWO STRANDS FLASHABOU PEARL UNDER A SINGLE GRIZZLY MARABOU (COLOUR TO SUIT) ON EITHER SIDE

PECTORAL FINS: COCK PHEASANT RUMP, GREY PARTRIDGE, HEN PHEASANT, GROUSE, SHOVELLER - ALL ARE GOOD

GILLS: GRIZZLY MARABOU DYED RED

COLLAR: STACKED DEER HAIR

HEAD: STACKED DEER HAIR, SHAPED

Dave Whitlock's Sculpin originally had a wing of hackle feathers tied Pukeko style over a bunch of red fox squirrel tail. This evolved to a wing of hackle feathers tied Matuku style. I conceived the idea of using rabbit and thought that I had come up with an original winner. I was then unaware of Rabbit Muddler 1. On 24 October 1996, I was browsing through an English fly fishing magazine and was aghast to find a photo of Whitlock's Sculpin which now incorporated rabbit as an evolutionary change from the hackle feather wing. Which one of us came to it first (if, indeed, either of us did) is not known, but I like to think that there are enough differences in any event to warrant my claim to this dressing.

Combining, as it does, the proven features of both Rabbit and Muddler Minnow, it might be expected to be an effective lure, and so it is. All the usual colour variations are available.

BULLY MUDDLER (M)

ORIGIN: KEITH DRAPER OF TAUPO

HOOK: 2-8, LONG SHANK

TAIL: (OPTIONAL) HACKLE WHISKS, COLOUR TO SUIT

BODY: CHENILLE

RIB: OVAL SILVER

WING: TWO SPLIT SECTIONS OF GROUSE TAIL

PECTORAL FINS: (OPTIONAL) TIPS FROM TWO GROUSE TAILS

COLLAR: SPUN AND PACKED DEER HAIR

HEAD: SPUN AND PACKED DEER HAIR

In splitting the grouse tail, the tip section is cut away.

It is this (plus one more) that can be used for the pectoral fins, if using.

Keith has only ever used this lure at night, preferring a brown or olive colouring, but feels there is no reason why it shouldn't work well during the day.

The lure is fished on a high density line with a short leader of about half a metre. The lure is retrieved very slowly, giving the line a quick pull and then pausing. This causes the lure to dart downwards and then slowly rise, giving the impression of an injured fish.

"Does it work?" Keith asks. "Give it a try and see. One dark night at Waitahanui something heavier than any trout I've ever felt before took my Bully Muddler and began a steady unstoppable run out into the lake. I had to clamp up eventually as it had no intention of stopping and the nylon parted."

When I reminded Keith of this incident he gazed wistfully into the middle distance, eyes glazed "I reckon that trout is still going", he said.

While I cannot relate a similar story, I can vouch for its effectiveness.

PUDDLER (O)

ORIGIN: BASED ON AN UNNAMED PATTERN CREATED BY PETRI PAJUNEN OF FINLAND
HOOK: NOT STATED BUT PROBABLY 2-8 LONG SHANK, ALTHOUGH THE TECHNIQUE CAN BE EMPLOYED IN VERY SMALL SIZES
TAIL: MARABOU
BODY: PALMERED POLECAT STRIPS
COLLAR: (OPTIONAL) SPUN DEER HAIR
HEAD: PALMERED STRIP OF DEER HAIR

For those who find spinning deer hair a somewhat daunting exercise, this method may appeal. Palmering a strip of deer hair (caribou in the example) produces an instant Muddler head. It is a good way of utilising the base stubs of cut deer hair swatches.

The Palmered hair can be packed to increase density, if desired, and the whole thing trimmed and clipped to your liking. Good Muddler heads can be produced in a fraction of the time taken using the conventional method. The same technique can be used in very small sizes to make the body of an Irresistible, for example.

The colouring used in the example has overtones of Hamill's Killer and Wisp, although any colour or combination of colours can be used.

The concept of Palmered Muddlers gave rise to the name I have given this lure. I believe the original lure on which this was based used Arctic Fox fur. That has a much longer fur length than Polecat, and if I were using Arctic Fox I would be inclined to omit the tail, as Petri does, particularly in the larger sizes. I have a preference for the shorter-fibred Polecat fur, particularly with the dark guard hairs.

In presenting this pattern, however, my focus is not on the lure but the technique of using deer hair in the manner described. In order to wind on a strip of deer hair on the skin, it is important that the skin be as thin and pliable as possible. The example has been tied on a Partridge Single Low Water size 2.

FUZZY BAMBI (O)

HOOK: 2-8 LONG SHANK (OPTIONAL, WEIGHTED)
TAIL: BUNCH OF MARABOU
BODY: SHORT SECTIONS OF PEARL MYLAR OR FISHSCALE
WING: SPUN DEER HAIR
HACKLE: RED DYED COCK IMMEDIATELY BEFORE SPINNING ON THE HEAD COLLAR
HEAD: SPUN AND PACKED DEER HAIR WITH OPTIONAL GOLD BEAD

MORE INFORMATION ABOUT THIS LURE IS ON PAGE 128

TYING KILLER LURES and THE SOUTH ISLAND WAY

Tying Killer style flies can be difficult and frustrating at any time. Keith Draper recounts using as many as 16 feathers in tying a Lord's Killer to his satisfaction. Hugh McDowell describes Killer style lures as "awkward, fiddly, exasperating, time-consuming things to construct..."

The problem stems mainly from the difficulty in getting the wing feather to lie nicely along the body and meeting over the top of the body with the wing feather on the opposite side. Some feathers tie in more easily than others, for example, the Shoveller feathers used in Brown Killer. Others can be a curse (Spa Special), but the problem is often not the inherent nature of the feather but the construction of the body. The most commonly used body material is chenille. When tying Killer style flies, a feather is often tied in at the bend on either side of the shank. The chenille is then tied in and wound back to about the mid-point and tied off. Another feather is tied in on either side at that point. Normally, the wing stems are tied in against the shank. The problem that then arises is that the feather is pushed away from the shank by the chenille, preventing the feather from lying nicely alongside the body. The same problem arises again at the head when the last set of feathers is tied in.

A number of methods have been devised to overcome this. Placing the feather stem against the chenille, rather than the shank, and then tying in, is one method. This also avoids the need to tie off the chenille and then re-tie it for the second body section. One tier I know builds up the tie-off point with thread so that the feather is tied in roughly on the same plane as the chenille.

One useful method which I often employ is to forsake the chenille and use a single strand of wool unwound from a length of, say, 3 ply wool, or, better still, use Uni Yarn or Micro (Ultra) chenille. These are all less bulky than the standard medium chenille and the feather lies flatter along the shank at the tie-in point. You can achieve a similar advantage using floss.

Another method which I, and other fly-tiers, adopt, is to tie in the wing feathers at the bend and at the head only, omitting the mid-section (see, for example, Duchess). Sometimes the nature of the feather will almost demand this method, as with Duchess and Orange Witch.

Then there are those who omit the body material completely, reasoning that a well-tied Killer so totally enwraps the body that it can't be seen anyway, so why have it? This does not satisfy those who feel a plumper body is more desirable. Garth Coghill, for one, likes plump bodies on his Killers, but he achieves this by tying in continuous sets of feathers for about the last third of the shank. A thin tinsel body makes up the first two-thirds in the event that the feathers part in the act of casting, allowing some colour to show (see, for example, Pluto).

One technique which sometimes overcomes the problem of fickle feathers is to tie the feathers in with the stems pointing towards the bend of the hook and the dull side of the feather facing out. Once tied in, and the stems trimmed, the tip of the feather is then pulled forward towards the bend so that the correct side of the feather is facing out. It is then bound in again at the original tie-in point.

And then there is the South Island way. The photos shows four well-known lures tied in a manner which is common in the South Island. Far from omitting or hiding the body material (and perhaps more importantly, the colour) it is accentuated. This is done by tying in the head and mid-point side feathers at an upward angle, quite markedly so in some cases. Some of Robert Bragg's ties I have seen are almost butterfly-like in appearance. I can easily achieve this effect, and often do, just trying to tie them conventionally! I sometimes wonder if the method evolved from some poor harassed individual justifying his inability to get the feathers to lie parallel to the shank. No doubt I am being unfair to someone, and it should be recognised that lures tied in this manner are very effective.

Not all Killer style lures are given this treatment, and the four lures shown, together with Bragg's Bully, are really the only ones which attract this style of tying. All four lures were tied by Peter Hart of Christchurch on No. 4 hooks. The angle of wing ascension is not as acute as some examples I have seen, but the body is exposed. For those who regard this as a desirable attribute this method of tying may commend itself.

While not wishing to become embroiled in a discussion on name derivation, I note that Peter has called the Kilwell No.1 a Walker's Killer, and the Mrs Simpson a Kilwell No.2. Keith Draper, Eddie Bosomworth, and others are of the view that Mrs Simpson was a South Island name for the Kilwell No. 1. Joe Frost of Turangi always called Kilwell No.1 a Mrs Simpson. Peter Hart's research suggests that the true Mrs Simpson is of English origin tied from the brown 'church window' plumage. He is adamant that Mrs Simpson is the name given to Kilwell No.2 in the South Island. Further confusion stems from the Mrs Simpson (Kea) originally tied up with Kea feathers in 1939, by Mona Carter at Tisdalls' in Christchurch. The confusion is compounded by John Giacon's assertion that Mrs Simpson was first tied by (and, by inference, originated from) one Selwyn Clark, an Auckland lawyer. However, Fred Fletcher, who created Fuzzy Wuzzy, and who saw that 'first' tie, describes it as being dressed with striped brown partridge feathers, which, of course, is Kilwell No.1.

O.S.("Budge") Hintz also saw that 'first' tie but says it was a Fuzzy Wuzzy, except that the Fuzzy Wuzzy correctly depicted in his book was incorrectly called Mrs Simpson. (Are you still with me!) Clark, himself, has confirmed to Keith Draper that that 'first' tie was indeed a Fuzzy Wuzzy. Keith offers the thought that an over-indulgence in apres fishing formalities can be the only explanation for Fred confusing his own creation for a Kilwell No.1. Whatever the reason, of all the claims made about the origin of Mrs Simpson, the one which credits Selwyn Clark with that honour is the easiest to refute.

That does not solve the riddle, or throw light on the English connection, if there was one. I have seen English publications which have hailed Mrs Simpson as a New Zealand lure. Keith Draper recounts how Jack Ramm, who used to live in Hawke's Bay, once said: "You know that fly you call a Mrs Simpson? Well it isn't. I remember when it first came out and we used to call it a Cock Pheasant Leslie." (1997)

Keith then points out that Leslie's Lure is tied with hen pheasant plumage, and supposes that someone probably tied up a Leslie's Lure using the cock feathers. I think this version has more credibility that most and I strongly suspect that it provides most of the answer. It vaguely supports Frank Lord's memory that Mrs Simpson originated with a Hastings angler. I doubt if we are going to get any closer to the truth than that, and I fear that the true origin of Mrs Simpson has been consigned to perpetual obscurity. What is beyond dispute, I believe, (having spoken at length with Frank Lord) is that Kilwell No. 2 was the creation of Frank Lord, by whatever name it may be known.

Equally so, Kilwell No.1 was created by Frank Lord. The name Walker's Killer is interesting. I thought I had the answer when someone told me that at the time Frank Lord created both of these lures he was running his own tackle shop in Rotorua. Employed in the shop was one Walker, from South Africa. At some stage, Walker returned to South Africa, and some time later Walker's Killer appeared on the South Island scene, purportedly tied with some exotic plumage that bore a striking similarity to a striped brown partridge. In fact, Frank Lord cannot recall employing anyone of that name and the account is probably apocryphal except that, even as I write, Walker's Killer continues to appear in overseas publications, described as a South African lure, and is identical in every respect to Kilwell No.1. No doubt that explains why Peter Hart refers to the Kilwell No. 2 as Mrs Simpson. Whether Walker's Killer is a plagiarism or a coincidence, I cannot say, but I do say that Frank Lord has the first claim, and it most certainly is not a Mrs Simpson, nor a Kilwell No. 2.

(There! I just got embroiled in a discussion on name derivation!)

FOR THE RECORD

Despite my best endeavours, I have been unable to track down a number of lures which I know existed in years long gone. In some cases I had the pattern but no name. In most cases I had a name but no pattern.

Bryn Hammond in *The New Zealand Encyclopaedia of Fly Fishing* (1988) had an entry on 'Bygone Flies'. Those old timers which neither of us have been able to track down are:

RANGATIRA
SUNSET GLORY
MAORI'S LURE

The mention of Rangatira "rings bells" with many older anglers but so far has failed to push any memory buttons. To the above list, I can add the following:

(Red) Rufus – not to be confused with Bronwyn Wilson's Rufus

Jock Patterson – possibly originating in Central Otago

Black Murderer – probably a Rotorua pattern.

Neptune } – sold by Tisdall's at least as late as 1958.

Pirate }

Okataina Lady – obviously a Rotorua lure. It was a Matuku pattern based somewhat on Parsons' Glory.

O'Rielly – a Taupo trolling lure popular at least until the early 1960s.

Apart from what I have written here, I have been unable to find any other information on these lures.

The following lures have no names but I have (or have seen) these lures and have been able to ascertain the pattern. It is possible, I guess, that someone may be able to match one of the above pattern-less name to one of the name-less patterns.

NO NAME 1 (O)

ORIGIN: NOT KNOWN
HOOK: PROBABLY 2-8
TAIL: GREEN PEACOCK HERL
BODY: FLAT SILVER TINSEL
RIB: OVAL SILVER
UNDERWING: SINGLE RED GOOSE WING FIBRE
WING: BUNCH OF BRONZE PEACOCK HERL
TOPPING: SINGLE RED GOOSE WING FIBRE
HACKLE: SOFT BLACK
HEAD: BLACK

I came across this among Alan Beamish-White's collection of old lures. He could not give me any information about it and thus far I have not been able to identify it. I would guess that it is a night lure.

NO NAME 2 (O)

ORIGIN: NOT KNOWN
HOOK: PROBABLY 2-8
TAIL: DARK GINGER HACKLE POINTS

BODY:	FLAT SILVER TINSEL
RIB:	OPPER WIRE
WING:	FURNACE (TWO PAIRS BACK TO BACK) TIED IN AT THE HEAD STREAMER STYLE
TOPPING:	PEACOCK HERL
HEAD:	RED

I came across this in an antique shop. I have not been able to identify it positively, but I believe it to be a South Island pattern, possibly from South Canterbury. It puts me in mind of the Hope series of lures.

RILEY'S GLORY (H)

ORIGIN:	BRIAN RILEY OF AUCKLAND
HOOK:	8-10
THREAD:	MEDIUM OLIVE
TAIL:	GOLDEN COCK PHEASANT RED RUMP WHISKS
BODY:	DEWHURST'S SYLKO PERLE NO. 5, M 10, 102
RIB:	SMALL FLAT GOLD TINSEL
HACKLE:	PALE HONEY TO GIVE A GREYISH WHITE COLOUR
HEAD:	OLIVE

This pattern appears in Tony Orman's *Angling Anthology*. An important aspect is that the hackle, when wet, covers the body like a veil, so it must slope back. It is a very good lure when fished along the edge of weed beds.

The problem with this pattern is that I have been unable to locate any Dewhurst's Sylko perle, far less the colour of the body material, which is identified by the numbers. My enquiries have extended as far as England without success. It is certain that the colour will be readily available in the makes of Perle currently widespread, particularly the DMC brand, but without even a hint as to the colour I am unable to suggest a substitute unless someone knows what colour combined with pale honey will give a greyish white. I have been unable to trace Brian Riley for his assistance. Tony Orman could not throw any light on the subject, and so it must remain as a matter of written record only, without illustration.

Robert Bragg's book *New Zealand Fishing Flies* (1997) is a lavish, limited edition production with a hefty price tag to match. It contains many photos of Bragg's framed collections of trout flies including a section of early lure patterns. There is considerable artistry in the presentation of these displays but unfortunately the photos suffer from the same complaint that I make of those contained in Keith Draper's books. The image size of individual lures is too small to ascertain the dressing in many cases. Some written patterns are given but without accompanying photos. Notes given in relation to many of the lures are cryptic to the point of confusion.

I was able to ascertain the dressing to a number of lures with varying degrees of certainty, and they are listed in the alphabetical section. The remainder have defied my scrutiny. For the sake of completeness only, I record the names of those lures in alphabetical order. This will perpetuate the inventory of New Zealand lures which this book has attempted to achieve. The reader will be informed but not enlightened.

BERRY'S SILVERY
CAPTAIN HOWE
CRIDGE'S FANCY
DINGO
DRAGON FLY LARVAE
DR. WATSON
ELIZABETH
GREEN PHEASANT
HAINE'S PATTERNS
INDIAN SUMMER
IRVING'S BULLY
JINKS
KELLY'S SILVERY
MEYER'S TERROR
MOBY DICK
NYMPHO
RED BULLY
RED SQUIRREL
SMYTHE'S BULLY
SNOOKS
STANDARD PHEASANT
TATTLE'S KILLER
TURKEY TIME
WILD IRISHMAN

Charles Nott of Havelock North, who gave us Harley's Bully, has two collections of framed Taupo lures. The collection of Old Taupo Lures was gathered together over many years by one John Lane who ultimately gave it to Charles Nott. The collection of 1974 lures were all tied by Charles Nott.

Charles died in late 1997 aged in his nineties. The framed collections are now held by his family, and were kindly made available to me by Charles's son, John Nott. Both sets of lure collections have been photographed in their entirety. I have photographed individual lures which have not otherwise appeared in this book. I have not come across any reference anywhere to most of them. In other cases, I have highlighted certain lures because of intrigue over dressings used or other areas of interest.

It was not possible to remove the lures from the glass frame enclosures, and some intuition and guesswork was employed in determining some of the patterns. The origins and hook size range are not known and have been omitted in all cases.

OLD TAUPO LURES

WHITE MATUKA (M)

BODY: WHITE
RIB: SILVER
WING: BITTERN FEATHERS
SIDE WING: BITTERN FEATHERS
HEAD: BLACK

(N.B. The possession and use of Bittern feathers is strictly prohibited)

WHITE KIWI (O)

BODY: WHITE WOOL, TIED THICKLY
RIB: NONE APPARENT
WING: KIWI FEATHERS TIED IN AT HEAD STREAMER STYLE
CHEEK: JUNGLE COCK
HEAD: BLACK

(N.B. The possession and use of Kiwi feathers is strictly prohibited)

AWAHOU (K)

TAIL: PHEASANT TAIL FIBRES
BODY: YELLOW WOOL, TIED THICKLY
RIB: NONE APPARENT
WING: HEN PHEASANT TIED IN AT THE HEAD
HEAD: BLACK

RED MATUKA (O)

BODY: RED
RIB: FLAT GOLD
WING: BITTERN FEATHERS TIED IN AT HEAD STREAMER STYLE
HEAD: RED

(N.B. The possession and use of Bittern feathers is strictly prohibited)

YELLOW KIWI (M)

BODY: YELLOW WOOL
RIB: OVAL GOLD
WING: KIWI FEATHERS TIED MATUKU STYLE
CHEEK: JUNGLE COCK
HEAD: BLACK

(N.B. The possession and use of Kiwi feathers is strictly prohibited)

RED SETTER (M)

BODY: ORANGE WOOL
RIB: OVAL SILVER
WING: GINGER
HACKLE: GINGER
HEAD: BLACK

An unusual treatment of an old favourite.

TINOPAI (O)

TAG: SILVER FOLLOWED WITH YELLOW FLOSS
BODY: YELLOW WOOL
RIB: OVAL SILVER
WING: TURKEY
HACKLE: YELLOW UNDER RED
HEAD: BLACK

A slightly different dressing from the one listed alphabetically.

KIRKLEY'S ABORTION ("K.A.") (O)

TAIL: RED WHISKS
BODY: FLAT SILVER TINSEL
RIB: OVAL SILVER
WING: BADGER TIED IN AT THE HEAD STREAMER STYLE
HACKLE: DARK NATURAL RED GAME
HEAD: BLACK

NAMELESS (O)

TAIL: RED WHISKS
BODY: RED FLOSS (ONE-THIRD); BLACK SEAL'S FUR (TWO-THIRDS)
RIB: OVAL SILVER (OVER BLACK BODY ONLY)
WING: TURKEY STRIPS
CHEEK: JUNGLE COCK
HACKLE: BLACK
HEAD: BLACK

MILL'S BLONDIE (O)

WING: WHITE HAIR OF SOME KIND

I am inclined to the view that it is natural rather than synthetic because the fibres taper to a fine point. Note that the hook itself is completely bare. The wing is tied on to a monofilament loop arrangement which we are told is now illegal. No doubt this method was designed to give greater mobility to the lure through the water.

McMILLAN (O)

TAG: OVAL SILVER
TAIL: GOLDEN PHEASANT CREST
BODY: YELLOW (ONE-THIRD), RED (TWO-THIRDS)
RIB: OVAL SILVER
WING: TURKEY
HACKLE: NATURAL RED, AT THROAT ONLY
HEAD: BLACK

BLACK DOCTOR (O)

TAG: OVAL GOLD
TAIL: GOLDEN PHEASANT CREST TOPPED WITH BLACK WISKS
BODY: RED FLOSS FOLLOWED BY GOLD FOLLOWED BY BLACK
RIB: OVAL GOLD
UNDERWING: GOLDEN PHEASANT CREST
WING: TEAL
SIDEWING: GOLDEN PHEASANT TIPPETS
TOPPING: GOLDEN PHEASANT CREST
CHEEK: JUNGLE COCK
HACKLE: BLACK, AT THROAT ONLY
HEAD: RED

TAUPO LURES 1974

PETER ROSS (O)

TAIL: GOLDEN PHEASANT TIPPETS
BODY: SILVER AND RED FLOSS
RIB: OVAL SILVER
WING: BRONZE MALLARD
HACKLE: BLACK
HEAD: BLACK

The original Peter Ross had a Teal wing

WHITE RAT (M)

TAIL: RED WHISKS
BODY: WHITE CHENILLE
RIB: OVAL SILVER
WING: STRIP OF (PRESUMABLY) MUSKRAT FUR
HACKLE: BADGER
HEAD: BLACK

SPUDDLER (O)

TAIL: GOLDEN PHEASANT TIPPETS
BODY: WHITE FLOSS, RED FLOSS
RIB: OVAL SILVER
WING: DARK GRIZZLE COCK
HACKLE: NATURAL RED
HEAD: SPUN DEER HAIR

HOPE (O)

TAIL: SQUIRREL TAIL, BLACK OR POSSIBLY GREY BARRED
BODY: YELLOW FLOSS
RIB: NONE APPARENT

WING: POSSIBLY SQUIRREL OR POSSUM TAIL - A SHORT BROWN TUFT AT THE MID-POINT AND A LONGER BLACK TUFT AT THE HEAD

HACKLE: YELLOW FLOSS AT THROAT

HEAD: BLACK

RUKI BUG (O)

BODY: DIFFICULT TO SAY - PROBABLY BLACK SEAL'S FUR TEASED OUT

RIB: OVAL SILVER

HEAD: BLACK

HATEPE BUG (O)

TAIL: POSSIBLY BROWN MINK

BODY: BLACK

RIB: OVAL SILVER

WING: POSSIBLY WHITE, PALMERED, AND CLIPPED SHORT

HEAD: BLACK

BRADSHAW'S FANCY (O)

TAG: BRIGHT CRIMSON FLOSS OR WOOL WITH A COUPLE OF TURNS AT THE HEAD

BODY: GREEN PEACOCK HERL

HACKLE: GREY

TOPPING: (SEE TAG)

HEAD: NONE APPARENT

ORANGE & CLARET BLACK RABBIT (M)

TAIL: GOLDEN PHEASANT TIPPETS

BODY: ORANGE AND CLARET CHENILLE

RIB: OVAL SILVER

WING: STRIP OF NATURAL BLACK RABBIT

HACKLE: BLACK, AT THROAT ONLY

HEAD: BLACK

BULLY (K)

TAIL: BLACK SQUIRREL TAIL

BODY: NOT VISIBLE

WING: DARK HEN GRIZZLE

HACKLE: YELLOW, AT THROAT ONLY

HEAD: BLACK

BUM FLY (O)

TAIL: PHEASANT TAIL FIBRES

BODY: GREEN WOOL

WING: (TIED IN AT HEAD) CAN'T IDENTIFY

MRS SIMPSON KEA (K)

ORIGIN: PROBABLY MONA CARTER OF CHRISTCHURCH

HOOK: 4-8

TAIL: THE ORANGE/RED UNDERWING OF A KEA TOPPED WITH BLACK SQUIRREL

BODY: WOOL, RED, YELLOW OR GREEN

WING: GREEN KEA PLUMAGE

HEAD: BLACK

Keith Draper recounts, in both his books, that in 1939, an angler took a kea skin in to Tisdalls' sports shop in Christchurch and wanted some flies tied from its plumage. Mona Carter came up with this lure which she called Mrs Simpson - then added Kea, perhaps to avoid confusion with whatever pattern then was known as Mrs Simpson.

However, on 29 December 1938, Alan Beamish-White of Rotorua recalls John Wells (Senior), the founder of Kilwell's in Rotorua, using a Killer style lure made of green kea feathers. It took a limit bag (10) in the Log Pool at Lake Okataina. He recalls that it was called Mrs Simpson because Wallis Simpson was a (metaphorical) killer.

It will be realised that this is some time prior to Mona Carter's creation. It was not too surprising that a lure might be called Mrs Simpson, as that name was extremely topical at the time following the abdication of Edward VIII in 1936 prior to his marriage to Wallis Simpson. It would be surprising if two lures were created within a year of each other both made from kea feathers and both called Mrs Simpson. That is a coincidence that takes some grasping. Alan Beamish-White has good reason to remember the date. It is his birthday. He is fairly sure (he won't swear on the bible), it was 1938 and not 1939 because John Wells was fishing. A year later the country was immersed in World War II. Frank Lord tied up these kea lures for

Alan's family who owned the lodge at Lake Okataina. The kea lures were kept for visiting VIPs. As many as 14 feathers were used in their construction and they were therefore very expensive. Frank could not confirm the year that he started tying them, but he does recall that John Wells served in the war, mainly in Fiji. That would seem to confirm Alan's memory of this lure being around in 1938, except for one thing. The Pacific did not become a theatre of interest until Japan entered the War. Troops did not go to Fiji until 1941 or 1942. I am confident that the first kea lure was tied by Mona Carter in 1939, and that it was in December of that same year that John Wells used it with such devastating effects.

The example photographed was kindly loaned to me by a colleague, John McDowell of Napier. It was among a collection of very old lures owned by his late father-in-law. Unfortunately it was tied without the tail underlay of red/orange underwing but is otherwise the genuine article. In that regard, I notice that the pattern in Keith Draper's book has the red/orange underwing as a topping over the squirrel tail. The only photo I have ever seen is in Keith Draper's first book (1971). That example was tied by Bob Bragg in the characteristic South Island style with raised wings. The photo clearly shows the red kea plumage under the squirrel tail and I have amended the pattern accordingly. The kea is a protected bird and you will have to look for substitutes to tie this up. Cock hackles dyed a deep orangey-red are available and are a good match for the tail underlay. For the wing, use olive dyed mallard or partridge.

PHOTOGRAPHY DETAILS

For those technically minded or just interested, all photos were taken using a combination of the following equipment:

CAMERAS:

CANON T90

CANON EOS 630

LENSES:

FD 85MM F1.2L

FD135MM F2

FD35-105MM F3.5

ACCESSORIES:

EXTENSION RINGS 31,21, AND 13MM, FD - EOS CONVERTER

TRIPOD:

CULLMAN

FILM:

FUJICHROME SENSIA ISO 100 AND 200

FUJICHROME VELVIA ISO 50

KODACHROME ELITE II ISO 200

I would estimate that in excess of 98% of all photos were taken using Fujichrome Sensia ISO 100.

All photos were taken in natural daylight. No flash or filters of any kind were used, although the judicious use of mirrors helped reflect light onto the subject in appropriate instances. For example, over Christmas/New Year 1996-97 I went camping, as always, at a private beach north of Napier. I set up a table at the back of the tent and passed the time between cyclones (true!) tying flies and photographing them. The photo of Barred Killer was taken in that tent. A clump of Scotch thistles was gathered from nearby and propped up in an empty beer can. My brother-in-law held a mirror by the tent 'window' and directed the light while I operated the camera.

Problems: Plenty! With close-up macro photography, depth of field (that part of the scene from front to back which remains in sharp focus) can be measured in millimetres.

Even though using very expensive optics, edge to edge sharpness was almost impossible to achieve, usually resulting in a 'softening' of the lure head.

Using available outdoor light meant days of waiting for the right conditions, and wind is a constant problem, particularly when photographing anything involving marabou which flutters in the merest puff of wind.

Trying to come up with a different setting for every lure exhausted my available creativity, but I was not displeased with the distance I travelled towards that goal. At least I successfully resisted the urge to resort to the cliche fly-in-a-vice technique.

In the end, whatever the problems and the limitations of my equipment, I enjoyed the challenge and the experience, and I hope the results find favour.

BIBLIOGRAPHY

I have consulted all of the following plus numerous other publications, many obscure, the details of which I have now forgotten.

Bragg, Robert K. *New Zealand Fishing Flies.* The Caxton Press, Christchurch. 1997.

Busch, Tony. *A Trout Fishing Guide to New Zealand's South Island.* David Bateman Ltd., Auckland. 1986.

Dawes, Mike. *The Flytier's Companion.* Swan Hill Press, London. 1989.

Draper, Keith. *Trout Flies in New Zealand.* Heinemann Reed, Auckland. 1971.

Draper, Keith. *New Zealand Trout Flies Traditional & Modern.* Reed Books, Auckland. 1997.

Hammond, Bryn. *The New Zealand Encyclopaedia of Fly Fishing.* Halcyon, Auckland. 1988.

Hickling, Harold (Vice-Admiral). *Freshwater Admiral.* A.H. & A.W. Reed, Wellington. 1960.

Hintz, O.S. *Trout at Taupo.* Max Reinhardt, London. 1955.

Kendrick, C. H. *Modern Fly Dressings.* Unity Press, Auckland. 1946.

Kent, John (Dr.). *North Island Trout Fishing Guide.* Heinemann Reed, Auckland. 1989.

Kilwell Ltd., Rotorua. Old tackle catalogues.

McDowell, Hugh. *New Zealand Fly Tying.* Heinemann Reed, Auckland. 1984.

Orman, Tony. *The Sport in Fishing.* A.H. & A.W. Reed, Wellington. 1979.

Orman, Tony (compiled by). *Trout & Salmon Sport in New Zealand.* A.H. & A.W. Reed, Wellington. 1980.

Parsons, John. *Deceiving Trout.* Halcyon, Auckland. 1988.

Parsons, John. *Four Seasons of Trout.* HarperCollins, Auckland. 1994.

Tichborne, Nancy and Bryan. New Zealand Trout Fly Calendars. New Zealand Calendar Co., Rotorua. 1987-1991.

Tichborne, Nancy and Bryan. *Anglers' Paradise.* The Bush Press, Auckland. 1990.

Tisdall, W.H. Ltd. Old tackle catalogues.

Various fishing magazines.

Veniard, John. *Reservoir and Lake Flies.* Black, London. 1970.

Whiting, N. (compiled by) *Fifty-Eight NZ Lure Patterns.* Daily Telegraph Print, Napier. About 1977.

Williams, A. Courtney. *A Dictionary of Trout Flies.* A. & C. Black, London. 1949.

POSTSCRIPT

If all the fish in the waters of the world were to disappear tomorrow, I would still continue to tie flies.

Jack Gartside

(Contributor to *The Art of the Trout Fly* by Judith Dunham 1988)

I understand precisely the sentiment expressed.

FLY TYING CREDITS

The following lists the tiers who tied up the various lures. In determining whether to list the tiers alphabetically or the lures alphabetically, it was considered more likely that an inquiry would centre on "who tied that lure?" It was therefore determined to list the lures alphabetically. As a general guide, the creator of a lure has tied his or her own pattern. In the various appendices, it is clear from the text who tied which lure. The credits below relate to the alphabetical section only. In all other cases (except GT Smelt, Silver) the author has tied the example shown. The hook size is shown in parenthesis.

ALBINO (1)	BARRY KENT	(#4)
ALBINO (3)	BRONWYN WILSON	(#4)
ALL BLACK	BARRY KENT	(#4)
ANNA'S BLUE GHOST	SUE CRAWFORD	(#4)
AURORA	MAUREEN BUTLER	(#6)
AWESOME AUCK	RITCHIE BUCHANAN	(#6)
BADGER SMELT	BRONWYN WILSON	(#6)
BALCARASTER	BRONWYN WILSON	(#4)
BALLARD'S BEAUTY	RAY PUNTER	(#4)
B AND B	BRONWYN WILSON	(#4)
BARRY'S SMELT	BARRY BIRCHELL	(PARTRIDGE D4A #4)
BASIL'S WHITEBAIT	BASIL JACKSON	(#12 LONG SHANK)
BETHLEHEM CAT	JOHN KENT	(#6)
BILL'S KILLER	BRONWYN WILSON	(#4)
BISHOP'S BLESSING	BRONWYN WILSON	(#4)
BLACK ARROW	JOHN MORTON	(#4)
BLACK BOOBIE	HUGH MCDOWELL	(#8)
BLACK MARABOU	JIM MCIVOR	(#6)
BLACK PETE	JOHN MORTON	(#4)
BLUE DUN MATUKU	TOM KEMPER	(#8)
BMS	MURRAY WILSON	(#8)
BOCKETT'S GHOST	JIM MCIVOR	(#6)
BOOBY	ALF ELLISON	(#6)
BOTTLETOP	MAUREEN BUTLER	(#6)
BROWN BOMBER	IVAN BODLEY	(#6)
BROWN KILLER	KEITH DRAPER	(#6)
BRUNTON NO.1	GARTH COGHILL	(#4)
BRUNTON NO.2	GARTH COGHILL	(#6)
BRUNTON RED	GARTH COGHILL	(#6)
BUDGIE	NIGEL WOOD	(#4)
BULLY	RON BERRY	(#6)
BULLY FLY	PAT O'KEEFE	(#6)
BUM FLY	PAT SWIFT	(#6)
BUM FLY VAR. (1)	BARRY KENT	(#6)
BUM FLY VAR. (2)	PAT SWIFT	(#4)
BUM FLY VAR. (3)	PAT O'KEEFE	(#6)
BUNNY	MEL KRIEGER	(#4)
BURGLAR	BRONWYN WILSON	(#4)
CASEY	BRONWYN WILSON	(#4)
CASUAL DRESS	MONTY WRIGHT	(#10S)
CHARLIE'S FAVOURITE	ALAN ANDERSON	(#8)
CHINAMAN	RITCHIE BUCHANAN	(#6)
CLAIRE'S CHARM	RAY PUNTER	(#4)
COACHMAN LURE	GARTH COGHILL	(#6)
COMETS	JIM MCIVOR	(#6)
CRAIG'S KILLER	CRAIG ADAMS	(#4)
CRAYFISH	BASIL JACKSON	(#6)
DAMSEL NYMPH NO.1	ROGER SMAILFS	(#8)
DAMSEL NYMPH NO.2	BARRY KENT	(#8 LONG SHANK)
DELUXE HARLER	PAT O'KEEFE	(#2)
DIANNE'S KILLER	PETER STOREY	(#4)
DIRTY HARRY	GARTH COGHILL	(#8)
DOLL FLY	PAT SWIFT	(#6)
DOUBLE PUFF	BRONWYN WILSON	(#4)
DRIFTER	KEITH DRAPER	(#6)
DUCHESS	BRONWYN WILSON	(#4)
ENGLAND'S DEMON	BRONWYN WILSON	(#4)
EPOXY SPRAT	GARTH COGHILL	(#4)
ETHIOPIAN	RITCHIE BUCAHANAN	(#6)
EWE WASP (OLD TIE)	PAT SWIFT	(#6)
EXOCET	DAVID DANNEFAERD	(#6)
FIREBALL	GARY KEMSLEY	(#6)
FRANCIS BUTCHER	FRANK CIOCHETTO	(#6)
FURRY BARRED WASP	BRONWYN WILSON	(#6)
FURRY BUTCHER	BRONWYN WILSON	(#6)
FURRY EWE WASP	BRONWYN WILSON	(#6)
GARY'S GREEN MARABOU	GARY KEMSLEY	(#6)
GILLIES LODGER	RITCHIE BUCHANAN	(#6)
GINGER MICK	BRONWYN WILSON	(#6)
GLO-BUG	BARRY KENT	(#14)
GOLDEN DEMON	PAT SWIFT	(#6)
GOLDIE HAWN	MAUREEN BUTLER	(#6)
GOTCHA	VIC NOVIS	(#4)
GREEN DOG	DAN HARTLEY	(#6)
GREEN FROG	RITCHIE BUCHANAN	(#6)
GREEN PARSONS	FRANK LORD	(#6)
GREEN PRINCE	BRONWYN WILSON	(#6)
GREEN SLEEVES	PAT SWIFT	(#6)
GREYFRIARS	MAUREEN BUTLER	(#6)
GRIZZLE SMELT	BRONWYN WILSON	(#6)
GRIZZLY BEAR	GERARD VAN WIJNBERGEN	(#6)
GUARDSMAN	KEITH DRAPER	(#4)
HAEMORRHOID	MONTY WRIGHT	(#2)
HAMILL'S KILLER	ADAM ROWBOTHAM	(#6)
HARRY	BRONWYN WILSON	(#4)
HAWKE AND POSSUM	BRONWYN WILSON	(#6)
HEN PHEASANT	KEITH DRAPER	(#4)
HERB'S GLOW SMELT	HERB SPANNAGL	(#8)
HOB NAILED BOOT	JOHN MORTON	(#6)
HOPE'S SILVERY	FRANK HARWOOD	(#4)
HUGHIE'S MALLARD	HUGH MCDOWELL	(#6)
HYDRO HUSTLER	FRANK HARWOOD	(#10)
IRISH REBEL	PAT O'KEEFE	(#6)

IRISH SETTER	TREVOR HALFORD	(#6)
ITALIAN STALLION	KARL DECKE	(#6)
JOCK MILLER	RAY PUNTER	(#6)
JOCK MILLER VAR.	RAY PUNTER	(#6)
JO JO JUGGINS	NIGEL BIRT	(#10)
KEELER	BRONWYN WILSON	(#6)
KEITH'S KRAWLIE	KEITH DRAPER	(#2)
KILWELL BLONDE	BRONWYN WILSON	(#4)
KILWELL NO.1	BRONWYN WILSON	(#6)
KILWELL NO.2	BRONWYN WILSON	(#6)
KOKAPU	BRONWYN WILSON	(#4)
LA GIACONDA	JOHN GIACON	(#8)
LAMPREY	MONTY WRIGHT	(#10 LONG SHANK)
LIMEY	MAUREEN BUTLER	(#6)
LISA	BRONWYN WILSON	(#4)
LISA SIMPSON	SUE CRAWFORD	(#6)
LITTLE GREEN FATALE	KARL DECKE	(#8)
LITTLE RAINBOW	PHIL STECK	(#6 4X LONG SHANK)
LOGAN'S LURE	RICHARD LOGAN	(#8)
LORD'S KILLER	PAT SWIFT	(#6)
LOU'S GREEN PARROT	ALF ELLISON	(#6)
MALLARD AND BLACK	EDDIE BOSOMWORTH	(#8)
MALLARD AND CLARET	PAT SWIFT	(#6)
MALLARD HEN	KEITH DRAPER	(#6)
MAORI ALL BLACK	MARU MANIOPOTU	(#6)
MAORI CHIEF	PAT SWIFT	(#6)
MARABOU KING VAR.	ALF ELLISON	(#4)
MARABOU KOURA	MAUREEN BUTLER	(#6)
MATUKU MUDDLER	HUGH MCDOWELL	(#4)
MELLOW YELLOW	JOHN MORTON	(#2)
MICHELLE'S MAGIC	PAT O'KEEFE	(#6)
MOHAKA NO.1	BARRY KENT	(#8)
MOHAKA SPECIAL	BARRY KENT	(#8)
MONSUM'S BULLY	MONTY WRIGHT	(#10)
MOONSHINE	BRONWYN WILSON	(#6)
MORTON'S SMELT	JOHN MORTON	(#6)
MR SIMPSON	PAT SWIFT	(#6)
MRS SIMPSON	PAT SWIFT	(#6)
MUSKRAT (1)	GRAEME HUGHES	(#2)
MUSKRAT (2)	ROB LIMMER	(#8)
NORTHERN RABBIT	BARRY BIRCHELL	(#4)
O'KEEFE'S KILLER	PAT O'KEEFE	(#6)
O'KEEFE'S SMELT	PAT O'KEEFE	(#6)
OLIVE SMELT	JIM MCIVOR	(#6)
ORANGE HAWKE	BRONWYN WILSON	(#6)
ORANGE ROUGHIE	RITCHIE BUCHANAN	(#6)
ORSIM	PAT SWIFT	(#4)
PADDLE TAIL	GARTH COGHILL	(#6)
PALAMINO	RON DOUGLAS	(#6)
PARADISE KILLER	HERB SPANNAGL	(#8)
PARADISE WRIGGLER	ROB LIMMER	(#8)
PARSON'S GLORY (OLD TIE)	PAT SWIFT	(#4)
PARSON'S GLORY (MODERN TIE)	PAT SWIFT	(#4)
PARSON'S GLORY VAR.	BARRY BIRCHELL	(#6)
PARSON'S SUNSET	HUGH MCDOWELL	(#4)

PEPPERMINT TWIST	MAUREEN BUTLER	(#6)
PETERKEN'S POACHER	GARTH COGHILL	(#6)
PETERKEN'S POSSUM	GARTH COGHILL	(#6)
PHANTOM BURGLAR	GEORGE GATCHELL	(#4)
PINK AND GREY	HERB SPANNAGL	(#8)
PINK DAWN	RON DOUGLAS	(#6)
PLUTO	GARTH COGHILL	(PARTRIDGE D4A#6)
PROSPECTOR	GARTH COGHILL	(#8)
PUNTER'S BLACK RABBIT	RAY PUNTER	(#6)
PURPLE MARABOU PRINCE	ALF ELLISON	(#6)
PURPLE PARSON'S GLORY	SUE CRAWFORD	(#4)
QUAIL	CAROL HARWOOD	(#10)
RABBIT BULLY	KEITH DRAPER	(#4)
RAINBOW TROUT	RITCHIE BUCHANAN	(#6)
RASTAFARIAN	RITCHIE BUCHANAN	(#6)
RECKLESS WILLIAM	GARTH COGHILL	(#8)
RECKLESS WILLIAM'S MATE	GARTH COGHILL	(#8)
REDFIN MATUKU	JIM MCIVOR	(#6)
RED SETTER (OLD TIE)	BRONWYN WILSON	(#6)
RED SHADOW	FRANK HARWOOD	(#4)
ROTODYERAN SPECIAL	HUGH MCDOWELL	(#4)
ROYAL COACHMAN LURE	PAT O'KEEFE	(#4)
RUSTLER	GARTH COGHILL	(PARTRIDGE D4A#6)
SILVER FITCH	JIM KELLER	(#8 LONG SHANK)
SILVER POSSUM	JIM KELLER	(#8 LONG SHANK)
SIMPLE SALMON	MAUREEN BUTLER	(#6)
SIMPSON FLY	ROB LIMMER	(#6 LONG SHANK)
SINGLE PUFF	BRONWYN WILSON	(#10)
SKINNY MAC	DAVE MCLELLAN	(#8)
SOUTHERNER'S COMFORT	JOHN MORTON	(#6)
SPLIT PARTRIDGE	GARTH COGHILL	(#6)
SPLIT TURKEY	PAT SWIFT	(#6)
SPOTTY GOLD	RITCHIE BUCHANAN	(#6)
STARLING	HERB SPANNAGL	(#8)
SUCCESS	BRONWYN WILSON	(#4)
SUNSET FLY	GRAHAM ANDREWS	(#4)
SUNSET RABBIT	GARY KEMSLEY	(#4)
TADPOLE	BARRY KENT	(#10)
TAGARTI	JACK MURRAY	(#6)
TAIL LIGHT	KEITH DRAPER	(#6)
THAT PURPLY BLUE THING	ALF ELLISON	(#4)
THE BOSS	ROGER SMAILES	(#6)
THE SMELT FLY	HUGH MCDOWELL	(#6)
TONGARIRO QUEEN	PAT SWIFT	(#6)
TURKEY (YELLOW AND RED)	GARTH COGHILL	(#4)
URCHIN	GARTH COGHILL	(#4)
WAIHORA	GARTH COGHILL	(#4)
WARDEN'S WORRY	BRONWYN WILSON	(#6)
WATER RAT	PAT O'KEEFE	(#10)
WHANGANUI SMELT	RITCHIE BUCHANAN	(#6)
WILLY'S WONDER	BRONWYN WILSON	(#6)
WILSON'S WUNDER	ERIC WILSON	(#6)
WOOSTER'S SILVERY	PROBABLY BILL WOOSTER	(#4)
YELLOW FUZZ	JOHN MORTON	(#4)
YELLOW RUDDEL	BARRY BIRCHALL	(#4)